'Writing with verve and great narrative d[...] [...] of adventure, brutality and moral ambigui[...] [...] down. A splendid book'   Fred Anderson [...]

46/38

'[a] captivating story of frontier conflict . . . Brumwell's story-telling skills balance his anger, making for an otherwise flawless study'   *Good Book Guide*

'Brumwell deftly pulls together a variety of sources and conflicting accounts in telling his tale, but he is equally adept at sketching the background of the Anglo-French conflict and the status of the Native Americans in the colonial wars. He makes it clear . . . that almost every event in the history of the colonization of the USA was a minor tragedy for the native tribes'

Samuel Blake, *Times Literary Supplement*

'A good, vivid account of the times'   *Regiment*

'[*White Devil*] . . . is a worthy accomplishment, for Rogers' brief, extraordinary career inspired both James Fenimore Cooper's *The Last of the Mohicans* and Kenneth Robert's *Northwest Passage* . . . he is rightly considered the founder of America's Modern Special Forces'   Raymond Seitz, *Sunday Telegraph*

Stephen Brumwell worked as a newspaper reporter before gaining a PhD in History from the University of Leeds. He is an expert on the British Army in eighteenth-century America and lectures in Britain and the USA. His doctoral thesis formed the basis of his first book, *Redcoats* (Cambridge University Press 2002), which won him terrific reviews. Married with a daughter, he lives in Amsterdam, where he is currently working on a biography of General Wolfe.

WHITE DEVIL

AN EPIC STORY OF REVENGE
FROM THE SAVAGE WAR THAT INSPIRED
THE LAST OF THE MOHICANS

STEPHEN BRUMWELL

PHOENIX

A PHOENIX PAPERBACK

First published in Great Britain in 2004
by Weidenfeld & Nicolson
This paperback edition published in 2005
by Phoenix,
an imprint of Orion Books Ltd,
Orion House, 5 Upper St Martin's Lane,
London WC2H 9EA

Design by Gwyn Lewis
Cartography by Peter Harper

A CIP catalogue record for this book
is available from the British Library.

ISBN 0 304 36255 7

Printed and bound in Great Britain by
by Clays Ltd, St Ives plc

www.orionbooks.co.uk

For Laura and Milly

Nous sommes touts Sauvages

GRAFFITO LEFT BY CANADIAN FUR TRADER,

ILLINOIS COUNTRY, 1680

Contents

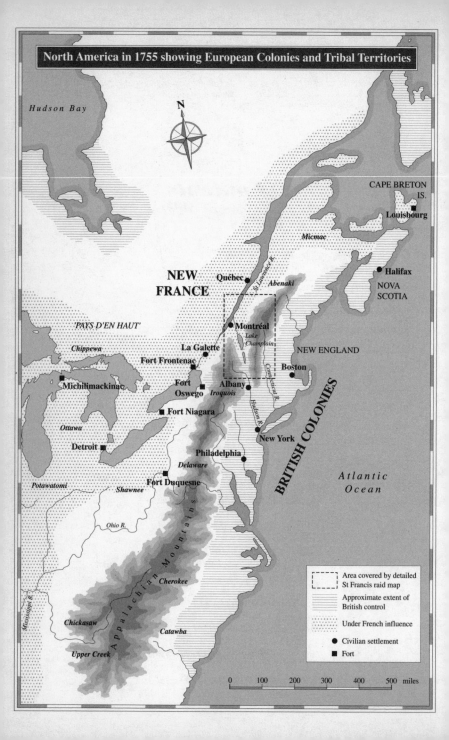

North America in 1755 showing European Colonies and Tribal Territories

Hudson Bay

N

CAPE BRETON
IS.
■ Louisbourg

Micmac

**NEW
FRANCE**

● Québec

St Lawrence R.

Abenaki

● Halifax

NOVA
SCOTIA

'PAYS D'EN HAUT'

Chippewa

● Montréal

*Lake
Champlain*

NEW ENGLAND

La Galette

Fort Frontenac

● Boston

■ Michilimackinac

Fort
Oswego ■

■ Albany

Iroquois

Champlain R.

■ Fort Niagara

Hudson R.

Ottawa

Detroit ■

● New York

Philadelphia ●

Delaware

*Atlantic
Ocean*

Potawatomi

■ Fort Duquesne

Shawnee

BRITISH COLONIES

Ohio R.

Appalachian Mountains

Cherokee

Mississippi R.

Chickasaw

Catawba

Upper Creek

┄┄ Area covered by detailed
St Francis raid map

Approximate extent of
British control

Under French influence

● Civilian settlement

■ Fort

0   100   200   300   400   500   miles

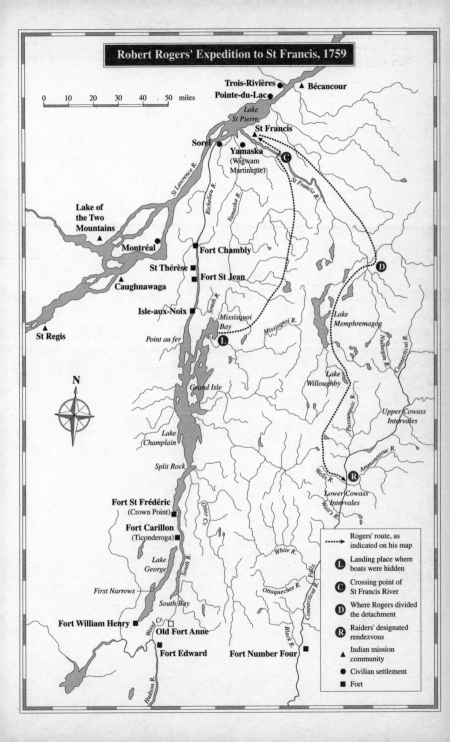

Robert Rogers' Expedition to St Francis, 1759

0 10 20 30 40 50 miles

Trois-Rivières
▲ **Bécancour**
Pointe-du-Lac
Lake St Pierre
▲ **St Francis**
Sorel
Yamaska
(Wigwam Martinique)
Ⓒ
St Lawrence R.
Richelieu R.
Yamaska R.
St Francis R.

Lake of the Two Mountains ▲
Montréal
■ **Fort Chambly**
St Thérèse ■
■ **Fort St Jean**
Ⓓ
Caughnawaga ▲
Isle-aux-Noix ■
South R.
Missisquoi Bay
Missisquoi R.
Lake Memphremagog

St Regis ▲
Point au fer
Ⓛ
Nulhegan R.
Connecticut R.

N
Grand Isle
Lake Willoughby
Upper Cowass Intervales

Lake Champlain
Passumpsic R.

Split Rock
Ammonoosuc R.
Ⓡ
Fort St Frédéric
(Crown Point)
Otter Cr.
Lower Cowass Intervales
Fort Carillon
(Ticonderoga)
Wells R.
Wait's R.

Lake George
White R.

First Narrows
Ottauquechee R.
Connecticut R.
Falls
South Bay

Fort William Henry
Wood Cr.
□ **Old Fort Anne**
Black R.

Fort Edward
Fort Number Four
Hudson R.

- - - → Rogers' route, as indicated on his map
Ⓛ Landing place where boats were hidden
Ⓒ Crossing point of St Francis River
Ⓓ Where Rogers divided the detachment
Ⓡ Raiders' designated rendezvous
▲ Indian mission community
● Civilian settlement
■ Fort

Preface

ST FRANCIS, 4.30 A.M., 4 OCTOBER, 1759.

THE VILLAGE LIES STILL. Beyond its boundaries lean figures lurk in the darkness, a bedraggled and motley company. Some are tribal warriors drawn from the native peoples of New England; their heads are shaven clean save for a tufted scalp-lock, their ears and noses sport ornaments of brass and silver. Greased and painted, they wear loose shirts and breech-clouts that leave their haunches bare. But most of the raiders are white men, clad in moccasins, coarse cloth leggings and short jackets of rough wool – the dark green of the rangers, the brick-red or brown of the British regulars and the midnight blue of the colonial provincial troops, all alike now tattered and filthy. Many wear Scots bonnets jammed down low on their brows; others sport leather or fur caps, or shapeless slouched hats cropped from once-elegant tricornes; here and there a bunch of leaves or a jaunty feather stand substitute for the smart cockade. Their faces are scored by scratches and swollen from the bites of insects. Beneath their beards and the layered dirt of the wilderness, all are gaunt with fatigue, hunger and fear.

For all their ragged appearance, these men are an élite fraternity. They have been carefully selected from amongst the fittest, keenest and wiliest fighters in the great British-American army that has slowly pushed back the frontiers of New France to the northern shores of Lake Champlain.

Their proud designation – chosen men – has been hard earned. During the past three weeks they have traversed some hundred and fifty miles of punishing country, much of it within the domain of a ruthless and skilful enemy. Gruelling terrain and an unrelenting pace have already made inroads upon manpower; dozens of their comrades have been sent back, disabled by accident, illness or sheer exhaustion. Others have simply disappeared amidst the trackless forests and swamps. Those that remain have slogged onwards in the dispiriting knowledge that the enemy is not only ahead, but also behind them. By now the hornets' nest has been well and truly stirred: Canada's French and Indian defenders are closing in upon them as inexorably as the jaws of a vice.

Each of these men knows that the destruction of the Abenaki village across the clearing is just one of many hurdles to be surmounted before they regain the safety of friendly territory once more. Those who survive the coming assault face an onerous retreat through the desolate wilds; on that long march homewards they will have to reckon with more inveterate foes than the French regular soldiers, Canadian militia and vengeful Indian warriors who will surely be snapping at their heels. After weeks away from base they are starving, their rations finished days before. Yet the woods are strangely barren of bird, beast and berry. The forest has already assumed its flaming fall livery; there's a marrow-numbing chill in the autumn air. The most experienced woodsmen amongst them know there will be as much to fear from hunger and exposure as from hostile muskets and scalping knives.

But now such demoralising thoughts must be laid aside: the raiders are within striking distance of their prey: for the moment at least, they are the hunters.

Swiftly and silently the command ready themselves. Blankets, packs and canteens are slipped from shoulders and left where they fall amongst the bushes; cartridges are ripped open and powder, ball and buckshot tipped down the barrels of muskets and rammed well home; priming is checked and fresh flints are coaxed between the jaws of hammers; bayonets are unsheathed and locked into place, hatchets and knives loosened in their straps and tugged snugly to hand.

These preparations over, the raiders advance stealthily to the fringes of the clearing and array themselves in a loose cordon that girds the silent village on three sides. On the fourth side, the wide and dark waters of the St Francis River flow swiftly down towards their confluence with the mighty St Lawrence. The banks of the river are high and steep, broken only by a path descending to the landing place. There's small prospect that the quarry can escape that way, but to be certain, a well-placed team of marksmen will ensure no one slips past.

Towards the right of the line there's a brief conference: a knot of officers and sergeants crane inwards, watching and listening intently as a tall, burly, blunt-featured man in his late twenties outlines the plan of attack one last time. This tough and confident young soldier is Robert Rogers. Through four years of bloody warfare his well-publicised exploits have made him a household name on both sides of the Atlantic. As a result of what is to happen on this October morning, and during the weeks that follow, his fame will reach its zenith; within the next six months, no corner of the English-speaking world will remain unfamiliar with the deeds of 'the brave Major Rogers'. The Abenakis of St Francis will also have cause to remember Robert Rogers, but when they do so it will be by a name of their own: Wobomagonda – White Devil.

The instructions that Major Rogers is now issuing to his men are simple and familiar; indeed, they've been drummed home often enough during the long war against New France. But there is no margin for error; Rogers jabs his broad hands through the air in abbreviated gestures of emphasis. Trickling back to their designated posts, the squad leaders brief their men. The night's orders are clear and concise; every man knows exactly what is expected of him. And so they hunker down to await the signal.

First hints of dawn bloody the skies. It is time.

Rising now, the ragged figures lope forwards. The raiders close swiftly upon the silent village like a clenching fist.

VIOLENCE WAS THE MAINSPRING OF North America's colonial frontier; of all the characters it propelled across that blood-streaked stage, few remain more enigmatic than Robert Rogers. At home in the wilderness, Rogers also wrote books that earned him the acclaim of London's literary critics. A noted scourge of Indians, he nevertheless admired them and shared much of their world-view. According to the *Dictionary of American Biography*, Rogers was the most romantic figure to emerge from that bitter conflict now known as the French and Indian War. His lifetime encapsulated peaks and troughs of fortune that would invite disbelief if they weren't corroborated by independent testimony. Whilst still a young man, Rogers' flair for waging the brutal war of the backwoods brought him celebrity; in a trajectory followed by many other natural-born fighters, the subsequent frustrations of peacetime exposed telling flaws and led to a dramatic fall from grace.

Of all the episodes embraced within Rogers' chequered career, none gained him greater fame than his 1759 raid upon the Abenaki village of St Francis, known to the French as St François, and to its native inhabitants as Odanak. The tale of this search-and-destroy mission, and the hardships undergone in its wake, captured the imagination of Rogers' contemporaries. It generated many column inches of dramatic newspaper copy – not only in the Boston and New York titles for which lurid tales of frontier massacre were standard fare, but also in the pages of Great Britain's metropolitan and provincial press.

Interest was rekindled in 1765 when Rogers published his *Journals* in London, recalling the savagery and hardships of frontier warfare in an unvarnished and functional prose that only heightened the impact of the grim vignettes studding the text. The extended narrative in the *Journals* of the St Francis operation was a case in point: despite Rogers' classic understatement, its dramatic potential was recognised and highlighted by contemporary chroniclers of the victorious struggle with France. Robert Rogers' *Journals* were well received; a second edition surfaced in Dublin four years later. In 1772, when he produced his massive history of the American war, the former army officer Thomas Mante grafted new details onto Rogers' version of events; they included an eye-witness account of cannibalism.

But any lingering fame surrounding Rogers and his daring raid was swiftly swamped by the tidal wave of revolution that engulfed British America in 1775. Like many other Americans, Rogers remained loyal to King George III. In the wake of the bitter War of Independence, there was no longer any place for him in his native land. Rogers died in 1795, exiled an ocean away from his beloved New England frontier. In coming years, the fledgling United States of America showed little interest in perpetuating his memory. The new republic had enough freshly minted heroes of its own, patriots who had chosen the cause of Liberty. Robert Rogers was nothing more than a tarnished warrior from a long-gone war.

But 'the brave Major Rogers' wasn't so easily forgotten. In the opening decades of the nineteenth century, men who'd served with him as young-sters still lived on in Massachusetts and New Hampshire. These former rangers were sought out and interviewed by local historians keen to preserve first-hand accounts of bygone frontier days. Those who recorded their vivid testimonies included the printer and journalist Luther Roby, who incorporated such recollections of the St Francis raid and other old-time fights in a new edition of Rogers' *Journals* which was published at Concord, New Hampshire, in 1831.

Neither was the memory of Rogers erased from the rugged Hudson and Champlain valleys that had witnessed so many of his clashes with the French and Indians. There the very landscape bore the indelible imprint of his name: Rogers' Island, Rogers' Rock and Rogers' Slide all testified to his enduring impact upon the wild, picturesque region.

This lasting legacy sparked the imagination of a young man destined to play a pivotal role in rehabilitating Rogers in the eyes of his country-men. In 1842, the eighteen-year-old Francis Parkman dedicated his summer vacation from Harvard to a physically challenging trek that also satisfied his passion for the past. By way of Albany and Lake George he moved up the Champlain Valley and across northern Vermont and New

Hampshire, following in the wake of armies that had fought for mastery of that same ground less than a century before. Part of his itinerary retraced the arduous steps of the St Francis raiders during their return from the village.

Two years later, when Parkman toured the Berkshire Hills of western Massachusetts, his growing interest in Rogers and his rangers turned into obsession. He noted snippets of folklore; when he met the venerable General Epaphras Hoyt at Williamstown, he could scarcely contain his excitement at learning that the general not only possessed journals and letters of great interest, but also a complete unpublished life of Rogers.

In coming years the tireless Parkman established himself as the pre-eminent historian of North America's colonial era, writing best-selling books that presented exhaustive archival research within vivid and readable narratives. He remained fascinated by the harsh lifestyle of Rogers and his rangers, but some four decades passed before he finally tackled the subject of his youthful enthusiasm within a full-blown account of the French and Indian War. The resulting study, *Montcalm and Wolfe*, is generally considered his best work. First published in 1884, it's remained in print ever since. The uncompromising nature of the guerrilla warfare encountered by the rangers during the bloody conflict with New France between 1755 and 1760 inspired some of Parkman's most powerful and effective prose: 'like Dürer's knight,' he wrote, 'the ranger walked out with a ghastly death ever at his side'. The book included a detailed treatment of the St Francis raid, with a note harking back to the author's sophomore sortie into Vermont. Through Parkman's literary skills and fertile imagination Robert Rogers was rescued from obscurity and belatedly restored to the pantheon of America's frontier heroes.

Today, the St Francis raid is perhaps best known from King Vidor's 1940 film, *Northwest Passage*, based upon Kenneth Roberts' robust historical novel of the same title. Roberts provided a vivid account of the horrors of colonial frontier warfare. The Technicolor movie, which employed spectacular wilderness locations and featured Spencer Tracy in the role of Rogers, likewise pulled few punches. And in an unusually even-handed treatment for the age in which it was written, the screenplay left no doubt that whites and Indians alike were capable of unbridled savagery.

Throughout King Vidor's film, Rogers and his rangers demonstrate the rugged individualism that's often taken to epitomise the American frontier spirit. This rough-hewn model continues to strike a chord with many; as Professor Fred Anderson has observed, Rogers and his rangers remain the subject of both military legend and popular fascination. Rogers is regarded as the founding father of the American Army's Special Forces units; according to their most devoted historian, Burt Garfield Loescher, Rogers' Rangers were the original Green Berets.

The continuing popular interest in Rogers and his corps is evident from the hundreds of modern-day enthusiasts – concentrated in North America, but scattered as far afield as the United Kingdom and Czech Republic – who seek to recreate the world of the rangers on weekend wilderness treks, who reconstruct those brutal times as re-enactors, and who write, produce or appear in television programmes on both sides of the Atlantic. But although long admired by re-enactors and military buffs, Rogers and his rangers have had a more mixed reception from professional historians: under their scrutiny, Rogers' reputation has undergone just such fluctuations as characterised his tempestuous life.

Since the 1970s, his standing as a superlative backwoods warrior has come under sniping fire: the respected Canadian military historian Colonel C.P. Stacey considered Rogers' Rangers were *probably not quite so formidable as they have been made out to be*; his countryman and leading scholar of the old French régime, W.J. Eccles, went further, roundly declaring them to be *highly overrated*.

And scholars of colonial America, particularly those concerned to give due weight to the previously neglected perspectives of Native Americans, mounted frontal attacks upon Rogers and his deeds; much of this was a reaction to the writings of Francis Parkman, who, for all his wide-ranging research, displayed the prejudices of a privileged white

Protestant Yankee: *his* Indians too often appeared as savages, pure and simple.

Perhaps unsurprisingly, Francis Jennings, Parkman's arch-critic, viewed Rogers with hostility. To Jennings, Parkman was a pariah who twisted the evidence to suit his own racist agenda. It followed that Parkman's great hero Rogers was nothing less than depraved: a brutal braggart, and an unashamed self-publicist whose celebrated raid upon St Francis amounted to little more than the massacre of defenceless women and children. Far from being an epic feat of hardihood and a shining example of the American frontier spirit, it was merely another sorry chapter in the dismal story of the destruction of the Indian by avaricious colonists. From the perspective of Rogers' critics, there was little to distinguish what happened at St Francis in 1759 from the infamous slaughter of Black Kettle's band of Cheyenne at the hands of the Colorado militia at Sand Creek in 1864, or the massacre of South Vietnamese villagers by men of the US Army's Americal Division at My Lai in 1968. Such assessments now colour the mainstream scholarly view of the raid; one popular textbook on colonial America concludes that it was 'one more demonstration of British inhumanity toward the native people'.

This uncompromising stance is shared by the descendants of Rogers' Abenaki victims: for them, his name will be forever linked with the grim events of 4 October, 1759. That was made clear to me in May 2002, during a conversation with Wes Red Hawk Dikeman, a Sokoki-St Francis Abenaki who recreates his people's dramatic past as a costumed interpreter at Fort Ticonderoga in upstate New York. Once a bitterly contested strong point on the Anglo-French frontier, the reconstructed fortress is now a popular tourist attraction. Over coffee in the fort's Loghouse restaurant, I quizzed Wes about prevailing Abenaki attitudes. A deeply knowledgeable man who strives to give the fort's visitors a balanced perspective upon the region's troubled past, Wes smiled and replied without hesitation: 'To the Abenaki people, Rogers will always be *White Devil*'.

SO FIRM BATTLE-LINES HAVE been set. The rivals are well entrenched: the St Francis raid was either a daring feat of arms, visiting a bloody but well-deserved retribution upon a ruthless foe, or a despicable massacre of innocents. Given these extreme viewpoints, it's perhaps unsurprising that few researchers have ventured out into the intervening no man's land in an effort to discover *exactly* what happened when Rogers' command fell upon St Francis. In consequence, even such basic facts as the date of the attack continue to be misrepresented in both popular and scholarly works. Equally striking is the lack of any serious effort to explain *why* St Francis was targeted to receive Rogers' attentions.

This book attempts to answer these questions – attempts, because it's highly unlikely that the full story of the raid can ever be told. Any account of the Indian experience of early America must be skewed by a hopeless imbalance of the evidence. The Indians had an oral culture, lacking independent written records, so their voices can usually be heard only through the distorting accounts of the white man.

While it's certainly true that the bulk of contemporary evidence for the St Francis raid comes from British and French records, here at least the Abenaki voice *can* be heard. That bloody episode generated some of the most credible and revealing of all Indian testimonies to survive from before the nineteenth century. Much credit for chronicling this precious evidence belongs to Gordon M. Day (1911–93). Armed with his trusty tape recorder, Day was indefatigable in documenting the tribe's memories before they were lost forever. As historians have increasingly recognised, *provided* it is subjected to careful analysis, such oral history can illuminate even long past events. Every effort has been made to use it here.

If Indian memories of the St Francis raid are unusually rich, the written European accounts remain undeniably problematic. The key contemporary source for the raid has always been Rogers' own published *Journals*; these reproduced the official report he wrote upon his return, adding explanatory comments. But Rogers' account raises questions of its own. In addition, no sooner had reports of his expedition filtered back to the settlements of New England than the facts became furred under a patina of rumour and hearsay. In the two and a half centuries since then, the legends have accrued like barnacles upon a sunken hulk. Even now the myth-making process continues, with the publication of spurious evidence further muddying the waters.

Because of this apparent dearth of genuine eyewitness accounts, the temptation to rely upon others that strain credulity has proved strong. But while the testimony of participants is scarce, enough exists to permit a more detailed reconstruction than has previously been attempted. Indeed, the emphasis hitherto placed upon dubious evidence, tales of lost treasure and attempts to plot every step that the raiders took on their route march to and from St Francis, has only deflected attention away from the true stories of those people enmeshed in these bloody events.

Fact *is* often stranger than fiction, and this overworked expression is undoubtedly justified when applied to the St Francis raid. That episode didn't occur in a vacuum: it coincided with the pivotal months of the decisive year in a conflict that decided the fate of North America. For that reason *White Devil* aims not only to trace the raid's causes, course and consequences, but to place it within the epic struggle for dominance of the continent.

The story unfolds through the reminiscences, reports and correspondence of participants, often using their own spellings and punctuation: these contemporary witnesses were men and women, soldiers and civilians, Europeans and Americans, whites and Indians. With this diverse cast of characters, it's necessary to say something about the terms used here for specific ethnic groups. In the interests of simplicity, the English-speaking inhabitants of Great Britain and her North American colonies are frequently characterised as British, or, following common French and Indian usage of the period, English. Similarly, French-speakers of both metropolitan and New France (the colony embracing Canada) are often labelled French. Where no specific tribal name is given to the aboriginal inhabitants of North America, the term Indian is used. This is not intended to imply any disrespect, nor to fly in the face of political correctness: although based upon a notorious misnomer, this terminology is so broadly accepted that it seems perverse not to use it here.

Whilst founded upon extensive research among both published and manuscript sources, this book is aimed squarely at anyone with a broad interest in the past. Keeping this general audience very much in mind, detailed discussion of controversial evidence has been restricted to the endnotes; these not only seek to complement the text, but also allow the interested reader to identify the sources used.

THIS IS A STARK AND BLOODY saga dominated by the *leitmotifs* of vengeance and survival. But it is also a tale of high courage, great fortitude and unexpected humanity. It's a true story from North America's shared past – one that deserves to be freed from the choking tentacles of legend and bias.

Stephen Brumwell
AMSTERDAM, 2004

CHAPTER ONE

Conflict and Coexistence

FOR THE INHABITANTS OF THE New Hampshire outpost known simply as Fort Number Four, the early summer of 1754 was a tense time.

The stockaded village, and the outlying farmsteads that sought its protection, marked the northern limit of British settlement in the fertile valley of the Connecticut River. Beyond it lay a swathe of mountains and forested wilderness, a dubious buffer zone between the territories claimed by the rival imperial powers of Britain and France. During more than a century of North American colonisation, the traditional animosities between these old enemies had been readily transplanted to the New World. By 1754, such tensions had already sparked three spasms of warfare that had echoed the more conventional fighting in far-off Europe; now there were rumours that the coming spring would herald a fourth bout of bloodshed.

The anxious residents of Fort Number Four included Susanna Johnson, a young mother of three; her foreboding at the gathering war clouds was exacerbated by her fears for the final stages of another pregnancy. But on 29 August, both the looming conflict and the hazards of impending child-birth were momentarily forgotten: Susanna's beloved husband James had returned safely from a successful three-month trading trip to Connecticut. Their log house was full of the stores he'd brought back, and their neighbours had gathered there to celebrate his homecoming.

The evening passed very cheerfully as the Johnsons and their guests feasted upon ripe watermelons and quaffed heady flip, a concoction of strong beer spiked with rum and seethed with a loggerhead, or red-hot poker, that made the liquor bubble and foam. At midnight the tipsy company finally dispersed, save for a spruce young spark who lingered on to pay court to Susanna's fourteen-year-old sister, Miriam.

Exhausted but happy, the Johnsons slept soundly, until they were awakened shortly before sunrise by loud knocking at the door: their friend Peter Labarree, axe on shoulder, had come to start the day's work.

But when James Johnson answered the summons, he found his neighbour – and eleven hostile Abenaki warriors at his heels.

James lunged for his guns; his cry of 'Indians! Indians!' was Susanna's first inkling of the attack. 'In an instant,' she recalled, 'a crowd of savages, fixed horribly for war, rushed furiously in.'

As Susanna screamed for mercy the war party swarmed through the house. Miriam was tumbled out of bed and James pinioned and bound. Susanna, faint and trembling, was led outside, where she saw Labarree likewise tied, along with their hired man, Ebenezer Farnsworth. The shocking scene was completed when her children – six-year-old Sylvanus, Susanna, four, and Polly, aged two – were dragged naked from the house.

Bundling up their plunder, and urged on by the thud of the fort's alarm guns, the Abenakis hustled their eight captives away. With Indians tugging at each arm, they were hurried unmercifully through thorny thickets. After a mile and a half, the heavily pregnant and panting Susanna was obliged to rest. A watching Indian drew his knife; it looked like the end had come for her – but instead, he merely slashed the band that constricted her bulging gown and pushed her onwards.

When Fort Number Four was three miles behind them, the Indians called a halt and captors and captives alike shared a breakfast of looted bread, raisins and apples. A horse the Johnsons recognised, Scoggin, wandered nearby; the Indians caught him so that Susanna, whose bare feet and legs were torn by thorns and spattered with blood, could ride.

The following morning, Susanna's woes were multiplied. At this most inconvenient of times, she was taken with the pangs of childbirth. More than forty years later when she published an account of her ordeal, Susanna summarised her predicament: 'fifteen or twenty miles from the abode of any civilized being, in the open wilderness, rendered cold by a rainy day, in one of the most perilous hours, and unsupplied with the least necessary that could yield convenience in the hazardous moment. My children were crying at a distance, where they were held by their masters, and only my husband and sister to attend me. None but mothers can figure to themselves my unhappy fortune.'

But as Susanna conceded, the Indians showed some pity by constructing a booth to shelter her from the elements. Throughout her memoir, she recorded episodes which showed that the Abenakis were far from oblivious to the well-being of their captives: whether they were motivated by humanity, or a simple desire to preserve valuable prisoners for sale to the French was something she remained uncertain about. That both sentiments were intermingled is suggested by the reaction of Susanna's Indian master – who 'evinced, at numerous times, a disposition that showed he was by no means devoid of compassion' – to the birth of her daughter. Looking in upon mother and baby in their crude arbour, he had clapped his hands with glee and exclaimed 'Two moneys for me! Two moneys for me!'

Having suppered on porridge and fire-baked cornmeal Johnny cakes, Susanna fell into an exhausted sleep. Next morning the group proceeded on its way. The miserable mother was incapable of producing milk for her baby, who was instead supported entirely by water gruel.

Tired, cold, dejected and frightened, the prisoners were chivvied on a hazardous and painful route march north-westwards across the Green Mountains of what is now Vermont. None of the Indians were inclined to abuse their captives, save for the youngest, who delighted in tormenting the teenaged Miriam by pulling her hair, treading on her gown, and numerous other boyish pranks. Susanna rode on Scoggin, but even so, she was frequently obliged to dismount and rest. By the fifth day of the journey, hunger had been added to their hardships. Abenaki hunting parties had returned empty-handed, and finally there was no alternative but to eat the faithful Scoggin: the hapless horse was swiftly shot, cooked and consumed. With a bewildering decorum, the Indians offered their prisoners the choicest steaks. What remained of the beast's flesh was dried and smoked; next morning, Scoggin's bones were pounded for marrow to make soup flavoured with roots from the woods.

Once the party had slurped down the broth, the Abenakis gave their war whoop and the exhausting march resumed. Obliged now to totter along on her own two feet, Susanna feared that she would be too weak to continue, but her master hitched up her petticoats with strips of bark and ordered her to 'munch' once more. It was too much; Susanna soon fainted, and the last thing she saw as she slipped into unconsciousness was an Indian raising his hatchet above her head to administer the *coup de grâce*.

Susanna woke to find her master berating the warrior who had so nearly destroyed his prize. Because she remained so feeble, a crude pack-saddle was constructed of bark so that James could carry his wife piggyback.

The party now followed the course of Otter Creek as it flowed down into Lake Champlain; a beaver pond formed in one of its branches meant that they all had to wade across. Waist-deep in chilly water, and at the limits of her endurance, Susanna passed out once more. James dragged her ashore, and the whole party halted. Susanna was again impressed by the humanity of her captors, who kindled a fire to warm the life back into her before they all moved on. As they forded a swift-flowing stream, Peter Labarree tripped and dropped Susanna's baby. She recalled, 'little did I expect to see the poor thing again.' But luck was with them, for Labarree clutched a corner of the child's blanket and plucked her to safety.

With this hazardous crossing now behind them, the mood of the captors suddenly changed: according to Susanna, they 'gave loud tokens of joy, by hallooing and yelling in a tremendous manner'. Their prisoners were obliged to join in a war dance around the fire; each was taught a song to perform. Susanna wasn't sure if this was some sort of religious ceremony, or for the amusement of her captors, but she found the whole proceedings both painful and offensive.

The captives were soon obliged to demonstrate their new skills for the benefit of seven other Indians; Susanna remembered that these warriors 'were received with great joy by our masters, who took great pleasure in introducing their prisoners'.

Now the swollen party continued its journey by water; shortly afterwards, at noon on the sixth day since that fatal morn at Fort Number Four, they arrived at the French stronghold of Fort St Frédéric, at the southern end of Lake Champlain.

James Johnson later reckoned they had travelled a hundred miles, and all eight – nine, now, counting the newborn – had survived the perils of the wilderness, a deliverance that his wife attributed 'to the blessing of that Providence whose smiles give life to creation'. She was not to know that their strange odyssey had barely begun.

FORT ST FRÉDÉRIC, OR CROWN POINT, as the British always called it, occupied a neck of land adjoining a channel linking the broad expanse of Lake Champlain with the narrower waterways to the south. With the notable exception of several short overland portages, across which boats or goods had to be laboriously manhandled, a continuous watercourse stretched from the Hudson to the St Lawrence, from British New York to French Montréal. In a region where land travel was proscribed by mountain, forest and marsh, this four-hundred-mile-long chain of rivers and lakes was both a vital trade route and an obligatory conduit for the movement of troops: Fort St Frédéric was a valve that regulated the flow of both.

Aware of the region's strategic importance, the French had established a stockaded post on the banks of Lake Champlain in 1731. Work on the stone fortress was begun in 1734 and completed two years later. Its construction coincided with a period of peace, and a village of soldier-settlers swiftly mushroomed around it; the descendants of the yellow Normandy roses that they planted to remind them of the old country still bloom today beneath the arc of the Champlain bridge.

By the standards of its own age, Fort St Frédéric was a curiously old-fashioned structure. At a time when military architects extolled the virtues of squat bastions that minimised the target presented to enemy cannon, its granite citadel soared to a height of four storeys. To many educated Frenchmen of the Enlightenment, this conspicuous chateau-like tower and the dark limestone ramparts that encircled it would have looked more at home in the pages of a medieval illuminated manuscript than in a modern manual of fortification.

Nor was the situation of the fortress all that a competent military engineer might desire. In 1754, the keen-eyed James Johnson noted the towering citadel's vulnerability to siege artillery, remarking that it was 'not tenable against proper battering pieces'. Indeed, the entire site was dominated by an adjoining hill. Five years earlier, the roaming Swedish scientist Peter Kalm had also identified the position's defensive flaws. Kalm was a botanist, not a soldier, but luckily for the historian, his interests extended far beyond North America's flora and fauna. He observed that the fort was built in the wrong place, adding that every visitor was immediately struck by the absurdity of its location.

Yet such criticisms assumed that any hostile force would be able to transport heavy siege guns to within effective range of the fort's walls. The logistical problems involved in such an operation were daunting; during the fighting that had erupted between 1744 and 1748, when the War of the Austrian Succession stirred bloody ripples in the Americas, that threat had failed to materialise. Indeed, far from advancing to Crown Point, the British colonies were obliged to remain on the defensive. During those years Fort St Frédéric established its sinister reputation as a base for French and Indian war parties striking south against the frontiers of New York and New England.

And for all its shortcomings, Fort St Frédéric was no puny stockade: its stout stone walls and bristling cannon looked impressive enough to the Indian allies of New France who beached their birch-bark canoes on the shoreline below. Its defences also offered concrete evidence to those who argued that His Most Christian Majesty King Louis XV of France, and not His Britannic Majesty King George II of Great Britain and Ireland, held sway over the extensive waters of Lake Champlain.

In 1713, at the end of the War of the Spanish Succession – or Queen Anne's War, as the English colonists called it – a peace treaty had fixed the boundary between the French and British domains at Split Rock, on the lake's western shore, some twenty miles north of Crown Point. The subsequent construction of Fort St Frédéric within land claimed by the colony of New York therefore represented a calculated act of defiance; its great jutting citadel was a fist brandished in the very teeth of the British.

By the time Peter Kalm visited the fort in 1749, in the aftermath of King George's War, the territorial battle-lines had shifted once again. The British now maintained that Canada's true boundary lay beyond the *northern* end of Lake Champlain, between Fort St Jean and Prairie de la Magdeleine. For their part, the French had nudged the hypothetical frontier far to the south. King Louis' claims now encompassed the entire length of the serene waterway that his countrymen had named Lake St Sacrement, and which optimistic New Yorkers later christened Lake George, in honour of their king. The merits of these rival claims would soon be tested by the forthcoming inevitable conflict.

When they arrived at Fort St Frédéric in September 1754, the Johnsons and their fellow captives were led before the commandant, Captain Paul-Louis Dazemard de Lusignan. Since his early teens, Lusignan had served in the independent companies of regular troops that provided a permanent garrison for New France; administered by the Navy Department responsible for the colonies, these units were known as the *Compagnies Franches de la Marine*. Whilst most of the rank and file were recruited in Europe, the officers, like Lusignan himself, were typically natives of Canada; they knew the country and were experienced in conducting military operations alongside those other mainstays of the colony's defences, militiamen drawn from the hardy *habitants*, and the Indian tribes allied with France.

Five years before, Peter Kalm had found Lusignan to be an urbane and courteous man. Although in very different circumstances, the haggard prisoners from Fort Number Four encountered similar hospitality, receiving plenty of brandy, a good dinner and a change of linen. After all that they had suffered, a grateful Susanna Johnson confessed that this was luxury indeed. Following an examination by Lusignan himself, the captives were shown to an apartment where they remained beyond the jurisdiction of their *savage masters*; throughout their stay, they were civilly treated. The Johnson children were all decently clothed, although Susanna awakened from a nap to find her baby – who now rejoiced in the apt, if singular, name of Elizabeth Captive Johnson – dressed so fantastically in the finicky French fashion that she failed at first to recognise her.

All of this unexpected kindness only heightened the prisoners' grief, bewilderment and mortification when, on the fourth day of their stay at Fort St Frédéric, they were returned to their Abenaki captors and led on board a vessel sailing northwards on Lake Champlain, through the waterway known to the Indians as *Caniad eri-Guarante* – the mouth or door of the country. Peter Kalm had undertaken that same journey years earlier; his usual careful notes on the changing landscape describe, to the left, on the lake's western side, the peaks of the Adirondacks towering above the very shoreline; to the east a belt of lowlands extending for some ten miles before giving way to the Green Mountains of Vermont. The entire countryside was mantled in thick forest. Kalm noted how the lake rapidly widened; within thirty miles of Crown Point it was already some twelve miles across and flecked with islands. Its waters were clear, and reportedly too deep to fathom with a line of two hundred yards. As the voyage continued, so the mountains receded, eventually giving way to tree-covered plains.

Like Kalm, the Johnsons and their captors followed the lake to its narrow and shallow northern limits, and then journeyed onwards into the very heart of French Canada by way of the Richelieu River. After a three-day journey they arrived at Fort St Jean. It was 16 September,

1754: just eighteen days since their abduction from Fort Number Four. The prisoners spent a comfortable night within the wooden stockade, followed by another at the older stone-built garrison of Chambly, twelve miles to the north; on both occasions they were turned over to their captors in the morning.

Arriving at the great St Lawrence River, they proceeded eastwards by canoe to Sorel, near the island-choked entrance to Lake St Pierre; here the kindly local priest tendered brandy and a blessing before they paddled wearily onwards. That afternoon, on 19 September, they disembarked at a barren heath. A fire was kindled, a dinner cooked and another war dance staged amidst more infernal yelling. The prisoners capered and hollered with their captors until they were hoarse. At last the party was nearing its final destination. The Abenakis orchestrated a suitably triumphant return to their home village. Everyone – captors and captives alike – was required to look their best: the prisoners had their cheeks, chins and foreheads daubed with a mixture of vermilion and bears' grease.

Within a mile of the village, the captives were taken to a French house for soup and bread. They must have wondered whether this frugal refreshment would be their last. As they grew closer to their village, two of the Abenakis went ahead to announce the party's arrival. Before long, whoops, yells, shrieks and screams resounded from all sides; the triumphant new arrivals reciprocated with enthusiasm.

Two hours before sunset, the party arrived at the landing place. As the terrified gaggle of adults and children stumbled ashore, the disconcerting hubbub rose to a crescendo. But this intimidating noise was the least of their worries. As Susanna recollected, 'a cloud of savages, of all sizes and sexes, soon appeared running towards us. When they reached the boats they formed themselves into a long parade, leaving a small space through which we must pass.'

The community towards which their exultant captors now thrust them bore a name that had long struck terror amongst the frontier settlements of New England and New York. As they prepared to enter the twin rows of the waiting gauntlet, the cringing captives braced themselves for a vicious beating. What else could they expect from the notorious St Francis Indians?

BY 1754, THE ABENAKI VILLAGE of St Francis possessed a justifiably fearsome reputation. For generations it had disgorged warriors whose raids had helped to check the northwards expansion of Britain's burgeoning colonies. During a half century of sporadic warfare, the St Francis Indians had torched countless frontier communities, killed and scalped numerous men, women and children, and herded droves of shocked and bewildered captives back to Canada. In the eyes of their prey they were a devilish crew and their village was a pernicious nest.

It was ironic that a community cast in such a murderous mould should have evolved as a haven for refugees from violence, but this was truly the case. For almost a century, the village had attracted a steady stream of migrants from many Indian groups. Though divided by differing tribal backgrounds and loyalties, these incomers nonetheless shared a bond that helped build a common identity: they all hailed from societies that had buckled under the strains imposed by an era of unprecedented strife.

For the Indian peoples of North America's eastern seaboard, that bleak new age had dawned long before Europeans even dreamed of invading their lands. The French, English, Dutch, Spanish and Swedish colonists who established precarious bridgeheads by the beginning of the seventeenth century had followed in the wake of an unseen but deadly advance guard, as fleeting contacts with visiting Old World fishermen had already exposed Native Americans to an array of previously unknown diseases. The Indians lacked immunity; entire communities were winnowed by influenza, measles, dysentery, typhoid and, above all, smallpox. The land that the first colonists believed virgin was in fact already widowed.* The subsequent settlement of Europeans and their African slaves only compounded the catastrophe: by 1650 some ninety per cent of the original Indian population had succumbed to epidemic illness.

* In the telling words of the ethno-historian Francis Jennings.

This biological holocaust left those who survived ill-prepared – either physically or psychologically – to resist the European onslaught when it eventually came. Armed conflict with the colonists, from Massachusetts to Virginia, resulted in the swift destruction of many weakened coastal tribes.

But even peaceful contacts with the incomers had disastrous consequences for the native peoples. The fur trade – through which Indian hunters provided pelts in exchange for Old World manufactured goods – had far-reaching effects; as they sought to satisfy the insatiable demand for furs, the woods were cleared of game. This virtual extinction of fur-bearing wildlife, combined with the colonists' wholesale felling of forests for settlement and farming, skewed the Indians' balanced relationship with their environment and destroyed their traditional economic system. Furs bought the European goods that Indians increasingly craved – including strong drink. English rum and French brandy exerted a baleful influence as endemic alcoholism corroded the very core of tribal society.

Competition for domination of the fur trade that guaranteed access to these coveted European wares triggered an escalation of inter-tribal warfare. The Indians swiftly adopted European military technology, which meant such conflicts were far bloodier than the ritualistic confrontations of old. Muskets and steel hatchets were deadlier than traditional bows and wooden clubs; the heavy casualties that resulted from the new warfare prompted calls for vengeance that fuelled a vicious circle of violence.

It was this mixture of bewildering change and ferocity that led to the formation of the Indian community of St Francis. The first great influx had followed King Philip's War: in 1675 and 1676 the hard-pressed tribes of southern New England, led by the Wampanoag chief Metacom, or King Philip, as the New Englanders had styled him, mounted a desperate bid to preserve their autonomy from the expanding colonial population. Protracted, bitter and brutal, the result was overwhelming victory for the colonists: the defeated Wampanoags and their Narragansett allies were shattered and dispersed.

Those who survived the cataclysm sought asylum amongst fellow Algonquian-speaking tribes; some approached the Mohegans and Mahicans of the Hudson Valley; others gravitated towards the Abenakis, whose territories ranged across northern New England from Vermont to Maine. The Abenakis – People of the Dawnland – already embraced a wide array of groups. Anthropologists have divided them on linguistic grounds into western and eastern Abenakis: the former included the Sokokis, Cowasucks, Missisquois, Winnipesaukees, Ossipees, Pennacooks and Pigwackets; the latter, the Kennebecs, Androscoggins and Penobscots. New Englanders, though, made no such distinction: they were all the Eastern Indians.

Although far from the epicentre of conflict, the Abenakis couldn't avoid getting entangled in King Philip's War. They had clashed with their hereditary Mohawk foes, members of the powerful Iroquois Confederacy from what is now upstate New York. Bitter enemies of the French, the Mohawks had become staunch allies of the English. In addition, a group of Indians surprised and massacred by New Englanders at Peskeompscut on the Connecticut River included a band of Sokoki Abenakis.

So the Abenakis had themselves contributed to the wave of displaced tribal peoples; Sokokis were amongst the refugees who now sought sanctuary at the site of the future mission of St Francis, joining a handful of relatives who had moved there during the previous decade. Other Abenakis were drawn to Schaghticoke on the Hudson River, where the colony of New York offered a refuge for Indians who might become valuable military allies. Many of those later drifted northwards to the village of St Francis.

The shock waves from Metacom's war reverberated long after he'd been run to ground and his severed head spiked atop a Plymouth watchtower. As a fresh surge of English settlement rippled up the Connecticut and Merrimack river valleys, other western Abenaki groups took evasive action. They withdrew to the rugged and wooded interior of the Green and White Mountains, or found sanctuary within the welcoming arms of New France.

The growing number of refugees who gravitated towards the settlement attractively situated upon the high bluffs bordering the St Francis River offered tempting potential converts for New France's black-robed Jesuit missionaries. In what had become an increasingly uncertain world for the Indians of the north-east, the French mission villages ranged along the St Lawrence Valley from Montréal to Québec offered both security and stability.

Unlike their Puritan counterparts in New England, the Jesuits had enjoyed considerable success in persuading Indians to embrace Christianity. The Black Robes travelled far and wide amongst the tribes, enduring terrible hardships and risking agonising deaths. They did not flinch from a martyrdom that Canada's fearsome Iroquois enemies were only too willing to grant them. When collared with necklaces of red-hot hatchet blades, or baptised with kettles of boiling water in mockery of their own rituals, the Black Robes displayed impressive courage. Such stoicism was also prized by their tormentors; a grudging acceptance followed. The sufferings the Black Robes endured in spreading the faith were recorded in gruesome detail and published in best-selling *Relations*; this helped to ensure that their evangelising received the financial support of good Catholics back in old France.

It was not bravery alone that underpinned the Jesuits' success; unlike the Puritans, they did not insist that Indian converts should abandon *all* of their own customs and beliefs. Although baptised as Christians, the so-called mission Indians retained their cultural identity; as a result, by the end of the seventeenth century the Jesuits were ministering to Indians from Nova Scotia to the Mississippi.

In 1700, the Jesuit mission of Saint François-de-Sales, established on the Chaudière River opposite Québec some seventeen years earlier, was relocated to the Saint Francis River to cater for the Indians who were congregating there. These disgruntled migrants bore deep-seated grudges: they had axes to grind, and needed little encouragement to wield them against the land-hungry English settlers.

Although New England had emerged triumphant from the ordeal of

King Philip's War, victory came at a terrible price: the lasting enmity of displaced and embittered native peoples. In coming years, they and their descendants would exact bloody vengeance for real and imagined wrongs.

THE OPPORTUNITY TO SETTLE old scores came soon enough. In 1689, the War of the League of Augsburg in Europe had triggered the first open confrontation between the North American colonies of England and France. During the conflict known as King William's War, the Abenakis – who were already embroiled in their own territorial disputes with Massachusetts – readily allied themselves with Canada and devastating Abenaki raids upon New England established a pattern that characterised succeeding imperial clashes. The Iroquois allies of the English did much of the fighting and suffered severely; in the future they avoided direct conflict with New France, protecting their own interests through a policy of wary neutrality.

When Queen Anne's War broke out in the summer of 1703, the inhabitants of the newly established mission village of St Francis cajoled other Abenakis and their Micmac relatives into taking part in raids on Maine. A year later, warriors from St Francis were prominent amongst a 200-strong force of mission Indians who joined the French in an assault on the Massachusetts frontier town of Deerfield. Much of the settlement was reduced to ashes; one hundred and fifty inhabitants were slain or captured; the massacre was etched upon the collective memory of the New Englanders.

A contingent of Mohawks – renowned for their hostility towards Canada – were amongst those who torched Deerfield; their presence was striking evidence of Jesuit activity; it also reflected the divisions that catholicism provoked within tribal villages, creating factions between converts and those traditionalists who scorned the Black Robes' teachings. From the 1660s onwards, Mohawks, many of them women for whom the cult of the Virgin Mary held particular appeal, began to migrate from the New York frontier to new missions around Montréal. Two communities emerged: Mohawks concentrated at Sault-Saint-Louis, better known from contemporary accounts as Caughnawaga, and another settlement administered by the Sulpicians, the Jesuits' rival order. In this mission, named after the Lake of the Two Mountains, Mohawks lived side by side with Algonquins and Nipissings.

As intensive farming exhausted surrounding soil, both missions drifted westwards in search of fresh land. The Black Robes were also keen to distance their charges from the corrupting influence of unruly Montréal. The transplanted Mohawks, together with other tribes of the St Lawrence Valley, became a key component in the armies of New France – they also engaged in a lucrative smuggling trade between Montréal and Albany; the close contact they maintained with their Iroquois brethren to the south added a perplexing twist to frontier politics.

Though the Anglo-French treaty of 1713 ushered in a lengthy era of peace between the imperial rivals, it did little to ease tensions between the Abenakis and their British neighbours. Continuing encroachment upon Indian lands meant violence was inevitable; during the 1720s, both eastern and western Abenakis fought in defence of their territories. On Maine's Kennebec River, resistance was kindled by Sébastien Rasles, the Jesuit missionary at Norridgewock. New Englanders burned the village in 1722, but Father Rasles escaped and his congregation swiftly retaliated against the nearest British settlements.

In a letter to his brother, Father Rasles told how the Abenakis' mode of warfare rendered even a handful of their warriors more formidable than a body of two or three thousand European soldiers. Upon entering enemy territory they divided into bands of thirty or forty; each party was given a hamlet or village *to eat*. Their strategy was devastatingly effective. Recalling a previous raid, Rasles explained that, 'Our two hundred and fifty warriors spread themselves over more than twenty leagues of country . . . and on the appointed day they made simultaneous attacks, very early in the morning. In one single day they ruined all the English; they killed more than two hundred, and took a hundred and fifty prisoners, while on their side only a few warriors were wounded, and these but slightly. They returned from this expedition to the village, each of them having two canoes laden with booty that he had taken.'

Yet for all their skill as raiders, the Abenakis were lackadaisical when it came to their own security; Father Rasles told his brother, 'the Savages, and especially the *Abnakis*, know not how to guard themselves against surprises'. Their raids prompted Massachusetts' Lieutenant Governor Samuel Shute to denounce the Abenakis as rebels and traitors: their scalps now carried a hefty bounty.

Such temptation stimulated a fresh attack upon Rasles' mission, in August 1724; this time the troublesome priest was not so lucky. He was killed in company with thirty of his flock; the head of the Jesuit missions in New France reported that the English and their tribal allies had pillaged and burned the village. They didn't spare the mission church, which was torched 'after a base profanation of the sacred vessels and of the adorable Body of Jesus Christ.' The 66-year-old Father Rasles endured equally shocking corporeal indignities: grieving villagers found his body riddled with bullets; his scalped skull was smashed by hatchet blows, the hollow eye-sockets and gaping mouth plugged with mud.

Following that raid, some hundred and fifty Norridgewock Abenakis sought the security of mission villages at St Francis and Bécancour, near Trois-Rivières; the embittered refugees bolstered both the size and prejudices of these already anglophobic communities.

To the west, in the Green Mountains and on the upper Connecticut Valley, the Abenaki war chief Grey Lock orchestrated a skilful guerrilla struggle against Massachusetts: his unremitting assaults halted the depredations on tribal lands. Grey Lock's warriors often operated from the fortified village of Missisquoi, a strong point surrounded by swamps at the northern head of Lake Champlain. Missisquoi, like St Francis, was a polyglot community of fragmented and disparate Indian peoples; the formidable Grey Lock was himself a refugee from one of the shattered communities in Massachusetts.

Grey Lock's war was waged without French aid, at a time of peace between the European powers; it underscored what the New England authorities were slow to grasp: the Abenakis, and the other Indians who fought alongside the French of Canada, were independent *allies*, not subject peoples. Father Rasles understood this: in 1722 he said, 'there is not one savage Tribe that will patiently endure to be regarded as under subjection to any Power whatsoever.' Whilst the Governor General of New France was *Onontio*, the acknowledged 'father' to his numerous Indian children, he did not enjoy their unquestioning filial devotion; the relationship was always conditional upon him fulfilling the role of indulgent parent, nurturing his cherished offspring through gifts, protection and other signs of favourable treatment. If his children squabbled, Onontio might intervene to separate them, but he never commanded their blind obedience. The failure of the familial metaphor to reflect reality created continual tensions between New France's governing order of soldier-statesmen and their capricious but indispensable Indian allies.

WHEN KING GEORGE'S WAR erupted in 1744, Abenakis from St Francis, Bécancour and Missisquoi swiftly consolidated their reputation as inveterate foes of the English. The pattern of raiding established in previous conflicts was now repeated with deadly effect.

On the exposed northern frontier, Britain's colonists, despite overwhelming weight of numbers, were forced into a defensive crouch. The fourteen British colonies along the eastern seaboard between Nova Scotia and Georgia mustered around one and a half million souls; New France, by contrast, embraced just seventy thousand widely scattered inhabitants. But the struggle was far from unequal: addicted to bickering amongst themselves, the British were incapable of presenting a united front. In addition, the amateur militias they traditionally relied upon for defence had long since lost their cutting edge. New France, in contrast, was a centralised régime with a single governor general, dominated by a military ethos that left it well honed for war. The resulting contest pitted a flabby and floundering heavyweight against a lean and skilful bantam capable of packing a stinging punch.

The experience of Fort Number Four, on the very cusp of settlement in New Hampshire, epitomised the plight of the British as they reeled back on the ropes under a barrage of French and Indian blows. Despite its uninspiring title (it was the fourth in a numbered sequence of plantations earmarked for settlement by the General Court of Massachusetts back in 1735), Number Four became a veritable backwoods Gibraltar. Throughout the spring and summer of 1746 its little garrison, commanded by the brave and experienced Captain Phineas Stevens, repelled repeated enemy assaults. The stockade was abandoned that autumn, but hard weather kept the French from returning to torch it; all through the winter the fort was held for King George by an aged spaniel and a domesticated cat, who provided a hearty welcome to Stevens and his men when they came back the following March.

Stevens was a wily frontier-fighter who'd learned much about Indian warfare after being captured by Grey Lock's raiders back in 1723. He was soon required to put this knowledge to good use. In early April 1747 his post endured a particularly determined two-day assault mounted by a substantial French and Indian war party led by Jean Baptiste Boucher de Niverville. Fire arrows and threats both failed to intimidate the garrison. Fort Number Four held out, but it was the exception that proved a very different rule: remorseless Abenaki raiding scoured settlers from Vermont, the upper Connecticut River Valley and the Massachusetts frontier.

Peace was announced at Aix-la-Chapelle in 1748, but once again the niceties of European diplomacy meant precious little to the Abenakis: *they* had not participated in the negotiations that ended hostilities; *they* could see no reason to stop raiding the British frontiers in quest of captives and vengeance. Viewing the distant Green Mountains from the surface of Lake Champlain in 1749, Peter Kalm reported that the Abenakis who wandered them remained the Englishman's worst enemy.

And of all the Abenakis ranged against the British, none were more inexorable than those from St Francis; British commentators increasingly used their name as a label for all the western Abenakis.

In the three Anglo-French conflicts between 1689 and 1748, the Abenakis were amongst the most effective, reliable and valued of Canada's

Indian allies. But for all their celebrated loyalty to New France, they also fought the British for reasons of their own: a determination to protect their remaining tribal lands, and a deep-seated desire to exact retribution for past wrongs. White observers who encountered the woodland tribes agreed that these traits lay at the very heart of their character: a burning spirit of independence went hand-in-hand with an unquenchable thirst for vengeance. One British soldier wrote, 'No people have a greater love of liberty, or affection to their relatives; but they are the most implacably vindictive people upon the earth, for they revenge the death of any relation, or any great affront, whenever occasion presents, let the distance of time or place be never so remote.'

In 1752, it was rumoured that the British planned to cut a road northwards from Fort Number Four to the Cowass Intervales, the Place of the White Pines, situated on the great Oxbow bend of the Connecticut River, near modern-day Newbury, Vermont. The fertile soil deposited by the floodplain of the sinuous river had long since made it attractive to seasonal Indian agriculturalists; it also occupied a strategically important site poised midway between Canada and New England. Although unoccupied in 1752, Cowass – Cohase, Cohose or Coös, as it was also known – remained a favoured destination for roaming Abenaki bands. The ground held the bones of their ancestors. It would not be surrendered without a fight.

At a conference held in Montréal that summer, the Abenakis left no doubt of their feelings towards this sacred land. In the presence of the Governor of Montréal, Charles Le Moyne de Longueuil, and delegates from the mission communities of Caughnawaga and the Lake of the Two Mountains, they reasserted their ownership of the region. Through their chief spokesman, Ateawanto, or Jerome Atecuando, the St Francis Indians delivered a warning to their old foe Captain Stevens, there representing the Governor of Massachusetts. Ateawanto's words vented a bitterness engendered by decades of suspicion and hostility: 'We hear on all sides that this Governor and the Bostonians say that the Abenakis are bad people. 'Tis in vain that we are taxed with having a bad heart; it is you, brother, that always attack us; your mouth is of sugar but your heart of gall; in truth, the moment you begin we are on our guard.'

Ateawanto's people did not seek war with the English, but they would tolerate no settlement beyond Fort Number Four. They would not surrender one single inch of land; nor would they allow the English to kill a single beaver, or take a single stick of timber from ground that had been given to them by the Master of Life himself. Any Englishman foolish enough to ignore that warning would surely die. For their part, the listening mission Iroquois delegates professed themselves charmed with the Abenakis' vigorous maintenance of their rights; should it prove necessary, they would aid them with all their might.

This blunt speech was not merely an expression of determination to resist British expansion; it also amounted to an Abenaki declaration of independence. Ateawanto told the Anglo-Americans that whilst his people were loyal allies of the King of France, from whom they had *received the Faith and all sorts of assistance in our necessities*, they now spoke on their own behalf as a people who remained entirely free.

Ateawanto's uncompromising words were hammered home the following January when a delegation of six Abenakis met Stevens at Fort Number Four to remind him that if the plans to settle Cowass went ahead, Number Four would burn. The Abenakis promised a *Strong War*: one that would enjoy the support of powerful tribal allies.

This was clearly no hollow boast: Massachusetts swiftly backed down, and directed Stevens to reassure the Abenakis that the colony had no intention of occupying Cowass. The authorities in Boston also cautioned Lieutenant Governor Benning Wentworth of New Hampshire against provoking Indian wrath. An expedition sent to blaze a trail to Cowass, by marking the bark of trees to indicate the path of a future road, was recalled when it struck the Connecticut River.

But by 1754, British desire to appease the Abenakis had been subsumed by growing concern that the French now intended to establish a fort at Cowass themselves, with another post at the head of the Kennebec River; such worrying rumours gained credence from escalating Anglo-French conflict in the Ohio Valley. It was widely believed that the French sought to establish a chain of posts, strung like beads on a necklace, stretching from Canada to the Mississippi; these forts – and the influence they could exert through trade with neighbouring Indians – threatened to pen the teeming British colonies within the constricted lowlands east of the great Appalachian Mountains.

Alarmed by these worrying developments, Governor Wentworth sent an expedition with orders to eject interlopers. Captain Peter Powers probed further into the wilderness than any previous British party, but his men found no sign of the French. Wentworth now begged his colony's elected representatives to seize the initiative and occupy Cowass before the opportunity was lost for good: a British fort there would not only provide a crucial bastion against Indian raiders from the north, but also an advanced base from which future offensives against Canada could be mounted. Although appreciating Wentworth's reasoning, New Hampshire's assembly doubted whether such a remote and exposed post could ever be maintained. Despite persistent stories of a Fort Wentworth, the governor's dream remained nothing more than that.

Against this broader canvas of increasing imperial tension, animosity between Abenakis and British settlers continued to smoulder. Resentments were fanned into flames after two St Francis Indians failed to return from a hunting trip to New Hampshire in 1753. Convinced that the inhabitants of Fort Number Four had treacherously killed the pair by treating them to poisoned rum, the tribe's angry young men demanded vengeance. The English received an ominous warning to take care of themselves; as frontier families would soon discover, these were no idle threats.

WITH THIS ACRIMONIOUS background, no British settler could have contemplated the whooping villagers of St Francis with anything other than extreme trepidation. The ordeal that now lay before the Johnsons and their fellow prisoners was horribly familiar, both from the popular published narratives of New Englanders who had returned from captivity amongst the Indians and the pages of the Jesuit *Relations*. Running the gauntlet could be a harrowing experience for those whose strength and spirit quailed beneath the sticks and stones of a particularly vengeful and vindictive community; prisoners stunned by the barrage of blows might lie where they fell until they were beaten lifeless; others suffered injuries that would dog them to the end of their days.

One man for whom the physical and mental scars of the gauntlet ran deep was a young English soldier named Henry Grace. Captured by the Micmacs of Nova Scotia during the early 1750s, Grace was subsequently sold to the St John's Indians, who took him with them on a convoluted hunting trip. Whenever his captors entered a new tribal territory, Grace was made to run the gauntlet, to make him *free of the country*. Whilst in the south-east, Grace endured a brutal drubbing at the hands of the Choctaws, who beat him black and blue. The Cherokees were scarcely more charitable, pelting him with sticks and stones. Years later, when safely back home in his native Hampshire, Grace recalled, 'One Stick stuck in my Back, and they almost beat one of my Eyes out, so that I could not see out of it for above a Month.'

When Grace encountered them, the Cherokees were believed to be favourably inclined towards the British, so the long-suffering redcoat had expected to fare far worse when his captors brought him to the notoriously hostile village of St Francis. As they approached the settlement the customary cry for a prisoner went up, and Grace's heart trembled in fear. Yet although he was once again obliged to *run the Gantlope*, to his considerable surprise and relief, he emerged unhurt.

For all their misgivings, the treatment meted out to the cowering captives from Fort Number Four was equally mild. Susanna Johnson said, 'We expected a severe beating before we got through; but we were agreeably disappointed when we found that each Indian only gave us a tap on the shoulder.' On this occasion the dreaded ordeal of running the gauntlet was a symbolic rite of initiation. Relieved at having escaped so lightly, the captives were taken to the homes of their masters.

This unexpected leniency from one of the most infamous tribes in colonial America was due to several factors: firstly, live and undamaged captives were valuable commodities; they commanded a ready market amongst the French, who could employ them as workers in labour-starved New France or ransom them back to the British authorities for a handsome dividend. By the mid-eighteenth century, captive-taking was a highly profitable variation upon traditional hunting practices, and provided a steady source of revenue for the Abenakis and other Indian communities. Secondly, women and children were always far less likely to be the focus of violence; though male captives could typically expect a rougher reception, like the redcoat Henry Grace, James Johnson, Peter Labarree and Ebenezer Farnsworth had all passed through the gauntlet with nothing worse than a token pat on the back.

Thirdly, the warriors who descended upon Fort Number Four that August morning had returned to St Francis unscathed, so the mood of their relatives remained undarkened by any emotional clamour for revenge. Had the raiders suffered casualties, grieving kin might have demanded blood for blood. In time of war, the fate awaiting male captives brought to mourning tribal villages would be very different.

There was a fourth factor: the Johnson party represented potential recruits for the tribal community. Through the long-established and widespread practice of adoption, captives could provide an invaluable transfusion of fresh blood. Women and children were especially suitable for bolstering populations weakened by war, disease and dispersal; females might find partners and produce offspring to further strengthen the tribe; youngsters were more likely to undergo rapid assimilation and utterly forget their white roots.

The prevalence of adoption amongst Canada's Indians left a strong impression upon the quizzical Swede Peter Kalm. In 1750, whilst scouring the countryside around Québec for his beloved plants, Kalm was guided by an Indian from the nearby Huron mission village of Lorette, an 'Englishman by birth, taken by the Indians thirty years ago when he was a boy and adopted by them according to their custom in the place of a relation of theirs killed by the enemy.' He had stayed with the tribe ever since, embracing both the Catholic faith and an Indian bride.

This was far from untypical; Kalm's British contemporaries were baffled and worried that many of those taken prisoner by the Indian nations, particularly young people, were loath to return to their own society. Even though their parents begged them to do so, the free life led by the Indians pleased them better. Kalm noted the startling consequence – that the Indian blood in Canada was very much mixed with European blood.

Of all the Indians in Canada, none had proved more adept at raiding and captive-taking than those of St Francis; more than any others, the St Francis Indians hated the English*. Exact totals are impossible to determine, but in the course of half a century or more, many of the captives taken to their village were subsequently adopted into the tribe. Thanks to this steady racial intermingling, St Francis was a veritable ethnic melting pot, a hybrid community sustained by Indian immigrants and English prisoners alike. This striking fact was soon made clear to Susanna Johnson.

Mother and baby had spent their first night in St Francis within a large wigwam, accompanied by two or three warriors and as many *squaws*. The other captives were dispersed throughout the town. That evening Susanna and her new housemates dined upon *hasty pudding* served in a large wooden bowl placed in the centre of the floor. The other women sat to eat by first kneeling and then sitting back on their heels; Susanna's attempts to mimic this posture caused her some indignation and them considerable amusement.

The following afternoon, Susanna and her baby were taken to the grand parade, where the villagers had assembled. A venerable chief stepped forward and the multitude subsided into respectful silence. He delivered a solemn and impressive speech: 'Not a breath was heard, and every spectator seemed to reverence what he said,' Susanna remembered. When the oration was over, her six-year-old son Sylvanus was brought

* The conclusion of Emma Lewis Coleman, who conducted exhaustive research into the background and fate of New Englanders captured during the French and Indian wars.

out and a number of blankets laid beside him. It became clear that Susanna's and her son's captors intended to exchange their respective prisoners. 'My master, being a hunter, wished for my son to attend him on his excursions,' she wrote. Each of the two Indians delivered up his goods with formality: Sylvanus and the blankets were reckoned a balance for Susanna, her baby and two large belts of wampum she had already been given by her master and his brother. These were items of considerable value and immense significance. Wampum consisted of white and purple beads made from the drilled shells of whelks and quahog clams, arranged in single strings or woven into belts. It was a coveted commodity that could be given as a gift or to emphasise the sincerity of treaties, agreements or other important statements. Because it was prized by Indians and was used to purchase furs from them, whites employed wampum as currency amongst themselves; although Indians did not regard wampum as money, its value made it a useful medium of economic exchange.

The transaction over, Susanna discovered that she had been adopted into the leading family of St Francis. Conscious of this distinction, the resilient and perceptive young mother expressed her gratitude and craved the indulgence of her new relatives whilst she learned their customs. But the peaceful mood was shattered by a grim reminder of exactly why the St Francis Indians maintained their fearsome reputation: the arrival of warriors triumphantly brandishing a pole bearing scalps prompted widespread rejoicing. The passage of four decades did nothing to diminish Susanna's outrage when she remembered the scene: 'Savage butchery upon murdered countrymen! The sight was horrid. As I retired to my new residence I could hear the savage yells that accompanied the war dance. I spent the night in sad reflection.'

Susanna's grief was heightened by the rapid dispersal of her loved ones: within days, James was taken to Montréal for sale to the French; her daughters Susanna and Polly and sister Miriam followed soon after; the remaining captives from Fort Number Four, Labarree and Farnsworth, ultimately joined them.

Alone now save for her baby and son, Susanna grew deeply depressed.

'In this strange land, without a prospect of relief, and with all my former trouble lying heavy upon me, disappointment and despair came well nigh being my executioners,' she wrote. Even now her sorrows were not over: there was a heart-rending scene when young Sylvanus was dragged away by his new master on a hunting expedition.

But the dejected Susanna could at least draw some small consolation from the knowledge that her own master, Joseph-Louis Gill, was an important and influential man. He was not only son-in-law to the *grand sachem*, but was wealthy, possessed a store of goods, and lived in a style far above the majority of his tribe. He often told Susanna that he had an English heart – and with good reason, for there was not a drop of Indian blood in his veins.

THE STORY OF JOSEPH-LOUIS GILL, the White Chief of the St Francis Indians, could have sprung directly from the overheated imagination of a Hollywood screenwriter. Born at St Francis in 1719, Joseph-Louis was the child of white captives Samuel Gill and Rosalie James, who had been abducted during separate Abenaki raids on Massachusetts and Maine. Taken to St Francis and adopted into the tribe, Samuel and Rosalie were later baptised as Roman Catholics and married in a ceremony conducted by the long-serving missionary Father Joseph Aubery. The couple spent the rest of their lives at St Francis, raising seven children, of whom Joseph-Louis was the eldest son.

Although distinguished by blond hair, Joseph-Louis' Yankee looks did nothing to prevent his acceptance within the tribe. Tall and strongly built, he was a formidable hunter. When aged about twenty-one, he married Marie-Jeanne Nanamaghemet, the daughter of one of the principal chiefs of the St Francis Abenakis. They had two sons, Xavier and Antoine; the adopted Susanna became particularly fond of her new 'brother' Antoine, whom she knew by the name of Sabatis.

In 1747, Joseph-Louis joined a war party of Abenakis and Canadians mustered to fight Miamis who were menacing the far-flung French outpost of Detroit. During this expedition he demonstrated his bravery when a medicine man caught a rattlesnake and challenged him to bite it. With the fearlessness and skill of a mongoose, Gill snapped the snake's spine with his teeth, then, for good measure, chewed open the rattler's belly and swallowed its still-throbbing heart. This impressive display did not go unappreciated by his own people; he was soon after elected a principal chief.

In September 1749 Gill was amongst five tribal leaders – including the famed orator Ateawanto – who signed a letter written by Father Aubery to the canons of the great Romanesque cathedral of Chartres in the very heart of France. This letter renewed the Abenakis' vow to Our Lady of Chartres and emphasised their desire to remain as the cathedral's spiritual children. It likewise expressed continuing gratitude for church ornaments given to the first converts at St Francis half a century before. Conspicuous amongst these treasured relics from old France was a handsome and weighty silver statue of the Virgin Mary; modelled upon a venerated image preserved in the famous underground church at Chartres, it had been donated by the canons after the Abenakis presented them with a collar crafted from wampum beads and porcupine quills.

Alongside his role as a principal chief of the St Francis Indians, Gill also held the post of *chef de la prière*; he was interpreter and middleman between the villagers and the Jesuits. The post demanded fluency in both Abenaki and French; as Susanna discovered, Gill also spoke some English. These accomplishments allowed him to straddle the world of the European and the Indian, and to act as cultural broker between them. Although a proven hunter and warrior – and apparently one of the raiders who descended upon Fort Number Four in August 1754 – by his mid-thirties, Gill was primarily a trader. That summer, when he bought Susanna Johnson and adopted her into his family, Joseph-Louis Gill was growing rich on his profits.

The community of which this 'white Indian' had become such a respected and successful member was far removed from the primitive tribal settlement of cliché. As Gordon M. Day pointed out, St Francis was *no irregular assemblage of squalid bark huts.* A French plan of 1704, drawn shortly after the Jesuit mission was established, already depicted a well-ordered community of some twenty substantial houses, ranged on three sides of a church and presbytery with an open area before them. This neat, rectangular settlement was enclosed within a defensive wooden palisade. By the mid-eighteenth century the village had relocated down-river and grown considerably. A military engineer who visited St Francis in 1752 counted more than fifty houses made of squared timbers covered with bark or boards. Another dozen homes were built in the French style, possibly of frame construction. Two years later, James Johnson estimated *near Fourty buildings of all Sorts*, including some built of stone.

When the Johnsons and their neighbours arrived as captives, the population of St Francis may have numbered some nine hundred men, women and children. Precise figures are difficult to determine because the community included groups that habitually drifted between different villages, but the settlement was clearly thriving. By 1754 any protective stockade had long since gone; unlike the beleaguered inhabitants of Fort Number Four, the villagers of St Francis felt no need to shelter behind man-made defences. Their security rested upon the bravery of their menfolk, predatory hunters and warriors long accustomed to raiding the distant English settlements in search of captives and glory. James Johnson reckoned these fighting men to number one hundred and twenty; this total included both St Francis Indians and *Shatacooks* recently absorbed from the dwindling settlement of Schaghticoke on the Hudson. It was unthinkable that the feeble Yankees would ever forsake the security of their forts to bring the fight to *them*.

Yet the settlers who inhabited the tattered fringes of British America were far from being mere helpless victims: for all the ingrained enmities that set them apart, the St Francis Abenakis and the colonists who faced them across the debatable lands between New England and New France shared much in common, and not just because of the racial intermingling from adopting captives into Indian tribes. They might not have acknowledged the fact, but the settlers who occupied the hazardous northern extremities of Britain's mainland American colonies were, in many respects, closer to their traditional Indian foes than to their own governments. Once again, it was the foreigner, Peter Kalm, who explained the phenomenon. Travelling through New Jersey in 1748, he remarked, 'The country, especially that along the coasts in the English colonies, is inhabited by Europeans, who in some places are already so numerous that few parts of Europe are more populous . . . In most parts you may travel twenty Swedish miles, or about a hundred and twenty English miles, from the coast, before you reach the first habitation of the Indians. And it is very possible for a person to have been at Philadelphia and other towns on the seashore for half a year without so much as seeing an Indian.' Kalm believed this would surprise his countrymen, who assumed that North America was almost wholly inhabited by 'savage' or heathen nations.

In coming decades the growing physical and psychological gulf between the needs and aspirations of the young and dynamic frontier and those of the old and increasingly remote Tidewater would become a familiar source of discord.

Unlike the townsfolk of Philadelphia, Boston or Portsmouth, those living in frontier settlements like Fort Number Four were well acquainted with Indians. Despite their cultural differences, they were bound together by the rugged natural environment in which they struggled for survival; alongside the conflict, there was at least some degree of coexistence. During spells of tenuous peace, the mutual hostility engendered by decades of massacre and betrayal could give way to wary acceptance, and even genuine friendship and respect. And many of those who sought a new life on the borders of Massachusetts and New Hampshire came from societies that shared core values with Indians: they too placed a particularly high priority upon independence and revenge.

Since the 1730s, there had been a steady push of population towards the frontiers of New England. Between 1710 and 1760, when the combined populations of Massachusetts, Rhode Island and Connecticut leaped from 100,000 to more than 400,000, good farmland became scarce and expensive. The northerly province of New Hampshire, with its seemingly limitless supply of prime timber and enough fertile soil to lure farmers, grew increasingly attractive. The provincial government was keen to encourage settlement and the establishment of regular townships, so land was competitively priced. The Connecticut, Merrimack and Piscataqua rivers all offered convenient routes into the interior, thus providing cheap transport, both for incoming settlers and for the produce they subsequently sought to export.

New Hampshire's expansion was initially fuelled by migrants from southern New England. Staunched during the colonial-Indian strife of Queen Anne's War, the population flow recommenced during the second quarter of the eighteenth century and by the late 1730s, settlers had begun to edge their way up the Connecticut River Valley.

But a distinctive source of New Hampshire's booming population came from Northern Ireland, many of them Scots who had earlier crossed the Irish Sea for a new life in the province of Ulster. Between 1718 and 1775 it is reckoned that at least 150,000 so-called Scotch-Irish immigrants took ship for America from Northern Ireland; this folk movement dwarfed all others that sailed across the Atlantic – with the significant exception of enslaved Africans.

Although the Scotch-Irish influx is associated primarily with the settlement of Pennsylvania, Virginia and North Carolina, its impact upon New Hampshire was far from negligible. A bridgehead settlement with the emotionally charged name of Londonderry, established in the lower Merrimack Valley, was a magnet for fresh waves of migrants and by 1730, according to one royal official, the province was already home to more than a thousand Scotch-Irish.

Like the Abenakis with whom they soon collided, many of these products of Great Britain's Celtic fringe were refugees. They included a hefty contingent of Presbyterians whose decision to quit Ulster was prompted by the religious intolerance of their Anglican neighbours. Others were displaced by chronic dearth; the spectre of famine that stalked Ireland after a succession of failed harvests in the late 1720s prompted Jonathan Swift's most biting satirical work; his *Modest Proposal* of 1729 suggested that the children of the poor might be sold for food, being capable of providing a wholesome and nourishing meal whether served 'stewed, roasted, baked or boiled', or indeed, 'in a fricassee or a ragôut'. Many of the immigrants from Ulster gravitated towards the far-flung frontier. In the opinion of most Tidewater contemporaries, that was the best place for them: the Scotch-Irish were seen as hard-drinking and quarrelsome, rough folk who preferred swords to plough-shares.

The Scotch-Irish undoubtedly shared other salient characteristics with the Abenakis of St Francis, Bécancour and Missisquoi: alongside their readiness to resort to violence, they likewise cherished notions of family honour and martial prowess, and were imbued with strong traditions of feuding and vendetta. Such characteristics were typical of many tribal border folk; indeed, amongst the Scotch-Irish were Anglo-Scots borderers, who had been forcibly resettled in Ulster during a prolonged drive to pacify their notoriously lawless homeland after the unification of the English and Scottish monarchies in 1603. The Scotch-Irish thus included *a double-distilled selection of some of the most disorderly inhabitants of a deeply disordered land* .*

The belligerent heritage of these hard, feuding, vengeful folk clearly heightened the potential for discord with North America's indigenous peoples, but shared values and codes of behaviour also helped to draw the seemingly disparate and irreconcilable societies closer together. This is shown by an episode from the early life of a notable frontiersman of Scotch-Irish stock, the Revolutionary war hero John Stark. In April 1752, whilst the teenaged Stark and Amos Eastman were on a beaver-trapping expedition to Baker's River, New Hampshire, they were captured by ten St Francis Indians: their crime was trespassing on tribal land. They were brought to St Francis where the young men of the village armed themselves with sticks and formed the customary gauntlet; Eastman got a vicious beating. The stalwart Stark was disinclined to share his friend's fate without at least hitting back; a colourful *Memoir* of his life tells how he 'snatched a club and made his way through the lines knocking the

---

* David Hackett Fischer.

Indians down, right and left whenever they came within his reach.' So Stark escaped with scarcely a blow; all the while the old men of St Francis sat at a distance enjoying the sport heartily.

Stark and Eastman remained at St Francis until early July, when they were ransomed – or redeemed – by Phineas Stevens. During that time Stark endeared himself further to his captors by deliberately bungling his designated chores. Sent to toil in the fields, he instead threw his tools into the river, declaring loftily that it was 'the business of Squaws and not warriors to hoe corn'. Far from being angered at Stark's defiance, the St Francis Indians were so impressed with his boldness that he was adopted into the tribe. Stark later recalled his captivity with both fondness and amusement: he had experienced more genuine kindness from the 'savages' of St Francis than he ever knew prisoners-of-war to receive from any civilised nation.

Other such bonds were forged between like-minded individuals who confronted each other in the rugged, contested region between New France and New England. Recalling his own early days hunting and trading on the dangerous New Hampshire frontier, another frontiersman of Scotch-Irish descent likewise painted a picture of cross-cultural interaction. He wrote: 'I could hardly avoid obtaining some knowledge of the manners, customs and language of the Indians as many of them resided in the neighbourhood and daily conversed and dealt with the English.'

This young man was Robert Rogers. The fourth son of James and Mary Rogers, he was born in November 1731 in the frontier town of Methuen, in the province of Massachusetts Bay. Little is known of his parents, although it's likely they were recent arrivals from Ulster.

In the spring of 1739, the Rogers joined the trickle of hardy settlers who were prepared to weigh the hazards of the frontier against the prize of land and freedom. They crossed the border into New Hampshire, following the course of the Merrimack River to Mountalona, the Great Meadow, where the family carved out a homestead. During King George's War, when French and Indian raiders filtered down from Canada to assail

New England's frontiers, they sought the protection of Rumford, a stockaded town some ten miles to the north. In the summer of 1746, after a patrol of militiamen was ambushed, fourteen-year-old Robert Rogers was amongst those who volunteered to take the place of the slain and pursue the raiders.

The following summer found young Robert enrolled in the militia, although these part-time soldiers failed to encounter their elusive enemy. The Rogers family went back to their homestead in the winter of 1747–8, but the move was premature; in the coming April, fresh French incursions once again obliged them to seek the sanctuary of Rumford's blockhouses. When the family eventually returned to Mountalona, they found nothing but ashes.

The war had barely subsided before James Rogers looked set to lose his land again, this time because of a convoluted boundary dispute between Massachusetts Bay and New Hampshire. In October 1748 a group of Scotch-Irish from the New Hampshire settlement of Londonderry had successfully petitioned for permission to establish a township on land encompassing Mountalona. James Rogers and a neighbour countered by claiming that they and their six sons had already purchased the land in question. In a final settlement, the pair were granted lots equal to those of each of the petitioners, with their two eldest sons to share another. The rest of their offspring received nothing.

But the restless Robert Rogers was not shaped for the life of a husbandman. In March 1753 he was one of the party sent by New Hampshire's governor on the perilous expedition to mark out the road to the fertile Cowass Intervales. Their guide, John Stark, remained undaunted by his recent encounter with the St Francis Indians, even when they passed the very spot where he had been captured just a year before.

In his published *Journals*, Robert Rogers was vague about his early years on the New Hampshire frontier, yet they were clearly formative ones. He recalled: 'my manner of life was such as led me to a general acquaintance both with the British and French settlements in North America and especially with the uncultivated desart [wilderness], the mountains, valleys, rivers, lakes and several passes that lay between and contiguous to the said settlements.'

Young Robert was not content with second-hand information from Indians and hunters; instead, he ranged the country himself. This experience not only gratified his curiosity; it also developed stamina and bequeathed a comprehensive knowledge of the techniques necessary to survive within such a punishing natural environment.

Rogers returned from the aborted expedition to the Connecticut River to find his father was dead. In 1844 the young Francis Parkman noted the enduring tradition that James Rogers was shot by a friend who mistook him for a bear. Later that year, Rogers bought land to the south at Merrimack. The following summer of 1754, when the escalating imperial crisis once again obliged the governor to call out the militia, Rogers served on patrols along the Merrimack River Valley.

On this front there were no clashes with the enemy. Elsewhere, the bloodshed had already begun. In the distant Ohio Valley an ambitious young Virginian militia officer named George Washington had instigated a savage little skirmish that left French corpses strewn across the forest floor. Through his bloody ambush, Washington had unwittingly kindled a conflagration that would reduce North America's previous conflicts to the status of petty squabbles. Robert Rogers and those others who followed the harsh existence of the New England frontier would need all of their hard-earned knowledge and endurance to survive it.

CHAPTER TWO

Making Reputations

THE ABENAKIS SLIPPED EASILY into this new war with the hated English. As they had never subscribed to the previous peace between the European monarchs and their North American colonies, to them it was just a continuation of ongoing hostilities – but in scale and intensity, this conflict was very different from those that had gone before. For the first time, the St Francis Abenakis and other Indians found themselves operating both against and alongside large numbers of trained professional troops from across the Atlantic; the resulting clashes between the martial systems and values of the Old and the New Worlds were bewildering and often unsatisfactory for all concerned.

There were Abenakis amongst the 130-strong contingent from the mission villages of Canada accompanying reinforcements sent to the Ohio Valley. For many Indian nations, this region had been a traditional refuge from strife in troubled times, but a collision of French and British interests now made it the flashpoint for a world war. The warriors from the St Lawrence arrived to find that fighting had already erupted: on 28 May, 1754, Washington's command and their local Iroquois allies bushwhacked a band of Frenchmen bivouacked within a rocky forest glen. Thirteen of the French were wounded, including their leader, Ensign Joseph Coulon de Villiers de Jumonville of *la Marine*; to the horror of Washington and his men, the Iroquois promptly tomahawked them where they lay.

It was in the wake of this bloody encounter that the Canadian mission Indians arrived at France's newly constructed post at the Forks of the Ohio River. This was Fort Duquesne, named in honour of the Governor General of New France, Ange Duquesne de Menneville, Marquis Duquesne. The commandant, Captain Claude-Pierre Pécaudy de Contrecoeur, now implored them to join the struggle against the Virginian aggressors; in a more personal plea the brother of the slain Jumonville, Captain Louis Coulon de Villiers, appealed for their help in exacting vengeance. After discussions, the majority agreed to accept the offered axe and to wield it against their 'father's' enemies.

On the afternoon of 3 July, 1754, Villiers' seven hundred Frenchmen and Indians emerged from the forest into an extensive natural clearing, where they found Washington's force holed up within a puny entrenchment bearing the apt name of Fort Necessity. The garrison consisted of four hundred men, a mixture of Virginian short-service provincial troops, and redcoats from the South Carolina independent companies. For several hours driving rain transformed Washington's shallow trenches into muddy rivulets and the enemies exchanged shots across the intervening meadow. With their casualties mounting, the dispirited defenders took solace in rum; like the earthen ramparts around them, their discipline eventually crumbled. Such attrition was too gradual for Villiers' Indian allies; their decision to decamp the next day persuaded the Frenchman to initiate negotiations with Washington and his officers. Articles of Capitulation were agreed that evening and the sodden and increasingly drunken defenders were granted the right to depart unmolested with their personal goods and weapons. In recognition of their resistance, they would be granted the honours of war: the defenders were permitted to march off proudly with standards flying, drums beating, and in possession of a token piece of artillery. That the cannon in question was an insignificant swivel gun did not matter a jot: it was the symbolism that counted.

For professional soldiers who valued their reputations, the honours of war were a hallowed formula that sugared the bitter pill of defeat –

but they meant nothing to the tribal warriors who now eyed the vanquished garrison. For his part, Villiers had rebuffed the Virginian incursion into the Ohio Valley and secured a major propaganda coup by duping Washington into admitting culpability for Jumonville's murder; in contrast, the Indian contingent had nothing to show for its efforts. Having travelled so far, these warriors required something more than the possession of a squalid encampment in the midst of the dripping forest: they needed concrete proof of their prowess, in the traditional form of captives, loot and scalps. When Washington's men moved out, the Indians descended upon them in search of such trophies. Demoralised and intimidated, the garrison allowed themselves to be plundered: two of the wounded and a trio of stupefied drunks were slain. Spooked by fear of an impending massacre, the remainder stampeded in flight; the pursuers took sixteen prisoners, later killing and scalping three of them.

This was an unfortunate and regrettable incident, but one for which the French acknowledged no responsibility: it was an inevitable consequence of a conflict in which *both* sides sought the services of tribal warriors. But the butchered invalids and inebriates of Fort Necessity were an ominous portent: in coming years, other more glaring infractions of established European codes of conduct would prompt similar Gallic shrugs.

Washington's humiliation only strengthened Great Britain's resolve to break France's choking grip upon her North American colonies. London's strategy for 1755 envisaged a policy of aggressive self-defence, with wide-ranging strikes against key enemy strong points. The elimination of Fort Duquesne was now a matter of national honour: the expedition sent against it was entrusted to the commander-in-chief himself, Major-General Edward Braddock, who headed a force composed of two regiments of redcoats backed by provincials from Virginia, Pennsylvania and North Carolina. Once he had secured his primary objective, Braddock was to unite with another army led by William Shirley, the Lieutenant Governor of Massachusetts; their combined forces would then advance to assault Niagara. A third army composed solely of colonial troops was allocated to Colonel William Johnson; this was to advance up the Hudson Valley against that hated symbol of Bourbon imperial pretensions, Fort St Frédéric at Crown Point. Finally, an expedition of New Englanders, stiffened with a sprinkling of redcoats, would sail to thwart the enemy in Nova Scotia, that troubled region called Acadia by the French.

New France once again looked to its heterogeneous Indian allies, both domesticated and otherwise, to help counter this ambitious four-pronged assault. Many warriors answered the call.

IN THE WAKE OF VILLIERS' TRIUMPH, some hundred warriors from Canada wintered at Fort Duquesne. By the following June, their numbers had doubled as others from the St Lawrence missions gravitated towards the likely epicentre of conflict. Still larger contingents of pro-French tribesmen converged upon the Forks of the Ohio from the upper country of the Great Lakes, the so-called *pays d'en haut*. These nations – Ottawas and Potawatomies, Menominees and Chippewas – remained largely beyond the influence of the Jesuit and Sulpician missionaries. In all, by early July 1755, there were around eight hundred assorted tribal warriors at Fort Duquesne; as his own garrison numbered no more than six hundred regulars and part-time militia, Captain Contrecoeur placed much faith in their services.

During those tense days, Contrecoeur received continuing reports of the remorseless advance of Braddock's army as it painstakingly hacked a path through the gloomy and primeval western Pennsylvanian forest. The size of the enemy's force remained vague, but there was no doubting its determination. As he finally neared his prize, Braddock split his command and forged ahead with the siege guns and a picked command of more than fourteen hundred men. By 9 July, the Anglo-American army had completed a hazardous double-crossing of the Monongahela River; they'd expected opposition there, but none materialised. The column now moved on with increasing confidence.

Braddock's advance guard was led by 35-year-old Lieutenant-Colonel Thomas Gage of the 44th Foot. The son of an Irish peer, Gage had been an army officer since his early twenties, fighting the French in Flanders and Jacobite rebels in Scotland. Despite this extensive and varied experience, Gage now made an elementary blunder: he neglected to occupy a hill that loomed upon his right and dominated the forest track the army had to follow.

What happened next is often described as an ambush, yet Braddock's column did not march blindly into some carefully baited trap. In fact, its leading elements collided with a force loping forward in hopes of catching the redcoats at the river; of its nine hundred men, more than two-thirds were Indians. These warriors had only been persuaded to participate through the persistent oratory of a respected Canadian officer, Daniel-Hyacinthe-Marie Liénard de Beaujeu. Both sides were surprised at the confrontation. Gage's redcoats reacted first. The élite grenadier companies that spearheaded the column opened fire with disciplined volleys; the range was long, but a lucky shot claimed Beaujeu. Soon British artillery pieces were brought into action. As musket balls and grapeshot rattled through the trees, the militiamen grew dismayed and disheartened; most of them fled. The Indians too hesitated, seemingly in awe of the thundering cannon. With triumphant cries of 'God Save the King' the bold British grenadiers advanced to complete their victory.

It was now, when all seemed lost, that a new leader emerged to galvanise the French and Indian resistance: Beaujeu's second-in-command, Jean-Daniel Dumas, a French-born captain of the colonial troops. Like so many others in this new war, Dumas had learned his trade during the previous decade's European campaigns. Since arriving in New France in 1750 he had bolstered this firm grounding in conventional warfare with fresh skills, including a flair for handling Canada's Indian allies. By his own account, Dumas rallied the regulars of *la Marine*; their hot fire staunched the British advance. Taking heart, the Indians now returned to the attack; they streaked along the flanks of the British column, swiftly seizing the knoll that Gage had failed to secure. From this position the Indians poured down a fire that obliged Gage's advance guard to give ground. Several British witnesses maintained that his command recoiled in confusion, thereby transmitting disorder to the main body following close behind.

Crouching behind trees and rocks, the Indians subjected the crumpled column to a withering crossfire that felled Braddock's men by the score. Crammed together on the road, they presented an unmissable target, while the Indians remained all but invisible to their opponents; from what little could be glimpsed of them it was clear that they sought to encircle their enemies. One British soldier, servant to an officer in the 48th Foot, reported that the Indians 'began to Ingage us in a half Moon and still Continued Surrounding us more and more.' As experienced Indian-fighters agreed, the skulking tactics that were now employed with such success against Braddock's men encapsulated the very essence of Indian warfare. The enveloping movements mimicked the techniques of the communal hunt; these were readily adapted to the needs of war. By fighting from cover, the Indians sought to inflict maximum casualties whilst minimising the risk to themselves. According to this cautious creed, a victory bought by a profligate outlay of tribal blood was a hollow triumph indeed.

Although scarcely seen, the Indians were far from unheard. As another humble redcoat, Duncan Cameron of the 44th Foot, recalled: 'these ravenous Hell hounds came yelping and screaming like so many Devils.' The war cries that resonated through the dismal forest represented another formidable weapon in the tribal arsenal: amidst the customary cacophony of battle – crashing musketry, throbbing drums and howling wounded – such spine-tingling whoops jangled nerves that were already frayed to breaking point. In combination, the physical and psychological elements of Indian warfare could eventually dissolve the courage of even the steadiest troops. Cameron was himself a veteran of several bloody engagements: within one twelve-month span of the last war he had faced massed French artillery at Fontenoy and slashing Highland broadswords on Culloden Moor. But the sights and sounds that assaulted his senses on that hot July afternoon near Fort Duquesne ensured that the Monongahela would remain the most shocking battle of them all.

After some two and a half hours of unrelenting punishment, the traumatised, bloodstained and smoke-grimed survivors of Braddock's command finally broke in desperate flight. This total rout of the King's troops at the hands of an inferior number of French-led 'savages' prompted considerable debate amongst military men and civilian pundits alike. In an official report on the disaster, Gage blamed the defeat squarely upon the cowardice of the rank and file: they had been demoralised by long marches and short rations, and discouraged by the locals' pessimistic predictions that if they engaged the Indians in their European manner of fighting they would be beaten. But Braddock's successor as commander-in-chief, William Shirley, remained sceptical of such simplistic explanations. Forwarding Gage's comments to Secretary-at-War Henry Fox, he felt obliged to observe that the causes of the troops' bad behaviour were not so distinct and clear as might be. Indeed, from all that eye-witnesses had told *him*, the confusion responsible for the men's 'Consternation & Stupidity' stemmed from the over-hasty retreat of the advance guard. Shirley also believed that the army's failure to secure the crucial high ground was a fatal oversight; had this been occupied, it was morally certain the battle would have been won.

Wrangling over responsibility for the defeat has continued ever since, but what remains beyond dispute is its overwhelming nature. Two-thirds of Braddock's men were killed or wounded; the general himself was amongst the dead. Those too badly injured to crawl off the field were slaughtered and scalped. A handful of prisoners had been taken, although for most of them this involved nothing more than a leap from the brisk frying pan of battle into the slow fire of the torture stake. As the sun began to set, the teenaged Pennsylvanian captive James Smith witnessed a disturbing scene from the ramparts of Fort Duquesne. A dozen pinioned prisoners, their faces and bodies blackened in token of approaching death, were burned on the banks of the Allegheny River. Before he turned away in shock and horror, Smith saw the Indians tormenting one of their victims with firebrands and red-hot irons; in response to his screams they yelled like infernal spirits.

Although the Jesuits and Sulpicians had taken pains to discourage such practices amongst their own neophytes, beyond the missions of Canada the torture of war captives by tribal warriors remained common. Smith's account of what he witnessed outside Fort Duquesne suggests the frenzied action of fighters heady with victory and looted rum; the fate of prisoners taken to tribal villages would be more ritualistic. Those rejected for adoption and marked down for death became actors in a grim drama with widespread audience participation. Men, women and children tortured their common enemy in gruesome ceremonies that could last for days. Such behaviour might be motivated by a desire to avenge and appease the restless spirit of a slain relative; it also subjected an enemy's physical and mental courage to the supreme test. The centre of all this attention was traditionally expected to play his part: whilst strength and resolution endured, he should mock his executioners' efforts and goad them with tales of the agonies he had formerly inflicted upon their people. It was a contest of wills, but one in which the ultimate result was never in doubt.

White observers did not share the cultural values and conditioning that underpinned such a response to pain. They were struck by the superhuman stoicism displayed by Indian victims of torture. Terrified British redcoats and Virginian provincials subjected to these protracted ordeals could not be expected to enter into the spirit of the event. For the Anglo-Americans, the treatment meted out to helpless prisoners-of-war reinforced existing perceptions of Indians. As 'savages', *they* at least possessed some justification for their excesses; the civilised Frenchmen who had failed to restrain them had no such excuse.

Indeed, amidst all the backbiting and recrimination that followed Braddock's defeat, there was one point upon which participants and commentators agreed: the unfortunate general and his followers had fallen victim to an unsporting combination of French and Indian treachery and barbarity. Such bloodthirsty confederates must be made to pay for their inhumanity.

THOSE WHO NOW BURNED TO avenge the shocking fate of Braddock's command included Captain William Eyre of the 44th Foot. It was thanks only to a rare expertise in engineering that Eyre had missed the massacre of his comrades on the Monongahela. Major-General Braddock had assigned him to the provincial army under William Johnson that was bound for Crown Point. In late July, when he heard the grim tidings from the Ohio, Eyre was struggling to organise the cumbersome train of artillery that would hopefully pound that notorious fortress into rubble. The captain feared that news of the disaster would dampen the spirits of the army's raw and undisciplined New Englanders and undermine Indian support; to prevent such damaging consequences it was imperative that *the Compliment* given to Braddock should be returned without delay.

Johnson, now with the provincial rank of major-general, began moving up the Hudson Valley during August. His army of three thousand colonials was joined by some three hundred Mohawks under their venerable chief Theyanoguin, known to the British as Old Hendrick. This formidable contribution from the senior tribe of the ostensibly neutral Iroquois League was striking evidence of Johnson's influence amongst them. Aged about forty in 1755, he was an Irishman who had crossed the Atlantic seventeen years earlier to oversee an estate owned by his uncle, Vice Admiral Sir Peter Warren. Johnson possessed a shrewd head for business; allied with the admiral's cash and connections, this expedited his rise to the rank of paramount farmer and trader in the Mohawk Valley on New York's exposed northern frontier.

During King George's War, Johnson's prominence brought other responsibilities, including appointment as Colonel to the Six Nations; ready access to colony funds earmarked to purchase the Iroquois' continuing goodwill enhanced his prestige amongst them. When a fresh conflict with France loomed in 1754, Johnson's celebrated expertise in Indian affairs guaranteed him a leading role in implementing Braddock's instructions to *cultivate ye best Harmony and Friendship possible* with the Indians; he received a commission for the 'Sole management and direction of the affairs of the Six Nations of Indians & their allies, to the end that the said Indians may be heartily engaged in & attached to the British Interest'.

William Johnson was a maverick. Although he amassed his own considerable fortune by exploiting the Iroquois through unscrupulous trading ventures and land deals, his ability to do so rested upon a genuine rapport; this extended to a string of liaisons with Indian women. Like few other Britons on the North American frontier, Johnson understood the Indians' character and concerns; in turn, he enjoyed their friendship and respect. It was this personal bond, and precious little besides, that had brought Old Hendrick and his Mohawks into the field to fight for King George.

At the Great Carrying Place – the point where the Hudson jinked westwards, making it necessary to disembark goods for the onward journey north to Montréal – Johnson instructed Captain Eyre to build a substantial strong point, designated Fort Edward in honour of one of the princes across the Atlantic. Before the base was completed, about half of the army marched for the lake that the French knew by the name of St Sacrement. When they reached its shores, on 28 August, Johnson dubbed the waterway Lake George. Having asserted his monarch's undoubted dominion, Johnson set his men to making good the claim by clearing the virgin forest in readiness for another fort.

Canada's defenders were confident that Johnson could be prevented from proceeding further. They took heart from events on the Ohio and signs that King Louis' ministers had not forgotten them. That spring, in response to reports that Britain had despatched professional troops across the Atlantic, France countered by reinforcing her own forces in North America. Six white-coated battalions of the regular army, the so-called *troupes de terre*, arrived in June. At their head was Major-General Jean-Armand, Baron Dieskau; mature in both years and experience, he had distinguished himself as a cavalryman under the leading soldier of the age, Marshall Maurice de Saxe.

The same convoy that ferried Dieskau and his men from Brest to Québec also delivered a new governor general. The man answerable to Versailles for the disparate territories that comprised New France would always face a daunting challenge, and Duquesne's successor arrived at the onset of an era of unprecedented turmoil. But Pierre de Rigaud de Vaudreuil de Cavagnial was uniquely qualified for the demanding task before him. Canadian by birth, Vaudreuil had served a lengthy apprenticeship in the colony troops before becoming governor of New France's sprawling southern territory of Louisiana. His life's ambition was to head the whole colony, and he lobbied officials in Paris to achieve that end. In finally securing this goal, Vaudreuil followed in a proud family tradition: his father had held that post during the opening decades of the century, earning a legendary reputation. It was a record that Vaudreuil was keen to both emulate and exploit.

Vaudreuil's return to New France coincided with the startling news of Braddock's elimination. Original plans for the colony's defence had envisaged a concentration of forces at Frontenac, at the north-eastern corner of Lake Ontario, ready for an attack upon the key British post of Oswego on the lake's southern shore. But the plunder harvested at the Monongahela included a copy of Whitehall's ambitious blueprint for the coming campaign; this illuminating document left no doubt that the rumoured threat to Crown Point was all too real.

As a result, Dieskau was sent to thwart Johnson on the Lake Champlain front. He was delighted at such an opportunity to further derange British hopes. Sniffing action, the old warhorse now began champing at the bit; as he prepared to quit Montréal for the army congregating at Crown Point, his chief fear was that the enemy would not wait for him.

Dieskau arrived at Fort St Frédéric in mid-August and spent the ensuing fortnight encamped beneath the fort's swart limestone walls. During that time he had a perplexing introduction to the peculiarities of North American campaigning. His command included some seven hundred Indians, almost half of them Iroquois from the missions at Caughnawaga and the Lake of the Two Mountains. Dieskau claimed that they were troublesome allies from the outset: they scouted only grudgingly, and even then returned without learning anything useful; in consequence, he doubted their very fidelity.

But the baron had no such gripes about the Abenakis. On 27 August they brought him a prisoner who divulged fateful intelligence: Johnson had left just five hundred men to hold Fort Edward. The unfinished post and its meagre garrison looked ripe for the plucking. Halving his available manpower, Dieskau selected a strike force of fourteen hundred men; some two hundred were crack grenadiers from the regulars, the balance was composed equally of Canadian militia and Indians.

After a tiring four-day approach by way of the muddy waters of South Bay and through the dense woods beyond, Dieskau was poised to pounce. To his undisguised exasperation, the Iroquois now refused to attack: they argued that the fort lay within English territory and therefore posed no threat. Following their lead, the Algonquins and Nipissings were equally reticent. The Abenakis alone were for pushing on: they had the greatest incentive for striking a vigorous blow against an enemy who menaced their tribal homelands. Surely the Iroquois would not abandon their brothers of St Francis? Abenaki oratory was persuasive and the troubled march continued until Dieskau's force neared its objective, when there was another unscheduled halt. The Iroquois now refused to assault a fortification mounting cannon; after further debate they agreed to attack Johnson's encampment at Lake George instead.

On the morning of 8 September, after marching fifteen miles towards this new target, Dieskau received word that Johnson had despatched a contingent to succour Fort Edward. The canny Saxon prepared an ambush on the wagon road connecting the two posts, deploying his force in what he characterised as a cul de sac. But his efforts to bag the enemy were only partially successful. In the baron's version of what happened next, it was the treacherous Iroquois who wrecked his plans. When the enemy column drew near it became apparent that the English were accompanied by numbers of Mohawks. Reluctant to massacre their kindred in such a cold-blooded fashion, the mission Iroquois allegedly betrayed the ambush by firing into the air.

Despite this warning, the ensuing scrimmage was bloody enough. The Mohawks at the column's head fought stoutly and suffered heavily. Prominent warriors were slain, including Old Hendrick himself. Age and girth obliged him to travel on horseback; he was bayoneted whilst pinned beneath his stricken mount.

In Dieskau's words, the enemy now doubled up like a pack of cards and fled pell-mell for the sanctuary of Johnson's lakeside encampment. Continuing Iroquois recalcitrance stalled the momentum of the pursuit: although Johnson's camp was fortified with nothing more than upturned bateaux and knee-high log barricades, they baulked at the unexpected sight of Eyre's artillery. According to a British observer, it was only this halt that prevented the French from tumbling into the camp along with the panic-stricken fugitives. Dieskau was justified in grumbling at such contrary behaviour; but for what ensued he had only himself to blame. Arraying his two hundred grenadiers in a single assault column, he sent them tramping forwards to storm the camp. With the sun glinting bravely upon their bristling bayonets, the dense clump of white-coats offered a fine mark for Eyre's siege cannon. This heavy metal now exacted retribution for Braddock's men: as one gunner reported, shot and shell opened *Lanes, Streets and Alleys* through the oncoming ranks.

The Frenchmen endured this pounding with a tenacity that impressed their opponents, but like the rest of Dieskau's motley army, they were ultimately driven from the field. As his command melted away the baron refused to budge: he believed himself dying, and with good reason; he was already prostrated by multiple leg wounds when one of the camp's defenders gratuitously shot him through the hips. Carried before Johnson, he was thereafter treated with scrupulous care and courtesy. This constant supervision was crucial for the baron's survival. A rueful Dieskau later recalled his predicament with grim humour. Several Indians had followed him to Johnson's tent; they gave him a furious look and spoke to Johnson with vehemence. When Dieskau observed that such behaviour scarcely suggested compassion, his host disclosed that the Mohawks wished to burn him in revenge for the death of their comrades. Johnson reassured his guest, and gave him an escort of a captain and fifty men. These safe-guards were definitely necessary: an Indian bluffed his way into the baron's tent, drew a sword from beneath his blanket and was attempt-ing to skewer him when an officer intervened.

Such persistence underscored the scale of Mohawk casualties. More than thirty warriors had been slain, and others injured. For the Indian allies of the French, the rambling fight was scarcely less disastrous. Trickling away from the lakeside camp, they returned to reclaim the packs and scalps left at the site of the morning's victorious ambush; there they clashed with a fresh force of New Hampshire and New York troops marching to Johnson's assistance; surprised and exhausted, they suffered severely. No account of their total losses survives, but they were clearly significant. Titus King, a captive held at St Francis, reported how that village alone lost ten warriors. By Indian standards this was a grievous toll; when news of the casualties arrived, King awoke to the sound of crying women.

Returning Indians were vocal in their condemnation of Dieskau's rashness. They poured out their grievances to Vaudreuil; he too was mortified that the baron had flouted meticulous rules of engagement in a frenzied hunt for glory. Plans were now afoot to create a bulwark for Crown Point by fortifying the Ticonderoga peninsula fifteen miles to the south. Here Lake George flowed into Lake Champlain, but the outlet was rendered impassable by cascades, so goods and boats had to be portaged via another short overland carry. In Vaudreuil's opinion, it was of infinite importance that this crucial spot be secured and fortified before the enemy seized it.

Had he known the mood of Johnson's army, the governor general might have been less anxious for the security of his colony. Coming so soon after the dismal news of Braddock's defeat, the Battle of Lake George had certainly administered a timely boost to Anglo-American morale, but though Johnson was acclaimed by the populace on both sides of the Atlantic and won a pension from Parliament and a knighthood from his grateful monarch, the immediate fruits of victory were less apparent to the officers and men at Lake George. In a detailed report to London, Johnson's aide-de-camp, Captain Peter Wraxall, gave a candid and pessimistic assessment of affairs. The provincials were nothing more than *raw Country Men*, he claimed: the fatigues of the campaign, approaching winter, the enemy's bravery and their own losses had all combined to produce a general and visible dejection amongst them; this mood manifested itself in a fondness for home and a marked reluctance to proceed any further towards French territory.

Under the circumstances, an assault upon Crown Point that season was out of the question. In addition, there were reports that the French were now digging in at Ticonderoga. In Wraxall's opinion the best that could be hoped for was to replace Johnson's makeshift encampment with a respectable fort, and to complete the works already started at Fort Edward. Both posts should be garrisoned, and the bulk of the troops disbanded in expectation of marching against Ticonderoga in the spring.

The crisis was compounded by an utter dearth of Indian allies. In keeping with custom, Johnson's Mohawks had lost no time in heading for home with their prisoners and scalps; they were keen to conduct the ceremonies required to appease the spirits of the warriors slain during the Bloody Morning Scout of 8 September. Their departure robbed the Lake George army of a priceless resource: they alone were believed capable of scouting and providing intelligence about the numbers and location of the enemy to the north. Without such information, the army was blind and helpless in the forested and mountainous wilderness. Increasingly desperate, Johnson turned to Colonel Joseph Blanchard of the New Hampshire Regiment. Did he know of any frontiersmen possessing the resolution and skill required to undertake such hazardous missions? One name came readily to Blanchard's mind.

FOR 24-YEAR-OLD ROBERT ROGERS, the swift escalation of warfare in 1755 was timely. During the previous autumn, he had become acquainted with a notorious counterfeiter; already a marked man in Boston, Owen Sullivan had subsequently shifted his activities to the currency-starved New Hampshire frontier. When the authorities in Portsmouth issued warrants for the arrest of nineteen suspected members of Sullivan's ring, Robert and his younger brother Richard were both named. In February 1755 preliminary hearings took place before examining justices. Robert pleaded his innocence but the magistrates remained suspicious; he was amongst ten men detained for trial. Forgery was then a capital crime; as a first-time offender, Rogers might expect to escape the hangman's rope, but there remained the painful and humiliating possibility of corporal punishment: with his ears cropped like clipped coins and both cheeks bearing the livid brand of *C* for counterfeiter, he would carry indelible marks of infamy.

Rogers was spared this ordeal: though undoubtedly involved in Sullivan's racket, he was a minor player and was soon released on bail; indeed, none of the accused ever stood trial. New England's guardians had weightier matters on their minds. Within days of Rogers' examination, Governor Shirley of Massachusetts appealed for volunteers to march against the French in Nova Scotia. The resulting upsurge of patriotic fervour provided Rogers with an opportunity to clear his name. Contacting a local recruiting officer, he promised to enlist a round score of men within New Hampshire's borders; he was remarkably adept in this task and rapidly raised two dozen recruits. This success stemmed from an unusual combination of traits: tradition maintains that Rogers was 'a man six feet in height, well proportioned, and one of the most active and athletic men of his time'; he was also intrepid and possessed a plausible manner of address. Big, strong, bold and articulate, Robert Rogers was clearly a man whom others would follow.

When New Hampshire soon after elected to raise a regiment of five hundred men of its own to join the strike against Crown Point, Rogers was ordered to Portsmouth to attend upon Governor Wentworth himself.

Despite protests from Massachusetts, the men that he had originally raised for *that* colony were instead turned over to Blanchard's New Hampshire Regiment. Unabashed by the furore he had provoked, Rogers blithely continued with his recruiting, eventually drumming up more than fifty men. This impressive tally entitled him to the rank of captain in the regiment's first company: that other seasoned woodsman, John Stark, became his lieutenant and right-hand man.

Blanchard's regiment received initial orders to watch the New Hampshire frontier; it was soon after redirected to rendezvous with Johnson's army on the Hudson. Rogers was out on scout when Dieskau launched his misguided assault on the lakeside camp, but he soon made amends for his absence. Within a week of the battle, Rogers and three companions clambered into a bateau and rowed stealthily down the west side of Lake George. It was the evening of 14 September, 1755.

This, the first of many such patrols that Rogers was to undertake during the next five years, gave some small hint of hardships and dangers to come. They paddled north for about twenty-five miles, then beached their craft and hid it in the bushes. Two of the party stayed to guard the boat and provisions whilst Rogers and the other man marched overland until they sighted Fort St Frédéric; many Indians were in the vicinity, amusing themselves at target practice. When night fell, Rogers infiltrated the French guards to explore the settlement that lay to the south of the fort. He discovered the beginnings of a gun battery, and an encampment containing five or six hundred men. With no prospect of securing a prisoner, and fearing that he and his companion had been detected, Rogers decided to withdraw. The return route took them within two miles of Ticonderoga, but as provisions were running short, there was no time to investigate the enemy's strength there.

Back at the landing place, they discovered that the two watchers had gone, taking both food and bateau with them. Rogers and his companion headed for the Lake George encampment without delay; they arrived ten days after first setting out, exhausted, freezing and starving.

Three days later Johnson ordered a fresh scout to reconnoitre

Ticonderoga. Rogers once again took to the lake, this time heading five men in a light birch-bark canoe. Passing sundry Indian fires, they put ashore some seven miles from the lower end of the lake. Rogers and two others continued towards the Carrying Place, where they crawled unnoticed through the enemy's outlying pickets to observe an encampment of about a thousand French and Indians. Probing onwards for a further mile and a half, Rogers and his men discovered a more substantial Grand Encampment. The promontory commanding both the pass from Lake George to Lake Champlain and the entrance of South Bay was plainly the focus of major activity. Large amounts of cut timber had been stockpiled and several cannon were already in position; appearances suggested that a fort was under construction; it was judged likely that some three thousand French and Indians were concentrated there.

Rogers was not content to simply gather intelligence; as they withdrew, he spotted a large canoe containing nine Indians and a Frenchman. This craft continued southwards, passing the point of land where Rogers had left his own canoe and its guards. Hurrying to the spot, all six prepared for the Indians' return; oblivious to the reception awaiting them, they paddled on. Rogers' squad gave them a salute of musketry; after some forty rounds had crossed the water half a dozen of the enemy lay dead or disabled. The survivors were pursued down the lake, but when their shrieks attracted three more canoes, Rogers gave up the chase and returned to camp that night, 29 September.

The reports that Rogers subsequently submitted to his colonel, and which Blanchard then forwarded to Johnson, were comprehensive and credible; their value was immense, particularly when set alongside those compiled by others. On 13 October, Captain William Symes ventured out with fifty men, travelling by land along the west side of the lake. He marched just three miles before encamping and despatching scouts; they returned without discovering anything. But the enemy found *them*: one of Symes' sentries was shot and scalped and left lying with a hatchet embedded in his skull. This grim marker cowed the captain's men; when all but thirteen refused to stand by him, he returned to camp.

Symes remained game to venture forth again – provided he was given *such materials as are fit for ye Purpose*. His plea went to the very heart of the problem: it was not easy to find volunteers with the nerve and endurance to penetrate a forbidding wilderness dominated by skilful and ruthless enemies; those with the qualities required to *lead* such patrols were scarcer still.

That autumn, as the rival armies warily consolidated their positions at either end of Lake George, it became clear that Robert Rogers was such a man.

Yet there were some who doubted the veracity of Rogers' reports; scepticism arose because his accounts of substantial enemy fortifications and major troop concentrations were used to justify Johnson's continuing failure to advance. William Shirley was impatient for the Lake George army to second its success over Dieskau by marching onwards against Crown Point. Knowing the precarious morale of their men, Johnson and his officers opposed any such move. In this increasingly partisan atmosphere, each new scrap of intelligence became fodder for one or other faction.

The debate was fuelled in mid-October when a French deserter swore that there were just four hundred troops at Ticonderoga, along with two hundred Canadian labourers. Some seized upon this news to suggest that Ticonderoga lay vulnerable to a *coup de main*. Writing from Albany, Goldsbrow Banyar, the deputy secretary of New York's provincial council, emphasised that such a blow would add much credit to Johnson's army, and bring it within reach of Crown Point. But Rogers soon reported a very different scenario. On 22 October he returned from another long-range patrol bearing the scalp of a Frenchman who had declined a summons to surrender, and intelligence that Ticonderoga was not only fortified, but also surrounded by encampments estimated to hold two thousand men. He had observed this from a mountain in plain sight of their fort. Banyar was irate that Johnson's council-of-war preferred Rogers' reports, based upon *the critical view* of Ticonderoga at three miles' distance, to those of deserters whose very lives hung upon the accuracy of their testimony. He cautioned Johnson against believing a single syllable of Rogers' information – but Johnson defended Rogers, praising both his bravery and honesty, in letters to the governors of Massachusetts and Connecticut. Loath as he was to undertake a risky winter campaign, the captain's stories of daunting enemy forces were exactly what Johnson wanted to hear.

By mid-November there was no longer any doubt that the French were ensconced at Ticonderoga. On 19 November, Rogers came in having seen barracks and storehouses and men busy at work. Named Carillon, that fortress now represented New France's southernmost bastion in the Champlain Valley; Ticonderoga, as the British always called it, would constitute the first obstacle to any future invasion of Canada by that route.

As 1755 drew to a close, it was clear that Johnson's army posed no such threat. The general and the bulk of his homesick provincials finally dispersed on 27 November, but not before voting to raise a body of seven hundred and fifty men to safeguard Fort Edward and Captain Eyre's new strong point on the shores of Lake George. This stout timber and earth structure, bolstered by four lozenge-shaped bastions, was named Fort William Henry. Each of the colonies contributing manpower to the winter defence force was permitted to nominate a captain: the New Hampshire men chose Robert Rogers.

IT WAS NOW, AS SNOW AND ICE put an end to conventional campaigning, that Rogers set about establishing the reputation that would soon make his name familiar throughout Britain's Atlantic empire. Colonial newspapers were quick to chronicle his activity and daring. During the autumn of 1755 they had noted the scouts sent out from Johnson's stymied army: their leader at first remained unidentified, but by early November the name of Captain Rogers was beginning to feature. Letters written from the Lake George camp sang his praises; these were snatched up for publication by the news-hungry east coast journals. On 12 February, 1756, the Boston *Weekly News-Letter* printed extracts of two letters from Albany that both reported Rogers' exploits: he had taken two prisoners within sight of Crown Point itself; discovering the tracks of a great number of French and Indians, the captain had prudently sent back six of his men to Fort William Henry so that due warning could be given of the raiders' approach. Later that month, Rogers' name cropped up again; once more, the report highlighted his zeal and tireless energy. Indeed, having returned from a scout to Crown Point, during which he burned a great many farmers' barns and slaughtered livestock, he stayed just a day within the sheltering ramparts of Fort William Henry before sallying forth with a fresh party of men.

As such glowing notices became a regular fixture in the news columns, so it was that plain Captain Rogers metamorphosed into *brave* Captain Rogers. Recognition of his efforts now brought material rewards. As the *News-Letter* informed its readers that same month, officers at Albany made a collection and presented Rogers with a handsome suit of clothes. Besides the smart new outfit there was a tidy sum to be laid out upon refreshments, for him and his men. Following suit, New York's elected General Assembly voted him 125 Spanish dollars, 'for the Services done to his Country in several late Excursions against the French and their Indians, near Crown-Point.'

Rogers' growing reputation as a vigorous and determined patrol leader also attracted the attention of William Shirley. The commander-in-chief summoned him down to Boston, and on 24 March, 1756, Rogers was commissioned captain of an independent company of rangers. Such troops had a lengthy pedigree in the English-speaking colonies; indeed, rangers led by Captain Benjamin Church had countered Metacom's warriors in the late 1670s. But it was Rogers, and the men under his command, who won the rangers their distinctive niche in American military history.

Rogers' company of sixty privates, three sergeants, an ensign and a lieutenant, was to be raised without delay. None were to be recruited except for those used to travelling and hunting, and in whose courage and fidelity he could trust. The stipulated rates of pay were unusually generous, and each man rated a bonus of ten Spanish dollars towards the cost of clothing, blankets and weapons. They were expected to earn every penny.

That summer Rogers put his men through their paces in a succession of scouts; one excursion in particular captured the public's attention. Towards the end of June Rogers ventured out at the head of fifty men in five light whaleboats. Rowing down Lake George for twenty-five miles, they landed and spent the next four days heaving their hulls over the intervening six-mile belt of mountainous terrain to reach the waters of South Bay. This deed alone proved Rogers *indefatigable for his country*, but there was more: on the night of 4 July his boats passed below the guns of Fort Carillon, coming so near that they heard the sentries calling 'All's well'. Two nights later they rowed past Crown Point and ten miles further down Lake Champlain, they concealed their boats upon the eastern shore. Lying low, they watched as numerous bateaux and a forty-ton schooner passed back and forth. When the coast was clear, Rogers and his men continued north for a further fifteen miles.

Learning that the schooner was anchored nearby, Rogers readied his whaleboats to board her, but before he could, two lighters came near; from one, the words of a warlike song rang across the water. In response the rangers blazed away, killing three of the boats' occupants outright and mortally wounding a fourth. In his *Journals*, Rogers said the injured man lived but a short time; this was true enough, but as the captain's post-raid report reveals, as the Frenchman couldn't march, it was decided to put an end to him to prevent discovery. Eight others were taken prisoner.

The French craft had been carrying wheat, flour, rice, wine and brandy: destroying the foodstuffs, Rogers' men carried ashore seven casks of liquor and cached them in a secure place. After staving the French boats, they rowed their own three miles to the far shore and there concealed them. The prisoners revealed that they were merely the foremost amongst a 500-strong convoy: Rogers thought it needless to tarry any longer without a stronger party. On 8 July they began a great looping march that crossed the headwaters of the Hudson and struck Lake George about twenty-five miles from Fort William Henry. As the prisoners were now exhausted, fourteen rangers forged ahead for help. A relief party responded, and on 15 July, all came safely in.

Such epic feats of daring and endurance did nothing to influence the course of the war, but they gave a welcome jolt to the jaded morale of Rogers' countrymen. Indeed, whilst 1755 had yielded a mixed bag of victory and defeat, 1756 brought nothing but gloom and disaster. Another projected provincial expedition against Crown Point, this time under the command of Major-General John Winslow, again failed to get anywhere near its objective. Such inactivity was depressing enough, but far worse was the news from the west. There, in a brisk and decisive campaign that offered a painful contrast to the bickering and dithering of the Anglo-Americans, a French force had destroyed the entrepôt of Oswego and snapped up its dejected garrison.

This bold scheme was the brainchild of Vaudreuil, but it was executed by Dieskau's successor, Major-General Louis-Joseph, the Marquis de Montcalm. The new field commander came from an old noble family boasting a proud tradition of military service to the Crown: his stocky frame already bore an impressive array of scars accumulated whilst fighting the Austrians in Bohemia and Italy. Montcalm had arrived in Canada that spring, accompanied by two more infantry battalions and a staff of officers who were all destined to play major roles in the defence of New France. His second-in-command, Brigadier-General François-Gaston, Duc de Lévis, was a native of Gascony, a province long noted for mellow wines and robust fighting men. Like his chief, the gallant Chevalier de Lévis had seen much active service during the War of the Austrian Succession. Next in the chain of command was Colonel François-Charles de Bourlamaque; the orphaned son of a grenadier captain, he too was no stranger to the smell of gun smoke. No less remarkable than any of these veterans was Montcalm's devoted young aide-de-camp, Captain Louis-Antoine de Bougainville. A true product of the Enlightenment, he was an accomplished mathematician who had recently authored an acclaimed treatise on integral calculus; on the eve of his arrival in Canada to fight the British these efforts had been recognised by his election to London's prestigious Royal Society.

Bougainville's curiosity was kindled by much that he encountered in North America, but nothing intrigued him more than the appearance and customs of Canada's Indian allies. Their behaviour was frequently frustrating and sometimes unsettling; he recorded much of it in his journal, employing a mixture of anthropological interest, sarcastic disdain and fascinated horror, all spiced with a certain dark humour.

But there was one such episode that Bougainville declined to note: the immediate aftermath of the fall of Oswego. Montcalm's army had numbered some three thousand men; of these, two hundred and fifty were Indians, mostly mission Iroquois and Abenakis. Under bombardment, Oswego's wretched garrison mounted only a token resistance before surrendering on 14 August. So feeble was the defence that Montcalm denied them the honours of war; unlike Washington's men at Fort Necessity, they were refused the prized privilege of marching away with martial trappings intact. Instead, they had to surrender themselves as prisoners-of-war and give up their weapons and regimental standards to the victors. But like Villiers three years before, Montcalm was incapable of persuading his tribal allies to abide by terms that did nothing to satisfy their needs. As an indignant British officer reported: 'No sooner had we deliver'd up our Arms, than both Officers and Soldiers were ordered to the Parade, there we stood, to be insulted by the Enemy Indians, who, not satisfied with taking away our Baggage, murther'd several of our Soldiers, as they stood on the Parade, and scalped all our sick in the Hospital.'

Just as Bougainville neglected to mention this butchery in his journal, so Montcalm omitted it from his official victory despatches; but there is no doubt that it happened. Soon after, one French officer confessed that the Indians had *supped full of horrors*; he regretted that it had proved impossible to prevent them from massacring more than a hundred persons who were included in the capitulation. Oswego's shocked and crestfallen defenders were marched off to the St Lawrence before shipment to Britain in exchange for French prisoners-of-war; details of their ordeal were therefore slow to surface, but they ultimately provided fresh ammunition for those who called for a day of reckoning with the French and their 'savage' allies.

THE FALL OF OSWEGO EPITOMISED the total failure of the Anglo-American war effort. Against this dour backdrop, the star of Robert Rogers shone all the brighter. Whilst aided by a distinct lack of home-grown heroes to share the spotlight, the rise of Rogers was expedited by a timely expansion of colonial newspapers. On the eve of war, British North America already possessed a venerable journalistic tradition. The first regular newspaper, the *Boston Weekly News-Letter*, began publication back in 1704. It was joined by the *Boston Gazette* in 1719 and by 1754, eleven English-language titles were strung along the eastern seaboard. Six years later there were eighteen.

Such phenomenal growth was closely linked to the escalating conflict with France; as the former printer's apprentice Isaiah Thomas later observed, this war in which the British colonies were so deeply interested increased the demand for public journals. With its negotiations, skirmishes, massacres, battles and sieges, it provided a long-running saga peopled by a cast of recognisable heroes and villains. Whilst some fell from view as combat or natural causes took their toll, Robert Rogers endured.

Newspapers were published weekly as a single sheet folded into four pages; their densely packed columns were black with domestic and foreign news items, all jostling for room alongside homely advertisements and local notices. With space at a premium, not even the vertical margins of the pages were sacrosanct; they were often encroached upon by breathless pre-deadline newsflashes hinting at detailed coverage to come. Special supplements were also common. These periodicals, readily available in urban coffee houses and taverns and rural ordinaries, enjoyed a wide readership; literacy levels in Britain's North American colonies were higher than in the old country; and even the unlettered might hear choice items read aloud and chewed over in taproom debates.

Publications born out of the war included the *New-Hampshire Gazette*. Introducing his first issue of 7 October, 1756, printer Daniel Fowle conceded that whilst it was possible for *Fondness of News* to be carried to an extreme, if ever a desire to keep abreast of events were justified, it was now, when the British nation was embarked upon a just and necessary struggle with a powerful enemy.

Fowle's patriotic sentiments suggested that the mother country and her colonial children were engaged in a unified effort against the common foe. The man sent from Britain to replace Shirley as commander-in-chief searched in vain for such consensus. John Campbell, Earl of Loudoun, had arrived in New York in July – too late to stave off disaster at distant Oswego. A Lowland Scot who could be as prickly as a thistle, Loudoun faced a Herculean task: not only was he obliged to revitalise the flagging war effort against Canada, but he had to do so with the ungrudging co-operation of independent-minded colonies that remained jealous of each other and intensely suspicious of his imperial authority.

Reporting to his political masters back in London, Loudoun remained unimpressed by most of the military resources at his disposal. The short-service colonial provincials could not be trusted against the enemy's regulars, while even the redcoat battalions were stuffed full of raw recruits, hundreds of them pressed into service against their will. In addition, the rangers authorised by Shirley were staggeringly expensive. But given the lack of Indian allies – save for a handful of Mohawks and a few stragglers from other tribes – they remained indispensable: 'for it is only by them,' he wrote, '[that] we can have Intelligence of what motion the Enemy are making; and by them, that we can secure our Camps and Marches from Surprizes.'

Indeed, it was Loudoun's opinion that no army could subsist in North America *without* rangers; if he could find enough good men, he intended to maintain five or six companies over the winter. Whilst Loudoun doubted the efficiency of most of Shirley's rangers, he had nothing but praise for those headed by Robert Rogers himself. His company alone had taken the field on schedule; and it was Rogers who had captured a much-needed prisoner within gunshot of Ticonderoga.

The novel circumstances in which Rogers secured this vital captive only increased the aura surrounding his name. The hapless Frenchman was plucked from his post by a combination of boldness and guile. In his *Journals*, Rogers said, 'I took five of my party and marched directly down the road in the middle of the day till we were challenged by the sentry. I answered in French, signifying that we were friends; the sentinel was thereby deceived, till I came close to him, when perceiving his mistake in great surprise he called, Qui êtes vous? I answered, Rogers, and led him from his post in great haste, cutting his breeches and coat from him that he might march with the greater ease and expedition.'

Press coverage was jocular in tone: Rogers had *boldly ventured up* and by *taking the advantage of a Grenadier Centinal . . . fairly brought him from his Post, without the least Noise.* Indeed, the reports of Rogers' scouts and skirmishes increasingly gave him a Robin Hood swagger, while the French became foils reminiscent of the Sheriff of Nottingham and his Norman minions.

These picaresque embellishments belied the importance of the deed. Loudoun had recently written that one prisoner was worth ten scalps; such a catch could yield certain accounts of the enemy's numbers and motions, by which they could govern their own. Rogers' captive proved a prime specimen. In a statement running to six pages, Laverdure, private in the grenadiers of Languedoc, gave information on everything from climatic conditions to troop strengths and strategy: there was ice in Lake Champlain until the beginning of May; Captain de Lusignan, the long-term commander at Crown Point, would preside at Ticonderoga that winter; and if Montcalm did not change his mind, his army would attack Fort William Henry in the spring. Upon the basis of this comprehensive testimony, corroborated by other scouting parties, Loudoun decided to withdraw the bulk of his troops into winter quarters.

Before Loudoun quit the frontier for New York, Rogers approached him with a proposal to expand the rangers' role. He wished to winter at

Fort Number Four; a strong presence there would not only baffle French and Indian incursions down the Connecticut Valley, but also provide a firm base from which to mount long-range strikes against Canada. Above all, Rogers hoped to lead the pick of the rangers on a raid to destroy the notorious village of St Francis. But Loudoun refused to sanction the risky scheme: he needed Rogers on the Lake George front, both to gather intelligence and to parry enemy thrusts against forts Edward and William Henry. These posts were garrisoned by men of the 44th and 48th Foot; hardened survivors of the Monongahela, they were now Loudoun's steadiest troops. To guard against surprise, each fort was allocated two companies of rangers.

Denied permission to implement his own ambitious plan, Rogers drew some consolation from an escalation of ranger operations in the Champlain Valley. He now began to lead larger scouts into enemy territory. One such reconnaissance in force departed from Fort William Henry on 17 January, 1757. With eighty-five officers and men drawn from the four ranging companies, Rogers headed down the frozen surface of Lake George. The going was hard: next morning, eleven men who had hurt themselves were sent back. The remainder pushed on. On 19 January, when they had covered some fifteen miles on the ice, the command left the lake, donned snowshoes, and moved ever deeper within enemy territory. Another two days brought them to Lake Champlain, at a point midway between Ticonderoga and Crown Point. Almost immediately, a sled was seen heading north. Lieutenant John Stark and a score of men sought to intercept it. Another eight or ten sleds now appeared and desperate attempts were made to recall Stark's runners before they revealed themselves. But it was too late. Spotting figures out on the ice, the sleds slewed around and headed back to Ticonderoga. Rogers' frantic pursuit took seven prisoners, but the rest escaped. Interrogated separately, the captives told a disquieting story: two hundred Canadians and forty-five Indians had recently arrived at Ticonderoga. This war party was well equipped and ready to march at a moment's warning. In addition, the neighbouring forts held nearly a thousand regulars.

Knowing that the fleeing sleigh-men would soon raise the alarm, Rogers ordered a rapid return to his previous encampment. By doubling back on his own tracks he flouted a cardinal rule of wilderness warfare: according to ranger John Shute, in doing so he overruled a council-of-war that recommended a different route, boldly claiming that the enemy would not dare to pursue him. But Rogers' decision rested upon more than mere bravado. Sixteen-year-old ranger Thomas Brown recalled that the snow was very deep; on their old well-trodden path the going underfoot would be firmer and faster. When they reached their last camp, they swiftly rekindled fires and dried muskets rendered useless by rain. Now able at least to defend themselves, they marched on in single Indian file, Rogers leading and Stark bringing up the rear. Early afternoon found the long line of snow-shoed rangers strung across a valley. An ominous clicking was heard; it betrayed the simultaneous cocking of many muskets. Seconds later the hammers fell and firing erupted all around. The rangers had marched directly into an ambush of about a hundred French regulars bolstered by militia and Indians, mostly Ottawas and Potawatomies.

The enemy, as Rogers reported, were arrayed in the familiar half-moon formation designed to surround them. In the rainy conditions, many of their muskets had misfired; although hampered by a lack of snowshoes, the French regulars floundered gamely onwards with their bayonets at the ready. After returning fire, Rogers ordered his men back across the valley. They were closely pursued, but under the covering musketry of the rearguard, ascended the slope and assumed a defensive position. Those with prisoners were ordered to kill them. A stubborn combat ensued. The enemy sought to turn the right flank, but were beaten back by a party placed in reserve for that very purpose. They now mounted a determined frontal assault. As Rogers and his men held the high ground and sheltered behind substantial pines, this too was rebuffed. Another flanking move was likewise thwarted by the mobile reserve. Firing continued hot until darkness.

Rogers suffered a glancing head wound at the onset of the action; before it ceased he also received a ball through the hand and wrist. John

Shute was stunned by a shot that furrowed his scalp; regaining consciousness, he witnessed a comrade cutting the ribbon from Rogers' pigtail and using it to plug his bleeding wrist. Although unable to load his own firearm, Rogers continued to encourage his men. Throughout the engagement the enemy had sought his party's surrender, alternating dire threats with offers of fair treatment. They called to Rogers by name, giving the strongest assurances of their esteem and friendship. His rangers responded by announcing their determination to fight on as long as there was two left to stand by each other. Ranger Stilson Eastman remembered that Stark threatened to shoot the first man who retired.

By nightfall Rogers and his command were in dire straights. They had suffered many casualties and their powder and shot was almost exhausted. The enemy, by contrast, could be readily reinforced from Ticonderoga: indeed, thirty-five fresh men joined them in the course of the engagement, bringing provisions and ammunition. Rogers resolved to retreat under cover of darkness; the withdrawal was successful. By the following morning the survivors were six miles south of the French advance guards on Lake George. The injured were now overcome with cold, fatigue and loss of blood. Stark and two colleagues volunteered to push ahead to Fort William Henry and secure a sled for their transportation. Remarkably, they arrived that same night. Next day, 23 January, the survivors encountered a relief party at the lake's First Narrows. Reduced to forty-eight effectives, the mauled command limped back to base that evening.

Rogers believed the enemy to consist of two hundred and fifty French and Indians, of which he supposed forty were killed, besides the prisoners, and many more wounded. These estimates of the enemy's strength and casualties were too high, but then so were French claims that Rogers left forty-two dead on the battlefield. In a common pattern, *both* sides exaggerated the damage that they had inflicted. French reports conceded eleven men killed outright and another twenty-seven wounded, some of them mortally. In his own official return, Rogers reckoned fourteen killed and nine wounded, with a further six missing or captured.

SEVERAL RANGERS LISTED AS killed were in fact prisoners, including young Thomas Brown, who provided an unflinching account of his experiences in a slim pamphlet offered to the public at a price of *8 Coppers*. Purchasers no doubt considered their pennies well spent, for Brown's is amongst the most vivid and convincing of all such narratives. It left no doubt about the sheer ferocity of frontier warfare – and of the quirks of fate that could mean the difference between life and death in the wilderness.

Throughout the fierce action of 21 January, Brown had exhibited a lodestone-like attraction for bullets. The enemy's very first shot pierced his body; at this, as he admitted with unusual candour, he: 'retir'd into the rear, to the Prisoner I had taken on the Lake, knocked him on the head and killed him, lest he should Escape and give Information to the Enemy.' Taking post behind a large pine, Brown fired off six or seven rounds before another ball shattered his musket. Half an hour later he was shot through the knee; when he turned to crawl to the rear, yet another round took him in the shoulder. By now it was dark and firing had ceased. Rogers chose this hiatus to escape with the well men; he neglected to inform the badly wounded, for fear that they would reveal his movements to the enemy.

Those abandoned alongside Brown included his captain, Thomas Speakman, and a volunteer from the 44th Foot named Robert Baker. The miserable trio huddled around a small fire. As Brown could barely walk and his companions were scarcely capable of movement, they resolved to surrender to the French, but before they could do so, an Indian approached; crawling beyond the firelight, Brown watched appalled as this warrior stripped the helpless Speakman and then scalped him alive. The same Indian foiled Baker's fumbling efforts to stab himself, and carried him off. Brown hoped for nothing better than to creep into the woods and there die unmolested. As he dragged himself over the snow the wretched Speakman begged him for a tomahawk, but Brown refused to abet this suicide, pointing out that the cold would finish him soon enough.

Skirting a cordon of French sentries, Brown hobbled into the darkness. Next morning he heard Indians shouting. Four warriors were pounding towards him. Weak from his wounds, he stumbled on; fearing Speakman's fate, Brown ignored his pursuers' levelled guns and calls to surrender: it was better to die quickly. But they refrained from shooting him down. Instead, as he related, they 'took me by the Neck and Kiss'd me.' Clamping dry leaves upon his wounds, they promptly turned about and ordered him to follow; back at the site of the previous day's fight, Brown was overjoyed to discover that Baker too had survived; another five of their comrades were likewise prisoners.

The exhausted captives were hauled to their feet and told to march the mile and a quarter to Ticonderoga, but Baker refused. When an Indian shoved him onwards he collapsed, sobbing. At this, another warrior grabbed the youngster by the hair and raised his tomahawk for the killing stroke. Filled with pity, Brown intervened; he took Baker upon his shoulders and they staggered together to Fort Carillon. Commandant Lusignan conducted their interrogation in person. The captain had lost none of the humanity noted by Susanna Johnson at Crown Point three years before; the prisoners' wounds were dressed and they received a reviving quart of claret.

In early March, Rigaud de Vaudreuil, the governor general's younger brother, arrived at Ticonderoga at the head of a formidable force destined to attack Fort William Henry. They aimed to take it by storm, and constructed scaling ladders to that end. Rigaud summoned Brown and offered a handsome reward in return for revealing the weak points in the fort's defences. Brown stoutly rejected these blandishments, although two others consented to go along as *pilots.* Rigaud's raid accomplished nothing more than the burning of boats and stores; the poor fellows who had agreed to act as guides were clapped in irons.

Like Susanna Johnson and her fellows, Brown remained the property of his Indian captors. On 27 March, 1757, they took him to Montréal. Brown's stubborn personality continued to influence his fate. He was tethered to a sledge loaded with provisions, and by the time they reached

Crown Point could barely walk. Tired of his burden, Brown asked three Indian women to climb aboard 'and pleasantly told them I wish'd I was able to draw 'em'. This defiant stance struck a chord with his captors and signalled a change in their attitude towards him. Promptly relieved from drudgery, Brown was now treated in a manner that suggested grooming for adoption. Removing his clothes, his captors gave him a blanket instead; next day they cut off his hair and painted him; finally, using needles and Indian ink, they tattooed the back of his hand with the image of one of the scaling ladders that Rigaud's men had fruitlessly lugged across the ice to Fort William Henry.

Brown accepted this outward transformation without complaint. He was wise to do so. Another prisoner who refused to allow the Indians to cut his hair in tribal fashion was burned at the stake. Love of life obliged Brown to join the powwowing and dancing about the anguished victim. Indeed, although French officers like Montcalm and Bougainville observed that the torture of captives was going out of fashion, and Canada's 'domesticated' Indians were no longer cruel in cold blood, members of the mission communities came into frequent contact with warriors from the *pays d'en haut* who had no intention of abandoning their traditional practices.

Upon approaching an Indian town some twenty miles from Montréal, Brown's captors made as many live shouts as they had prisoners, and as many dead ones as they had scalps. The villagers issued forth and stripped Brown naked; in another variation upon the gauntlet ritual, they pointed out a wigwam, told him to run to it, and pursued him all the way with sticks and stones.

Brown's Indian master hailed from the Mississippi country, and it was to that far-flung region that he was ultimately taken. Two weeks into the journey they tarried at an Indian town some two hundred miles from the Ohio. On the third night there, one warrior developed a murderous grudge against the young New Englander. He aimed to push Brown into the fire, and when he nimbly vaulted the flames, subjected him to repeated punches and head-butts. Provoked beyond bearing, Brown finally retaliated with a shrewd blow that sent his assailant sprawling. At this the other Indians laughed, and called him *a good Fellow*.

Such behaviour indicated that the teenaged ranger would adapt well enough to tribal life, and when the Indians finally arrived at their destination in late August, he was ordered to live with a woman who was to be his mother. Brown stayed with her throughout the ensuing winter, hunting and dressing skins.

In the spring of 1758, a *voyageur* arrived to trade; he needed hands for the return trip to Montréal and Brown persuaded his mistress to let him go along. Back in Canada, he became a farm labourer, working in exchange for food and clothing. But the life was hard; he fared no better than a slave. In September, Brown and another English lad – a prisoner toiling upon a neighbouring farm – made a pact to escape home together. Given the great swathe of wild and trackless terrain before them, this was a desperate venture. Elaborate preparations were made. As Brown was allowed the use of a gun to shoot pigeons, he split and dried his feathered victims, then concealed them in the woods. He and his companion set off as arranged, but after just a week their hoarded provisions gave out; for the next fifteen days they survived upon roots, worms and suchlike. Brown's accomplice grew ever weaker; a shared meal of three frogs failed to revive him.

Thomas Brown now struggled to overcome a powerful taboo: should he use his gunflint to kindle a fire and then cook and eat the body of his dead friend? He resolved upon a compromise: cutting as much flesh as possible from the bones, he tied the meat in a handkerchief for future use. After burying the remains, Brown continued on his way. He was now nearing the end of his own strength; but although he believed himself to be dying, Brown refused to turn cannibal and partake of his friend's flesh. As he was commending his soul to God, a partridge landed nearby; this he shot and ate, along with two pigeons. His firing drew a distant response.

Staggering towards the sound of the guns he encountered three Canadians; he posed as a Dutchman in the French regulars and was taken to Crown Point, but the commandant there quickly recognised him. Sent back to Montréal under escort, Brown now faced his angry Canadian master; a French officer billeted upon the same house was his protector – but even he chided Brown for his foolishness in attempting so impossible a task, crossing the wilderness that divided New England from New France.

Thomas Brown finally returned to Albany in November 1758. During his absence, the Champlain Valley had witnessed fighting of unprecedented intensity; but whilst both forts Carillon and St Frédéric stood defiant beneath the white standard of the Bourbons, Fort William Henry was now nothing more than hummocks of charred timber and blackened sand.

THIS LATEST DISASTER HAD befallen the British despite a hefty reinforcement of redcoats from across the Atlantic. Loudoun had originally hoped to lead most of them against Québec, at the very heart of New France. This target would have obliged Vaudreuil to maintain substantial defensive forces in the St Lawrence Valley. However, the emergence of a new ministry in London, fronted by the forceful William Pitt, had heralded a significant shift in strategy. Loudoun was now ordered to make the fortress of Louisbourg on Cape Breton Island his first objective. With its substantial garrison, Louisbourg could fend for itself; in Loudoun's absence, the bulk of Canada's manpower was therefore freed to take the offensive. Rigaud's winter raid had already probed the defences of Fort William Henry; it was now time to subject them to a full-scale siege.

As Loudoun and his task force concentrated at distant Halifax, Nova Scotia, the New York frontier remained in the keeping of Major-General Daniel Webb. A lacklustre and timid officer, he commanded provincials stiffened by just two battalions of regulars. As Loudoun had feared, his warships were slow to assemble; they didn't arrive until 9 July and by then, superior French squadrons were already on station. Whilst Loudoun and his officers debated the viability of attacking Louisbourg, Vaudreuil sent Montcalm against Fort William Henry.

The marquis' army of more than eight thousand men reflected the diversity of New France's military resources – it consisted of disciplined white-coated regulars of the *troupes de terre*, seasoned Canadian militia and woods-wise Indians. Totalling some two thousand warriors, the tribal contingent was the largest yet mustered under the lilies of King Louis; more than half had travelled from the far west, lured by tales of the plunder and glory lately harvested at Oswego. Some came from lands so distant that no interpreter could decipher their language. To Bougainville's eyes, the dress, ornaments, dances and songs of these different nations all looked alike: they went naked save for a breechclout and painted their bodies black, red and blue; heads were shaved and ornamented with feathers, ears stretched to accommodate rings of brass; they toted lances and bows, with arrows carried in buffalo skin quivers. Himself inclined to portliness, Bougainville considered them to be 'erect, well made, and almost all of great height'.

Bougainville also believed these warriors of the *pays d'en haut* to be more biddable than the 'domesticated' tribes of Canada. Because they had travelled so far to fight, they did not relax and go home whenever they made a strike, and they retained greater respect for the French, whom they saw less often. It was very different with the Abenakis: he grumbled that they were amongst the most unmanageable and insolent of all the Indians. But Bougainville also conceded them to be both brave and implacable against the English. No fewer than two hundred and forty-five of them joined the expedition against Fort William Henry: this represented a substantial tribal contribution, ranking behind only the mission Iroquois and Ottawas. More than a hundred of the Abenakis were from St Francis; Bécancour and Missisquoi together supplied a like number; the balance were Penobscots from Panaouamaské, in what is now Maine.

Accompanying the Abenakis was the new missionary at St Francis, 33-year-old Pierre-Joseph-Antoine Roubaud. A native of Avignon, he had entered the local Jesuit college at the age of thirteen. According to his tutors, as a novice young Pierre lacked both prudence and judgement, but he possessed a rare flair for teaching, and although far from robust, he did not shirk the notorious rigours of Canada's missions.

By July 1757 Roubaud had already spent more than a year with the St Francis Abenakis. In now joining them on the warpath he hoped to combat the undesirable influence of the pagan westerners. Roubaud's weapons in this religious war included a mobile chapel and a supply of holy oils. He did not hesitate to deploy them. On Sunday 24 July, as Montcalm's army concentrated at Ticonderoga, he conducted a formal mass, exhorting his charges to 'do honour to their religion by their conduct in the presence of so many Idolatrous Tribes'.

Roubaud's fears were not unfounded. Shortly before he administered communion to his flock, others of Montcalm's Indian allies slaughtered a force of New Jersey provincials that had ventured upon Lake George to reconnoitre the French army. Within hours, exultant warriors returned to camp with tethered batches of terrified prisoners. The provincials' bateaux had been carrying rum. Shocking scenes followed. Roubaud's tent was pitched in the midst of the Ottawas' camp. Upon arriving there he noticed a large fire. Wooden stakes were set upright, as if for a feast. One was most certainly underway: Indians were devouring the flesh of a captive *with a famished avidity*. The remains of his half-eaten carcass lay nearby. Ten other prisoners were forced to witness these proceedings. Roubaud attempted to halt the meal, but a young Ottawa made it clear in broken French that his words were wasted: 'Thou have French taste; me Savage, this meat good for me,' he said. Roubaud was not alone in recording these ghastly sights: Bougainville believed that at least three prisoners were put in the pot and eaten.

Shutting himself away in his tent, the distraught Roubaud took consolation from the knowledge that even when they were plunged deepest in the darkness of paganism, the Abenakis never deserved the odious name of cannibals. Some thirty years earlier, Sébastien Rasles had heard the Penobscots talk metaphorically of eating enemy villages. Amongst some other tribes, the consumption of foes could prove all too literal. Captain Pierre Pouchot of the *troupes de terre*, who became familiar with the Iroquois and other nations during stints as commandant of Fort Niagara during the 1750s, maintained that whilst cannibalism certainly existed, it was restricted to rites of vengeance: 'It is solely through bravado & to harden their hearts that they sometimes consume such food,' he explained. These rituals were performed with such repugnance that young warriors were known to swiftly vomit up what they had eaten. Like the prolonged torture of captives, such practices were typically loaded with deeper significance; by devouring a vanquished enemy, the victors may have sought to conquer his spirit and absorb his strength. If, as Roubaud claimed, the Ottawas ate human flesh with an undisguised relish, they were exceptional amongst the tribes of the north-eastern woodlands.

AT THE END OF JULY MONTCALM'S great host moved south via Lake George and its flanking forest; when he arrived before Fort William Henry on 3 August, Montcalm summonsed the garrison's commander and urged him to surrender without delay. This was a standard opening gambit of conventional siege warfare, but Montcalm weighted it with an additional warning; given the vast number of Indians accompanying his force, it might prove impossible to restrain them once their blood had been shed. Undaunted, and anticipating prompt assistance from nearby Fort Edward, Lieutenant-Colonel George Monroe of the 35th Foot spurned the offer. According to Bougainville, as this formal parley ended, an Abenaki made a menacing contribution of his own. In bad but very clear French he shouted a grim promise: 'Ah, you won't surrender; well, fire first; my father will then fire his great guns: then take care to defend yourself, for if I capture you, you will get no quarter.'

Monroe's garrison of regular and provincial troops staged a stubborn defence, but as the anonymous Abenaki had predicted, Montcalm's great guns proved too much for Eyre's fortifications. On 9 August, when it became clear that he could expect no relief from the south, Monroe agreed to capitulate. Unlike Oswego's dispirited defenders, his command was deemed worthy of the honours of war; although bound by an agreement not to serve against King Louis for eighteen months, they would be permitted to march off unmolested.

Cheated of their spoils, Montcalm's tribal allies once more decided to impose their own surrender terms. Father Roubaud witnessed the *bloody catastrophe* that followed. That afternoon, as the French took formal possession of the fort with all the martial etiquette appropriate to such an occasion, warriors clambered in through the empty gun embrasures and proceeded to kill the sick and wounded remaining within the fortifications. One Indian emerged clutching a severed head, 'which he displayed as the most splendid prize that he could have secured.'

As Roubaud recalled, this was but a very faint prelude to the cruel tragedy enacted next day, when the defeated garrison and their camp followers eventually marched out of the entrenchment. Those bringing up the rear of the column bore the brunt of the massacre. Initiated by only a few 'savages', the butchery soon spread to others, who 'struck, right and left, heavy blows of the hatchet on those who fell into their hands.' As the English offered no resistance, the killing quickly abated. Roubaud estimated the slain at forty or fifty; the true total was considerably higher. The Indians henceforth concentrated upon taking prisoners. Numbers of Frenchmen sought to protect the panic-stricken survivors; the Chevalier de Lévis was conspicuous amongst them, repeatedly thrusting himself into the worst scrimmages. When Montcalm arrived upon the scene, he too employed entreaties and threats in an effort to calm the situation. Roubaud played his part by retrieving a baby from the arms of a Huron warrior. He redeemed the child with a scalp donated by one of his Abenakis.

Writing to Loudoun, the embarrassed Montcalm sought to excuse the whole sorry episode. He blamed the disorder squarely upon the improper conduct of the garrison; they gave the Indians rum, whilst their obvious terror only made their assailants bolder. But the marquis added: 'I look upon it as a real misfortune to have had along with me the Abenakis of Panaoske [Panaouamaské] in Acadia, who imagined to have complaints on account of some bad treatment.'

Montcalm may have been seeking scapegoats for an episode that was destined to sully his honourable name, but it is not improbable that just such a deep-rooted desire for vengeance played some part in these events. Roubaud claimed that the Indians he spoke with afterwards sought to justify their actions by the law of retaliation. The Abenakis in particular had cause to seek revenge; during the previous winter, it was rumoured that some of their warriors had died by treacherous blows in the English forts of Acadia. Whether or not this was indeed so, the Penobscots of Panaouamaské already possessed long-standing grievances against the Massachusetts troops who formed the largest single unit in Monroe's unlucky garrison. Two years previously their province's lieutenant governor, Spencer Phips, proclaimed the Penobscots to be enemies, rebels and traitors to His Majesty King George II. The colony's treasury offered generous bounties to their killers: scalps of adult males earned the taker forty pounds, those of women and boys under the age of twelve brought in twenty. Faced with such genocidal policies, the band of Penobscots with Montcalm's victorious army may have considered themselves entitled to some small measure of satisfaction.

Whilst the causes and magnitude of the massacre at Fort William Henry remain controversial, its consequences were never in doubt: it swiftly became the most notorious French infraction of the internationally recognised Laws of War. Much Anglo-American newspaper coverage was predictably hysterical. The most gruesome and exaggerated accounts soon gained the currency of fact. Harking back to the aftermath of Braddock's defeat and the fall of Oswego, commentators now detected a clear pattern of cruelty and barbarity. Outraged editorials demanded vengeance against the French and their 'savage' allies: in future it would be necessary to make some severe examples amongst these inhuman enemies.

Amidst this general clamour, some nursed more personal grudges; they included Robert Rogers. Appointed to Loudoun's futile Cape Breton expedition, he had played no role at Fort William Henry, but his brother Richard captained one of the ranging companies assigned to the fort; it was a sickly garrison and he died of smallpox shortly before the siege began. However, as Rogers observed bitterly, 'such was the cruelty and rage of the enemy after their conquest that they dug him up out of his grave and scalped him.'

But Richard Rogers and the other uncomplaining dead of Fort William Henry wrought a dreadful vengeance upon their desecrators. Ottawas, Chippewas and Potawatomies carried home more than scalps: they also transmitted the smallpox virus. A devastating epidemic soon raged amongst them. More than a year would pass before the formidable warriors of the *pays d'en haut* recovered their strength and rallied once again to Onontio's aid.

CHAPTER THREE

The Ranging Way of War

IN THE DISMAL AFTERMATH OF the summer of 1757, Britain's military planners sought to ensure that the mistakes of the last campaign in North America would not be repeated. The shameful failure to prevent the fall of Fort William Henry, and the inaction of the vast force assembled to move against Louisbourg, dragged the prestige of British soldiers to an all-time low in the eyes of the colonists they had been sent to defend. Battalion upon battalion of regulars had arrived in North America, but nothing had been done with them; as far as the colonials were concerned, the growing numbers of redcoats had actually made things worse. As one commentator observed, 'the more we are strengthened from Great Britain, the more ground we lose against the French ... this great number of regular troops have been of no service for want of proper management.'

The man at whom the brunt of such withering criticism was directed was Lord Loudoun. He devoted much thought to the formulation of a strategy through which the overwhelming resources of the Anglo-Americans could be made to tell against the French. Loudoun did not lack advice, gratuitous or otherwise. One unsolicited analysis was prepared by the litigious new Lieutenant Governor of Massachusetts, Thomas Pownall, who believed that French control of inland waterways gave them easy and uninterrupted communication to posts from which offensive operations could be readily mounted against the English colonies. It was this advantage that had allowed Montcalm to exploit Loudoun's absence in Nova Scotia and fall upon Fort William Henry with such speed. If the sprawling British Army was to become anything more than a defensive force belatedly reacting against French strikes, it would be necessary to occupy the enemy by staging *simultaneous* assaults upon Canada via Lake Champlain and the St Lawrence River: Pownall argued that without two fleets and two armies, nothing could be achieved.

Loudoun regarded Pownall as an irritating humbug whose knowledge of North America was extremely superficial and frequently erroneous, yet the strategy that he evolved for the coming year's campaign shared much of Pownall's thinking: Loudoun aimed to divide the enemy's forces, and attack them in more places than one. The general envisaged a triple- rather than a double-pronged offensive. He would take personal command of the force aimed at Ticonderoga and Crown Point whilst Major-General Peregrine Hopson co-ordinated another amphibious strike against Louisbourg; in addition, a smaller expedition would be sent to the Ohio theatre to sever links between Canada and New France's southern sector on the Mississippi. Although Loudoun was removed from office before he had the opportunity to personally implement this ambitious plan, it provided the strategic blueprint for future British campaigns in North America.

But a viable strategy was just one ingredient in the recipe for victory. As astute officers like Loudoun's right-hand man, Colonel John Forbes, appreciated, the success of any paper plan ultimately rested upon the combat effectiveness of the soldiers who were required to translate words into deeds. In consequence, much attention was devoted to the evolution of a tactical doctrine that would permit regular British soldiers to tackle the French and Indians they would surely encounter amidst the forests of the interior wilderness.

So far, the only troops who had proved capable of fighting Canada's irregulars on anything approaching equal terms were the American rangers, so Loudoun and his staff sought ways to spread their expertise throughout the army as a whole. Before the start of the disastrous 1757 campaign, Forbes had urged that every junior officer and soldier be made familiar with the manner of *Wood fighting*, in which individuals sought cover behind *tree stumps or stone.* That summer the army was already implementing a simple drill intended to cope with forest ambush situations; at the terse order *tree all!* every man was enjoined to scatter for shelter. Forbes also made another significant recommendation: 'I should think it would not be amiss that the Regular army knew the mornoevres and ruzes made use of by our Rangers when they go a Scouting.'

When Loudoun's army returned from Halifax, Forbes' suggestions were implemented. Amongst the regulars who now joined Rogers and his men on their repeated patrols through the hazardous no-man's-land that stretched between Fort Edward and Ticonderoga was Colonel George Augustus, Viscount Howe. The eldest of three brothers who were destined to make their mark upon American history, Howe was rumoured to be a grandson of King George I. Despite this illustrious – if illegitimate – pedigree, Howe was no silk-cushioned courtier, but a tough professional soldier who led by example. Howe also possessed considerable personal charm; in a war in which relations between British officers and their colonial counterparts were all too frequently strained, this won him the esteem of Americans of all ranks. Such devotees included Robert Rogers, who was proud to report that Lord Howe 'expressed his good opinion of us very generously'.

As part of the drive to propagate ranger skills, volunteers from the regular regiments were formed into a special cadet force to learn ranging techniques under Rogers' personal supervision. Young gentlemen keen to demonstrate both their zeal for the service and their suitability for an officer's commission were schooled in the rangers' methods of marching, retreating, ambushing and fighting, so they would be better qualified for any future service against the enemy they had to contend with. These volunteers would hopefully disseminate their newfound expertise when they returned to their parent units.

It was at this time that Robert Rogers compiled his famous rules for the ranging service. Described by his biographer as the first written manual of irregular warfare in the New World, these instructions represented a codification of techniques already tested during two years of guerrilla warfare. For example, small patrols were recommended to march in single file, with one man forward twenty yards, and another at a similar distance on each flank to prevent surprise. If pursued by the enemy, Rogers advised making a circle till you came to your own tracks, and there forming an ambush to receive them.

Such survival skills had been employed by Indian-fighters since the days of King Philip's War in the 1670s; one of the most effective of these, the canny Captain Benjamin Church of Massachusetts, had already detailed his methods in his diary of that conflict, first published in 1716. Church's success derived from observing and imitating the tactics of the Indians themselves. The captain's memoirs provided numerous examples of his techniques, but the essence of his creed was to *march thin and scatter*, thereby denying Indian marksmen the easy targets to which they had become accustomed.

Whilst Rogers undoubtedly built upon an existing store of indigenous knowledge, the rules that he prepared in 1757 provided the clearest, fullest and most systematic introduction to that peculiar brand of warfare waged in the woods of North America. With their emphasis upon intelligence and security, fire and movement, ambush and evasion, Rogers' Rules for Ranging have a curiously modern ring: they embody timeless principles that remain central to the ethos of modern Special Forces – not least the US Army's own élite Rangers, who proudly trace their lineage back to Rogers' companies of the Seven Years' War. In a simplified form – apparently based upon a passage in Kenneth Roberts' novel *Northwest Passage* – the rules were issued to US ground troops embarking upon active service in Vietnam during the 1960s.

But rules were one thing, reality quite another; Rogers was quick to acknowledge that written instructions were only *guidelines*. After ten pages of such hints, he emphasised that there remained a thousand occurrences and circumstances for which no established procedure existed; at these times every man's reason and judgement must be his guide. Above all, it was essential for the commander of such troops to 'preserve a firmness and presence of mind on every occasion'.

This final maxim embodied the most important rule of all.

ROGERS' RULES FOR RANGING were not written merely for the enlightenment of bewildered British soldiers needing tuition in the rudiments of American irregular warfare. In Rogers' own manuscript copy, presented to Lord Loudoun, he emphasised that they were also intended to enhance the performance of the rangers themselves; they had been compiled so that *errors may be avoided & want of greater Regularity if found necessary pointed out to them for their observation and Improvement.*

Rogers may have sensed a gathering storm; he had good reason for caution. That winter found the rangers embroiled in a string of controversies that threatened their very existence.

Captain-Lieutenant Henry Pringle of the 27th Foot, or Inniskilling Regiment, maintained a regular correspondence with his family back in Ireland throughout a lengthy and colourful military career. On 15 December, 1757, shortly after Rogers' return from a scout to Ticonderoga, Pringle – who was then based at Fort Edward – wrote a vivid description of the famous captain and his corps:

> You may perhaps ask who these rangers are? They are Independent Companies; the officers pay is the same as the regulars, the men's near 2 shill[ing]s a day sterl[ing], to scout, as they term it, thro' the woods – in short, they are created Indians, & the only proper troops to oppose to them. They are good men, but badly disciplined. They dress & live like the Indians, & are well acquainted with the woods. There are many of them Irish, & their Commanding Officer, Rogers (who dined with me this very day) was born in the County of Antrim. He is a very resolute clever fellow, & has several times, as he terms it, banged the Indians & the French heartily. The last time *he came across them*, he killed them 90. They shoot amazingly well, all Ball, & mostly with riffled Barrels. One of their Officers the other day, at four shots

with four balls, killed a brace of Deer, a Pheasant, & a pair of wild ducks. The latter he killed at one shot. They, as well as the Indians, go out every now & then about six men together, upon a scout to shoot men, for 15 or 20 days; & carry their provisions & blankets upon their backs.

Pringle's letter provides an unusually candid glimpse of the tough, convivial and cocksure Robert Rogers and a snap-shot of a fighting formation that was already famous.

An Ulsterman himself, Pringle clearly felt an affinity with Rogers and his men; although Rogers was born in Massachusetts, Pringle's reference to Antrim hints at his parents' origins. It was from the hardy Scotch-Irish who flooded into the country that the original core of Rogers' Rangers had been recruited; subsequent recruits, also including many recent immigrants from Ireland, were picked up throughout New England, and especially in Boston.

Alongside numerous representatives of Britain's Celtic fringe, the ranging companies also fielded manpower that reflected the diversity of colonial American society. They mustered not only native-born Indians, but also men of African origin who had been brought to the Americas under duress. Boston Burn, for example, who served under Rogers in 1758, was the slave of James Burn of Westford, Massachusetts; he was captured whilst out on scout that February. And an advertisement in the *New-York Mercury* during the summer of 1759 reported that a *Negro Man* named Jacob, who had been arrested for pilfering, was being held in the jail at Goshen in Orange County; although the *Mercury* presumed him to be a runaway, Jacob maintained that he had spent three years in Rogers' Rangers, and that his former master had granted him his freedom in recognition of that fact. Jacob's appearance certainly supported his claim. Besides tribal scarring – *a Cut on each Cheek in his own Country* – he displayed a gunshot wound to his right wrist. When taken up, he was in possession of an iron-mounted gun and was wearing an outfit strongly suggestive of the rangers: a green jacket lined with red, buckskin breeches and blue Indian stockings. Described as a spry able fellow aged between twenty-five and thirty, Jacob was clearly something of a dandy: his fine white shirts sported decorative ruffles, or chitterlings, and his handkerchief was of spotted silk.

Such detailed contemporary descriptions of individual rangers are frustratingly rare and the whole question of ranger costume continues to generate debate. The issue is complicated by the fact that Rogers' Rangers were never an officially recognised battalion, but rather a loose conglomeration of independent companies grouped under the overall command of Rogers. Different companies wore their own individual outfits, and these changed over time as threadbare clothing was replaced.

As one unusually observant British officer noted in 1757, the ranging companies assembled at Halifax, Nova Scotia had no designated dress, but simply wore their usual clothes cut short. But whilst there was never a prescribed uniform for *all* of Rogers' Rangers – still less the natty suits of fringed green buckskin and matching forage caps sported by Spencer Tracy and his merry men in the movie of *Northwest Passage* – certain items of dress appear regularly enough in contemporary accounts to provide a reasonable idea of what constituted typical ranger garb. Ranger coats were often short, and green in colour, as were waistcoats. Other typical components of ranger apparel were Indian leggings and moccasins; the presence of both items on a drowned corpse in October 1759 was enough to prompt speculation that the man concerned was a deserter from the rangers.

As many rangers had Scotch-Irish roots, the blue woollen bonnet worn by both Highland and Lowland Scots remained popular; in the spring of 1758, an agent for one Albany clothing company felt sure that 'a parcel of Scotch Bonnets would sell well, as the Rangers who can get them wear nothing else when they go out'. Peaked jockey caps, either purpose-made from hardened leather or improvised from cut-down felt tricorne hats, also featured. During winter months the basic kit was augmented by extra waistcoats, blanket-coats, fur caps and mittens, all intended to stave off frostbite. Though details remain imprecise, the general picture is clear enough: rangers wore practical, hard-wearing clothing that wouldn't be cumbersome or constricting in the woods, in sombre colours to offer a reasonable degree of concealment.

The rangers at Fort Edward in December 1757 apparently wore a more drastic version of Indian dress than native-style leggings and moccasins. White men who came into contact with Indians on the frontiers needed little prompting to mimic their fashions, so some rangers might have adopted such traditional tribal trappings as tattoos, beaded belts and quill-decorated pouches. A strong Indian influence was also detected by an eyewitness during the siege of Louisbourg the following spring: the rangers, together with the British Highlanders and regular light infantry, were dubbed *the English savages* by the French. However, whilst the light infantry were undoubtedly a rough-looking crew, compared with the cut-throat rangers, they looked like *artificial savages*.

Pringle's ranger companions made notable use of rifles; the hawk-eyed frontiersman, with long rifle carried casually in the crook of his arm and capable of awesome feats of marksmanship, is a figure familiar from James Fenimore Cooper's *The Last of the Mohicans*, but despite this iconic image, and Pringle's eyewitness account, most rangers typically used the smoothbore musket, or firelock. In key respects the humble musket was a far handier combat weapon. Although the rifle was more accurate and longer-ranged, and therefore the perfect precision tool for the hunter, it was less suited to the close-quarter bush fighting experienced by the rangers. Not only could a smoothbore be loaded far more swiftly, it was also capable of firing buckshot and mounting a bayonet. For the ranger faced with a rapidly closing line of whooping Indians or determined French regulars, such considerations were not without weight.

By modern standards the musket was an inefficient weapon, prone to misfires and wildly inaccurate at a range of anything over one hundred yards, but, within its limits, and as the era's lengthy casualty lists confirm, it was an effective enough weapon. Practice actually made a difference; the attention devoted to target-shooting by Indians, rangers and regular troops alike maximised the musket's performance at the relatively close ranges characteristic of both forest fighting and the open battlefield.

Regular and ranger officers used lighter muskets known as fusils or fuzees; simpler patterns were available to the rank and file, and possibly saw service within the ranging companies. Some rangers may have used the shorter carbines employed by the British Highland regiments and the Royal Artillery. Even the standard-issue British Long Land Pattern musket – the famous Brown Bess shouldered by generations of redcoats – could be adapted into a lighter, handier weapon by simply sawing several inches off its 46-inch barrel. This technique was employed by the regulars themselves on Lake George and elsewhere in 1758; it was officially recognised ten years later when the Long Land Pattern began to be replaced by shorter versions that served the British Army well throughout the Revolutionary and Napoleonic Wars.

Though the rifles that so impressed Pringle in December 1757 were probably primarily for hunting game, some of the provincial troops from the Virginian and Pennsylvania frontiers employed rifles as weapons, and the British Army issued small numbers of them itself. The fifty regular volunteers who served as cadets with Rogers' Rangers that autumn were all issued with *Riffle-barrel Fuzees*, though they were ordered to return these weapons to the Ordnance Stores when they rejoined their parent units in November.*

Whatever the finer details of their clothing and weaponry, the rangers were clearly distinct from both the long-service British redcoats and the short-term provincial troops raised by the individual colonies. Those ranger units who were actually in the pay of the Crown rather than the colonies were regarded as independent companies of the regular army – but despite this designation, the units that formed Rogers' Rangers were never formally placed upon the regular establishment; as a result, they were not recorded within the pages of the annual *Army List* that catalogued every far-flung unit of the British Army from the fashionable Guards to the decrepit Invalids.

Regardless of status, the rangers were unusually expensive. In early

---

* Metal detector explorations of suspected ranger skirmish sites have unearthed both musket *and* rifle balls.

1757, the pay for privates under Rogers' command had been fixed at two shillings and sixpence New York currency per day; this was equivalent to one shilling and five and a half pence sterling – more than double the pay of the humble redcoat. For cash-strapped British commanders, the hefty ranger wage bill was a powerful incentive to investigate cheaper alternatives.

This desire to supplant the rangers with other troops capable of undertaking scouting duties was only encouraged by another factor that Henry Pringle highlighted: their notorious unruliness. When Pringle penned his letter in mid-December 1757, the question of ranger discipline – or rather, the lack of it – had become a favourite topic for debate in British Army circles. During the previous month, things had come to a head when Captain James Abercrombie of the Black Watch, aide-de-camp to and nephew of Loudoun's second-in-command, Major-General James Abercromby, accompanied a ranger patrol to Ticonderoga. Abercrombie returned livid at the lax discipline he witnessed.

According to the captain, the scout's failure to secure a prisoner stemmed solely from the blatant misbehaviour of the rangers. When a French woodcutter spotted them and took to his heels, Captain John Stark had *set up the Indian hollow*, at which the whole party jumped up and yelled as if hell had broken loose, and all fell a-firing at a few men running away. The exasperated Abercrombie struggled to restore order, knocking down several of the rangers and damning their officers for a set of scoundrels. When the scout withdrew, it was left to Abercrombie and some of his fellow regulars to form the rearguard.

Abercrombie was not some red-faced professional soldier venting his prejudices at the shortcomings of amateur colonials; he was a highly motivated officer who had previously accompanied the rangers on scouts and wished for nothing more than to take the war to the enemy. Moreover, he admired Rogers and felt sure that if he had been with them, they could not have failed; indeed, he was the only ranger officer who knew anything of the country.

His uncle General Abercromby felt that this episode – and other circumstances – demonstrated the need to remould the rangers into a respectable body of men under proper discipline; he believed that objective could be achieved by transforming one company of each redcoat battalion into rangers.

The Ticonderoga scout had been bad enough, but worse was to follow. On 6 December, just a week before Pringle wrote his letter, the rangers at Fort Edward mutinied in protest at the flogging of two of their comrades. Brutal corporal punishment was an accepted fact of life in the British Army; hard-bitten redcoats displayed the scars inflicted by the cat-of-nine-tails as a mark of caste; some even wagered upon the number of lashes they could accumulate within a specified period. But for the rangers, the whipping post was a hated symbol of oppression and degradation; when two of them received a 'gentle correction' for stealing rum, others seized an axe and hacked the post down. After the culprits were arrested, their comrades gathered in an attempt to rescue them. A witness heard several rangers say 'they did not like the Whipping post, and if the Rangers were to be flogged there wou'd be no more Rangers.'

The commander at Fort Edward, Lieutenant-Colonel William Haviland, was outraged. After hearing the evidence of a preliminary court of inquiry he was adamant that the ringleaders should be court-martialled and severely punished: 'unless they are got the better of, it is better to be without them,' he proclaimed. Rogers countered by warning Haviland that most of his men would desert if the matter were pursued. Personally, Haviland replied, he would be glad to see the back of such a riotous sort of people, but if any ranger were caught absconding, he would surely hang as a warning to the rest. This threat failed to stop nine men deserting, apparently in protest at the imposition of military justice.

Haviland's anger at the rangers' behaviour was understandable enough from the perspective of an officer steeped in the uncompromising disciplinary code of the regular army, but he displayed a blinkered approach on shooting practice that was at odds with the realistic doctrines espoused by forward-thinking officers like Forbes and Howe. He grumbled that the rangers wasted too much ammunition in target-shooting; Rogers countered by maintaining that his people could not do without practising at marks. Neither man was prepared to back down. Haviland managed to put a stop to the constant firing on the island in the Hudson where the ranging companies were based, but no sooner did the rangers get into the woods than they made them ring. This friction between Rogers and Haviland sparked damaging consequences.

Rogers was sick with scurvy when this discipline crisis exploded; those in authority were not slow to make the connection between these two events. For all his concerns over the conduct of the rangers, Abercromby, like his nephew, had no doubts about the worth of their forceful young leader. He told Loudoun: 'With regard to Rogers himself, I do think him so necessary and Usefull a man, that I should be extreamly sorry to part with him, and rather than that, I [would] give him some encouragement to Continue diligent and hearty in the Service.' Without Rogers, he added, the four companies of rangers at Fort Edward would be good for nothing.

Recovered from his illness, Rogers set about re-establishing the reputation of his corps by heading a reconnaissance in strength. On 17 December, 1757, he led a hundred and fifty men on a scout to Fort Carillon in quest of a prisoner; after taking two captives, he torched stockpiles of wood and slaughtered seventeen cattle while the garrison looked on. Rogers rubbed salt in French wounds when he left a note impaled upon the horns of one of his bovine victims, politely thanking Carillon's commandant for the fresh meat he had sent him, and forwarding his compliments to the Marquis de Montcalm. It was exactly the kind of exploit that endeared Rogers to newspaper readers in Boston and New York. The French were less amused.

While Commissary Jean-Baptiste Doreil condemned the prank as 'an ill-timed and very low piece of braggadocio', Rogers revelled in his growing notoriety. When an equally experienced enemy officer of partisans arrived at Fort Edward to discuss an exchange of prisoners, Rogers could not resist ribbing him about the fresh meat they let him eat at Carillon. His butt was Lieutenant Wolff, a half-pay officer who was once a sergeant in the *troupes de terre*. A man of like kidney to Rogers, he responded by cautioning him to be careful of himself when he came again. It was advice that Rogers would have done well to heed.

FOR ALL THE CRITICISMS OF THE unruly rangers, Britain's commander in North America was obliged to keep them in pay whilst he struggled to train regular troops capable of taking their place. Early in the new year, Loudoun decided upon a major expansion of his ranging arm: he authorised Rogers to recruit five new companies, more than five hundred men. Four companies were to be raised in New England; these were to provide themselves with good warm clothing, uniform in every company, and likewise decent blankets. The fifth company, recruited from the Mohegans of Connecticut, was to be dressed in all respects in the *true Indian fashion*. All, white and Indian alike, were to be 'able-bodied, well acquainted with the woods, used to hunting, and every way qualified for the Ranging service.' Loudoun also accepted the services of some fifty Mahicans from the settlement of Stockbridge in Massachusetts; these warriors enlisted under their own officers, including Captain Jacob Cheeksaunkun and Lieutenant Jacob Naunauphtaunk.

The demand for specialist forest fighters had been underlined by the continuing problems of the regulars in absorbing the lessons of war in the North American wilderness. For troops schooled in the conventional conditions of Flanders and Germany, the learning curve was long, steep and slippery with blood. The bewildering conditions of New World warfare had been all too clear to the redcoats who marched into the Pennsylvanian backwoods with Braddock in 1755; British soldiers sent across the Atlantic in subsequent years found them no less disconcerting.

The wave of reinforcements that disembarked at New York in 1757 had included Henry Pringle's own unit, the 27th Foot; according to disgruntled soldiers who were drafted from its ranks into the newly formed Royal American Regiment, this was a *Good Old Regt*; it dated back to the major expansion of the British Army at the beginning of King William's great war with Louis XIV of France in 1689. More recently it had participated in the ill-fated Anglo-American expedition against Spain's Caribbean empire; sent out to reinforce the army winnowed by tropical disease in 1742–3, the 27th lost most of its manpower to the same invisible killers. The ruined regiment was rebuilt in time to oppose Bonnie Prince Charlie's Jacobite rebellion, only to be routed by his Highlanders at Falkirk in January 1746. The humiliated battalion regained its nerve, participating in the crushing Hanoverian victory at Culloden three months later.

In 1757, the Inniskilling Regiment had formed part of the task force that assembled at Halifax for the descent upon Louisbourg; when that operation was cancelled, the regiment went into winter quarters at Fort Edward. It was there, in the new year, that the men of the 27th received their short, sharp initiation into the brutal realities of American frontier warfare.

On Tuesday 8 February, 1758, the battalion's commanding officer, Lieutenant-Colonel Haviland, sent out a sergeant and twenty-four men as a covering party for woodcutters seeking timber to build barracks. According to Major Eyre Massy, the snow on the ground was upwards of four foot deep. The group had gone no more than two hundred yards beyond the fort's outlying blockhouses when a party of Indians – believed to be more than a hundred strong – descended upon them.

The sergeant fired three rounds before he was dragged off and scalped. Another soldier was shot through both thighs but stood his ground and when any of the enemy came near him, he *presented his Firelock and came to a Recover*; his instinctive survival technique meant he lived to tell the tale. Massy reported that his men had fired a great many shots at the Indians, and had behaved well, but unlike their assailants they had no snowshoes: straying off the beaten path they sank waist-deep in the drifts and were butchered like sheep. No fewer than fourteen were killed; another four were wounded and five reported missing. Several woodcutters were also slain.

This brutally effective ambush had been sprung by an ensign in the *troupes de la Marine*: Jean-Baptiste Levrault de Langis Montegron, better known to his English-speaking enemies as Langy, was amongst the most capable of a formidable band of guerrilla leaders who fought doggedly to preserve New France. Langis returned to Carillon with three prisoners who provided valuable information regarding British plans and dispositions; his raiders also brought back twenty-three scalps. One of these grisly trophies belonged to a British soldier who later rose up from where he lay in the bloody snow and reeled into Fort Edward. There he confronted his astonished officers and declared: 'by God Gentlemen I have lost my night Cap'. This shocking spectre was subsequently *four or five times out of his Senses*, the newspapers reported, although they were optimistic of his recovery.

This unfortunate soldier was probably Hugh Smith, who came before the board of Chelsea's Royal Hospital to be examined for his army pension on 27 March, 1759. Smith, who was aged thirty and from Taunton in Somerset, was working as a tailor before he took the King's shilling and joined the 27th back in 1743; at the time of his enlistment he was just fourteen years old. The hospital's register of applicants reported Smith as *Scalp'd by the Indians in America*; his unusually traumatic ordeal no doubt gained him a sympathetic hearing and, unlike most pensioners, who were placed upon the out-pension and had to fend for themselves in the civilian community on a measly dole of five pence a day, he was allotted accommodation within Chelsea Hospital itself. A German aristocrat who visited the Hospital three years later noted that the four hundred and fifty pensioners dined together in the great hall. Each man received a daily ration of one pound of meat and another of bread, plus a quarter-pound of cheese, two pints of beer and a penny for tobacco. There, under fading and tattered standards and guidons wrested from the French and Bavarians at Blenheim more than half a century before, veterans of more recent conflicts supped their ale, smoked their pipes and pondered the vagaries of the soldiers' lot.

IN AN EFFORT TO AVOID JUST SUCH lopsided encounters as had cost Hugh Smith his scalp, Loudoun continued to encourage volunteers from the regulars to join the rangers' arduous scouts. So, on 10 March, 1758, when Rogers left Fort Edward bound for Carillon at the head of ten officers and a hundred and sixty-two other ranks drawn from four ranging companies, he was accompanied by eight volunteers from the 27th Foot, amongst them, Captain-Lieutenant Pringle.

Rogers embarked upon this scout with grave misgivings – reflecting the baleful legacy of his recent spat with Haviland. At the end of February, Haviland had despatched a patrol under Captain Israel Putnam of the Connecticut provincials; at the same time, he publicly announced that upon Putnam's return Rogers would lead out a stronger party of four hundred rangers. Whilst this scout was away, the French captured a servant belonging to one of the rangers' sutlers, and a man of Putnam's party deserted to the enemy; to make matters even worse, his advance scouts reported the presence of an estimated six hundred Indians clustered near Ticonderoga.

Rogers was convinced that either the prisoner or the deserter had revealed Haviland's intention to send *him* against the French. However, not only did Haviland insist that the reconnaissance must proceed, but he halved its strength. Rogers fretted that the security of his patrol was compromised; meanwhile, the swingeing reduction in numbers left it vulnerable to interception by a stronger French force. He later confessed: 'I entered upon this service and viewed this small detachment of brave men march out with no little concern and uneasiness of mind.'

On their first night the party encamped at the Halfway Brook, midway to Lake George. The next day, 11 March, they reached the frozen lake's First Narrows and there made camp for the night. Rogers remained nervous. A party was sent three miles ahead to search for the enemy. They found nothing, but sentries were posted on the land and parties sent to patrol the lake all through the night.

At sunrise the march continued; after advancing three miles, Rogers spotted a dog skittering across the ice. A patrol probed an island thought likely to conceal lurking hostiles. Once again, nothing was found. Nerves stretched ever tighter, Rogers resolved to quit the conspicuous surface of the lake and halt upon land on its western side, at Sabbath Day Point. Parties scrutinised the snow-covered landscape through telescopes, or *perspective glasses*. The main body crunched stolidly onwards across the ice in pitch-darkness. An advance guard under Lieutenant William Phillips glided ahead on skates. When they arrived within eight miles of the French outposts at Carillon, one of Phillips' skaters returned and advised Rogers to halt; soon afterwards, Phillips himself appeared: he believed he had seen firelight on the eastern shore, but could not be certain. Sent back to investigate with another officer, Phillips returned convinced that he had discovered an enemy encampment. Concealing their sleds and packs in a thicket, the rangers marched to attack this unsuspecting enemy, yet when they came near the spot there was nothing to be seen; it seemed that their eyes had played tricks upon them. Rogers conjectured that they had mistaken 'some bleach patches of snow, or pieces of rotten wood, for fire (which in the night, at a distance, resembles it).' Frustrated at chasing phantoms, his men returned to their packs and another fireless night in the chill and forbidding forest.

Despite Rogers' lingering fears that a prisoner or deserter had warned the garrison at Fort Carillon of his coming, this was not the case – yet the French *were* forewarned, albeit in a very different fashion. That same day, 12 March, a formidable raiding party of some two hundred mission Iroquois and Nipissings, along with forty Canadians, had arrived at Carillon under the command of *Sieur* de La Durantaye, an ensign in *la Marine*. The warriors sought rest and refreshment before continuing on their way southwards and the fort's commandant, Captain Louis-Philippe d'Hébécourt obligingly provided them with food and brandy. Returning to their encampment, they began to drink. One of the Indians, described by Captain Malartic of the *troupes de terre* as an *old sorcerer*, fell into a trance and divined that the English were nearby. Two Abenakis soon uncovered the truth of this revelation by reporting fresh tracks on the ice; a scout subsequently confirmed the presence of a substantial British patrol. The mission Indians were spoiling for a fight; they were joined by Canadians and volunteers from the regulars keen to punctuate the tedious routine of garrison life. On 13 March this assorted band of two hundred and fifty or more fighters marched for the lake; their leaders included the seasoned Ensign Langis.

Rogers was unaware of this alarming development. That morning he consulted his officers on how they should continue their march; all agreed that the surface of Lake George was now too risky and they should instead don snowshoes and proceed by land. They marched down the lake's western side, hugging the back of a mountain range that screened them from the French advance guards. The halt was called at noon, and the command rested until three, allowing time for the fort's customary day patrol to return to base. Rogers planned to set ambushes on paths during the night and spring them in the morning. The rangers pushed onwards in two divisions, one headed by Captain Charles Bulkley, the other by Rogers himself; a rearguard was commanded by ensigns James White and Joseph Wait. They marched with a rivulet close to their left flank and the sheltering mountain on the right.

Rogers calculated that any hostile force in the area would follow the firm path created by the stream's frozen surface; the surrounding snow was four feet deep and the going difficult, even for men equipped with snowshoes. Sure enough, after pushing on for another mile and a half, Rogers' advance guard reported that the enemy – a party of one hundred, mostly Indians – was marching up the rivulet towards them. The rangers shed their packs and prepared for action. Rogers' line simply faced to the left, taking cover amidst rocky and wooded ground. The rangers held their fire until the straggling enemy column was nearly level with their left flank, thereby giving every man a target. When Rogers fired, the whole line delivered a stunning blast of musketry. Rogers later claimed that this salvo killed more than forty Indians; although this was certainly an exaggeration, the point-blank volley obliged their vanguard, under La Durantaye's command, to recoil in confusion. About half of Rogers' men gave chase; others began to scalp the fallen.

Rogers and his men believed that they had executed the perfect ambush. They swiftly realised their mistake. As Rogers reported: 'we soon found that the party we had engaged, were only the advance Guards of the Enemy.' Their main body now came up in great numbers to join the action.

In a matter of seconds the tables were turned with a vengeance. Langis launched a counter-attack at the head of a strong party of Indians. This well-timed riposte caught the jubilant rangers off-guard; fifty of them swiftly dropped. The shocked survivors fell back to their old position. Here, as Rogers wrote in his official report, 'they stood and fought with the greatest Intrepidity and Bravery imaginable; insomuch, that in a very short Time, the Enemy were forced to retreat a second Time.'

Rogers lacked the manpower to exploit this temporary success, and the French and Indians soon returned to the fray, pushing hard in the front and on both flanks. So far the mountain had protected the rangers' rear, but the enemy now sent parties to gain the high ground and turn their position. Lieutenant Phillips rebuffed the threat on the right, while Lieutenant Edward Crofton covered the left. Though hampered by their unfamiliar snowshoes, Henry Pringle and another volunteer from the 27th, Lieutenant Boyle Roche, led eight men to Crofton's support; Rogers acknowledged that all acted with great bravery.

The fight was now reaching a crisis: 'the Enemy pushed on so close in the Front,' Rogers reported, 'that the parties were not more than 20 Yards a part, and oftentimes intermix'd with each other.' After an hour and a half of almost constant firing, his command finally broke and scattered. Phillips' party was surrounded and faced extermination; if the enemy proved willing to grant *good quarters*, he would surrender. When they received the strongest assurances of this, he and his men laid down their arms. They would have done better to fight it out. The Indians were in no mood for mercy; having discovered a chief's scalp in the breast of a ranger officer's jacket, they wanted vengeance. Although Phillips survived, most of his men were not so lucky. They were 'inhumanly tied up to trees and hewn to pieces in a most barbarous and shocking manner.' There was a great harvest of a hundred and fourteen scalps. According to Montcalm, the Indians took just three prisoners – and those only to furnish what they styled *live letters* to their 'father', Governor General Vaudreuil.

With all resistance now over, Rogers considered it prudent to retreat and bring off as many of his people as possible. The Indians pursued closely enough to drag down several of the fugitives. To their surprise and relief, Pringle and Roche were not followed. Seeing a fire kindled below, Pringle conjectured that the Indians must have found the rum in the rangers' canteens and set to celebrating their victory.

When they reached Lake George that evening, Rogers and the remnants of his command collected several injured survivors and carried them to the hidden sleds; from there he sent an express to Fort Edward seeking help to bring in his wounded. The weary survivors spent a miserable night without fire or blankets. Next morning they returned up the lake, meeting John Stark at Sloop Island, six miles north of the desolate site of Fort William Henry. On the following evening, 15 March, what was left of Rogers' command limped into Fort Edward. A grim roll call followed: of the one hundred and eighty men who had set out five days before, no fewer than one hundred and thirty were marked down as killed or missing: the cream of four veteran ranging companies. It would be difficult to replace these experienced officers, sergeants and privates with men of equal calibre.

Of the eight-strong detachment from the 27th Foot, three lived to tell the tale. Pringle and Roche spent a week wandering aimlessly in the ice-encrusted wilderness, sustained only by bark, berries, a small Bologna sausage and a little ginger. Numb with cold and fatigue, they survived their final, fireless night in the open by shambling around a tree in an effort to stay awake. Their ranger guide, who had long since lost his mind, wandered off to die in the snow. Frosted like icemen, the famished pair finally stumbled up to Fort Carillon on 20 March. French officers rushed out to grab them before the Indians could. The regiment's other survivor, Francis Creed, nephew of the regiment's colonel, Lord Edward Blakeney, was the only one of the 27th's three young volunteers to escape;

he received the highest praise from Rogers and soon after was rewarded with a commission in the rangers. Five years later, the loss of another of the volunteers, sixteen-year-old John Wrightson, was recalled with mingled grief and guilt by the soldier-uncle who had brought him over to America. The lad had sought adventure and advancement, only to be killed and scalped by the Indians, like so many before him.

The French were exultant. They had trounced a detachment of picked men commanded by the enemy's *most famous partizan*. Rogers' own jacket, along with his orders and captain's commission, had been found on the field. Some believed that Rogers himself was amongst the bodies that now lay stark and stiffening in the blood-stained snow; even if the famous captain had escaped the carnage, others reasoned, surely he would perish from cold and hunger as he wandered almost naked in the woods? But not for the first or last time, such reports of Rogers' death proved to be premature.

In his official report of what became known as the Battle on Snowshoes, Rogers remained frustratingly vague about the circumstances of his own escape; this quickly gave rise to extraordinary stories that later became embedded in the region's folklore: the two most popular variations both have Rogers retreating over the mountains at the rear of the rangers' position to the brink of a yawning precipice above the frozen surface of Lake George. In the first version, the wily ranger removes his snowshoes, replaces them back-to-front and then carefully retraces his steps, or takes a different path, thereby leaving the impression that he has plummeted headlong.*

The second is more spectacular still: in this, he does not double back at the cliff's edge but quite literally takes the plunge, using his snowshoes to slide to safety. Anyone viewing the sheer and bare expanse of rock in question must share the scepticism of those of Rogers' contemporaries who doubted whether any mortal could make such a descent without breaking his neck. The contemporary press, usually so diligent

* This particular exploit has parallels in others credited to several figures in Britain's medieval history; celebrated fugitives such as King Robert the Bruce of Scotland reputedly fooled pursuers by the simple expedient of reversing their horseshoes.

in recording his every deed, failed to mention either version of this particular escapade, yet there was clearly some basis for the stories: by 1760 the spot was already known as Rogers' Leap. When Francis Parkman visited Lake George in 1842, Rogers' Slide was a noted landmark; it retains that name today.

Robert Rogers was becoming a legend in his own lifetime. Still, there was no disguising the fact that he had suffered a stunning defeat. In the immediate aftermath of the fight there was no hint of criticism. One of the new publications spawned by the war, *The American Magazine*, informed its readers that his men had behaved with the most signal calmness and bravery during the whole action. Indeed, although the famous Captain Rogers had been worsted, he and his rangers deserved recognition for their readiness to seek out the enemy. An editorial continued: 'We have been the more particular in this account, as we shall in all others of the like kind; that posterity may find in our magazine materials sufficient for the history of the present times, and for doing justice to the memories of the brave men who have signalised themselves in their country's service, at a period when national virtue seems at a low ebb.'

In coming weeks, the accuracy of Rogers' version of events came under closer scrutiny. His post-combat report not only reckoned the enemy to be at least 700-strong, but estimated that his men had killed a hundred of them, and wounded as many more. Both claims were wild exaggerations. Although La Durantaye and Langis possessed a numerical edge, they probably outnumbered Rogers' command by fewer than a hundred men. French sources tallied their own losses far lower than Rogers claimed: Montcalm reported eight killed and seventeen wounded; Frenchmen captured by the Stockbridge ranger Captain Jacob and interrogated separately all agreed upon a dozen fatalities. However, this quibbling over numbers ignores one important factor: for the Indians who had borne the brunt of the action, such losses were heavy enough; as Montcalm noted, they were not accustomed to lose their warriors. Bougainville, who had been adopted by the Iroquois of Caughnawaga, noted the elaborate condolence ceremonies by which Vaudreuil sought to cover the dead of the tribe. Slaves were provided as substitutes for the slain and decorative gorgets and medals were distributed to those who had distinguished themselves, in the hope that this largesse would encourage them to avenge their losses still further.

Glaring discrepancies in the various reports of the snowshoe fight caused some British commentators to question both Rogers' prowess and his honesty. Reporting the French prisoners' testimony to Lord Loudoun, the army surgeon Richard Huck explained: 'Rogers since this Intelligence begins to fall into Disrepute. My high opinion of him is wavering. Here are Reasons to doubt his Veracity.' Huck believed that only the return of Captain Pringle and Lieutenant Roche would allow a better judgement of Rogers' courage and conduct.

Though it was more than a year before Pringle rejoined his regiment, on 28 March, whilst still a captive at Carillon, he wrote a lengthy letter to Haviland that went a long way towards silencing Rogers' critics; he felt obliged to assure his lieutenant-colonel that the combat had been very unequal from the start. Indeed 'such dispositions were formed by the enemy (who discovered us long enough before), it was impossible for a party so weak as ours to hope for even a retreat.' This unequivocal and soldier-like verdict, from a King's officer of unblemished character, cleared Rogers' name.

Throughout the rumour and backbiting, Rogers had never forfeited the friendship and confidence of men in high places. When he returned from *the late unfortunate scout*, he was sent down to Albany to fill the yawning gaps in the ranger ranks; there he became reacquainted with the charismatic Lord Howe, who gave him a very friendly reception and advanced the cash needed to pay his recruits. Howe gladly allowed Rogers to travel to New York to wait upon Major-General Abercromby, who had now replaced the unlucky Loudoun as commander-in-chief in North America. It was from Abercromby himself that Rogers received the ultimate vote of approval: by a commission dated 6 April, 1758, which expressed the greatest confidence in Rogers' loyalty, courage and skill, he was promoted to major of the rangers in His Majesty's Service. Rogers had long been known as *the Major* to his men and the press alike, but this formal recognition of rank was vindication indeed.

That spring, as another vast Anglo-American army slowly coalesced at Albany, Rogers' stock, and that of his unruly rangers, had never been higher. The major now commanded a contingent of six hundred troops, including the two Indian companies. Like Benjamin Church before him, Rogers valued the services of Indian warriors; he appreciated their combat and scouting skills and was quick to praise them in both his intelligence reports and published *Journals*.

Alongside the familiar rangers, Abercromby's army included a newly raised regular battalion of five hundred men that sought to emulate and ultimately replace them; this formation began recruiting in December 1757 after Loudoun approved an initiative proposed by Lieutenant-Colonel Thomas Gage of the 44th Foot – that same officer who had commanded Braddock's advance guard at the Monongahela. Gage's scheme won favour because it aimed to provide a cheaper and more highly disciplined alternative to the rangers.

Five of the ensigns' commissions went to gentlemen volunteers who had recently won their spurs as cadets under Rogers' supervision. Gage's Light Infantry mustered a mixture of men drafted from Loudoun's redcoat battalions and recruits drummed up in the colonies; many locals enlisted under the mistaken belief that they would receive ranger pay. Smooth-talking recruiting officers did nothing to disabuse them of this notion; it was further encouraged by the fact that the regiment wore brown coats instead of regulation red. Numbered the 80th Regiment of Light Armed Foot, it was the British Army's first officially recognised unit of light infantry. The rank and file were a wild bunch; if the army's court-martial records are any indication, they were every bit as unbridled as the rangers themselves.

Alongside these specialists, the entire force that was preparing to batter its way through the gates of Canada had begun to reflect the increasing influence of the rangers. By Abercromby's orders, officers were banned from taking to the field with any baggage more cumbersome than a small portmanteau, blanket and bearskin. The women who usually washed the soldiers' clothes were to be left behind; every man must scrub his own linen. Blacksmiths were busy sawing down the barrels of muskets for use in the woods, while redcoats and provincials alike had been ordered to modify their uniforms to meet the requirements of forest warfare: tricorne hats were cropped of their brims and worn slouched, and the long tails of uniform coats docked short. The regimental barbers played their part in this transformation: it was now *an Army of round heads* – no small matter in an age when men grew their hair long and wore it tied back in a queue. One officer, the future Revolutionary war general Horatio Gates, believed that the Germans in the ranks of the Royal American Regiment would sooner have parted with their scalps than with their long plaited pigtails.

Rogers' aristocratic friend Lord Howe was the driving spirit behind this revolution. Celebrated alike for his robust soldier-like constitution, his bold enterprising spirit and every other military accomplishment, he led by personal example. Howe's 55th Foot was a model corps; he had sacrificed his own fine head of hair, and was in the habit of going himself to the brook, and washing his own linen. And it was not just a question of appearances. According to one admirer, the brigadier had been schooling his own regulars in bush fighting; they were, he claimed, almost as dexterous at it as the rangers themselves.

All were agreed that the tough but charming Howe was exactly what the Anglo-American war effort needed. In appointing him as second-in-command to the expedition, Pitt trusted his youth and enthusiasm would animate the ponderous Abercromby. British hopes for the coming campaign increasingly rested upon Howe's athletic shoulders.

AS THE ARMY PREPARED TO MOVE down Lake George, Rogers and his rangers came into their own. On 8 June, Howe ordered him out with fifty men to reconnoitre Ticonderoga and beyond. Proceeding by whaleboat, they took a plan of the landing place at the north end of the lake.

Whilst Rogers and a few others were sketching the fort, the enemy fell upon his main party; they fought their way clear with the loss of eight men. In coming weeks, repeated ranger scouts probed northwards to establish the clearest possible picture of French defences. This essential service helped to cement Rogers' position and to quash any lingering doubts over his worth. As Dr Huck explained in another of his gossip-laden letters to Loudoun: 'It has been pretty much in Vogue lately to decry all Rangers and Rogers has come in for his share of Discredit. Parties therefore of regular Troops commanded by such Officers as were judged the properest for that service have been sent out to procure Intelligence, but returned without getting any Thing, for which they blamed the Guides, and I believe are not a little sick of these Experiments.'

At the end of June, Abercromby arrived at the lake with the rest of the army. There, by the mounded ruins of the ill-fated Fort William Henry, they remained until 5 July, when the entire host, some sixteen thousand strong, embarked in bateaux for Ticonderoga. It was an awesome sight: a vast armada of redcoats, provincials, rangers and armed boatmen choked the lake from shore to shore. Rogers and his men formed the left of the advance guard. At daybreak on 6 July they made a landing. To the surprise of many there was no opposition.

In fact, the French had expected a landing further south, and had left a rearguard of three hundred men to oppose it. With the British now between them and Fort Carillon, this party sought to regain its own lines by taking a loop through the woods; it was guided by Rogers' old enemy, Ensign Langis. But in an episode that underlines the potential for even the most experienced forest fighter to become disoriented in the wilderness, the French party lost its way and, at about 4.00 p.m. on that hot July day, it collided with the British advance guard led by Howe. A brisk skirmish erupted; outgunned and surrounded, the French were swiftly routed. More than one hundred and sixty were captured and many others killed and wounded.

British casualties were trifling in number – but momentous in consequence: first to fall had been the gallant Howe himself. Determined that the French should not thwart the march of Abercromby's main body, he had pushed forward with Gage's Light Infantry and the provincials. Reaching the brow of a hill as the fighting flared, Howe was struck by a ball that punched through his lungs and heart before shattering his backbone. An officer six yards away reported that 'he fell on his Back and never moved, only his Hands quivered an instant.' In his *Journals*, Rogers claimed that the loss of the noble and brave brigadier sapped the army's morale, producing *an almost general consternation and languor*; General Abercromby himself admitted that he had felt Howe's death most heavily. Rogers had more reason to mourn than most: the Anglo-American cause had been robbed of a popular and dynamic leader, but he and his rangers had also lost their most powerful patron.

Howe's fall was not the only disturbing consequence of that brief bush fight. Distant gunshots and blood-curdling whoops unnerved the columns of redcoats and provincials who were laboriously threading their way up through the woods from the landing place. Imagining just such an Indian onslaught as had massacred Braddock's men on the Monongahela three years before, many of them panicked and stampeded back to their boats. Their officers were aghast. Reporting this *little Scramble*, one of them drew a worrying conclusion: 'I am more than ever convinced that numbers of our People cannot hear a great deal of firing round them coolly. I mean when they hear & do not See.'

The embarrassing episode underlined the limitations of Howe's much-heralded reforms; it would take more than cut-down uniforms and novel manoeuvres to turn British regulars or American provincials into skilled forest fighters. For all their faults, Rogers and his rangers would now be needed more than ever.

The Frenchmen worsted in the skirmish of 6 July had bought a crucial breathing space for their comrades; as Abercromby's shaken army sought to regain its equilibrium, Montcalm's troops worked frantically to construct a defensive line across the peninsula upon which Fort Carillon was built. In Bougainville's opinion, this precious time was the saving of them and the colony. By the following evening Montcalm's regulars had completed an eight-foot high breastwork of logs which was itself screened by a mass of felled fir and oak trees, their tangled and sharpened branches presenting a daunting barrier to attackers.

Abercromby was confident that the French fortifications could be taken by direct infantry assault. His decision to attack without delay was based upon the advice of his engineers and prompted by intelligence that Montcalm hourly expected to be reinforced by another three thousand men.

The attack went in just after noon on 8 July. Deployed as skirmishers with the other light troops, Rogers and his men were sent forward to flush out the French irregulars and to cover the main assault; these marksmen's fire was *most murderous*, Bougainville reported. Now it was the turn of the British regulars: the same troops whose nerve had recently failed them amongst the woods showed no such trepidation now. Arrayed three-deep and with shouldered arms, they emerged from the trees and marched stoically into a maelstrom of musketry and grapeshot. All afternoon they sought a way through the maze of branches and storm of bullets. The French inside the breastwork could not help but admire their courage as they coolly shot them down. One column composed of grenadiers and Highlanders returned unceasingly to the attack, becoming neither discouraged nor broken. The red-coated battalions all suffered heavily, none more so than the Black Watch. One of the Highlanders' officers, Lieutenant William Grant, recalled that their ardour was so very extraordinary that they could not be brought off while they had a single shot remaining. A musket ball shattered Grant's fusil in his hand; soon after he was shot through the thigh and had to be carried off by two of his men. In all, the regiment lost five hundred and one men killed and wounded, a casualty rate of fifty per cent. Well might Grant ask, 'when shall we have so fine a regiment again?'

With nearly two thousand killed, wounded and missing, Abercromby's shattered army straggled back to the landing place. As dusk fell Rogers was ordered to cover the retreat. But there was no pursuit to oppose. With scarcely a handful of Indians, Montcalm did not dare risk his regulars in a potentially bewildering bush fight. Convinced that the enemy would try again next day, he instead set his weary men to perfecting their defences. When scouts confirmed that the enemy was gone the breastwork's powder-grimed defenders finally emerged to marvel at the extent of their victory. The Anglo-Americans had clearly experienced a crushing reversal of fortune. Shoes left mired in the mud bore silent witness to their disorderly withdrawal. Bloodied, shocked and grieving for its slain, the great host that had set out with such high expectations now returned dejected to its old ground at the southern end of Lake George. On 10 July, Major Eyre reported rumours that Fort William Henry was to be rebuilt, although he could not credit them. As to what the future held, who could say? 'A few Days Ago every thing looked cheerful, now the Contrary,' he wrote.

Such despondency mirrored the mood throughout British North America, but nowhere did the bleak tidings from Lake George prompt greater grief and consternation than in the Massachusetts township of Lancaster. Here, at a safe remove from the ravaged frontier, Susanna Johnson had recently begun to rebuild her life after finally returning from imprisonment in Canada.

Following her capture four years before, Susanna's sojourn amongst the St Francis Indians had, in the end, been brief; within months she was permitted to leave the village for Montréal; she never returned to her Abenaki family.

James Johnson journeyed to New England on an unsuccessful mission to raise their ransoms. With Britain and France once again on the brink of war, the captain returned to a hostile reception in Canada. James, Susanna, daughter Polly and baby Captive were all confined within the foetid bounds of Québec's prison; miraculously, they survived the scourge of smallpox. With her elder daughter, Susanna, and her sister Miriam held at Montréal, and young Sylvanus kept a-hunting at St Francis, Susanna worried away the months.

In 1756, an appeal to Governor Vaudreuil brought a transfer to the milder régime of Québec's civil jail, where, that December Susanna gave birth to a son who lived just a few hours. Soon after, she received word of her father's death: Moses Willard was killed when Indians raided his farm at Fort Number Four; his son limped to the safety of the stockade with a spear dangling from his thigh. This glut of grief plunged Susanna into a decline.

But at the start of 1757, the family's prospects gradually improved. Vaudreuil again interceded on their behalf, allowing Miriam to join them from Montréal. That summer Susanna and James were separated once more. Susanna, along with her two daughters and sister, was shipped to England to be formally exchanged for French prisoners-of-war. They reached *old Plymouth* on 19 August. There, the long-suffering frontier family attracted much attention; their many inquisitive friends were eager to hear their dramatic story at first hand.

Well-wishers helped to get the Johnsons home; in the early hours of New Year's Day, 1758, Susanna was reunited with her husband James; after protracted negotiations, he too had been freed. In New as in old England, Susanna became something of a celebrity. The unusual circumstances of her captivity – not least the birth of Captive in the wilderness between Fort Number Four and Crown Point – generated considerable interest. Noting the family's return, the *New-Hampshire Gazette* hoped that a narrative of the calamities they had undergone would soon be forthcoming.

That spring, James Johnson was called away to settle his accounts; whilst he was embarked upon this errand, Lieutenant Governor Pownall of Massachusetts persuaded him to accept a commission in the colony's troops. As a captain in Colonel Oliver Partridge's rangers, James joined Abercromby's expedition against Ticonderoga, and on 8 July he was killed fighting for his country during the frenzied but fruitless assault upon Montcalm's breastwork. He had been a free man for scarcely six months.

After all the trials and tribulations of the past four years, this latest blow was too cruel for even the indomitable Susanna to endure. 'The cup of sorrow was now replete with bitter drops,' she wrote. 'All my former miseries were lost in the affliction of a widow.'

THE FRENCH NEGLECTED NO opportunity to exploit their unexpected victory over Abercromby's great army. On 11 July, Rigaud de Vaudreuil arrived at Ticonderoga at the head of the anticipated reinforcement of Canadians and Indians. There were now four hundred and seventy of the latter, including Iroquois, Abenakis, Hurons and Ottawas; all were disgruntled at missing an opportunity to acquire glory, booty and scalps and within days they were running amok. A council called to halt the depredations had no effect. According to Bougainville, young Abenakis were the ringleaders, having not the least submission to the old men and the chiefs, either in peace or in war. A score or more of them soon departed on a scouting party, returning days later with a handful of scalps. Meanwhile, a larger detachment left to mount a strike against the British supply depot at Halfway Brook. The garrison was lured out, but the impatient Indians sprang their ambush too soon. They returned on 21 July with eight prisoners and twenty scalps and promptly demanded to go home.

On 24 July, Captain La Corne Saint-Luc left with another body of nearly four hundred Indians and two hundred Canadians. His departure had been delayed for two days – because of a lacrosse tournament between the Abenakis and Iroquois. The game was played with a ball and sticks curved in the shape of a crosier; it was this fancied resemblance to a bishop's staff that inspired the French name for the tribal sport. The stakes in this grudge-match were high: one thousand crowns worth of wampum in belts and strings. Amongst the Indians, lacrosse was a serious business; it could result in broken bones and even the occasional death; it was not for nothing that the Cherokees dubbed it *the little brother of war*.

The mission communities clustered around Montréal were particular aficionados; a 1743 plan of the settlement at the Lake of the Two Mountains shows an extensive lacrosse field. The neighbouring Caughnawagas were no less dedicated to the game and long remained so; a team of Mohawks from the village toured Britain in 1876. Their dazzling exhibition matches sparked the interest that led to the sport's adoption, in a slightly less violent form, by British schoolgirls. Even that glum widow Queen Victoria considered the game *very pretty* to watch. It is unlikely that she would have used the same words to describe the Abenaki-Iroquois clash of July 1758.

Bougainville failed to record the outcome of that sporting fixture, but he did note the return of La Corne's raiders on 30 July. Two days earlier they had fallen upon a convoy of provision wagons between Fort Edward and the Halfway Brook. The wagons were hauling rum and the attack degenerated into a frenzied massacre. New Hampshire provincial troops were ordered to the scene, but they were reluctant to intervene. Those soldiers who eventually came up encountered a grisly sight: the rough track was strewn with butchered oxen and the mutilated bodies of men, women and children. Such wanton slaughter, committed with apparent impunity within ten miles of a major concentration of British forces, goaded the morose Abercromby into action.

Rogers was given seven hundred men and directed to intercept the raiders as they returned north. La Corne's party had too great a lead; they gave him the slip, but on 31 July, as Rogers was returning, he received fresh orders to make a sweep embracing the South and East Bays of Lake Champlain before returning by way of Fort Edward. This swinging dragnet snared nothing until the morning of 8 August, when the party marched from its camp near the site of the old Fort Anne. Reduced by sickness, the patrol now mustered five hundred and thirty rank and file.

The command was strung out in a straggling Indian file stretching back for nearly a mile. Israel Putnam, now a major, took the lead with a body of Connecticut provincials; the centre, composed of men from Gage's Light Infantry and volunteers from other regular units, was under Captain James Dalyell; Rogers brought up the rear with his own rangers.

The French, a mixed force of some four hundred and fifty Indians, Canadians and colonial regulars under the skilful partisan Lieutenant Joseph Marin, were warned of the column's approach by an unforgivable breach of discipline: several officers demonstrating their marksmanship by shooting at pigeons for a wager. Alerted by this blunder, Marin swiftly prepared an ambush. Employing typical Indian tactics, he formed his men into a crescent ready to lay down a withering crossfire.

The head of the column walked blithely into the trap. Putnam and three of his men were captured; the rest recoiled in confusion. The British regulars – who were clearly gaining confidence in forest fighting – held firm. Their stand gave Rogers time to wheel his rangers up to the right flank. Both sides now blazed away at each other from horseshoe-shaped firing lines.

According to one account, the first crucial phase of the fight centred upon the redcoats' efforts to dislodge their opponents from behind a fallen tree. In an extraordinary incident, a formidable Indian sachem, six feet four inches tall, jumped upon the trunk, killed two men and defied all efforts to bring him down. A mettlesome officer of the 46th Foot drew blood from the giant's head with the butt of his fusil; he was about to receive a tomahawk blow for his pains when Rogers himself blasted the warrior from his perch.

Rogers was thinking as well as fighting having posted a hundred men to a small hill on the right flank and then sent to Fort Edward for reinforcements. One of the provincials testified to both the major's tactical awareness and his highly individual brand of leadership: Rogers 'hallooed to the French and said, "Come up you French dogs like men." And then he hallooed to the officer on the hill and asked him if he wanted more men, if he did he should have 500, which was to frighten the French. And they did not stand it but a little while longer but hallooed to get together and run off as fast as they could.'

In his *Journals*, Rogers was reticent about his own actions, but he praised the vigour and resolution of the men who had served alongside him. During an hour of fighting they had forced the enemy to retreat, 'which they did with such caution in small scattering parties as gave us no great opportunity to distress them by a pursuit.'

The hard-fought combat left the area strewn with dead. Rogers buried his own slain: a scout sent to the scene some days later counted upwards of a hundred bodies and believed there were many more about, but in the summer heat it was no place to linger. As usual, both sides sought to inflate the casualties they had inflicted, and to minimise their own, but whatever the merits of the respective claims, it was an important success for the British – one in which Rogers had played a prominent role. Captain Dalyell told Abercromby that Rogers had acted *with great Calmness, and officerlike*; the general, in turn, made a point of reporting the major's merits to Prime Minister Pitt: Rogers' name was once again on the tongues of some of the most influential men in the British Empire. Another officer identified the real significance of the fight when he observed that the French and Indian losses had made them *backwards [in] their Scouting ever Since*.

Abercromby was clearly delighted with the outcome of the action: in General Orders he thanked the officers and men concerned for their good behaviour. He now hoped they were 'satisfy'd that Indians are a Despicable Enemy, against Men who will do their Duty.'

As the summer drew to a close there was news of other successes that did something to balance the great disaster before the lines of Ticonderoga. A force despatched by Abercromby under the command of Colonel John Bradstreet had succeeded in destroying the key French base of Frontenac; this was a double blow, as it also undermined the credibility of the French in the eyes of their Indian allies. And at the end of August it was finally confirmed that the army sent against Louisbourg under Major-General Jeffery Amherst had captured that vital fortress. In its fortified camp at the head of Lake George, Abercromby's army gave a celebratory *feu de joi*. Rogers marked the occasion with a gesture of his own: he treated his company to a barrel of wine as a token of his dependence upon their loyalty and bravery, and to mark the good behaviour of the rangers who had served with Amherst on Cape Breton.

Under the original plan of operations, it had been envisaged that Amherst should push ahead against Québec once Louisbourg had fallen. The fortified town had held out long enough to scupper that plan; but there remained a possibility that Amherst's victorious battalions might join forces with Abercromby for another crack at Ticonderoga.

Louisbourg surrendered on 26 July. Amherst landed at Boston, at the head of five regiments, on 12 September, but further progress was retarded after the townsfolk insisted upon plying the victorious redcoats with New England rum. When Amherst finally marched out four days later, each battalion was obliged to leave men behind to round up the drunks and bring them along when they were sober. Amherst's force eventually rendezvoused with Abercromby's Lake George army on 5 October; by then it was too late to mount a fresh strike against Ticonderoga. Amherst returned immediately to Halifax by way of New York; there, on 9 November, he unsealed orders from London informing him of his appointment as commander-in-chief in Abercromby's place.

According to Captain Abercrombie, Amherst's reinforcements could have arrived at Lake George six weeks earlier, had a vital letter not gone astray: shortly after the bloody repulse before Ticonderoga, his uncle, Major-General Abercromby, had written to Amherst requesting all the troops he could spare. Unfortunately, Governor Pownall of Massachusetts had lost or mislaid the letter; as Abercrombie reported in December, the hapless Pownall acknowledged receipt of the despatches, 'but cannot tell by whom or when they were sent & they have never yet come to hand'.

It was a farcical end to a frustrating year. Generals had come and gone, but Robert Rogers and his rangers remained; the coming year would see the major reach the height of his fame.

CHAPTER FOUR

Amherst and Wolfe

AS THE GRUELLING WAR AGAINST New France entered its fourth year, Robert Rogers found himself with new commanders to obey, new companions to converse with, and a new apprenticeship to serve. He lost no time in establishing contact with the latest commander-in-chief, offering to pay a personal visit to Amherst's headquarters in New York. But the general was adamant that Rogers should stay put at Fort Edward, where he was needed to counter French raids.

Amherst's reply, as tendered by his aristocratic young adjutant general, Colonel Roger Townshend, was businesslike but cool. These same qualities characterised Amherst himself: an efficient and methodical soldier with an austere and aloof temperament. The general's personal journal does little to refute this image of a meticulous but essentially unimaginative man – yet such impressions can be misleading; the testimony of his officers showed a very different side. As he awaited his orders from Whitehall for the coming campaign, Amherst launched his own charm offensive upon New York society. That arch-gossip, the army surgeon Dr Huck noted, '[Amherst] dances at all assemblies and private Dances, gives Balls, and makes New York vastly gay.' Captain Abercrombie, who remained as aide-de-camp to his uncle's successor, also remarked upon Amherst's dancing techniques.

When Jeffery Amherst set his nimble feet upon the North American continent he already enjoyed a high reputation as the conqueror of Louis-bourg; his victorious campaign on Cape Breton had provided a clear-cut success to offset Abercromby's dismal failure before Montcalm's impenetrable breastwork at Ticonderoga. Amherst's appointment to head the Louisbourg army had been a gamble. He was an experienced staff officer and administrator, but had never before held a field command. His selection owed much to the patronage and friendship of Field Marshal John Lord Ligonier, under whom he had served as aide-de-camp during the bloody European campaigns of the War of the Austrian Succession. In October 1757, when Ligonier replaced the disgraced Duke of Cumberland as commander-in-chief of the British Army, he did not forget his protégé. With Pitt's backing, Amherst was fast-tracked from colonel to major-general and despatched across the Atlantic. Amherst's conduct before Louisbourg had vindicated his backers; a risky but spectacularly successful assault landing amidst the pounding surf of Gabarous Bay was followed by a careful textbook siege. With the army safely ashore, the operation progressed to its inevitable conclusion, chivvied along by the energetic presence of the fiery Brigadier-General James Wolfe. Amherst bolstered his reputation as a safe pair of hands who could be entrusted to mastermind the logistical intricacies of complex operations; Wolfe emerged as a forceful and courageous officer in the mould of the much-lamented Lord Howe: a commander guaranteed to lead from the front and prove relentless in pursuit of his objectives.

William Pitt's orders for the new campaigning season sought to exploit the contrasting strengths of these two very different soldiers, resurrecting the well-tried formula of an attack upon multiple fronts. Raised to the local rank of major-general, Wolfe was to co-operate with the Royal Navy in an amphibious operation against Québec; meanwhile, Amherst, as commander-in-chief, would orchestrate his own *Irruption into Canada*, via either Crown Point, or La Galette – on the St Lawrence facing Lake Ontario – or by both routes if practicable. Circumstances permitting, he was then to attack Montréal or Québec – or both places successively. On the Lake Ontario front, Pitt also urged the re-establishment of Oswego and a drive against Niagara; a success there would not only secure dominion of the lake, but also sever communications between Canada and the remainder of New France.

Wolfe was subordinate to Amherst, but Pitt's detailed instructions left no doubt that his strike against Québec was the year's flagship operation. As overall commander in North America, it was Amherst's responsibility to ensure that the troops, stores, guns and transport ships required for Wolfe's campaign were all ready to depart on schedule. Amherst was directed to open his own campaign by 1 May, because, said Pitt, 'nothing can contribute so much to the Success of the Operations to be undertaken in different Parts of No. America, and particularly of the Attempt on Quebeck, as putting the Forces early in Motion, on the other Frontiers of Canada, and thereby distracting the Enemy, and obliging them to divide their Strength.'

Pitt's directions were clear: the key to the success of the coming campaign would be *co-operation* between the two main armies on the St Lawrence and Lake George fronts. Writing to Amherst from England on the same day that Pitt penned his orders, Wolfe left no doubt that he envisaged a truly joint operation: he could not promise to take Québec, but if the fleet carried his army up the St Lawrence, he guaranteed to *find employment for a good part of the Force of Canada*, thereby rendering Amherst's road to Montréal less difficult and dangerous. Provided that France couldn't reinforce her troops in Canada from Europe, Wolfe saw no reason why he and Amherst should not be able to unite for their destruction.

Wolfe refined his ideas whilst sailing to North America; now he hoped to send sloops and schooners far enough up the St Lawrence to favour Amherst's attack upon Montréal, or a junction with his own army. Writing to Amherst, Wolfe had no doubt that the French would initially enjoy naval superiority on Lake Champlain; however, as Vaudreuil appreciated the importance of Québec, it was likely that he would allocate the bulk of the forces there, 'which makes me judge & hope that Tyconderoga & Crown Point will soon fall into your hands,' Wolfe added.

When he arrived at Louisbourg, Wolfe explained his thinking to his favourite uncle Walter. If the enemy at Québec were strong, audacious and well commanded, he would proceed with the utmost caution and cir-cumspection, so giving Amherst time to bring his numerical superior-ity to bear; however, should Québec's defenders prove more timid, he would 'Push them with more vivacity, that we may be able before the summer is gone to assist the Commander-in-chief'.

PITT'S ORDERS FOR THE COMING operations included the strong rec-ommendation that Amherst should field as many rangers as possible; this directive showed how strongly these distinctive – if controversial – troops had consolidated their position within Britain's American Army. In 1759 there would be more rangers in British pay than ever before: Wolfe and Amherst were each allocated six companies, and the latter's command also included two companies of Stockbridge Indians.

Not every British officer in North America shared this high opinion of the rangers: as well as the familiar gripes about drunkenness and insubordination, there were growing misgivings that the standard of recruits was dropping to an unacceptable level. After the heavy casualties of the past three years, seasoned woodsmen were not so easy to find; men enlisted on the Boston waterfront weren't calculated to fill their moccasins. Wolfe was characteristically blunt about the four raw com-panies of New England rangers assigned to his command: he consid-ered them to be *the worst soldiers in the universe.* The ranging companies earmarked for Amherst's army did not lack critics either: on 19 June, Dr Huck observed: 'Rogers's Rangers are far from compleat and have so many Boys among them that they are not worth a Farthing'. He was equally scathing about the Stockbridge Indians, believing they would be of little service. James Abercrombie was his usual forthright self: 'Our Rangers are worse than ever & we have the two Jacobs Companys who do nothing,' he wrote. On the other hand, Abercrombie considered Gage's Light Infantry to be vastly improved; he felt the rangers should be broken up and that corps augmented in their place. But in the midst of all this grousing an exception was made of Robert Rogers himself; Wolfe would have liked the celebrated major to join his army on the St Lawrence, but Amherst was loath to let him go.

Besides laying the logistical foundations for Wolfe's campaign, Jeffery Amherst was obliged to grapple with the vexing minutiae of his own. Wolfe's task was daunting enough, but Amherst also faced his share of problems. Unlike the force bound for the St Lawrence, which was composed almost exclusively of veteran British regular troops, Amherst also commanded thousands of volunteers raised by the northern colonies.

These provincials were notoriously slow to muster and march; as expected, the colonies failed to assemble their troop quotas by Pitt's projected deadline. This, together with the massive logistical task of transporting and stockpiling provisions for a substantial army, and then assembling enough boats to ferry it down Lake George, meant Amherst's advance units didn't head north from Fort Edward until 21 June. That evening they reached the southern end of Lake George and set up camp on what was now all too familiar ground for many; some succumbed to a superstitious sense of foreboding. Captain William Amherst, the general's brother, reported the provincials' belief that Lake George was enchanted. For some obscure reason, the army's slang name for Ticonderoga was *Bogus* – a powerful blend of unsweetened beer and rum; on 19 July, the Connecticut soldier Robert Webster noted in his diary that one of his comrades, Jonathan Corbin, had 'confessed that he was afraid to go to Boges'. Webster added harshly: 'Set his name down for a coward.' But it's unlikely that the honest but wretched Corbin was the only soldier to contemplate the coming campaign with trepidation.

Amherst waited a further month whilst preparations were completed for the move against Ticonderoga. The customary scouts pushed down the lake in quest of intelligence; laggard regular and provincial units marched into camp, and ever more artillery and ration wagons trundled up the road from Fort Edward. The next phase of the advance would be via the limpid waters of Lake George. No effort was spared to ease the army's passage: fragile bateaux that had taken a battering en route from Albany were overhauled; rafts to ferry the cannon to demolish the French forts were built from scratch; and to safeguard the whole impressive but unwieldy flotilla, substantial vessels capable of delivering broadsides were also needed. No sooner had the army pitched camp than Captain Joshua Loring of the Royal Navy began to raise and refit a sloop that had been deliberately sunk at the ignominious conclusion of the previous year's campaign.

Workmen also started constructing a radeau, or floating gun battery; this crucial craft was finished on 20 July and optimistically christened the *Invincible*. Her blunt, ugly lines were unlikely to gladden the heart of a sailor, but the eight heavy guns that she mounted provided a reassuring sight for the men who began to embark in their bateaux and whaleboats at first light the following morning. The flotilla moved down the lake in four long columns. Night found it moored beneath the bare rock-face of Rogers' Slide. Next day the fleet proceeded towards Ticonderoga. That morning the troops landed, encountering only slight resistance as they skirmished forward to seize dominating high ground.

The French forces on the Lake Champlain front consisted of some three thousand regulars, militia and Indians commanded by Brigadier-General Bourlamaque. His troops did not know that he was under strict instructions to forgo any heroic but costly last stand; instead, his inglorious task was to hold Carillon for long enough to oblige Amherst to begin the formalities of a siege; he would then retire again, first to Fort St Frédéric at Crown Point and then to Isle-aux-Noix. There, amongst the mosquito-infested marshes, he was finally to fight in earnest.

Bourlamaque was not impressed with the defensive potential of Isle-aux-Noix, which he'd inspected on his journey to Carillon. However extensive its fortifications and gun batteries might become, it was poorly sited. An enemy could easily outflank it, either by bypassing it on land, or simply disembarking at Missisquoi Bay and following a short portage route connecting with the South River, which ran into the Richelieu below the island fortress. The vulnerability of Lake Champlain's north-eastern corner had already prompted the Abenakis to abandon their fort at Grey Lock's old village of Missisquoi. Although it formed the

Richelieu's first line of defence, Isle-aux-Noix was incapable of shielding the posts of St Jean or Chambly – neither of which possessed its natural or manmade strengths.

On 23 July, British patrols discovered that the French had abandoned the formidable breastwork upon which Abercromby's army had flung itself in vain a year before. This came as a huge relief to many of Amherst's men, who included veterans from units mauled during the bungled assault. The stout log wall against which they had so recently struggled in vain now provided the delighted Anglo-Americans with a ready-made bulwark against the guns of Fort Carillon itself.

Obedient to his orders, Bourlamaque and the bulk of his army withdrew down Lake Champlain to Crown Point, leaving a skeleton force of four hundred men to hold the fort. But Amherst was taking no chances, and over the next three days his men sapped forward, methodically digging zigzag trenches and establishing gun batteries; shells lobbed from the fort's mortars kept them on edge.

On the evening of 26 July, Amherst's gun emplacements were finally preparing to retaliate when three French deserters appeared in the British lines and revealed that the garrison had decamped after setting fire to the fort and mining its defences. Amherst offered the trio a hundred guineas to return and cut the fuses, but they refused; it was a wise decision. Soon after, the warm night air was split asunder as the powder magazine detonated in spectacular fashion, sending debris rocketing skywards.

Amherst's army had gained Ticonderoga in exchange for a mere handful of slain; to the grief of many, they included his personable young adjutant general, Colonel Townshend, who was bisected by a cannon ball whilst reconnoitring the fort's defences. His memorial in Westminster Abbey, which features two Indian warriors, is one of the most striking to be found in that congested shrine to Britain's imperial past.

The capture of the famous fortress of Ticonderoga at such little cost was a considerable achievement, and a tribute to Amherst's meticulous planning. His army must have feared a repetition of the previous summer's carnage; any sense of anti-climax was heavily outweighed by heartfelt relief. This sentiment was expressed by Major Alexander Campbell of Montgomery's Highlanders, who wrote to his father from Ticonderoga on 27 July: '. . . what Gratitude is due from his Country to our General, I leave every true Brittain to judge, who has by his Conduct reduced the strongest [fort] the French have in Canada, att the Expence of not above a Dozen lives, the army loves and I may say adors him, and are almost sure of success, in every thing he orders them to undertake.' That same day, Major Allan Campbell of the Black Watch told his brother Duncan that the troops had such faith in Amherst's abilities that they would surmount all difficulties; their confidence was justified, for he was *as good a man as lives and a very Great Officer*.

To maintain the momentum of his advance, it was essential that Amherst push on without delay: his ability to further operations depended upon the speed with which he could assemble a flotilla to take control of Lake Champlain. He'd known this for a long time, but he could not begin building such a fleet until Ticonderoga was in British hands: unlike the bateaux and whaleboats, which could be landed from Lake George, transported across the peninsula and refloated on Lake Champlain, the *Invincible* and the sloop *Halifax* were too unwieldy to be portaged via the Carrying Place. Amherst's scouts at Crown Point reported the presence of a French schooner and two smaller sloops; to proceed against Canada by water, Amherst had to build new vessels of force himself.

On 27 July, as the fire-blackened ruins of the French fort smouldered, Captain Loring was ordered to repair the Ticonderoga sawmill so that work could begin on the construction of a brigantine. But progress remained painstakingly slow: three key officers – the logistics expert Colonel John Bradstreet, the naval officer Loring and the artilleryman Major Thomas Ord – were at loggerheads; some thought the general should have taken a sterner hand and made them work together. Even Amherst's aide-de-camp James Abercrombie thought his chief *rather too good natured to deal with these people*; he told his erstwhile commander Lord Loudoun that the army had been so slow to set out that he feared Ticonderoga would be the high point of the campaign.

On 1 August, before Loring's brig was ready, reports arrived that the French had now abandoned Crown Point, but Amherst told Pitt that this made no difference to his plans; he was already doing his utmost to move forward, although heavy rain had stymied efforts to haul boats over the Carrying Place. Three days later, in the early hours of 4 August, Amherst's army at last embarked aboard bateaux and whaleboats and headed north, rowing into the teeth of a strong wind. That same evening, Amherst made an unopposed landing at Crown Point. Major Campbell of Montgomery's Highlanders remained ecstatic at their progress: 'The French fly everywhere before our Victorious General,' he wrote to his father. Incredibly, the army had taken possession of that famed place without the loss of a single man.

The great citadel of Fort St Frédéric – that conspicuous symbol of French power in the Champlain Valley – had been blasted into rubble by Bourlamaque's engineers. Amherst contemplated the surrounding ramparts, all that remained intact of the fabled fortress, then instructed his own engineers to identify a suitable site for another, even more formidable stronghold. He told Pitt that the conquest of Crown Point would secure 'all His Majesty's Dominions that are behind it from the Inroads of the Enemy and the scalping party's that have infested the whole Country.' Amherst had no intention of relinquishing what he had won. He added: 'I shall take fast hold of it, and not neglect at the same time to forward every measure I can to enable me to pass Lake Champlain.'

The colonial press shared the general's euphoria at the elimination of a stronghold that had so long intimidated the frontier inhabitants of New York and New England. After printing Amherst's despatch to Pitt, the *New-York Gazette* added an editorial that emphasised the significance of the conquest: poised midway between the rival bases of Montréal and Albany, Crown Point had 'effectually covered all Canada, by blocking up our passage into that Country, whilst it led the French directly into New-England and New York'. With both Ticonderoga and Crown Point now in British hands, settlers driven from their Hudson Valley homes by the ravages of the enemy could return and live there safely. As an incentive to these homesteaders, Amherst had asked New York's lieutenant governor, James De Lancey, to announce that those choosing to settle between Fort Edward and Lake George would find several spots of cleared land with the wooden huts previously occupied by his own victorious army. Besides ready-made accommodation, De Lancey promised a rent-free start for those who strove to establish townships on this previously dangerous ground. After so much terror and bloodshed, it looked like a new era of peace was beckoning at last.

TRUE TO HIS PLEDGE TO PITT, Amherst lost no time in building a powerful new fortification at Crown Point. Laid out on ground overlooking the ruins of its poorly sited predecessor, the pentagonal stronghold was designed by Lieutenant-Colonel William Eyre, the man who, just four years earlier had drawn up the plans for the ill-fated Fort William Henry. The fall of that post in the summer of 1757, and the massacre that followed, had marked a humiliating low point in the Anglo-American war effort: now it was the French who were on the run.

Gangs of provincials and redcoats sweated and cursed as they toiled to transform Eyre's ambitious design into reality. By 9 August, some four hundred men were already at work; within weeks, there were no fewer than three thousand men felling timbers for the log ramparts and other construction works. The new fort dwarfed the old French post. Methodical as always, Jeffery Amherst was taking no chances. The bastions, ditches and outlying redoubts of Crown Point would convince onlookers that this land now belonged to His Britannic Majesty, King George II.

Amherst was determined to keep what he had conquered: while the frontiers of New France were being rolled back to their pre-war limits, there was no guarantee that old France would not retain the rump of Canada at any subsequent peace settlement. Should that happen, future French war parties that sought to follow the old route up Lake Champlain would find their path blocked by one of the most powerful artillery fortifications in the Americas.

But there were those who thought Amherst's huge new fort had become an obsession, and that his defensive mentality was at odds with broader strategic objectives. Officers who had delighted in the summer's bloodless conquests now began to fear that Amherst's campaign was running out of steam, and that the hard-pressed Wolfe would be left in the lurch. After all, Pitt's strategy for 1759 had assumed that Britain's armies would support each other by dividing the enemy. Wolfe faced the bulk of the French army; having made Amherst's job easier, he had every right to expect that the commander-in-chief would now do all in his power to help *him* by diverting Québec's defenders to other sectors.

Writing to Loudoun on 4 August, Richard Huck credited the French withdrawal from Ticonderoga on their being hard pushed at Québec. Huck added: 'The New Yorkers who are licentious enough begin to say, that if Wolf succeeds not it is our Faults'. The doctor was convinced that Amherst was acting on instructions, otherwise they'd have gone on much more swiftly.

James Abercrombie feared Amherst had no thoughts of further conquest. By repairing Ticonderoga, and building Crown Point on a scale set to rival the famed citadel of Lille in northern France, the general appeared to be announcing his intention to dig in for the winter. Once Bourlamaque grasped that fact, he could release troops that might tip the precarious balance against Wolfe. Were the aggressive Abercrombie to have his way, the army would by now have been menacing St Jean. If no such efforts were made to pin down French forces, and thereby 'prevent the whole from opposing the main object', then Wolfe would have every right to claim that he was not supported as he should be. In consequence, Abercrombie warned, dust would cover the laurels they had so easily gained.

Disquiet at Amherst's failure to push forwards in support of Wolfe surfaced in the colonial press. A letter from the Grand Army at Crown Point, reporting the prevailing belief that any further advance into Canada would depend upon Wolfe's success at Québec, prompted a critical editorial in several newspapers, voicing growing impatience at the fact that neither Amherst's army, nor another force detached under the recently promoted Brigadier-General Gage, was yet moving against Montréal. In contrast to these officers, who faced little real opposition, Wolfe was opposed by fully three-quarters of the *Force of Canada*. Only a diversionary attack by Amherst or Gage could give Wolfe a fighting chance.

The soundness of such logic had been demonstrated by the immediate consequences of Niagara's capture by the British in late July; no sooner had news reached Québec, on 9 August, than Montcalm was obliged to weaken his own army to reinforce the threatened rapids sector facing Lake Ontario. That very same night, Montcalm's valued second-in-command, Brigadier-General Lévis, was sent to take command of the situation there. He was followed by a force of eight hundred regulars and militia; as Montcalm observed, this was a considerable deduction from a little army that was obliged to keep watch from Jacques Cartier to Montmorency Falls.

Even though his own sprawling Grand Army was now stalled at the southern end of Lake Champlain, Amherst held high hopes that Gage and his independent command would mount just the kind of vigorous advance that a growing body of opinion now demanded. Gage had been sent north on 28 July, after Amherst received intelligence that Brigadier-General John Prideaux had been killed in the siege lines before Niagara. If he found Niagara and Oswego already in British hands, Gage was to build a fleet on Lake Ontario and then advance to take La Galette. On 1 August, after learning that Crown Point had been abandoned by the French, Amherst sent fresh orders; Gage should now attack La Galette without delay, and then push on rapidly against Montréal. Two weeks later Amherst reiterated his commands. He had no reason to doubt that Gage would obey them to the letter.

AMHERST WAS RELUCTANT TO move until he knew the fate of Wolfe's army: should Wolfe be defeated before Québec, or forced to lift the siege, Amherst might find himself deep within New France and facing a far stronger force than he'd encountered previously. A more vigorous commander would have pushed forward regardless, in the determined – if reckless – fashion demanded by Captain Abercrombie; but Amherst was not that kind of general.*

Despite his own problems at Québec, Wolfe had not forgotten *his* pledge to co-operate with Amherst. In early August he sent Brigadier-General James Murray up the river beyond Québec, directing him to assist Rear Admiral Holmes in the destruction of the French ships, if they could be got at, in order to open a communication with Amherst. When Murray landed at Deschambault on 18 August he took prisoners who divulged news of Niagara's surrender. From intercepted letters it was also discovered that the enemy had abandoned Ticonderoga and Crown Point and retired to Isle-aux-Noix; it was now widely believed that Amherst was making active preparations to cross Lake Champlain and fall upon Bourlamaque's army.

But while the bold Wolfe knew at least something of Amherst's progress, his cautious commander remained unaware of developments on the St Lawrence. Rumours periodically rippled through the army, but these were hopelessly vague and contradictory: at Ticonderoga on 3 August, Massachusetts provincial Lemuel Wood employed his eccentric prose to report the optimistic camp news that 'general montcalm is falen into ye hands of genarl woolf'. He claimed that Wolfe had virtually destroyed Québec, and 'had Run upon them in there trenches 5 or 6 times and Drove them out by ye Point of ye Bayonet.' Just five days later very different reports were circulating. It was now rumoured that Wolfe had been driven off from Québec. By 8 September, Wood recorded a disconcerting newsflash: 'general woolf is Routed and Drove 10 miles back and left 500 men on ye spot but Had Entrenched again and was Determined to stand it . . .'

As summer shaded into autumn, it became imperative that Amherst

---

* In a perceptive analysis, historian John Shy attributes Amherst's extreme caution during these weeks to an unwillingness to blot the pristine copybook that he had maintained ever since his triumphant siege of Louisbourg. In Professor Shy's opinion, Amherst's behaviour in 1759 makes sense, granted one unflattering assumption: 'he expected Wolfe to fail, and did not mean to have himself deeply committed in Canada when it happened'.

have accurate intelligence of Wolfe's progress. To reach Wolfe by land meant a hazardous trek through enemy-held territory. The day after the army arrived at Crown Point, the general had proposed that one of Rogers' men should try to get through to Wolfe; he could find no volunteers. But the general was determined: two days later, on 7 August, Amherst penned a despatch to Wolfe, and ranger ensign Benjamin Hutchins agreed to carry it. Hutchins was confident that he could easily reach Québec by way of the Kennebec River, although, as Amherst observed, it was a roundabout journey that would take up much time.

Besides providing Wolfe with a lengthy account of the capture of Niagara, Amherst's message confirmed his own possession of Ticonderoga and Crown Point. He also mentioned that his younger brother William had been sent to England with the victory despatches; unfortunately, he had taken with him a copy of the cipher – or code – that the general had intended to use when writing to Wolfe. Amherst ended his letter with a plea, a promise and a rallying cry: 'I Want to hear from You. You may depend upon my doing all I can for effectually Reducing Canada. Now is the time.'

For the intrepid Ensign Hutchins and his three companions, the trip from Crown Point to Québec and back again was rather more roundabout than even the pessimistic Amherst could have imagined. Dodging hostile patrols, they arrived in Wolfe's camp on 3 September, 'near starved, and near tired out with rubbing thro' the Brush, & c which tore their Cloaths to pieces.' However, their report of Amherst's conquests diffused a universal joy throughout the whole camp; the ebullient tone of the general's despatch raised hopes that Amherst was just a week's march away. Few of Wolfe's men now doubted that they would soon administer a *finishing stroke* to New France.

Having succeeded in delivering their morale-boosting message, Hutchins and his weary companions now had to carry Wolfe's reply back to Amherst. They embarked from the British camp at Point Lévis in a Boston ship on the evening of 7 September. It was not destined to be a smooth passage to New England.

After quitting the St Lawrence River, their sloop was overhauled by a French privateer whilst still twelve leagues off Halifax. Unleashing a volley of small-arms fire that killed the helmsman, the French boarded and robbed them of everything they had. As a precaution, Hutchins jettisoned Wolfe's answer to Amherst. They eventually made it to Halifax, and travelled from there to Boston. It was not until 11.00 p.m. on 9 October, more than two months after his departure, that Hutchins returned to Crown Point, in company with Major Robert Stobo.

Despite all the hardships encountered on the trip, thanks to Hutchins' decision to consign the despatches to the deep, the frustrated Amherst was not a whit the wiser about Wolfe's intentions. Major Stobo ventured his own assessment, although this was not encouraging: 'Wolfe had got with allmost his whole Army above the Town & he thinks he will not take it.'

But Hutchins was not the only messenger to seek a way to Wolfe; on 8 August, the day after he had set out from Crown Point, a regular officer, Captain Quinton Kennedy of the 17th Foot, stepped forward and offered to go himself, by a much quicker route. Amherst was swift to accept. Kennedy would be accompanied on his mission by another British Army officer, Lieutenant Archibald Hamilton of the Royal Regiment, along with the Stockbridge Mahican ranger Captain Jacob Cheeksaunkun and a handful of his warriors.

For a regular officer, Quinton Kennedy was unusually well qualified for the task in hand; his willingness to learn and use wilderness warfare had long since gained the attention of his superiors and made him a minor celebrity whose exploits, like Rogers', were followed by newspaper readers on both sides of the Atlantic.

A Lowland Scot, Kennedy had come to America with Major-General Edward Braddock in 1755. That July, as a subaltern in the 44th Foot, he had a bewildering and bloody introduction to wilderness warfare on the Monongahela; he was amongst the many officers wounded that day.

Nothing daunted by this unnerving baptism of fire, the following summer Lieutenant Kennedy participated in a raid that probed deep within enemy territory to the Richelieu River itself. He headed a motley contingent of some sixty Mohawks and Highlanders from the newly arrived Black Watch. Kennedy returned to the camp at Lake George on 20 September: during the forty-day raid, his party had torched a large quantity of *Naval and Warlike* stores that the French had accumulated on Lake Champlain, and burned down a tavern near St Jean. His trophies included the scalp of a servant killed by the Mohawks and two prisoners – the tavern's landlady and an 'Old Swiss' – who provided valuable intelligence. Lord Loudoun was impressed, and related the exploit to the Duke of Cumberland himself. The hardships undergone during Kennedy's hazardous foray had clearly been severe; Loudoun conceded that the capture of the prisoners was a bold deed; they were taken within one mile of a French camp and the raiders were pursued for five days by about three hundred Indians. The general wrote: 'I never saw People so thoroughly wore out, as those People are; the Indians are but just alive; Lieutenant Kennedy is better than they are, but extremely weak.' The French landlady was rumoured to have been handsome, but an arduous month-long trek through the wilderness, in which Kennedy's party were so short of provisions that some of them proposed to eat her, had, unsurprisingly, taken its toll on her looks.

Such covert operations brought Kennedy into unusually close contact with the British Army's Native American allies – his acquaintances back in Ayrshire were no doubt surprised to read in the columns of the *Scots Magazine* that he had married an *Indian squaw*, whose tribe had made him a king. Kennedy had learned the language of his wife's people, and could paint and dress himself in true Indian fashion; it was hoped that his unorthodox alliance would serve a useful diplomatic function by fostering links between the British and their dwindling band of Indian adherents.

When it was decided to raise Gage's Light Infantry, the ambitious, wily and woods-crafty Kennedy was an obvious candidate for a captaincy. As a specialist wartime unit, Gage's was unlikely to survive the peacetime reductions, so Kennedy's subsequent transfer to an old established line regiment – just days before Amherst sent him to establish contact with Wolfe – was a canny move.

Kennedy and his companions left Crown Point without delay on 8 August. As well as a copy of Amherst's despatch for Wolfe, Kennedy also carried separate 'Instructions'. He was to go first of all to the settlements of the Eastern Indians, and inform their chiefs of the progress of Amherst's mighty army. Kennedy was empowered to extend the hand of friendship on the general's behalf – on condition that the Abenakis opted out of the war. Should they adopt such a neutral stance, Amherst said he had no 'Intention of dispossessing or annoying them'. In fact, he would 'protect and Defend their persons & properties and secure unto them the peaceable and quiet possession thereof.' As a finishing touch, Jacob Cheeksaunkun carried a 'long Broad Belt of Wampum, to deliver with the General's Speech to the St Francois Indians.' Valued at £5 16s 8d, this would offer formal and binding proof of Amherst's sincerity. Once he had the Abenakis' answer to the proposal, Kennedy was to continue on his way and inform Wolfe of Amherst's orders to treat these Indians as friends and allies. He would then report back to Amherst.

These instructions were clearly a device intended to grease Kennedy's path to the St Lawrence; although strenuous efforts were later made to deny the fact, Amherst sent Kennedy into the wilderness on the same errand as Hutchins: his primary objective was the establishment of contact with Wolfe, not the initiation of some benevolent tribal diplomacy. Writing to Thomas Gage from Crown Point later that month, Amherst was blunt about his motives: 'I Doubt not but I shall by one Avenue or the other, Succeed in Acquainting Mr Wolfe of the operations on this side, & that I may soon get information of his progress, from which my motions here must be guided.' And as Amherst confided to Pitt, the plan to send Kennedy through the Indian settlements to the south of the St Lawrence River with a proposal was probably the quickest method of conveying intelligence to Wolfe.

And any lingering doubts over the real reason for the mission are quashed by a covering note, written on the reverse of the duplicate of the Instructions, sent to Pitt: these were, Amherst explained, to serve Kennedy 'by way of Credential in case he should be stopped by any of the Enemy Indians in his way to M. General Wolfe, across Lake Champlain'. If all went according to plan, and Kennedy reached Wolfe unmolested, the Instructions would not even be invoked.

For such a crucial undercover operation, Kennedy's departure was scarcely cloaked in secrecy. Back at Ticonderoga on 10 August, that diligent journalist Lemuel Wood duly noted the news that 'Cap Canada [had left Crown Point] with an Expres to general wolf to go Strat Down to Quebeck'. True to past form, Kennedy was painted like an Indian; Wood chipped in the rumour that Amherst had offered Kennedy no less than four hundred guineas to make the trip. But there was a more worrying breach of security than Wood's tortured scribblings: on the evening of 21 August, three British deserters arrived by boat at the new French base of Isle-aux-Noix: alongside reports of frantic ship- and fort-building at Crown Point, one of the trio disclosed the fact that an officer and ten Indians had recently left with letters to Wolfe at Québec.

Three days after Kennedy's departure down Lake Champlain, a party of rangers came into camp bearing a note from the intrepid captain reporting that he had seen three enemy vessels – a brigantine, a schooner and a topsail sloop – as he lay on the eastern shore below Corlear's Rock. Despite this close shave, Kennedy was confident that his own party had escaped detection; he now planned to proceed by water for a further night before striking into the woods. When the rest of the scout returned from St Jean on 19 August they could add little more, except that: 'Capt Kennedy parted with them up Mischiscoy Bay, & that as they came back they saw three of the Enemys Vessels lying at the same Place as before.'

NOTHING MORE WAS HEARD of Kennedy for another three weeks. In the interim, the miniature French navy that he had avoided on the dangerous waters of Lake Champlain continued to prevent Amherst's formidable army from advancing to Montréal. Its elimination now became more urgent than ever. With this end in mind, Amherst called upon the unusual talents of Sergeant-Major Joseph Hopkins of Rogers' Rangers.

On 1 September a scout led by Hopkins had returned with three prisoners, netted by a ruse worthy of Rogers himself. The sergeant-major and his six-strong squad had lurked in the bushes near Isle-aux-Noix for several days before he hit upon a cunning plan. The *New-York Gazette* relished the story:

> [Hopkins] observed three Soldiers go to Swim in the Lake, close by four armed Vessels; he immediately stripped himself and went into swim likewise, his Party lying conceal'd; He swam along till he came to the three Soldiers, when he enter'd into a familiar Discourse with them in French, which the Serjeant spoke fluently; among the rest that he told them, he said that where he enter'd to swim, there was such a prodigious Number of Fish that he could hardly get along for them: The three Soldiers were extremely anxious to be shewn the Place, which the Serjeant undertook, and swam along with them to the Place where his Men lay in Ambush, when they rush'd out upon the poor Frenchmen and made them all three Prisoners, under the Muzzles of the Guns of the arm'd Vessels, and in Sight of some hundreds of the Enemy.

When Hopkins brought his prisoners before Amherst, the general was 'exceedingly pleased with the Affair, and told the Serjeant, He was obliged to him for catching such Fish.' As related in the *Gazette*, the tale conveys a mischievous ballad flavour; it comes as no surprise that Amherst's own journal contents itself with a dry comment recording the return of Sergeant Hopkins and his prisoners.

Described as Germans by birth, and *very stupid, ignorant, starved Fellows*, these hapless soldiers of *la Marine* nonetheless provided useful information: they confirmed the presence of extensive fortifications at Isle-aux-Noix; more worryingly, they corroborated Hopkins' report that the French had now escalated the naval arms race by launching another sloop capable of mounting sixteen guns. Amherst decreed the British would build their own sloop of equal force, but the overworked sawmill at Ticonderoga was unable to take the strain. It was continually out of order, which led to frustrating delays.

Amherst now turned to increasingly desperate remedies. Constructed of tar-bound timbers and rigged with rope, the wooden sailing ship of the eighteenth century was always vulnerable to fire; Amherst therefore decided to burn the new French sloop as she lay anchored at Isle-aux-Noix. The versatile Sergeant-Major Hopkins was now sent back onto the troubled waters of Lake Champlain with orders to destroy the vessel in a commando-style raid. Amherst was confident that, with *proper precaution and resolution*, the sloop could be torched.

Accompanied by ten men, including four of the army's strongest swimmers, the long-suffering Hopkins set out on the night of 4 September. He was to proceed by whaleboat, travelling only after dark. His party was equipped with eighteen days' provisions and an array of rudimentary incendiary devices – *fire darts & hand Carcasses* * – prepared by that truculent gunner, Major Ord. Amherst gave detailed instructions for their employment: when the darts were screwed into the hull and the carcasses ready, they should all be lit together using a match carried in a *dark Lanthorn*. Hopkins' men were to avoid *putting themselves in any hurry from the blaze*, but should instead feed it by igniting any remaining carcasses and thrusting them through the sloop's cabin windows and gun ports, or tossing them onto the deck. In Amherst's considered opinion, it was best to strike at dead of night.

On the evening of 11 September, Sergeant Hopkins' raiders made a bold attempt to implement the general's hazardous plan. As a French officer reported in his journal, this was no token effort. That night the alarm was sounded after an 'English group tried to set fire to the barque'. One pair of swimmers actually succeeded in attaching an incendiary device to the hull. Sergeant-Major Joel Munson of the Connecticut provincials had been entrusted with the crucial *Combustibles* needed to ignite it; he swam gently towards his objective with them carried precariously in

---

* 'Carcasses' were ironwork baskets filled with rags and other combustible material, impregnated with mealed gunpowder, oil, pitch and tallow to burn more readily.

a little box fixed to his head. Despite this cumbersome arrangement, Munson almost accomplished his design, but was spotted before he could set the device ablaze. Under fire both from the guards aboard the ship and in the camp ashore, the raiders somehow managed to dodge the bullets that pattered around them. Munson dived and swam alternately for his life, escaping with no more than a grazed thigh. Hopkins' men left behind a barrel of inflammable material that was found bobbing on the river. At dawn a French detachment was sent out in pursuit; they discovered the tracks of five men, but returned empty-handed save for the raiders' bacon and biscuits.

Hopkins arrived back at Crown Point on 14 September and reported to Amherst; in his journal, the general blamed the disappointing result upon Hopkins' decision to strike at 10.00 p.m. rather than the stipulated hour. Amherst wrote: 'If they had more punctually obeyed my orders and done it at two in the morning they probably had succeeded.' The commander-in-chief pedantically recorded the loss of the combustibles and two blankets that had been left behind. Amherst's verdict gave scant recognition to the risks run by Hopkins and his men. Although strong swimmers they did not possess the equipment and expertise of trained frogmen; and as Joel Munson had discovered, Major Ord's crude and unwieldy incendiary devices were scarcely limpet mines.

By the time he wrote his dismissive report, Amherst had already resolved upon another way to take the war into French territory. The operation he instigated was no less risky than Hopkins' amphibious raid, but far more ambitious in scale. Its results would be very different.

ON 10 SEPTEMBER, SOME THREE weeks after Quinton Kennedy and his escort had melted into the woods beyond Missisquoi Bay, Amherst finally received word of them, though it was not what he wished to hear. That day a flag of truce from Brigadier-General Bourlamaque forwarded a letter from the Marquis de Montcalm: Captain Kennedy and Lieutenant Hamilton were both prisoners. There was also a jocular letter penned by Bougainville – now a colonel and Knight of the Order of St Louis –

to his good friend Captain Abercrombie. Written at Québec on 30 August, it indicated that the city remained in French hands.

Abercrombie was sent to sift out when and how Captain Kennedy was taken – and whether he had reached Wolfe; disappointingly, Captain Disserat of the *Régiment de la Reine* revealed that Kennedy had been taken by some of the St Francis Indians who were out hunting, whilst he was still en route to Wolfe.

Although couched in the scrupulously polite tones employed by one European officer to another, Montcalm's letter registered surprise at the unorthodox nature of the mission undertaken by Kennedy and Hamilton. Both officers were out of uniform when captured; as such they risked being treated as spies. Though Montcalm did not mention it, he would have been within his rights to hang them both.* The marquis had no intention of pursuing the letter of the Laws of War. A gallant soldier of the traditional school, he found the savageries of New World warfare hard to stomach. Montcalm accordingly took pains to reassure Amherst of 'the inseperable generosity of our two nations': however culpable and misguided they might be, Kennedy and Hamilton would receive the courtesies due to officers and gentlemen. They would be exchanged for others of their kind when the occasion arose. For his part, Amherst remained unabashed at the detection of his subterfuge. He had no doubt that his officers would be returned to him as he was unable to regard them as anything other than bona fide prisoners-of-war.

But how exactly had Kennedy's vital mission come to such an abrupt and ignominious end? After quitting Lake Champlain, the captain's command had used the Missisquoi Bay portage; as Bourlamaque had warned, this route was a weak spot that simply side-stepped the defences of Isle-aux-Noix. Once through the *Maska woods*, they followed the Yamaska River, a sinuous waterway that ultimately joined the St

---

* In October 1780, at the height of the American War of Independence, George Washington took just such a stern line with another British Army officer captured whilst engaged in espionage; the debonair Major John André was duly executed before a tearful crowd, and the future first president of the United States of America thereby incurred the lasting enmity of many British officers.

Lawrence, although not before passing Yamaska, a transitory French and Indian settlement better known to the British by the curious name of Wigwam Martinique. Kennedy's chosen course also veered dangerously close to the notorious village of St Francis.

Thanks to the three British deserters who had arrived at Bourlamaque's camp on 21 August, the French were well aware that an attempt to infiltrate their lines was under way. When this news reached Montréal, Rigaud, the governor general's brother, had lost no time in writing to alert the missionary at St Francis and urging him to send out his Indians.

On 24 August prowling hunters from St Francis confronted the two British officers and their seven Mahican guides. Taken by surprise, Captain Kennedy and his companions had at first sought to flee into the woods, but once it became clear that escape was impossible, they made every sort of appeal, even offering money, in a desperate bid to persuade the St Francis Indians to let them continue on their way to Wolfe. But pleading and bribery alike were all in vain: as Vaudreuil triumphantly reported, the Abenakis had proved incorruptible.

Amherst's invitation to the Abenakis to remain neutral, or, as Rigaud put it, *to sit on their tails*, was found; but neither Rigaud nor anyone else doubted that Kennedy's elaborate 'Instructions' were anything more than a cynical pretext: they were well aware that the principal objective of the mission was to ferry intelligence from Amherst to Wolfe. New France's leading civil administrator, Intendant François Bigot, believed that the officers must have been given their secret instructions for Wolfe verbally. This assumption was not entirely inaccurate; according to the Abenakis, as soon as the Britons and their Indian guides realised that flight was no longer an option, they promptly ate their letters.

Although successful in devouring Amherst's crucial despatches to Wolfe, Kennedy and his band failed to destroy another valuable source of information that they'd been carrying: two tin canisters contained a batch of letters from officers in Amherst's army to their friends serving with Wolfe. Dated at Crown Point on 8 August, these expressed the confident hope that the officers of both forces would soon be drinking good

French wine together in Montréal. Alongside such boastful banter, the same correspondence revealed important intelligence. According to Vaudreuil, one apparently well-informed British officer let slip that Amherst had not yet decided whether to attack the French at St Jean – a disclosure that suggested innocence of the fresh fortifications at Isle-aux-Noix. Even more significant was the frank admission that every-thing now hinged upon Wolfe's fortunes at Québec.

Following their capture, Quinton Kennedy and his men were first taken to St Francis, then subsequently escorted to Trois-Rivières, some twenty miles to the north-east; there, all were sent aboard a frigate and clapped in irons – a procedure that Montcalm believed to be warranted because the British officers were in disguise and carrying letters.

As Montcalm had been at pains to assure Amherst, and as Vaudreuil subsequently emphasised, although Kennedy and Hamilton could justi-fiably have been subjected to the greatest rigours, they were swiftly freed from their shackles and treated as befitted their birth and rank. But even so, lurid stories of the officers' mistreatment quickly circulated within the British Army – given the regrettable breaches of the Laws of War that had characterised the fighting in North America, including the slaughter of women and children and the ritual torture of captives, it was scarcely surprising such tales were believed. Even the chivalrous Montcalm could be held responsible for perpetrating an act of the *most cruel and refined barbarity* against one of the captive officers: according to rumour, the marquis had invited the victim to dine at his table, only to deliver him up to the Indians, who subjected him to fiendish tortures and cut off one of his ears.

There was no truth in the story;* however, the scrupulous courtesies extended to the officers of King George II were not afforded to their Indian guides. They remained in fetters aboard ship and as the Canadian winter began to bite, endured many hardships. But one among them was

---

* This may owe something to the reputed fate of Captain Robert Jenkins at the hands of sadistic Spanish coastguards in 1731. That episode provided the curious name for the conflict that erupted between Britain and Spain eight years later – 'The War of Jenkins' Ear'.

treated far more harshly. Although all of the Indians taken with Kennedy are described in French sources as *Loups*, or Mahicans, they actually included a former St Francis Indian who had joined the Mahicans of Stockbridge in about 1752; probably named Peter, he had taken a wife of that tribe and she had borne him a child. When Peter was captured with Kennedy, the St Francis clan to which he had formerly belonged offered him a stark choice: return to the fold or face the consequences. Peter was faithful to his new allegiance and forfeited his life.

The fact that Kennedy's party had probed so deeply behind French lines before interception caused considerable concern; their discovery far down the Yamaska focused attention upon the need to tighten security in that sector. Governor Vaudreuil sent a courier to Lévis, respectfully suggesting that it would be prudent for constant patrols to cover the Missisquoi Bay portage, the Yamaska woods, and anywhere else an English party or spy might be able to penetrate.

Amidst these calls for heightened vigilance, the capture of the famous Captain Kennedy and his companions gave Canada's embattled defenders a rare cause for celebration. Vaudreuil in particular was ecstatic at this demonstration of the Abenakis' unswerving devotion to New France. He hoped the Chevalier de Lévis would agree that these trusty allies deserved a reward worth far more than the British bribes they had so contemptuously spurned.

But this same loyalty was destined to cost the St Francis Indians dear.

CHAPTER FIVE

Chosen Men

THURSDAY 13 SEPTEMBER, 1759, was a red-letter day for the destiny of North America. By 11 o'clock that morning James Wolfe had found a hero's death on the Plains of Abraham before the walls of Québec. The ambitious young general succumbed to multiple gunshot wounds, but not before he witnessed the Marquis de Montcalm's army utterly routed, blasted apart by the disciplined firepower of his veteran battalions. The redcoats who fought under Wolfe that day included survivors of both General Braddock's defeat on the Monongahela and the notorious massacre at Fort William Henry. These men had butchered comrades to avenge; with fixed bayonets they emerged from the sulphurous smoke of their own volleys and prepared to settle old scores in person.

Faced with this oncoming line of steel, the shocked survivors of the French regular regiments took to their heels. Exploiting the bushes and scrub that flanked the battlefield, Canadian and Indian sharpshooters skirmished to cover their retreat: because of their stubborn stand, much of Montcalm's broken army escaped to fight another day. Wolfe's victory was nonetheless a hammer blow that shattered the morale of Québec's defenders. Its impact was only heightened by a lack of leadership: conspicuous on horseback, Montcalm had been mortally wounded by British grapeshot as he struggled to rally his men. The marquis lingered on for a day and a night; now beyond caring for the fate of New France, he was heartsick that he would never again see his beloved wife and children in sun-drenched Provence. His death left a vacuum that was not easily filled: Québec surrendered on 18 September.

Two hundred miles to the south-west at Crown Point, Jeffery Amherst and the thousands of soldiers who laboured upon his sprawling fort were oblivious to these momentous events. Though it was more than a month before news of Québec's conquest finally reached the commander-in-chief and his Grand Army on Lake Champlain, there too, the immortal 13 September, 1759, was not without significance: that same day Robert Rogers quit camp at the head of a formidable force of picked men. The major had orders to execute a mission that was much to his liking: at long last, he was to strike back against those troublesome raiders, the Abenakis of St Francis.

Two days earlier, Amherst had received confirmation of Captain Kennedy's capture by the St Francis Indians; since then, events had moved swiftly. As Kennedy's mission had plainly come to nought, the question of securing Abenaki neutrality – if it had ever been a serious proposition – no longer mattered. Amherst was now free to adopt a very different policy. Although neither his personal journal nor his lengthy official despatch to William Pitt betray any hint of indignation at this vexing turn of events, the interception of Kennedy before he had even reached Wolfe clearly rankled with the general. Amherst, who prided himself on his reputation as a British officer and a gentleman whose conduct was above reproach, may also have been irritated by Montcalm's reminder that he had acted unethically by disguising his officers in Indian dress and sending them abroad as messengers.

Such criticisms mattered to Amherst; some months later, New York and New England newspapers carried a statement that sought to clear him of any taint of duplicity. This read:

> We are credibly informed, that notwithstanding the many reports that
> have been spread some Time ago of Capt. Kennedy's being sent by
> Gen. Amherst with an Express to General Wolfe, that it was not so,
> but that he was sent with a Flag of truce to the Indian Town of St

Francis, with overtures of Peace, proposed to them by Gen. Amherst, and try to bring them over to English Interest: But they, contrary to all the Rules of War, (even the Savages themselves have heretofore held Flags of Truce sacred) immediately on his arrival, seized Capt. Kennedy, and the few others that were with him, and carried them Prisoners to Montreal: Intelligence of which afterwards coming to the General's Ears, he was so exasperated against them for their inhumanity, that he immediately propos'd the destruction of their Town to Major Rogers, who willingly undertook the Adventure.

In his own *Journals*, Rogers noted Amherst's exasperation at the ungenerous, inhumane treatment encountered by Kennedy's party. It was this flagrant flouting of a flag of truce by those very Indians to whom the peace overtures had been addressed that determined the general to *chastise these savages with some severity*. Rogers was likely indulging in more than a little sarcasm here; given the underhand nature of their mission, Kennedy and Hamilton had escaped very lightly indeed, and if anyone had been guilty of abusing a flag of truce, it was not the *savages*, but Jeffery Amherst himself.

Whether or not his rage was justified or genuine, Amherst lost little time in orchestrating his vengeance. Within forty-eight hours of the news of Kennedy's ignominious fate arriving at Crown Point, a plan for retribution had been devised and set in motion. Despite the newspaper proclamation, it is clear from a subsequent letter of Rogers that the scheme of going against that place was not Amherst's but his own: he exploited the general's pique to dust down and resurrect his long-cherished plans for the destruction of St Francis. The speed with which the proposal was implemented shows that the major's thinking mirrored his commander's mood.

However, while Rogers' intentions were fixed firmly upon the notorious village itself, Amherst's journal entry for 12 September suggests that this was not the sole target in *his* sights. In fact, the general recorded that Rogers' command was to 'go & destroy the St Francis Indian Settlements *and* the French settlements on the South side of the River St Lawrence.'

Whatever personal satisfaction Amherst may have derived from unleashing Rogers upon the ungenerous inhabitants of St Francis, the commander-in-chief believed that the operation could also help to achieve his wider strategic goals. Given his signal failure to press forward and support Wolfe with the Grand Army, this raid was one way in which he could be seen to be promoting something of an offensive. Although Rogers was to take just two hundred and twenty chosen men, they were enough to deliver a winding blow to the soft underbelly of New France.

The major's prospective targets were strung along the St Lawrence Valley, from Yamaska in the west to Bécancour in the east; the potential for disruption was considerable. As the bulk of French troops were apparently preoccupied with the defence of Québec, these settlements were clearly vulnerable; just as the fall of Niagara had left Montcalm with no option but to rush reinforcements to shore up the threatened Rapids sector, so fresh strikes south of the St Lawrence might be expected to prompt a further diversion of manpower from the crucial Québec front.

But for Amherst, the most important benefit of all would be Rogers' contribution to his own pet scheme for bringing the war to a rapid and triumphant conclusion. He held high hopes that Brigadier-General Gage would execute his urgent instructions to take La Galette as swiftly as possible and then push forward against Montréal. Amherst reasoned that Rogers' foray south of the St Lawrence would deflect French attention from the Lake Ontario front, and thereby ease Gage's progress. Later that month he revealed his thinking in a letter to Lieutenant Governor De Lancey of New York: 'Major Rogers is out, Chiefly intended to hinder the Enemy from Sending anything towards La Galette till our Fleet can make their Appearance.'

ROGERS' AUDACIOUS PLAN was finalised on 12 September. The speed with which it was concocted showed that the expedition had never been far from the major's thoughts. There was now no time to lose in assembling a body of men with sufficient stamina and courage to survive such a physically demanding and hazardous mission. They were picked from amongst the toughest, keenest and most experienced of the fighters to be found in Amherst's army: one newspaper reported that Rogers 'chose 250, Part of his Rangers included, and as many more to complete his number, as were willing to go, and be approv'd of by him'.

The nucleus of Rogers' command was the best of his own rangers, amongst them some twenty-five Mahican and Mohegan Indians; with several of their relatives languishing in captivity because of the Abenakis' actions, the Stockbridge warriors had a powerful personal incentive to retaliate. However, it is by no means certain that Rogers' Rangers formed an overwhelming majority of the St Francis raiders: at that very moment, when skilled rangers were needed more urgently than ever before, the corps was languishing at low ebb. In September 1759, Rogers' companies fielded all too few seasoned woodsmen of the calibre of those who had marched out from Fort Edward to fight the Battle on Snowshoes eighteen months before. Such bloody combats had taken a heavy toll, with scores of veterans killed in action or disabled and discharged through wounds or illness; many others were prisoners in enemy hands. This grim attrition was compounded by desertion: on 31 August, Rogers compiled a list of twenty-seven rangers who had absconded since the end of May; three weeks later this lengthy rogues' roll-call was given prominence within the pages of the *Boston News-Letter*. Drawn from the provinces of New Hampshire, Massachusetts and New York, the deserters included men from all six of the companies that comprised Major Rogers' Rangers. No fewer than four were sergeants; this desertion of men responsible for the discipline of others was particularly worrying. Rogers offered a reward of ten dollars for the apprehension of every private man, with a handsome thirty for the non-coms.

Losses through combat and desertion were but part of the problem; many of those men who remained failed to meet the standards demanded by the notoriously onerous ranging service. Prime Minister Pitt's orders to expand the rangers ready for that year's ambitious campaigns had highlighted a dire shortage of suitable material; by the early summer, British officers were already complaining that the ranging companies were stuffed with *mere boys*. These recruits left so much to be desired that it had been necessary to bolster the rangers with hefty drafts of the best men that the provincial regiments could supply.

But Rogers could at least rely upon the proven leadership of combat-hardened ranger officers who had risen up through the ranks. For example, Captain Joseph Wait had been serving as a corporal in John Burk's company of Massachusetts' provincial rangers when he first came to the notice of Rogers; Lord Loudoun gave him an ensign's commission in Rogers' own company on Valentine's Day, 1758. This trust was justified; within weeks Wait distinguished himself during the Battle on Snowshoes.

The ranger subalterns selected for the raid included William Hendrick Phillips, a mature man from the Albany area, of Dutch, French and Indian stock. Phillips enlisted with Rogers back in June 1756 and had already earned promotion to sergeant by that October. His gallant conduct during the fierce skirmish between Ticonderoga and Crown Point in January 1757 won him an ensign's commission; by the time of the second, and bloodier, snowshoe fight, Phillips had risen to first lieutenant. One of the few prisoners to be spared by the French Indians that day, Phillips subsequently escaped from New France – only to find that his officer's berth had been filled. Nothing daunted, he stepped forward again to serve the 1759 campaign as a volunteer in Rogers' company.

Although some of the fittest provincials had already been absorbed into the understrength ranging companies, Rogers' fresh call for volunteers gave an opportunity for others to join them. The British high command in North America thought little of the provincials as fighting men, and had increasingly consigned them to irksome fatigue duties, so for colonials bored with felling logs and heaving them up to Amherst's new fort, Rogers' mission offered action and excitement – with the added incentive of generous ranger pay. Those who accepted the major's challenge included nine 'Jersey Blues' from Colonel Peter Schuyler's New Jersey Regiment, led by Captain Amos Ogden, a veteran whose service stretched back to the 1756 siege of Oswego; remarkably, he had succeeded in emerging from that disastrous episode with a high reputation. For the operation against St Francis, Ogden was placed in overall command of a contingent of provincials drawn from five regiments: besides his own men there were others from the Connecticut units of Eleazar Fitch and Nathan Whiting; the Massachusetts' battalion commanded by Timothy Ruggles; and Henry Babcock's Rhode Islanders. Fitch's contribution included Corporal Frederick Curtiss, who would provide a dramatic eyewitness account of coming events. The provincial role was significant, but should not be exaggerated; as Curtiss was at pains to emphasise, he alone of his company went with Major Rogers.

The great army gathered at Crown Point placed a more obvious source of well-trained and highly motivated manpower at Rogers' disposal: the British regulars. By the late summer of 1759 these redcoats had acquired considerable knowledge of forest fighting. Amherst's regulars had been in America for two years or more; they were veterans, having seen active service at the siege of Louisbourg, the bloody assault on Ticonderoga, or Brigadier-General John Forbes' drive against Fort Duquesne.

Since their emergence in 1758, the regular light infantry had gained extensive experience of scouting on long and punishing patrols, often operating alongside the rangers. Amherst's army had no shortage of these specialists: both Gage's Light Infantry, and a temporary battalion composed of the brigaded light companies from the six redcoat regiments at Crown Point, gave Rogers a pool of disciplined and seasoned soldiers from whom to select his raiders. The major's detachment therefore included a party of light infantry from various units, commanded by Lieutenant James Dunbar of Gage's regiment.

Much like the frontiers it had been sent to defend, Britain's regular army in North America mustered a disproportionate number of Scots and Irish. Such representatives of the Celtic fringe were prominent amongst the redcoats who joined the St Francis raiders. The Inniskilling Regiment had forged particularly close links with the rangers over the past two years; the men it now contributed to Rogers' command included Hugh Wallace. Like Francis Creed before him, he was a young gentleman volunteer who calculated that his coming services would help to secure him an officer's commission. Another known representative of the 27th Foot was Private Andrew McNeal; surviving regimental rolls suggest that he was joined by more of his comrades. The redcoats who marched with Rogers also numbered men from the Royal Regiment, or Royal Scots, the British Army's senior line regiment, which boasted a pedigree so venerable that the colonial press was already using its nickname of Pontius Pilate's Bodyguard. The Royal's contribution included Captain Manley Williams, a veteran of Louisbourg who commanded the battalion's light company.

Rogers also drew manpower from both of the kilted units on Lake Champlain – the famous Black Watch and the newly raised Montgomery's Highlanders. Amongst the latter, according to his own colourful *Memoirs*, was Private Robert Kirkwood. Like many others in Montgomery's regiment, Kirkwood was not himself a Highlander, having been born in the Lowland shire of Ayr. A cooper by trade, Kirkwood had come to North America with his raw regiment in 1757. There, he soon underwent experiences that may have caused him to regret his decision to leave his barrels and take the King's shilling. In the summer of 1758, Montgomery's battalion had been assigned to the force that marched for the Forks of the Ohio. That September, Kirkwood joined an advanced party under the command of Major James Grant that was sent to harass Fort Duquesne. The gallant Grant possessed ample experience of European campaigning, but nothing he had encountered on the bloody battlefields of Flanders had prepared him for what could happen in the Pennsylvanian wilderness. The major's attempt to reconnoitre the fort at night was woefully mismanaged, and his regulars and provincials were scattered with heavy losses.

Lamed by a blast of buckshot, Kirkwood was taken prisoner by the Shawnee allies of the French. The blood-curdling scenes that followed gave further proof of the stark extremes of treatment that could befall male war-captives. Tied to a post and with wood heaped around him, Kirkwood steeled himself to face a slow death by fire. But luck was on his side: he was picked to take the place of a warrior killed some months earlier whilst fighting the Cherokees. Adopted into the tribe, Kirkwood was taken by his new brother to watch the war dance. To his unspeakable grief and terror, he witnessed five other captives burned to death in a most cruel manner.

Kirkwood was thereafter treated with great kindness, but although he took to the privileged lifestyle of tribal hunter readily enough, the tough young Scot hankered after his old calling. When the Shawnees sent a war party against the Cherokees in the following spring, he grabbed the opportunity to give his new family the slip and managed to rejoin his regiment at Lancaster, Pennsylvania, in the early summer of 1759 – in good time to participate in Amherst's methodical advance down the Champlain Valley: his recent experiences bequeathed him exactly the credentials that Major Rogers now sought as he assembled the detachment he would lead against St Francis.

AMERICAN OR BRITON, INDIAN or white man, ranger, regular or provincial, once approved by Rogers, the chosen men underwent a rigorous inspection to ensure that they were properly equipped for the mission that lay ahead of them. The Mohegans and Mahicans wore their own tribal dress, itself by now a mixture of native and European influences; the white rangers and soldiers were clad in stout jackets worn over waistcoats and checked shirts. With autumn fast approaching, the entire command would have toted blankets, rolled and worn bandolier-fashion, or draped about the body for warmth. Rations and spare clothing were carried in haversacks, either slung over a shoulder or worn high on the back as the Indians did. From another strap hung a wooden or regulation British tin canteen, containing a quart of full-strength or diluted rum.

In keeping with the first of Rogers' own Rules for Ranging, each man paraded with his firelock, sixty rounds of powder and ball, and a hatchet. Bayonets and knives were also carried. Out on scout a man's life depended upon the quality of his weapons and ammunition; both were subjected to minute scrutiny by inspecting officers. Rogers' men carried not only powder horns and loose ball, but also leather cartridge boxes. These held ready-made rounds of ammunition, with each roll of cartridge paper containing a ball and sufficient powder to both prime the musket and propel its projectile. Powder horns – often engraved scrimshaw fashion with the names of their owners, bellicose mottoes, maps and other decorative devices – could be used for careful loading and priming when time and circumstances permitted, but cartridges were essential for rapid fire.

At Rogers' initiative the raiders were issued with fresh kit: this would be an unusually demanding scout. The major took it upon himself to provide four hundred new pairs of moccasins – two to each man – and the same number of footings to slip inside them. He also ordered two hundred pairs of the Indian leggings that were a trademark of the rangers and that had also been adopted by the British light infantry. Wrapped around the legs from ankle to mid-thigh, these coloured lengths of coarse cloth gave protection against bushes and undergrowth. In addition, Rogers paid for a hundred and two hatchets, complete with cases and belts, and twenty tumplines – Indian-style straps for carrying heavy loads that were worn slung across the chest or forehead. The total cost of all this gear was £339 6s 0d in New York currency.

Rogers had picked his men and equipped them as best he could. Their fate now depended upon several factors. Much would hinge upon their individual courage and endurance; luck would likewise play a part. But above all, their survival rested upon the judgement and determination of one man: Major Robert Rogers himself.

ON 13 SEPTEMBER, 1759, Rogers received the following instructions:

> You are this night to set out with the detachment as ordered
> yesterday, viz. Of 200 men, which you will take under your
> command, and proceed to Misisquey Bay, from whence you will
> march and attack the enemy's settlements on the south side of
> the river St. Lawrence, in such a manner as you shall judge

most effectual to disgrace the enemy, and for the success and honour of his Majesty's arms.

Remember the barbarities that have been committed by the enemy's Indian scoundrels on every occasion, where they had an opportunity of showing their infamous cruelties on the King's subjects, which they have done without mercy. Take your revenge, but don't forget that tho' those villains have dastardly and promiscuously murdered the women and children of all ages, it is my orders that no women or children are killed or hurt.

When you have executed your intended services, you will return with your detachment to camp, or join me wherever the army may be.

Your's, & c. Jeff Amherst.

Amherst's order made it clear that this retribution should not be visited upon the innocent: revenge was to fall solely upon the fighting men, those same warriors who had earned such a notorious reputation. Amherst felt uncomfortable with Indians; this uneasiness – which is apparent throughout his journals – was ultimately subsumed by a burning hatred. But Jeffery Amherst was not an innately cruel man; there is no reason to doubt that in September 1759 the general meant exactly what he said when he ordered Rogers to discriminate between warriors and their families.

Throughout the war the British high command had sought to minimise the suffering of non-combatants. That June, as he prepared for his campaign on Lake George, Amherst had issued strict instructions 'that no scouting parties, or others in the army under his command, shall (whatsoever opportunities they may have) scalp any women or children belonging to the enemy; they are to bring them away if they can; if not, they are to leave them unhurt.' The following month, as he contemplated his task of subduing Québec, James Wolfe had warned his troops that anyone offering violence to a woman would suffer death.

Although undoubtedly motivated by humanity, this stance was also adopted to retain a moral advantage over the French, who had already besmirched their own record by failing to prevent massacres at Oswego and Fort William Henry, not to mention the indiscriminate raiding of just such allies as the St Francis Indians themselves. Amherst and his officers had no intention of laying themselves open to the same allegation of war crimes.

Yet even if followed to the letter, Amherst's instructions made it clear that the enemy Indians were to be treated differently from conventional foes. French regulars anticipated humane treatment once they had surrendered to His Britannic Majesty's arms, but Indian warriors could expect no such mercy. Because Indians waged a mode of warfare that failed to conform to European notions of acceptable conduct, they were deemed to lie beyond the protection of the Laws of War.

And despite their calls to save the women and children, Amherst's orders remained dangerously ambiguous; once their blood was up, men exhorted to slake their thirst for vengeance might find it difficult to differentiate between the innocent and the guilty.

THAT NIGHT, AS ORDERED, Major Rogers and his detachment set out from Crown Point. The two hundred or more men and their supplies were packed into seventeen whaleboats. These light but sturdy craft, similar to those employed by the whalemen of Nantucket as they plied their bloody trade to Greenland and beyond, had long been favoured by the rangers for their scarcely less hazardous voyages on lakes George and Champlain. Whaleboats typically mounted between five and seven sweeps, plus a steering oar at the stern. For the St Francis expedition each boat held a dozen or so men and the rowers would have worked in two relays. It is likely that these craft were collected and loaded within the confines of a small bay that lay between Orchard Point and Porter's Point; unlike the exposed and shallow beach directly below the old French fort, this provided at least some degree of cover from the eyes of enemy scouts.

Security was a crucial consideration: Quinton Kennedy's mission to Wolfe had been compromised by a lamentable failure to maintain it. With desertion of the bored and disgruntled troops at Crown Point a nagging problem, it was imperative that no such breach of intelligence should forewarn the French of the major's coming. Amherst and Rogers alone knew of the raid's objectives. According to Rogers, a deliberate effort was made to throw up a smokescreen that would cloak the target and wrong-foot the enemy. With the aim that the 'expedition might be carried on with the utmost secrecy,' he wrote, 'it was put into public orders that I was to march a different way, [while] at the same time I had private instructions to proceed directly to St. Francis.'

Still, there was no hiding the fact that a sizeable scout was in the offing, and the camp was soon buzzing with rumour. Soldiers' journals suggest that information was leaked and swiftly disseminated via the usual conduits of campfire gossip. The same day that Rogers and his men left Crown Point, Robert Webster of the 4th Connecticut Regiment recorded the fact in his diary: he reckoned the raiders to be 500-strong, and gave their destination as *Suagothel*. By the following day, Lemuel Wood at Ticonderoga had also learned of Rogers' departure. He believed the scout to consist of four hundred men who were heading for an Indian town near St Jean. Both Webster and Wood were more accurate when they recorded that the command had left Crown Point carrying provisions for thirty days.

All this intelligence filtered along the Hudson Valley to Albany; from there, couriers fed it to the news-hungry coastal periodicals. On 27 September, the *Boston News-Letter* duly reported intelligence from Crown Point, dated 14 September, that 'Rogers went out Yesterday with a large scout of 250 Men'. The *Boston Evening-Post* subsequently quoted a letter from Amherst's camp indicating that the major was making for Montréal.

Robert Webster's mysterious 'Suagothel' was probably his own twisted rendering of an all-too-real place: he meant Oswegatchie, as La Galette was sometimes known. If so, Amherst's policy of disinformation was proving successful: the *Boston Gazette* of 1 October reported the rumour that Rogers intended to join forces with Sir William Johnson, 'who had march'd with 3000 Men to attack Oswegatchi'. Whilst Amherst was certainly hoping that the major's scout would indeed assist an attack upon La Galette, he anticipated that it would do so by delivering a diversionary coup far to the east. But by the time the *Gazette* started speculating upon Rogers' whereabouts, he and his men were already closing in upon their true objective.

UNDER COVER OF DARKNESS, Rogers' chain of whaleboats uncoiled into the expanse of Lake Champlain. The major's own Rules recommended the technique calculated to guarantee mutual support: the boat adjacent to the last, or sternmost, was to wait for her, and the third likewise for the second, and so on. Not only did this prevent the long column of craft from becoming strung out and separated, but it also enabled the individual crews to offer each other prompt assistance in an emergency.

In setting out after sundown Rogers followed another key maxim. As he explained in rule number twenty-four of his twenty-eight commandments, by embarking in the evening 'you will then have the whole night before you, to pass undiscovered by any parties of the enemy, on hills, or other places, which command a prospect of the lake or river you are upon.'

But the greatest danger that Rogers now faced was prowling the surface of the lake itself. To reach Missisquoi Bay, some eighty miles to the north, Rogers had first to run the gauntlet of the French flotilla that continued to dominate the lake. Commanded by the former privateer Joannis-Galand d'Olabaratz, this numbered the topsail schooner *La Vigilant*, and a trio of sloops – *La Musquelongy*, *La Brochette* and *L'Esturgeon*. A fourth sloop, *La Waggon* – the same vessel that the intrepid Sergeant-Major Hopkins and his swimmers had attempted to burn just two days before – remained anchored and unrigged at Isle-aux-Noix. The four vessels already scouring Lake Champlain mounted a total of thirty-four carriage guns, ranging in weight of shot from four to twelve pounds. Even the least of them possessed sufficient firepower to blast Rogers' vulnerable whaleboats into driftwood. For close-range work the French ships also carried side-mounted swivel guns; loaded with musket balls and scrap iron, these crude, oversized shotguns could wreak havoc upon the crowded crew of a smaller craft.

The greatest risk of detection lay within the first twenty miles of Lake Champlain. Before the lake widened a succession of constricted choke points had to be negotiated, and more than two hundred men in seventeen heavily laden whaleboats could not easily sneak through these narrows. If d'Olabaratz and his lookouts lived up to their flagship's proud name, the raiders from the south would be forced to abandon all hope of continuing their journey by water.

Rogers acknowledged the problem in his *Journals*: 'It was extremely difficult while we kept the water . . . to pass undiscovered by the enemy, who were then cruising in great numbers upon the lake.' He claimed that the French had supplemented their gunships with other more unortho-dox defences: they 'had prepared certain vessels, on purpose to decoy any party of ours that might come that way, armed with all manner of machines and implements for their destruction.'

Faced with such hazards, and obliged now to travel by night alone, the coming of dawn on 14 September forced Rogers to conceal his command amidst the marshes lining the lake's eastern rim; the whale-boats were probably dragged ashore at Buttonmould Bay. Stealth was the key, with the journey north conducted in a cautious, creeping fashion. By the following day Rogers' force was reported to be taking shelter within the reed-clogged entrance to Otter Creek, just twelve miles beyond Crown Point. There, Rogers was said to be waiting for a dark night, fog or some other opportunity to slip past *La Vigilant* and two of the sloops that were now cruising off the entrance to the river.

This intelligence reached Amherst three days later, on the night of 18 September, being delivered by one of the provincial officers, Captain Butterfield. He had returned from the major's party with seven men who were taken ill. Within days of setting out, Rogers' command had been hit by a chain of minor disasters. Shortly after Butterfield's return, Captain Williams of the Royal Regiment likewise arrived in camp. According to Rogers, the captain was accidentally burnt with gunpowder; despite his injuries, he only turned back with great reluctance. Williams was accompanied by more than a score of men – four regulars, three rangers, two provincials and no less than thirteen Indians. And that wasn't all. The next day two Highlanders who had been wounded by a firelock accidentally going off, were brought in by *another* seven rangers.

Just days into his mission, Rogers had already lost forty-one men – almost a fifth of his available manpower. A sorry chapter of accidents lay behind this alarming attrition, although all were part and parcel of eighteenth-century warfare. Manley Williams, for instance, had been laid low in circumstances that were frighteningly familiar to soldiers throughout the long reign of the flintlock musket: he tripped and fell whilst carrying a loaded weapon. As news-sheets later reported, Williams and 'a few more were wounded in stepping over some Logs by their Pieces going off.' The captain 'tore his Hand and Arm to such a Manner that he with 4 or 5 Men return'd back to Crown Point.'

Then, as now, mishaps involving firearms were a fact of army life. At Lake George in August 1758, Major-General Abercromby was so exasperated by the number of accidental discharges that he was prepared to admit of no more excuses; for the future, any man whose piece went off accidentally could expect to be court-martialled. Abercromby was particularly incensed because an order had been issued for the use of Hammer Caps – leather covers intended to prevent gunflints from generating sparks. Yet accidents remained so common that a soldier who killed his comrade by an over-casual attitude to safety could usually expect to escape unpunished. A court martial held at Louisbourg that same month heard two typical cases. John Hobbins of the 40th Foot was rubbing away at a tenacious speck of grime near the trigger of his musket when the gun discharged and killed Charles Robinson; and John Stratton of the Royal Regiment slew Alexander Bane of the 22nd whilst checking the firing mechanism of a repaired weapon he had just collected from the stores. Probing the barrel with his ramrod, Stratton concluded that the musket was unloaded; he then proceeded to test the priming pan. It was a fatal error: in *going to shoot the pan, he accidentally shot the man*. Hobbins and Stratton were both acquitted after the court returned verdicts of accidental death. If these incidents were so common in camp, it is scarcely surprising that they should be even more so under the tense conditions of a scout into hostile territory.

Such accidents could prove all the more deadly because it was far from unknown for a single ball to punch its way through more than one body; hence Rogers' own Rules recommended that patrolling rangers should maintain 'such a distance from each other as to prevent one shot from killing two men'. With a gaping bore of .75 of an inch, Brown Bess was especially murderous. A dramatic demonstration of her capabilities had been given at Fort Edward in June 1758 when an edgy redcoat sentry opened fire upon approaching rangers who failed to hear his challenge and give the password: Conrad Humph's aim was both true and deadly; his ball passed clean through *both* Sergeant David Kerr and another ranger following behind him.

It is therefore possible that Williams, and the two Highlanders brought into Crown Point before him, were all wounded by the same close-range discharge. One of the Scots, a man of the Black Watch, was so badly injured that he died soon after.

The wounded and sick were a worrying drain on manpower, not only for the loss they represented in themselves, but because of the hale men needed to carry them back to Crown Point. At this early stage in his mission Rogers was clearly loath to abandon men to die in the wilderness; some of those sent off with the badly injured may have proved unequal to the rigours of the scout, and been already suffering from exhaustion or exposure themselves.

The rapid return of no less than half of the Indians who had accompanied Rogers suggests that contagious disease was at work; one warrior had already fallen sick on the day after Rogers set out, so it is unlikely that fatigue was to blame in that instance. Great Anglo-American army camps like that established at Crown Point in 1759 were veritable breeding grounds for epidemics. Just as Old World diseases had swept through Indian populations during the sixteenth and seventeenth centuries, so provincial farm boys with no immunity to measles or smallpox succumbed to contagions spread by hardened city dwellers from the urbanised east coast and Europe. Journals kept by soldiers at Crown Point indicate that by late summer, disease was already taking a steady toll of Amherst's manpower. On 28 August, Robert Webster of the Connecticut troops noted an ominous development: his regiment was very sickly; his subsequent journal entries record a steady succession of deaths from illness. The New Jersey Regiment was also hard hit by disease, and as Captain Ogden and nine of his Jersey Blues had accompanied Rogers, they may have been the source of the mystery illness that robbed the major of so many of his most valuable scouts.

When all these assorted invalids returned to Crown Point, the camp was already discussing rumours that the brave Major Rogers had encountered a roving party of three hundred French and Indians. Following *a smart Engagement*, he had secured a complete victory, bagging one hundred scalps and as many prisoners for the loss of just three men – though it was said that the major himself was either killed or wounded. The clash apparently occurred about twenty miles from Crown Point; a party had been sent out to bring in the prisoners.

All was fabrication. Whether this latest tall story was further evidence of efforts to screen Rogers' real objective by a deliberate policy of disinformation, or simply another example of galloping camp gossip, remains unclear. On 19 September the same rumour had been carefully noted by the avid, if barely literate, Lemuel Wood; the following day, he was equally quick to dismiss it as *northing but a sham*. But these dramatic reports brought forth a revealing rebuttal from a correspondent in Albany. He emphasised that the intelligence was unfounded, even though it allegedly originated with a regular officer at Crown Point. However, it was an established fact that Rogers *had* gone out with a large party of picked men. The letter writer added a robust vote of confidence in the major's abilities: 'we make no Scruple of judging, that his Conduct will be such as to perpetuate the Character which has been so justly given him of being a *Brave Man*, notwithstanding any Thing wrote from Crown Point with a view to depreciate it.'

THE STEADY STREAM OF SICK, wounded and dying men who staggered into Crown Point so soon after Rogers' departure did little to raise Amherst's hopes for the mission's success. Truth be told, the general was already depressed by a succession of demoralising reports from other fronts. On 19 September he had received a letter from Louisbourg, enclosing a copy of another from Wolfe at Québec. Carrying a date of 11 August, this suggested that Wolfe was pessimistic about his chances of taking the city; he penned his letter knowing nothing of developments on the Lake Champlain front. Amherst himself remained innocent of Wolfe's fate; with Kennedy snared by the Abenakis, and no word from Ensign Hutchins, the lack of liaison between the two armies was now more worrying than ever. Amherst's despondency was only heightened by the problems that continually beset the crucial Ticonderoga sawmill. Although recently repaired, the crank had swiftly broken; as the mill supplied all of the army's planking, including that required to construct the fleet that would hopefully gain supremacy of Lake Champlain, this latest mechanical failure was a serious blow.

But these reports only served to further darken Amherst's mood: he had recently heard news that was far more dispiriting. On 18 September a despatch arrived from Brigadier Gage. Its contents left the general dumbfounded: in the teeth of direct orders, Gage had abandoned all efforts to take La Galette.

Amherst was livid. Writing to Gage on the 21 September he left no doubt about his displeasure. As it was now too late in the season to reverse Gage's decision, Amherst had no option but to 'give over the thoughts of that very Advantagious Post La Galette, that might have been taken without a possibility of the Enemys Obstructing it.' In the pages of his personal journal the general gave full vent to his anger and frustration:

Gage had disregarded his positive orders; he'd created difficulties where none existed; indeed, the disobedient brigadier might not receive another such opportunity as long as he lived.

Thomas Gage had forfeited his commander's esteem and respect. In his official despatch to Pitt, Amherst registered his great concern at Gage's actions. This rebuke amounted to a crushing reprimand and drew forth a stern reply from the Prime Minister: the king himself was concerned at Gage's failure to execute the plan that Amherst had so prudently concerted.

This opprobrium was justified: rather than obeying his orders and seizing a weak position, Gage had confined himself to strengthening the posts of Niagara and Oswego, and their communications with the Mohawk Valley. Having done so, he found time to join Sir William Johnson in a spot of fishing and duck hunting.

Some of Amherst's anger against Gage may be explained by his own sense of guilt at having done so little to support Wolfe's campaign on the St Lawrence. The caution displayed by the general and his brigadier alike apparently stemmed from the same sense of uncertainty regarding developments at Québec: Gage had told Johnson that everything depended on General Wolfe; but by failing to push onwards to Montréal with determination, *both* men had made Wolfe's task more difficult.

Gage lost his nerve on 11 September; at exactly the same time Wolfe resolved upon a last-ditch effort to take Québec; and at Crown Point, Rogers was lobbying Amherst for a chance to strike at St Francis. Amherst had intended that Rogers' raid would support Gage in his undertaking against La Galette. Now that Gage had baulked at the first hurdle, the strike against St Francis assumed even greater significance. With Amherst's own army still stalled at the southern end of Lake Champlain by a lack of intelligence, shipping and resolution, Rogers and his dwindling band represented the general's only active task force. But if Amherst was bitterly disappointed in Thomas Gage, he retained his faith in Robert Rogers. Here at least was one soldier who could be trusted to obey orders. In the very same despatch in which he castigated the wretched brigadier,

Amherst voiced his confidence in the celebrated major. Despite the losses that had weakened his detachment, Amherst assured the Prime Minister that Rogers had 'men enough left to Execute the Service he is sent on'.

JEFFERY AMHERST'S TRUST was not misplaced. Despite its discouraging start, Rogers had no intention of abandoning his mission.

The last news of Rogers had been brought into Crown Point by Captain Butterfield; he left the major and his men sheltering within the marshy mouth of Otter Creek. Heading south on 15 September, the captain noted that the French vessels had shifted their patrolling pattern; like him, they were now moving towards Crown Point. This crucial development gave Rogers his opportunity to pass through the narrows and proceed down the lake.

With so many of the command already sent back, the whaleboat crews were reduced to nine or ten men each, so those remaining now faced more back-breaking hours at the oars. They kept close to the lake's eastern shore – ready to dive for cover if the French ships hove in to sight – and maintained their previous rhythm, rowing by night and resting up on land during the dangerous daylight hours.

As the lake widened, so their prospects of escaping detection by the French fleet improved. Roughly midway along its length, Champlain's surface was bisected by the elongated bulk of Grand Isle; the western channel led to the Richelieu River, the eastern terminated in Missisquoi Bay. By passing over the sandbar lying across the entrance to the East Bay, Rogers' shallow whaleboats gained some protection against direct pursuit by more substantial vessels.

But there were other hazards; in bad weather the lake could generate waves capable of swamping craft far larger then Rogers' frail whaleboats; during the nineteenth century, sizeable paddle steamers foundered in its depths. Autumn was also closing in. At Ticonderoga on 17 September, Lemuel Wood reported that the weather was *Very stormy Last night and to Day*; at Crown Point, Robert Webster also recorded a very stormy day, *as cold as you please*. Amherst too noted that it was beginning to grow cold: he had already ordered flannel waistcoats, leggings and socks for the regulars, and the increasingly homesick provincials were badly in need of cloaks to keep them warm. But if conditions were grim at the forts, for Rogers' men out on the lake they were undoubtedly far worse. Wind, spray and fog could chill a man to his very marrow. Things were little better on land, as there was no prospect of lighting fires to dry clothes, heat rations, warm numb fingers or revive flagging spirits: the fear of discovery was already too great.

Throughout New England and New York there had been other portents of unusually cold weather on the horizon. One sure sign of a hard winter ahead was an alarming influx of bears into inhabited regions where they were rarely seen. By late August, the New England frontier was under assault from more bears than anyone could remember. At Brentwood in New Hampshire, marauding beasts killed two children out gathering beans, and a few days later at Chester, in the same province, another bear crept up upon an unsuspecting woman and clawed off the back of her gown. From Boston, it was reported that some of these voracious animals had even ventured down to the seaport towns; one of the boldest had been slain within two miles of Boston itself. The problem only worsened: from Albany came great complaints that roaming bears were claiming sheep, hogs and calves and devouring whole fields of Indian corn. Efforts to repel this unprecedented invasion had resulted in a further crop of human fatalities; one man, Daniel Royce of Wellington in Connecticut was shot dead after being mistaken for a rambling bear.

Driven by instinct, the bears had moved south in search of sustenance. In obedience to their orders, Rogers and his men pressed onwards into the unwelcoming northern wilderness that these same creatures had forsaken. On the tenth day of the operation, during the early hours of 23 September, Rogers and his command pulled into the shelter of Missisquoi Bay. It had rained heavily all that night; they must have been soaked to the skin.

The final moments, as the leading whaleboats skirted the tree-lined shore in search of a suitable landing place, jarred upon nerves that were already strung taut. Had the French and Indians been tracking them from the shore? Were they at that very moment perfecting their ambush, cocking hammers and taking leisurely aim along the barrels of their fusils? It was dark and eerily silent; but without warning all that might change as the woods spouted scores of pyrotechnic muzzle flashes and the air resounded with the crash of musketry and spine-tingling war cries. Tightly packed and fumbling at their oars, the raiders were sitting targets.

But the woods remained silent. The whaleboats were swiftly beached, manhandled ashore and cached in the brush. Rogers intended to execute his mission and then retrace his steps to the hidden boats. Part of what now remained of the precious rations, enough to get them back from Missisquoi Bay to Crown Point, was stowed with the boats and two trusty Indians placed nearby to watch over them. As Rogers remembered, these warriors were 'to lie at a distance in sight of the boats . . . till I came back except [that] the enemy found them; in which case they were with all possible speed to follow on my track and give me intelligence.'

Rogers was destined to see these warriors sooner than he expected: although unopposed, the stealthy landfall of the whaleboats had not gone entirely unnoticed.

FOLLOWING QUÉBEC'S FALL ON 18 September, the defeated French army had been herded off by the ever-resourceful Governor General Vaudreuil; it regrouped above the Jacques Cartier River, some thirty-two miles to the west. Montcalm's competent and pugnacious subordinate, the Chevalier de Lévis, now assumed command of the dispirited French regulars and militia and sought to rebuild their battered morale.

Although it delivered a major Anglo-American war aim, and a leg-endary battle honour for the British Army, the capture of Québec was not the decisive victory that Wolfe had sought. He had aimed for nothing less than the total destruction of the city's defenders; but the bulk of them had slipped away to fight another day. Québec's conquerors now faced the problem of consolidating their position and surviving the harsh

Canadian winter amidst the crumbling ruins created by their own bombardment. For their part, the French at Jacques Cartier remained content to keep the redcoats under observation whilst frostbite and scurvy slowly took their toll.

Ironically, Québec's fall meant there were more French forces available to dispute any belated advance by Amherst. That autumn, New France's Lake Champlain front was thick with patrols. Everything that the French commanders had gleaned from British deserters and the letters found with Kennedy's party indicated that Amherst was waiting for news of Wolfe before he moved forward. Now that Québec had succumbed to British arms, they braced themselves to meet the expected assault from the south.

Quinton Kennedy's capture drew attention to the vulnerable Missisquoi Bay sector, and the route by which the British could reach St Jean without tackling the prickly fortress of Isle-aux-Noix; a detailed journal kept at that island stronghold by Captain Nicolas des Méloizes of *la Marine* chronicles the intensive patrolling that followed. On 16 September, Brigadier Bourlamaque headed a band of regulars, militia and Indians on his own reconnaissance mission to Missisquoi Bay. He returned convinced that it was indeed a major weak point in his defences. Reporting his scout to Lévis, he added: 'I would like to be in Mr. Amherst's place. I would launch an attack that way without difficulty.' On 20 and 21 September, further patrols had been sent to the bay; both returned next day, having seen nothing suspicious.

With all this frenzied enemy activity, Rogers was exceptionally lucky to escape immediate detection. But it wasn't long before the French realised that another British party was on the loose behind their lines: this time it was no mere brace of bumbling messengers and their escort, but a powerful strike-force capable of wreaking havoc. On 23 September – the very same day that Rogers marched inland after hiding his boats – one of Bourlamaque's officers, the veteran La Durantaye of *la Marine*, ordered yet another reconnaissance to Missisquoi Bay. French persistence now paid off; the scout came back that evening, bringing a British-made oar retrieved from the lake. This crucial discovery confirmed intelligence from Indian hunters who had heard a boat on the water the previous night.

The next morning, La Durantaye marched to the bay with forty men to investigate further; he was accompanied by that famed bush fighter, Ensign Langis: this was the same formidable partnership that had inflicted such a bloody check to Rogers and his rangers at the Battle on Snowshoes in March 1758. The wily pair soon found the seventeen whaleboats. Some were stove in and burned on the spot, others dragged to the Missisquoi portage.

The sheer number of boats left no doubt that a substantial raiding party was at large, but the French did not yet know it was led by the infamous Major Rogers. Although whaleboats belonging to Rogers' Rangers had been labelled as such during previous campaigns, there is no evidence that similar markings were retained for the St Francis raid; had this been the case, the French officers who found the hidden craft would surely have reported that they were dealing with their old rival; yet they did not do so.

Bourlamaque learned of the cached boats on 25 September. Conjecturing that the raiders might be making for Québec or St Francis, he despatched a courier to warn Rigaud at Montréal. The unflappable brigadier lost no time in mustering a rapid reaction force from amongst the troops concentrated at Isle-aux-Noix. At dawn next day a detachment of three hundred men left camp with enough food for five days. Runners reported back the following day; it was estimated that the intruders numbered between two hundred and two hundred and forty men; their tracks suggested they were heading for Chambly, Yamaska or St Francis. That evening Bourlamaque sent out a further fifty men with enough supplies to enable the original pursuit force to stay out for another eight days.

The canny Bourlamaque swiftly put two and two together. Reporting these troubling developments to Lévis on 27 September, he believed that the English might ultimately intend to reach Québec; but given their suspected route, surely the raiders were bent upon retaliation for the recent capture of Kennedy and Hamilton by the St Francis Abenakis? 'All appearances indicate that they want to punish Saint-Francois for its loyalty,' he wrote. Besides alerting Rigaud at Montréal, Bourlamaque had also written to Paul-Joseph Le Moyne de Longueuil, an officer in *la Marine* and Governor of Trois-Rivières, so that men could be sent to Yamaska and St Francis. Another courier had gone to rouse the missionary at St Francis; no doubt Lévis would reinforce both villages if they were unable to defend themselves. Bourlamaque had not written to Vaudreuil; he begged that Lévis would warn the governor general of developments.

Two days later Bourlamaque wrote to Lévis once again. He had just heard the shocking news of the British victory at Québec, and composed this latest despatch in a mood of some dismay. Intelligence reports had left no doubt that Amherst would only move once he knew the outcome of events on the St Lawrence; Bourlamaque therefore believed that an Anglo-American thrust towards the Richelieu River was now imminent. He was confident of defending Isle-aux-Noix, but could not say as much for Missisquoi Bay.

Despite this increased threat from the south, Bourlamaque had not forgotten the enemy party that had *already* penetrated his sector. Besides the detachment sent on the raiders' trail, another four hundred men now lay in ambush where the whaleboats had been found. Should these same English prove foolish enough to return the way that they had come, a hot reception would await them.

Brigadier Bourlamaque had done everything in his power to counter the intruders: if all went to plan, and others played their parts, they would be intercepted and exterminated.

CHAPTER SIX

Search and Destroy

MEASURED BY CROW'S FLIGHT, the village of St Francis lay some seventy-five miles north-east of Missisquoi Bay – but Rogers and his men did not possess wings, and neither geography nor the enemy permitted such a direct approach: they now faced a march of more than a hundred miles to reach their objective.

After ten tense nights spent negotiating the length of Lake Champlain, the major's men were no doubt relieved to leave its perilous waters behind them at last. Yet whilst technically back on dry land, it would be more than a week before they once again felt firm ground beneath their moccasins.

Rogers left no daily written itinerary of his subsequent movements, but this void can be filled thanks to a truly remarkable survival – a detailed map of his expedition that he later prepared for General Amherst. This fascinating relic of frontier history was long believed to be lost. In 1970 it finally resurfaced in the catalogue of a New York auction house, and now resides in a private North American collection. It provides a comprehensive and surprisingly accurate rendering of rivers and lakes; topography is also depicted, although in a more impressionistic fashion. Rogers employed a dotted line to indicate his route onwards from Missisquoi Bay, and used symbols to mark many of his camps and halting places. As Rogers also included a scale, it is possible to gain at least some idea of the distances covered during various phases of the operation. Complete with annotations and observations, Rogers' chart is a unique and richly evocative document – an authentic counterpart to Flint's map from *Treasure Island*.

Striking inland from his landing place on the morning of 23 September, Rogers initially headed due east; after some twenty miles, as his map reveals, he swung on a north-easterly tack. This route had much in its favour, giving the widest possible berth to Isle-aux-Noix, where Bourlamaque's troops were concentrated, and also avoiding the northerly Yamaska River trail that Kennedy had followed to disaster.

As he marched ever deeper into enemy territory, Rogers reversed the procedure adopted on the lake; the raiders now moved in daylight and rested up during the hours of darkness. The first day's march, undertaken by men still weary from their final night on the water, covered just eight miles; they made only marginally better progress next day, pushing on for another nine or ten. There was a good reason for this sluggish pace. The looping course chosen by Rogers was not without its own disadvantages and dangers: from the outset, as the map shows, his command was obliged to negotiate strength-sapping bogs.

The mosquito-ridden marshes were bad enough, but other circumstances now dampened the raiders' spirits still further. On the evening of the second day after leaving Missisquoi Bay, the two Indians who had been left behind to watch over the hidden whaleboats and provisions caught up with them. They gasped out a disconcerting message: about four hundred French had discovered the boats – and half of them were already hot on their trail.

Employing his characteristic understatement, Rogers recorded his reaction to this grim news: 'This unlucky circumstance (it may well be supposed) put us into some consternation.' Overcoming their initial dismay at this alarming turn of events, the major and his officers considered their options. First, they could confront their pursuers and fight it out in the swamps. But even if the French were worsted, the outlook for the raiders was bleak; they were far behind enemy lines and cut off from any source of assistance; the French, by contrast, were on their own ground and could expect to be reinforced by *any numbers they pleased*. No, standing and fighting offered little realistic hope of survival, let alone of completing the mission.

The loss of the whaleboats and the provisions cached with them ruled out the second option – withdrawal back up Lake Champlain. The situation was desperate, but they were tough and determined men under a leader of proven courage. They agreed upon a third response – the boldest course of all. Rogers recalled: 'It was however resolved to prosecute our design at all adventures, and, when we had accomplished it, to attempt a retreat (the only possible way we could think of) by way of No. 4.'

This was an extraordinarily daring stratagem. For the new plan to enjoy any chance of success fresh supplies must be sent to await them on the return leg of their march. Lieutenant Andrew McMullen of the rangers, who had lamed himself in an earlier accident, was ordered to return overland to Crown Point and inform Amherst of developments. Rogers requested the general to send provisions to 'Ammonoosuc River at the end of Coos Intervales on Connecticut River, that being the way I should return, if at all.' The Ammonoosuc enters the Connecticut from the east, directly opposite where the Wells River joins from the west; this conspicuous junction would, Rogers hoped, provide an unmistakeable landmark in the wilderness. The proposed rallying point was itself some sixty miles north of the nearest British settlement at Fort Number Four.

If at all . . . As Rogers and his men knew only too well, the odds of reaching the proposed rendezvous on the Connecticut were now stacked heavily against them. Even if they could shake off pursuit, their route was taking them ever further into the heart of enemy territory. The French now knew that a sizeable enemy force was on the loose; they would surely realise that St Francis presented a prime target and take pains to protect it. And even if the raiders reached the village, and fulfilled their orders to chastise its notorious inhabitants, what then? The best that could be hoped for was a fighting retreat across more than two hundred miles of unforgiving wilderness terrain with a vengeful and ruthless enemy snapping at their very heels. *If at all . . .*

McMullen, an Irishman who had first set foot in North America five years before, was sent hobbling on his way, escorted by another half dozen of the major's dwindling band. 'This being done,' Rogers wrote, 'we determined if possible to outmarch our pursuers and effect our design upon St Francis before they could overtake us.' Such determination offered a marked contrast to the attitude displayed by another officer recently sent upon a detached operation: whilst Brigadier Gage prevaricated in the face of imagined difficulties, the resolute Major Rogers pushed ever onwards into the maw of hazards that were all too real.

THE INJURED MCMULLEN undertook his own dangerous mission with a determination worthy of Rogers himself. He completed the journey – trekking across a hundred miles of forest, mountain and marsh, whilst evading enemy patrols – in nine days, limping into Crown Point camp on 3 October. By the lieutenant's reckoning, when he left Rogers the major was already about forty miles beyond *Mischiscove Bay*; if, as Rogers' *Journals* suggests, his Indian runners reached him on the evening of 25 September, he would actually have been just twenty miles to the north-east of Missisquoi Bay. Either way, Amherst duly noted the fact that Rogers 'intended to pursue the orders I had given him and thought of returning by No 4.'

The next day, ranger Lieutenant Samuel Stevens was despatched to Fort Number Four with a letter to the provincial officer who commanded there: Major Benjamin Bellows was directed to supply Stevens with provisions sufficient to sustain Major Rogers and his party – now reported to be 170-strong – from the designated intersection of the Wells and Ammonoosuc with the Connecticut, down to Fort Number Four. Bellows was also to give Stevens enough men to help carry the stores up to Wells River. The lieutenant's instructions from Amherst were clear: upon arrival at the specified rendezvous, Stevens was to 'there Remain with Said party, so long as You shall think there is any probability of Major

Rogers returning that way; at the Expiration of Which, You will Return with said provisions & party to No. 4 & Deliver them back to Mr Bellows and Yourself immediately thereafter Return to this Camp.'

Samuel Stevens was an experienced officer who had been promoted from the ranks. A native of New Hampshire, he was well acquainted with the region around Fort Number Four; Rogers had earlier recommended him to Amherst to command a squad of twenty rangers sent to that key frontier post during the winter of 1758–9. There was no reason to believe that he would not heed his unequivocal instructions.

FOR ANOTHER FULL WEEK AFTER McMullen's departure, Rogers and his remaining men continued their grim trek through the wet and sunken ground. In his *Journals*, Rogers reported that a total of nine days were spent in struggling through this spruce bog. For most of that time the water was nearly a foot deep. Yet the pace was unrelenting. In a bid to outdistance pursuit, they marched before daybreak and continued until after dark. The men were permanently damp; sodden moccasins and leggings would have swiftly rotted, along with the flesh beneath them. Even when they finally rested at night, there was precious little relief from the waterlogged wastes around them. In an effort to at least sleep in the dry, they cut branches from the trees and improvised hammocks. A newspaper reported how the major and his men 'were obliged to fell saplins, and lay them across each other, in form of a Raft, and cover them over with boughs and Leaves to keep themselves from the Wet.' The same account estimated that this dismal morass stretched for at least fifty miles.

As Rogers' men splashed and floundered through the seemingly endless bogs, they must have cursed their leader's choice of route. However, the very nature of the terrain, and the pace that they maintained in crossing it, was too much for the party that Bourlamaque had sent in pursuit from Missisquoi Bay. Although the major's Indian scouts had reported otherwise, this force had not actually set out until the morning of 26 September, so Rogers had a head start of some seventy-two hours. Unable to track the raiders through the squelching mire, Langis' men had eventually given up the chase. They did so with reluctance, and only arrived back at Isle-aux-Noix on 4 October, nine days after setting out; as Captain Méloizes noted in his journal, they'd returned without discovering *anything* more about the English who had arrived in the whaleboats.

Oblivious to this development, Rogers and his raiders waded ever onwards through the dispiriting swamplands. At long last, on the tenth day after quitting Lake Champlain, their determination was rewarded. They emerged from the marshes to find themselves finally upon dry land. It was 3 October, 1759.

But they now faced another formidable natural barrier: the St Francis River itself. Though Rogers estimated that they struck the river about fifteen miles above the village, they were actually somewhat closer. As his men were on the south bank, and their objective lay across the river, it was imperative that they cross it without delay. Fear of an enemy pursuit-force coming up behind them added an extra urgency to the situation; nobody wanted to fight with a swift-flowing river at his back. There was also the very real danger that the manoeuvre might be opposed: hostiles concealed amongst the trees lining the far bank could shoot them down at their leisure as they sought a way over.

Abenaki oral tradition provides a vital clue to what happened next. On that same day, so the old story goes, some St Francis women who were washing clothes in the river noticed chips of wood floating past; but although they reported this unusual phenomenon to their menfolk, nothing was done. All this suggests the following scenario: Rogers at first contemplated ferrying his weary command across the river by raft; indeed, his men actually began to construct rafts, but soon abandoned the enterprise through fear that it would betray them. Not only was there a danger of flying woodchips drifting downriver to the village, but also that the noise of axes thudding into tree trunks could carry through the forest. The first hazard was real enough: Rogers and his men were fortunate that the washerwomen's warning fell upon deaf ears.

Rafting the St Francis River was plainly too risky, but Robert Rogers once again kept his nerve – and his initiative. His map shows that he marched his command several miles upriver – *away* from St Francis – before attempting a crossing where the river was swifter, but narrower and more fordable. In his *Journals* Rogers noted that the operation of fording the river 'was attended with no small difficulty'. As the water was five feet deep and flowing swiftly, the major placed his tallest men upstream, thereby forming a living lifeline for their stockier comrades: the human chain was strung across the rushing St Francis River, with each man beard-deep in the foaming waters. In this fashion, by holding on to each other, the entire command crossed over safely with the loss of nothing more than a few muskets – and several of those were soon retrieved from the river bottom.

As they emerged dripping and gasping upon the far bank, anxiously scanning the woods for any sign of the enemy, all must have marvelled at their continuing good fortune. Like the nail-biting landing at Missisquoi Bay, the hazardous crossing had been conducted without the slightest sign of opposition. They were now just hours from their target, yet still they had not been obliged to fight. As they shook themselves down, checked their weapons and ammunition, and stepped out upon the final phase of the long march to St Francis, they must surely have wondered how much longer their remarkable luck would last.

BUT WHERE *WERE* THE DEFENDERS of New France? Since 25 September, when Brigadier Bourlamaque had sent couriers scuttling off with warnings that a substantial force of raiders was at large, considerable efforts had been taken to thwart them. Besides the troops that Bourlamaque himself had unleashed upon their trail and placed in ambush at the landing place in Missisquoi Bay, other forces were mobilised to intercept the raiders before they could do any mischief. On 27 September, Rigaud wrote to Bourlamaque from Montréal acknowledging the receipt of his letter. He reassured the brigadier that he had lost no time in likewise sending messengers to Longueuil at Trois-Rivières and to his brother,

Governor General Vaudreuil, forwarded Bourlamaque's intelligence reports of the estimated strength of the British detachment, and his thoughts about its likely objectives. Rigaud had no doubt that both his brother and Longueuil would take all necessary precautions to cut the enemy's route.

But a week later there was still no clue as to the intruders' whereabouts. Writing to Bourlamaque from Montréal on 3 October, Governor Vaudreuil himself was now extremely impatient for hard news of the mysterious English who had hidden their boats at Missisquoi Bay and then apparently vanished into thin air. Despite the worrying uncertainty, all possible measures had been taken to deal with the raiders. That same day Vaudreuil informed Lévis: 'I have sent all the St Francis Abenakis and a number of sturdy Canadians out in search of the English who were in these barges.' Abenaki warriors from the mission village of Bécancour, together with another contingent formed from the hardiest of the Canadian militia, were also ready and waiting. Vaudreuil was sure these experienced forces would prove sufficient to check the raiders.

In the crisis triggered by the unexpected news of Québec's fall, the unwelcome presence of some two hundred Englishmen was just one of many problems facing Vaudreuil and the other men charged with the defence of New France's shrinking perimeters. At his headquarters at Jacques Cartier, the Chevalier de Lévis as commander-in-chief, faced the mammoth task of rebuilding the army that had recently run so shamefully from Wolfe's redcoats on the Plains of Abraham. At Isle-aux-Noix, Bourlamaque, his second-in-command, was preoccupied with preparations for meeting the major assault that was now looming; convinced that Amherst must surely have heard of the dramatic developments at Québec, he was bracing himself for an attack upon his island stronghold within the next six to eight days. Bourlamaque was increasingly anxious that the four hundred men left in ambush at Missisquoi Bay were now themselves at risk of being cut off by the advance of overwhelming Anglo-American forces from Crown Point. Vaudreuil appreciated the situation; if Bourlamaque had received no word of the rogue English force by 5 October, he should recall his men from their precarious outpost.

Although Vaudreuil believed that he had done everything necessary to counter the unknown enemy rampaging unchecked through the colony, his dispositions were fatally flawed. Ironically, these errors were another legacy of Quinton Kennedy's failed mission to Wolfe. The captain and his companions penetrated as far as they did before discovery by following the line of the Yamaska River; their capture, which had been heralded as a major coup for Canada's embattled defenders, had drawn attention to the vulnerability of that sector. Assuming that the British raiding party would seek to exploit the same route, approaching by way of Wigwam Martinique, the detachments formed from the St Francis and Bécancour Abenakis, and the élite of the colony's militiamen, were posted to ambush them there.

AT THE VERY TIME THAT Vaudreuil was positioning his forces like pieces on a chessboard, Robert Rogers and his bedraggled band of rangers, regulars and provincials were moving ever closer to the village of St Francis. As Rogers related with evident relief, the command now had good dry ground to march upon. Progress was rapid, and that same evening they finally sighted their objective. The major himself clambered up a tree and located the village; one newspaper reported that he 'saw the Smoak about 5 or 6 Miles distant'. Moving on to within two or three miles of his target, Rogers called another halt. It was now time to take stock of his force.

The twenty demanding days since setting out from Crown Point had exacted a heavy toll: Rogers' command, including officers, now numbered just one hundred and forty-two men. No less than forty-one sick and wounded were sent back within days of setting out; another six had returned with McMullen after Rogers learned that the French had thwarted his plan to withdraw by Lake Champlain. Others had been lost along the way; and as the raiders moved ever farther from their base, so the prospects for those who succumbed to illness, exposure or exhaustion grew correspondingly bleak. The grinding nine-day march through the swamps clearly claimed its victims – newspapers later stated that several of the major's men perished within them.

Those who remained were in poor condition, dishevelled and drawn with fatigue. They were also ravenously hungry, their rations having run out during the last days of the long slog across the bogs. The Connecticut corporal Frederick Curtiss recalled that by the time they reached St Francis, 'after about Twenty Days Travail & Passage By Land & Water,' they'd already marched for no fewer than 'Three Days without Provision'.

At 8.00 p.m. on 3 October, in company with Ensign Elias Avery of the Connecticut provincials and Lieutenant George Turner of the rangers, Major Rogers left his detachment to go ahead and reconnoitre the village. In his absence, Captain Ogden of the Jersey Blues took command. Newspapers reported that Rogers donned disguise, entered the village and brazenly mingled with its unsuspecting inhabitants. Indeed, 'he went through the Town, and was spoke to several Times by the Indians, but was not discovered, as he was dress'd like one of them.' The major was highly satisfied with what he discovered, finding the Indians in a *high frolic or dance*.

According to another report, the inhabitants were 'singing and having the War Dance, as the whole Town intended to come up the River on a Scout the next Day.' One British newspaper added a further twist to the tale: Rogers had 'learnt that the Indians had Intelligence of his being out, and intended to attack him; and concluded that if they did know he was near, they would be engaged in performing their War-Dance, would all get drunk, and it would be a proper Time to surprise them.' Dancing there certainly was, but the occasion was more innocent. Ogden later claimed that the inhabitants had assembled to celebrate a wedding, and although the captain did not witness the scene, other sources give the same explanation for the festivities. Rogers reputedly stayed until 2.00 a.m. before leaving the Indians to their merrymaking and returning to his waiting men.

At first sight, the story of Rogers' daring reconnaissance appears incredible:* having overcome so many hardships to arrive undetected within striking distance of his target, why would he risk compromising the entire operation through an act of unnecessary bravado? And just how easy would it be for a burly white man, of six feet in height, to pass unnoticed through a gathering of his deadly enemies? Yet St Francis was a hybrid community in which English captives and mixed-race inhabitants were commonplace; French-Canadians would also have been a familiar sight. Rogers could speak French, so language was no barrier to such an escapade, and as his previous exploits indicate, the major was much given to self-promotion or what his enemies characterised as braggadocio. Such a daring undertaking would not have been out of character. And there was no reason why even Rogers' most inveterate opponents should have recognised him in the flesh. He was certainly notorious throughout New France; but by the very nature of the warfare in which he had made his name, precious few of his enemies were in a position to put a face to it.

MAJOR ROGERS AND HIS TWO companions were not the only men of his command to rub shoulders with the inhabitants of St Francis during that last carefree evening of dancing and celebration. Another interloper, one of Rogers' own Indian rangers, also entered the village, although his object for doing so could not have been more different to the major's.

This episode is vividly described within the rich oral traditions of the St Francis Abenakis.‡ According to Theophile Panadis, on the eve of Rogers' attack, the inhabitants of St Francis were celebrating their recent return from hunting by holding dances in the village's largest house. That night, Panadis related, 'there came a strange Indian who called himself a *Mahigan*.' He warned the Abenakis that they were to be exterminated

---

* Similar exploits have been credited to charismatic leaders throughout history. For example, on the eve of his decisive victory over the Great Army of the Danes at Edington in 878, the Anglo-Saxon warrior king Alfred the Great reputedly infiltrated the enemy camp disguised as a juggler, gaining both valuable intelligence – and applause for his performance.

‡ As recorded and translated from Abenaki by Gordon M. Day during the mid-twentieth century.

in the early morning; they should evacuate the elderly, women and children without delay. So the Abenaki men took their families and the sick to a place a few miles off called Siboseck then returned ready to defend the village, choosing the same large building as their stronghold.

Another St Francis Abenaki told much the same story: Elvine Obomsawin Royce related the tale passed down by her aunt's grandmother, who was a young girl in October 1759. In her version the dancers were celebrating the successful gathering of the harvest, rather than the hunters' return. Now and then the celebrants left the council house to smoke their pipes, rest and enjoy the cool night air. One young girl lingered in the dark after the others went in. She was about to rejoin the dance when a stranger stopped her. Speaking in an Indian tongue, he told her that he was a friend, and that she should not be afraid. He too brought a stark warning: enemies were lurking in the *little woods*. When the Abenakis retired for the night, these men would come to kill everyone and burn the village. The narrative continued: 'And surely the young woman went in to the council house, the dancing place, and she warned the other Indians what he told. She warned what she had been warned. And some did not believe her, because she was so young, because she was a child.'

But others heeded the warning, stopped dancing, fetched their children and took them to a safe hiding place. The girl's father gathered all the youngsters together in the darkness, but his own daughter had been left behind; he returned and found the child calmly singing to herself whilst gazing from the window of her home. Scooping her up, he took her to join the others at their refuge in a ravine at a place called the Pines: 'And there they hid, the Indians, the Abenakis'.

Although differing in detail, both narratives share crucial components: the dancing in the large council house on the eve of the raid; the last-minute warning delivered by the Indian stranger, and the subsequent evacuation of many villagers to a secret bolt-hole. These enduring tribal traditions receive striking corroboration from verifiable facts. Whether staged to mark the gathering of the harvest, the return of hunters, the despatch of a war party, or, as seems most likely, to celebrate a wedding, there was clearly a dance in progress on the night of 3–4 October, 1759. And there is no doubt that Rogers' raiding party included Mahicans – a tribe possessing strong links with the St Francis Indians. There had long been a two-way traffic between the communities, with Mahicans from the refugee village of Schaghticoke in New York continuing to gravitate towards St Francis up until the very eve of the present war; and Peter, who had been killed by the St Francis Indians after he was captured in company with Quinton Kennedy, died because he was perceived as a defector to the Mahicans.

With this background, the story of the mysterious warning becomes increasingly plausible: it would not be the first occasion during the war that tribal blood ties had outweighed allegiance to a cause; to the dismay and disgust of European officers like Baron Dieskau, Indians had proved reluctant to kill potential relatives, and equally keen to warn them of impending danger.

But if the St Francis Abenakis *were* warned of the looming onslaught, why didn't they prepare a devastating ambush for their attackers? The answer is not hard to find: on the morning of 4 October, 1759, St Francis was a village denuded of its fighting men. By order of Governor General Vaudreuil, some warriors had been sent off to intercept the raiders on their anticipated approach route; others of the village's menfolk, who had fought against Wolfe at Québec, remained with the main French army under the Chevalier de Lévis. St Francis lay virtually defenceless, and the villagers themselves were all too aware of this fact. Alerted to the coming attack, most of them simply abandoned their homes and hid nearby.

The infamous community of St Francis was now left in the keeping of those who were too old, infirm, stubborn or befuddled by the night's drinking to leave, or who simply refused to credit the far-fetched rumours that an enemy force had penetrated the very vitals of New France and was now poised to pounce upon them. It was they who would be obliged to answer for the sins of the St Francis Indians.

AT 3.00 A.M. ON 4 OCTOBER, an hour after returning from St Francis, Rogers marched his troops forward until they were within five hundred yards of the village. The raiders shed their packs and formed up for the attack in three divisions: Rogers himself commanded the right of the line; Lieutenant Dunbar of the regular light infantry held the centre; and the provincial Captain Ogden headed the left. In addition, the major's best marksmen were deployed to shoot down anyone seeking to flee the village. Robert Kirkwood of Montgomery's Highlanders said the raiders were instructed to advance 'by two and two, and place ourselves severally at each house'. The signal to attack was to be a shot fired by Major Rogers himself. At that, Kirkwood recalled, 'we were to fire the town at once and kill everyone without mercy.'

Half an hour before daybreak, at about 5.00 a.m., the three groups of raiders moved against the village in unison. Their revels finally at an end, the remaining inhabitants were now fast asleep. There was no lookout to shout a frantic warning; no clanging alarm bell sounding from the mission church. With not so much as a picket fence to bar their way, the paired attackers swiftly took up their stations. In the recollection of Kirkwood, someone's gun went off by accident, 'which made us begin without the right signal'. But the blunder was irrelevant – surprise was total.

The slumbering inhabitants of St Francis received a rude awakening – if they woke at all. In the jocular words of the *New-York Gazette*, Rogers' men 'never stood to ask Entrance, but burst open their Doors, and saluted them with Tomahawks and Bayonets.' One pair of rangers teamed up two of the stoutest men of their time, Lieutenant Jacob Farrington and Sergeant Benjamin Bradley. Posted to the house where the wedding had so recently been celebrated, they barged against the door with such violence that the hinges gave way. Carried headlong by his own momentum, Bradley fell in amongst the Indians who lay sleeping on the floor. All were killed before they could make any show of resistance.

It was the same story elsewhere as houses were systematically broken open and their occupants slaughtered. Some were shot as they lay in their beds; others, who sought to escape via back ways, were tomahawked or bayoneted. Major Rogers seemed to be everywhere, encouraging his men and issuing orders, while Captain Ogden was no less zealous. One ball passed through his body and another wounded him in the head; for good measure the captain's powder horn was shot away from where it hung at his hip. None of this hindered him from doing his duty. Ogden bound up the wound in his side with a handkerchief; when several men expressed concern at his injuries he responded that he was merely scratched and urged them on to the attack.

The onslaught was overwhelming, the defence short-lived. Rogers himself reported that the enemy *had not time to recover themselves*, or even to take up their weapons. There is a hint in the story told by Theophile Panadis that some of the men who had remained behind despite the warning held out in the large council house where the previous night's dance had been staged.* But if there was such a stand, it was all-too-quickly over.

In his orders to Rogers, Amherst had enjoined the major and his men to take their revenge upon the St Francis Indians; the general had also specified that no women or children should be harmed. But a surprise attack upon an enemy village, particularly before sunrise, was scarcely the occasion for such discrimination; amidst the resulting pandemonium, any flitting shape became a potential target. When they fell upon the village, Rogers and his men had no reason to disbelieve that it contained a substantial complement of fighting men from one of the most feared tribes on the North American continent. Their first priority was to maximise the vital element of surprise, striking fast and hard enough to subdue all resistance.

The consequences were all too predictable: the well-disciplined assault swiftly degenerated into an uncontrolled massacre. As the frank account published by one English newspaper noted, Rogers' 'Orders were to spare all the Women and Children, but they were little attended to.'

* Intriguing support for the story was discovered when the building was finally demolished in the early years of the twentieth century: its window and doorframes were pocked with old lead bullets.

Driven by a mixture of adrenalin and bloodlust, the raiders were not in merciful mood. Their pent-up fears and hatreds found release in a killing spree.

Indians who attempted to run from the scene were shot down immediately by the marksmen posted for that very purpose. Others who reached their canoes and desperately sought to paddle to safety across the St Francis River had no more success. Forty of Rogers' men pursued them, sinking canoes and occupants alike; according to Captain Ogden, the fleeing villagers had attempted to carry off their children with them; in consequence, they also suffered.

Shortly after sunrise Rogers ordered the village to be put to the torch. All the houses were set ablaze, except for three that stored corn; this would provide vital sustenance for the major's hungry men. As the fire took hold upon the substantial wooden houses it became apparent that some of the inhabitants had concealed themselves in their lofts and cellars. These places of refuge now became death traps; the raiders heard the dreadful cries and screeches of those who were penned within the burning buildings. The *Boston Gazette* revelled in the sufferings: 'those miserable wretches, when they perceived their houses on fire, and themselves like to be made the fuel: The sword without, which prevented all escapes, and the fire within rendered their situation most unhappy, most miserable.' Robert Kirkwood recalled the same grim choice: 'those whom the flames did not devour, were either shot or tomohawk'd.'

The clemency recommended by Amherst was the exception to a far more ruthless rule. According to Rogers, just twenty captives were taken. The lucky ones included the children of a white man who had married a *squaw*. They had heeded the following fatherly advice: if ever they fell into the hands of the English, they were to drop to their knees and cry 'quarter'. This, the sole word of English that they knew, sufficed to save their lives.

Quarter was also offered to a *French priest* found in a house adjoining the Chapel. He was 'desired to surrender, and promised good usage; but he refused, and perished in the flames.' In his official despatch to William

Pitt, General Amherst had numbered a priest amongst those who burned to death, but the identity of this defiant cleric – if cleric he was – remains a mystery. Father Roubaud was at Trois-Rivières at the time of the attack; his assistant, Father Jean-Baptiste de La Brosse – the parish priest at Yamaska, or Wigwam Martinique – seemingly travelled to St Francis in Roubaud's absence to conduct the wedding celebrated on the eve of the raid. La Brosse did not die a martyr's death in the inferno of the burning mission; the parish register at Yamaska shows that he was back there by 6 October. But though he escaped the grim fate of Sébastien Rasles at Norridgewock in 1724, the ordeal must have left La Brosse traumatised; many years later, Rogers himself revealed that a priest had been led forth from the church with a rope around his neck.

Before it collapsed in flames, the mission church was ransacked. Good Protestants all, Rogers' men fell upon its popish trappings with icono-clastic relish. The consecrated Hosts were scattered and stomped under-foot, the furnishings destroyed or stolen. During his long stint as missionary to St Francis, Roubaud's predecessor, Father Aubery, had taken great pains to enrich the church with fine sacred objects. These included cloth-of-gold draperies; copper candlesticks plated with silver; a banner painted with life-sized depictions of Christ on one side and the Virgin Mary on the other and embroidered with gold and silver wire. This last had been a lavish gift to Aubery from no less a personage than Marie Leczinska, the dull but devout Polish queen of that licentious monarch, Louis XV. One of the mission's most prized possessions, a silver shirt in a reliquary, succumbed to the blaze. But the solid silver statue of the Virgin – that donated by the Canons of Chartres more than half of century before – was snatched up and carried off as booty.

It was not only the church that offered opportunities for plunder. Despite its modest size, St Francis was reported to be extremely rich. It contained 'English Goods, and vast Quantities of Wampum, and likewise considerable of Silver and Gold.' The *New-York Gazette* maintained that such wealth had been purchased by *our poor People's Scalps*; it nonethe-less remained a tempting distraction for the major's men, and he took steps to curb the looting before it jeopardised the discipline and security of his command. Rogers later informed Amherst that he 'set Fire to the Houses as soon as we had Dispatched the Generality of the Indians to prevent the Party from Plundering.' Newspapers speculated that the speed with which the village was torched denied most of the raiders an opportunity to garner much loot. Captain Ogden reported that it was the prospect of the long journey home that had obliged them to abandon the spoils; otherwise, they could have brought off thousands of pounds worth of Indian goods. In spite of this, some men secured considerable plunder. Besides the ranger who had grabbed the silver image of the Virgin (which was said to weigh ten pounds), another was rumoured to have bagged a hundred and seventy guineas. And of course, there were valuable scalps to be harvested from the dead.

By about 7.00 a.m., Rogers reported, the *affair* was completely over. Of those sleeping within the village when the raiders struck some two hours earlier, a bare handful had succeeded in escaping. These shocked and wounded fugitives would convey the first news of the disaster to the French.

The losses sustained by the attackers were insignificant. Just one man – a Stockbridge Indian – had been killed. Besides the badly injured Ogden, only six others were wounded, all of them lightly. These statistics underlined the one-sided nature of the night's encounter. By the standards of European warfare, the assault had been unusually ruthless. When one Edinburgh-based journal reprinted the *Boston Gazette*'s gory account of the episode, it felt obliged to add a prefatory note warning its readers of shocking proceedings on different sides; as far as the publishers of the *Scots Magazine* were concerned, there was little to choose between the unrestrained behaviour of Rogers' men and that of the 'savages' they had punished so thoroughly.

Colonial journalists had no such scruples: they freely acknowledged that the treatment meted out to the inhabitants of St Francis was indeed severe, but if ever such draconian measures were justified, surely it was here? Had not these very same Indians long proved a scourge to the frontier settlements of Massachusetts and New Hampshire? Were they not guilty of more inhumanities, bloodshed and murdering than perhaps any tribe on the continent? The St Francis Indians had now been punished for their cruelty, for 'a just providence never design'd that those blood-thirsty Heathen should go down to the grave in peace.'

In the eyes of vengeful New Englanders, the guilt of the St Francis Indians was common knowledge, but if further proof was needed it could be provided by that same brave band who had administered their well-deserved nemesis. Upon entering the village, Rogers' men saw some six or seven hundred English scalps; wafting in the wind, they hung from poles erected over the doors of the houses and atop other prominent buildings. On the testimony of Captain Ogden, it was even reported that the mission church itself was bedecked with more of the gruesome trophies – a lurid detail at odds with the Jesuits' reputation for humanity.

Rogers also cited the notorious reputation of the St Francis Indians to justify his brutal treatment of them. For nearly a century, he explained in his *Journals*, they had harassed New England's frontier, slaughtering men, women and children in a most barbarous manner. To his personal knowledge, during the previous six years alone, they had killed or captured no less than four hundred New Englanders.

But the major's men had now exacted ample retribution. Some, like Lieutenant Nathan Brigham of Ruggles' Massachusetts' Regiment, who volunteered for the mission to avenge comrades massacred at Fort William Henry, had grasped the opportunity to settle personal scores. As a vivid contemporary ballad about the raid reveals, the notorious events of 1757 were certainly prominent amongst the grievances recalled to justify Rogers' severity:

> *The Indians he both cut & tore*
> *who soon began to howl and roar*
> *fort willian Henry they did cry*
> *To think upon their cruelty*

> *When at Lake George the English their*
> *They did in pieces cut and tare*
> *And now for their own cruelty*
> *In they same manner they must dy.*

In all, the newspapers reckoned the combined effects of lead, steel, fire and water had claimed the lives of three hundred or more Indians; Rogers himself informed Amherst that the raid had killed at least two hundred. But the major's tally of the losses he had inflicted was wildly inaccurate: French reports compiled in the aftermath of the attack consistently numbered the dead at just thirty; and of these, two-thirds were women and children.

It was not unknown for Rogers to exaggerate his enemies' casualties. In this instance, however, the major's calculations may have reflected his own impression of the village's population, based upon his risky personal reconnaissance of the previous evening; this was conducted *before* many of the villagers had heeded the tidings of an impending attack and sought refuge nearby. Rogers probably took that estimate, subtracted the twenty captives, and assumed the rest to be dead. But bickering over the butcher's bill misses the point. Indians sought to wage war at minimum risk to their own people; they expected to inflict casualties, not suffer them – least of all on their home turf. Even if numbered in tens rather than hundreds, Rogers' victims were numerous enough to be mourned – and *avenged*.

The raiders who descended upon St Francis that morning were impressed with the beautiful situation of the village. Those who had imagined a squalid conglomeration of fragile wigwams were also surprised to find that 'it was regular built with Timber and Boards, in two Rows, with a fine large Church, at the Head of the Town.' Houses and church alike had now been reduced to smouldering ruins; the village's streets were strewn with the scalped bodies of its men, women and children; the very air polluted by the reek of their charred flesh.

Surveying the carnage that he had helped to create, Robert Kirkwood pronounced a grim epitaph: 'thus the inhumanity of these savages was rewarded with a calamity, dreadful indeed, but justly deserved. This was I believe the bloodiest scene in all America, our revenge being completed.'

OF THE SCORE-STRONG HUDDLE of shocked and bewildered prisoners, many were elderly. According to Rogers, all save five – two Indian boys and three girls – were allowed to go their own way. In reality, *six* prisoners were retained by Rogers. They included no less than three members of the family of Chief Joseph-Louis Gill: his sons Xavier and Antoine, whom Susanna Johnson knew as Sabatis, and his wife, Marie-Jeanne. The relatives of such a prominent member of the St Francis tribe would make useful hostages and provide valuable bargaining counters in a crisis.

The raiders also recaptured five 'English' captives whom Rogers placed under his own care. Three of them were rangers, although their names are unknown. Another was a German girl aged about twenty; likewise unnamed, she had been taken prisoner when French and Indian raiders burned the Mohawk Valley settlement of German Flats in November 1757. The fifth of the liberated captives, described in newspaper reports simply as *a poor Man*, was actually George Barnes. A former provincial soldier from Durham, New Hampshire, Barnes later lodged a petition requesting compensation for his wartime losses. The petition told how he had been taken prisoner near Lake George in 1756, and brought into St Francis; there he suffered severely, being stripped of his clothes and beaten with staves and clubs when forced to run the gauntlet. Barnes had remained as a captive until Rogers freed him so unexpectedly.

Whilst his men hurriedly loaded themselves with corn from the storehouses, Rogers personally interrogated prisoners and freed captives alike in the hope of gleaning firm intelligence of enemy dispositions. What he learned was not encouraging. Rogers summarised it in his official report to Amherst: 'That a party of 300 French and some Indians were about four miles down the river below us; and that our boats were waylaid, which I had reason to believe was true as they told the exact number and the place where I had left them at; that a party of 200 French and fifteen Indians had, three days before I attacked the town, gone up the river Wigwam Martinique, supposing that was the place I had intended to attack.'

These revelations mingled fact with rumour. There *was* a force poised to intercept Rogers and his men some ten miles off at Wigwam Martinique, but the report that another substantial French party lay just four miles downstream near the mouth of the St Francis River was plainly false. Had such a formidable body of troops actually been ready and waiting so near to St Francis, it could have been alerted by refugees from the village *before* the pre-dawn attack; and even if there had been no alarm from some fleeing villager, a force so close at hand would surely have been roused into action by the assault itself. Whilst it is unlikely that the sound of gunfire, screams and war cries would have carried through the intervening woods, the smoke and flames of the burning village, and bodies and debris drifting downriver, would have provided unmistakable evidence that the elusive raiders had finally struck.

The young German woman released by the raiders gave a more plausible explanation: the St Francis Indians had received intelligence of the major's design against them, and were to have been joined the day *after* he attacked them by four hundred Canadians.

Whatever their exact location, it was all-too-clear that substantial hostile forces would soon be converging upon St Francis; the major and his men could not afford to dally there any longer. In addition, the prisoners' news finally quashed any lingering hopes of a withdrawal by way of Missisquoi Bay. When Rogers called his officers together to confer upon the route of retreat they all agreed that 'there was no other way for us to return with safety but by No. 4 on Connecticut River'.

Measured in a direct line, the distance from St Francis to Fort Number Four was approximately two hundred miles – *twice* as far as they had already marched from Missisquoi Bay. Once again, there was no straight, firm and level path to follow; their homeward route would be far more convoluted, taking them across a rugged, desolate and uncharted wilderness where few white men had gone before. The prospect was daunting enough for men who were fit and fresh, let alone those who had heaved upon oars and foot-slogged for nearly three weeks; and at the end of that journey they had enjoyed no more respite than a few tense hours of waiting before the frantic assault and the frenzied killing that followed.

Robert Rogers and what remained of his command were bone-weary, but the major urged his men up and onwards. If anything further was needed to keep them marching, it was the growing realisation of what they had done at St Francis: the fate of those who fell into the hands of its avengers would not be pretty. Shouldering muskets and packs, the tattered, smoke-blackened and blood-streaked raiders stepped out upon the next hazardous stage of their gruelling trek.

CHAPTER SEVEN

Retreat and Pursuit

ROGERS AND HIS MEN HAD fallen upon St Francis like a thunderbolt. The flash and rumble of their strike left New France's defenders momentarily stunned, but shock and disbelief were soon subsumed by other emotions: humiliation, anger and grief all coalesced into a dominating clamour for vengeance.

News of the mission's bloody fate spread with surprising speed. The nearest town of any consequence was Trois-Rivières, about twenty miles to the north-east on the far side of the St Lawrence. Its governor, Longueuil, received tidings of the attack around noon that same day. Governor General Vaudreuil at Montréal, and the Chevalier de Lévis at Jacques Cartier – respectively fifty miles westward and seventy miles to the east – both heard the news on the following day, 5 October; Bourlamaque, at far-flung Isle-aux-Noix, was told on the morning of the 6th.

When Rogers struck, Canada was fighting for its very survival. The men grappling with the unenviable task of keeping the territory French had much else to occupy their time and thoughts: the colony's inhabitants were starving and surly; one British army was already ensconced at Québec and another was daily expected to mount a major invasion from the south. But even amidst this escalating crisis, the destruction of St Francis warranted the attention of hard-pressed generals and officials.

It was clear that something had gone badly awry with the internal security of New France. Despite all the warnings and all the measures taken to intercept and exterminate them, the mysterious English had succeeded in landing a devastating blow. And that was not all: having ravaged St Francis with seeming impunity they had been permitted to go unmolested upon their way. The unknown enemy who had destroyed that venerable mission village, home to Canada's most loyal tribal allies, could not be allowed to escape unpunished. There were questions of honour and prestige to consider; not least of these was the régime's standing in the eyes of the 'domesticated' Indians who were so crucial to its defence: it was imperative that the attack be avenged.

No one believed this more strongly than Vaudreuil, who had learned of the disaster in dramatic fashion from the lips of five wounded survivors. Weary from their ordeal and subsequent journey, these pitiful refugees confirmed that their village had been totally destroyed. There were many slain or wounded, although they didn't yet know whether their missionary was amongst the dead or whether he'd been herded off into captivity. Following this interview, Vaudreuil wrote to Lévis: 'You will no doubt have heard that, yesterday morning, the detachment of just over 200 English, in pursuit of whom I had sent the strong Canadians as well as Bécancourt's and St Francis' Abenakis, were able to reach St Francis without being discovered and set fire to it.' He added: 'It appears that the Abenakis did not follow the route of the English, and instead took the Maska [Yamaska] route.'

It was at Vaudreuil's bidding that St Francis had been stripped of manpower in a misguided bid to ambush the raiders en route to their target; now he shrugged off all responsibility for what had subsequently befallen the defenceless village. If anything, he reasoned, the inhabitants had brought the misfortune down upon themselves. As Vaudreuil informed Bourlamaque, they had wantonly ignored warnings of impending danger. Indeed, not only the St Francis Indians but also the Frenchmen whom Vaudreuil sent to join them, had behaved irresponsibly: on the eve of the attack they had amused themselves by dancing late into the night; when the assault came at daybreak they remained fast asleep. It was all very unfortunate.

Vaudreuil clearly considered that he had done everything possible to prevent the disaster. With rather more justification, Bourlamaque adopted a similar view of his own role in events. As he wrote to Lévis, it was not *his* fault that St Francis had been destroyed, after all, had he not sent prompt warnings to Rigaud, and another to the missionary of St Francis himself? The chevalier reassured Bourlamaque that he had no reason to reproach himself; indeed, he'd taken all possible steps to warn that an enemy party was roaming across country towards the St Lawrence. Sadly, the brigadier's best efforts had been in vain; all appearances suggested that St Francis had succumbed to a surprise attack. Lévis, who had learned of that regrettable outcome by a courier from Longueuil, had no idea what had since become of the raiders. Having already got so far, it was possible that they might forge onwards to establish contact with the victorious British Army at Québec. The chevalier's own forces lay between them and *that* objective; and thanks to Bourlamaque's careful dispositions, Lévis remained sanguine that they would be cut off and destroyed if they turned back and sought to retrace their steps to Missisquoi Bay.

That first week of October 1759 had seen considerable activity at the island fortress of Isle-aux-Noix. Concerned at the growing likelihood of an advance by Amherst down Lake Champlain, Bourlamaque had recently recalled the four hundred men placed in ambush at the spot where Rogers had left his boats. However, when he learned that those same raiders who'd eluded Langis' trackers had since sacked St Francis, Bourlamaque lost no time in forming a fresh detachment of three hundred and sixteen soldiers, militia and Indians and sending them to Missisquoi Bay to await their return.

This same naive assumption that the enemy would attempt to regain Crown Point by retrieving their hidden boats also dominated Vaudreuil's thinking; in the days following the destruction of St Francis it became a fixation. Vaudreuil trusted that Bourlamaque would maintain at least five or six hundred men there, while the brigadier was also to conduct reconnaissance patrols ahead of where the withdrawing raiders might be expected to pass. So convinced was Vaudreuil that they would retreat via the bay that he sent Bourlamaque a reinforcement of Algonquins, Abenakis and Iroquois to bolster the existing force of Indians at Isle-aux-Noix. Writing to Lévis on 7 October, the governor general felt able to flatter himself that the English would be caught and cut to ribbons: some Abenakis were already in direct pursuit; those who escaped them must surely be snared in Bourlamaque's trap.

There was, of course, one major flaw in Vaudreuil's master plan: Rogers already knew that his whaleboats had been discovered and did not intend to return to them; instead, he'd long since resolved to retreat by way of Fort Number Four on the Connecticut River, and had already advised Amherst of that fact.

It had also been more difficult to organise a pursuit force than the governor general's confident despatches indicated. A contemporary French account of that year's campaign later reported that a party of two hundred Indians rushed to vengeance; but the surviving Abenakis were anything but hot on the heels of the raiders. In his personal journal, Lévis grumbled: 'It took a long time to send a group in pursuit. The savages were there but they were late.' Although a response force *was* mustered and sent after the raiders, it had been no easy matter to assemble the necessary manpower. Efforts to orchestrate a pursuit had begun immediately that news of the raid reached Trois-Rivières, but were hampered by a chronic dearth of fighting men in the vicinity. After scouring the city and the neighbouring community of Pointe-du-Lac, Longueuil could scrape together no more than sixty regulars and militia.

These three-score fighters compensated in experience and motivation for what they lacked in numbers. They also enjoyed the leadership of one of the most formidable soldiers in New France: having led the French and Indians who massacred Braddock's column on the Monongahela back in 1755, Captain Jean-Daniel Dumas was a partisan of impeccable pedigree. More recently, as adjutant general of the colonial troops, Dumas had commanded the *Compagnies Franches de la Marine* and militia during the siege of Québec; at the battle of the Plains, Dumas and his Canadians fought the dogged rearguard action that permitted so many of Montcalm's routed regulars to escape the field. If any man in Canada could be relied upon to visit retribution upon those who had burned St Francis, it was Dumas.

The captain and his posse set out from Trois-Rivières on 4 October, heading first for Yamaska. This was a logical enough gambit if Dumas hoped to augment his meagre force: according to the captives interrogated by Rogers earlier that same day, some two hundred French and fifteen Indians were still lying in wait for him there.

Dumas moved as swiftly as he could, but it was only on the afternoon of 5 October – more than a day after Rogers' men had left St Francis – that his command finally reached the smouldering ruins of the village. A few wary Abenaki men who emerged from the surrounding woods were persuaded to swell his force.

Amongst those who contemplated the wreckage of the mission was its priest, Father Roubaud. He'd arrived at Trois-Rivières on the eve of the raid, and was there to hear the shocking news that his church had been torched and dozens of his faithful congregation butchered or burned in their homes; he reached the scene at midnight on 4 October. The priest was shocked by what he found: 'Nothing was left of the village but embers. My house, the church, everything had been consumed,' he recalled. Even Roubaud, the respected spiritual leader, struggled to instil order amongst chaos. Two days passed before he was able to gather *his savages* in pursuit of their village's destroyers. The intrepid priest was already a hardened campaigner; having ministered to his Abenakis in the field at Fort William Henry and throughout the protracted siege of Québec, Roubaud was no stranger to danger and bloodshed, but as he kicked through the ashes of his parish he now had stronger personal cause to shepherd his flock as they once more followed the warpath.

WITH HIS SURVIVING COMMAND of one hundred and forty men, swollen now by knots of prisoners and freed captives, Major Rogers had set out from St Francis on the morning of 4 October. One newspaper report timed his departure at about 11.00 a.m.; this was already four hours after the major claimed the attack and destruction of the village to be completely over, and it is unlikely that he lingered any longer.

The route indicated on Rogers' own map shows that he marched in a south-easterly direction, moving up the St Francis River and remaining upon its north side. His course paralleled that of the river itself, but at some distance; the map's scale suggests that the detachment followed a line several miles to the north. Such a precaution not only minimised the risk of detection from enemy parties travelling the river by canoe, but also avoided the labour of negotiating bends in the river's winding course.

In his official report to Amherst, Rogers maintained that he 'marched the detachment eight days in a body.' At the end of that time they were drawing close to the northern head of Lake Memphremagog, some seventy miles from St Francis. At first glance, an average pace of nine miles a day seems unduly tardy for men with such pressing reasons for haste, but circumstances left little option. Rogers and his men were covering hard country, and the further they marched from St Francis the harder it became. By the fourth day at the latest they would have encountered the rugged foothills of the Appalachians. A trackless wilderness sprawled before them. Beneath the foliage of the endless forest lay an unforgiving landscape: jumbled mountains, slick boulders, sheer ravines, serpentine streams, concealed deadfalls and treacherous swamps. Such terrain represented tough going for soldiers who were rested, fit, warm and well fed. But Rogers and his chosen men enjoyed none of these advantages. They had now been *on party* for a full month. During that time their physical and mental endurance had been pushed to the limit by punishing forced marches, while their numbing fatigue was only exacerbated by the constant, nagging fear of ambush; and if the French and Indians caught them, those who died swiftly would be the lucky ones.

With their clothing and moccasins torn and mouldering from the countless miles traversed since quitting Crown Point camp, the major's men were now more vulnerable than ever to the cold, wet and stormy weather that had dogged the entire operation and which was worsening by the day. More baleful still was the spectre of starvation. Many of the raiders were hungry before they even reached St Francis, and the corn that they found there did not sustain them for long; if, as seems likely, this was stored on the husk or in kernel form, it would have been of limited value to men who lacked the time to grind it. In any event, even simple Johnny cakes prepared from a moistened mixture of ground corn, nuts and berries required baking, and fires were unthinkable for men who could not afford to betray their presence by a glimmer of flame or the sight and whiff of woodsmoke.

It was near Lake Memphremagog, Rogers reported, that 'provisions began to grow scarce'. This was an ominous development. In the eight days since quitting St Francis the detachment had marched hard, but they were not even halfway to their objective on the Connecticut River. The ration crisis was compounded by the fact that some of the raiders had found space in their packs for plunder at the expense of food. One of the regulars commanded by Lieutenant Dunbar later landed himself in trouble after allegedly claiming that Rogers had enforced a redistribution of the remaining corn: the major ordered the arrest of Sergeant Robert Lewis of Gage's Light Infantry 'for aspersing my Character by spreading a False Report that I took away from Dunbar's party provisions and gave it away to others who had loaded themselves with Plunder after the place was destroy'd.'

For all Rogers' efforts to prevent plundering by torching the village without delay, it is clear that some of his men succumbed to the lure of loot. This ranged from wampum necklaces and hard cash to the fabled silver Madonna of Chartres. According to Ogden, the greater part was discarded before they arrived at Connecticut River. Stories of riches taken at St Francis, and then jettisoned or cached by men for whom it had become a burden, were subsequently enshrined in the region's folklore. During the nineteenth century, a spate of finds suggested a veritable treasure trail along the reputed line of the raiders' retreat. In 1827 an incense holder was discovered on an island in the Watopeka River where it empties into the St Francis near modern Windsor, Québec; some eleven years later a local man uncovered a large image of a saint at the mouth of the Magog River; a pair of gleaming golden candlesticks were retrieved from a swamp near Lake Memphremagog; and a farmer who was lucky enough to find a hoard of gold coins used them to pay for a new barn. At the time, it was naturally assumed that these items reflected the spoils of St Francis. Some of the finds may indeed have come from the ransacked mission; but despite Father Aubery's best efforts to beautify his church, it was scarcely rich enough to explain them all. As Rogers' biographer John Cuneo observed, the yarns spun around the St Francis raid featured 'enough gold and silver candlestick holders to equip the most elaborate Old World cathedral'.

Men keen to distance themselves from pursuit enjoyed precious little opportunity to augment their dwindling food-stocks by halting to hunt along the way. In any event, the woods were empty of game: the bears whose far-ranging forays to the south had excited such comment during the previous month remained conspicuous by their absence. Such creatures as yet inhabited the bleak northern wastes were unlikely to remain oblivious to the blundering approach of seven-score exhausted and desperate men.

The worsening food crisis obliged Rogers to make a fateful decision. Within striking distance of Lake Memphremagog, he resolved to split his command. At a point approximating to the location of modern Sherbrooke, the major's map carries the following annotation: 'I parted hear the detachment into Small Companies'. Each group was given a capable guide. Some of the parties were ordered to head for the mouth of the Ammonoosuc River, the point where Rogers expected to find the provisions that he had requested from Amherst whilst outward bound for St Francis, others to make for Crown Point – the best route for hunting. It is probable that every party possessed at least one compass to aid their navigations; a British lieutenant who gave a detailed description of Rogers' men at Halifax, Nova Scotia, in 1757, noted that ranger officers usually carried 'a small compass fixed in the bottom of their powder-horns, by which to direct them, when they happen to lose themselves in the woods'.

Rogers parted his detachment in the hope that a number of smaller groups would stand a better chance of bagging game than one unwieldy body. This was a dangerous gamble: a single command of one hundred and forty men represented a formidable force, capable of rebuffing anything less than a sizeable war band; penny packets of twenty or ten offered easier pickings for Dumas' hunters. Prompted by stark necessity, the major's decision may have been bolstered by a conviction that he had now shaken off pursuit. If so, he misjudged the determination of the men unleashed upon his trail. The consequences were all too soon apparent.

Just two days after the detachment divided, the enemy struck. A twenty-strong party under Lieutenant Dunbar of Gage's Light Infantry was overhauled and overwhelmed. Dunbar was killed, along with ten of his men. Lieutenant Turner of the rangers was likewise reckoned amongst those slain or taken prisoner. The remaining eight men of the party made their escape, and later informed Rogers of what had befallen them.

At much the same time that Dunbar's command was obliterated, Ensign Avery of Fitche's Connecticut Regiment found the tracks of Rogers' own group and followed in his wake. However, as Rogers related, 'a party of the enemy came upon them, and took seven of his party prisoners.' Two of those captured managed to break free and rejoined the major the following morning. The ensign, with what remained of his squad, now marched in company with Rogers.

Nothing is known of the fate of Dunbar and his men beyond the sparse details that Rogers later related to Amherst. However, a remarkable documentary survival makes it possible to learn far more about the circumstances of the attack upon Avery's party, and the subsequent treatment of those who fell into enemy hands. One who lived to tell the tale left a vivid, if untutored, account of his ordeal.

After 'nine days travail in an unknown wilderness,' Corporal Frederick Curtiss remembered, he and his seven companions were in a poor way. Whatever corn they'd taken from St Francis had long since gone; at the close of the ninth day they were resting, 'being much enfeebled by travail & destitute of provision save mushrooms & beach leaves for four or five days then past.' In this pitiful state they were surprised by about twenty or thirty Indians who had been awaiting just such an opportunity to strike. Caught off guard, they only spotted the enemy when they were within a few feet of them; exhausted and famished, Curtiss and his comrades were in no condition to resist.

Whilst some of the Indians covered them with their guns, Curtiss recalled, 'others seized upon us [so] that we had us no opportunity for defence or flight & so made us all prisoners stript us of our cloathes & tyed us to trees.' One of the bound captives, a man named Ballard, was stabbed to death there and then. Curtiss and the others were untied and marched for about two miles before their captors made camp. In the course of the coming night, two of the prisoners succeeded in making their escape: these were the lucky pair whose deliverance was noted by Rogers.

On the following day, Curtiss and the others continued to a spot where the Indians went about building their canoes. This was the last occasion upon which Curtiss saw his fellow prisoners alive, with the exception of one other man, Moses Jones. The Indians now prepared their canoes for the return trip to St Francis. Curtiss was understandably vague regarding geographical details, but it seems likely that they travelled via the St Francis River itself. As soon as the canoes were loaded they departed, one after the other. It was fortunate for Curtiss that he was not amongst the first to embark. In fact, his canoe was the last of all, 'in which went four Indians & an Indian Inglishman who first seized me.' This startling revelation confirms that St Francis hosted the most extreme form of the 'white Indian' phenomenon: renegades who not only adopted the Indians' lifestyle, but who fought alongside them against their own countrymen.

Throughout what must have proved a harrowing journey, Curtiss remained fast-bound. If his captors retained any rations, they were disinclined to share them; the trip lasted for five long days and during this time he was again obliged to resort to his frugal woodland diet of mushrooms and beech leaves. Curtiss returned to the scorched ruins of St Francis – the village he had so recently helped to destroy – during the hours of darkness. Here, a grim sight met his eyes. Those prisoners who arrived before him, during daylight, had fared badly: five of them now lay dead on the ground. An onlooker, described only as a Dutchman, explained that these men had been *killed outright.*

According to an anonymous French journal, the pursuing Indians who descended upon Rogers' parties 'massacred some forty and carried off 10 prisoners to their village'. At St Francis, the same account maintained, some of these captives 'fell a victim to the fury of the Indian women, notwithstanding the efforts the Canadians could make to save them.' All of this suggests a frenzied lynching at the hands of a mob of grieving relatives; here was no protracted and ritualistic torture reminiscent of the more lurid passages of the New England captivity narratives or the Jesuit *Relations*, but something far more spontaneous.

It seemed at first as if Frederick Curtiss was destined to join the bloodied corpses that lay sprawled before him. The sober words of his testimony do nothing to diminish the drama of the moment: 'Upon seeing me the Indians which were numerously gathered to the place demanded me to be Slain right out. But my indian master being a Captain among them as he told me, who Could Talk inglish Well, he answerd them no, [saying] Let it alone till morning. His Squaw also Interposed for me & Quieted them for ye present time.'

Momentarily satisfied, the Abenakis lay down to sleep. Knowing that Curtiss was to be sacrificed in the morning, the Dutchman was moved to pity; he hired the same renegade Englishman who had first laid hold of the corporal to carry him off by canoe that night. His Indian *master and mistress* were privy to the plan and gave it their blessing. There could be no better illustration of the complex web of relationships and loyalties embraced within the hybrid village of St Francis: Curtiss, the 'English' soldier, had been snared by a fellow countryman living amongst the Abenakis; yet it was Indians with ample reason to hate him who helped to save his life.

So, having remained at the site of the village for just three night-marish hours, Curtiss was paddled some four or five miles to a French settlement – probably that located where the St Francis River emptied into Lake St Pierre – and there he surrendered himself to the protection of the inhabitants.

But the ordeal of Frederick Curtiss was not yet over. Determined upon exacting vengeance, several Abenakis pursued him to the house where he had sought refuge. Entering the building, one of them attempted to knife him. Curtiss dodged the blade. He fled to the side of the dwelling, where the French owner unlocked a door to another room, hustled him inside and then bolted it shut. His fellow survivor Moses Jones was brought to the same safe house. Two days later the two fugitives were carried by water down to Trois-Rivières; their subsequent confinement was close, but it finally placed them beyond the reach of those who sought to avenge the dead of St Francis.

THE PARTIES LED BY AVERY and Dunbar were run to ground as they headed for the appointed rendezvous on the Connecticut River; their assailants likely belonged to the force led by Dumas. After all the hardships of a long and punishing chase they at least enjoyed the satisfaction of the kill; Bourlamaque's troops, sent out after tidings of the raid first reached his camp at Isle-aux-Noix, hunted for their quarry in vain.

According to the detailed journal kept by Captain Méloizes of *la Marine*, four days after this force left camp a militiaman arrived and reported that the detachment had given up all hope of the enemy raiders returning to their whaleboats at Missisquoi Bay. Its commander, that experienced guerrilla-fighter Ensign Langis, was instead attempting to get ahead of the English, thereby cutting their likely route to Crown Point. He intended to march for two days and then lie in wait for them.

On 14 October, eight days after setting out, Langis' Indians and Canadians returned to camp. They brought vexing news: everything indicated that the hostile party had *already* passed on its way. The tracks of one small band of some nine to ten men were discovered extending for four to five leagues in a southerly direction, as if making for Crown Point. They also found an old campfire; the embers were still warm, but the men who had kindled it were gone. Later that day the rest of the crestfallen detachment came in.

Though Langis' frustrated scouts clearly believed that the tracks they detected belonged to the men who had burned St Francis, this was scarcely possible. Rogers had not divided his command until he was near Lake Memphremagog: how could any of his parties have covered the intervening wilderness, to reach a point some distance south of Missisquoi Bay, just two days later? It is far more likely that the mysterious tracks belonged to another British party – perhaps one of the ranger patrols that were routinely despatched from Crown Point to gather intelligence regarding French dispositions. On 9 October, Amherst had pushed out two such scouts, each consisting of a sergeant and six men, to trawl the east and west sides of Isle-aux-Noix for a prisoner capable of providing information.

Despite their failure to catch the English raiders, Bourlamaque was no doubt grateful for the safe return of Langis' men. By the time they arrived back in camp the brigadier's attention was firmly fixed upon an even more pressing matter: Amherst had finally resumed his lumbering assault upon New France.

ON THE AFTERNOON OF 11 October, at much the same time that Robert Rogers made the fateful decision to split his command, Major-General Jeffery Amherst led his Grand Army down Lake Champlain.

At long last the fighting ships upon which his security depended had been completed. Leaving all his provincial regiments to hold the burgeoning fort of Crown Point, the general embarked his regulars, rangers and Indians – a compact field force of some 4,500 men. Despite the advanced season Amherst was resolved to try to demolish the French fleet; in addition, as he explained to Lord Ligonier, he retained some hopes of staging a diversionary attack upon Isle-aux-Noix, and then detaching half his force to surprise Montréal.

Screened by Gage's Light Infantry, the army embarked in bateaux and proceeded down the lake in four columns; they were escorted by two new vessels that the general reckoned carried sufficient firepower to tackle the French flotilla – the *Duke of Cumberland* brig, and the *Boscawen* sloop. Both sailed with a fair wind to scour the lake for the enemy. The army rowed in their wake, and at night followed a lantern hoisted aboard the floating artillery platform, or radeau, that marked the centre of the whole flotilla; this carried Amherst himself and was named the *Ligonier* in honour of his venerable mentor back in Whitehall.

Next day the sound of gunfire prompted rumours that the rival naval squadrons had clashed; gunshots there'd certainly been, but they were directed at an unlucky boatload of Highlanders who strayed too close to the French ships and were captured for their pains. With darkness the weather worsened; the wind blew so hard that Amherst ordered his men to seek shelter in a bay on the western shore. On 13 October, the army remained stymied whilst a storm raged all day. Meanwhile, the British brig and sloop had not been idle. Amherst received letters from the naval commodore, Captain Loring, and his own vigorous aide-de-camp, Captain Abercrombie; at daybreak on 12 October, when about halfway down the lake, they had spotted the French schooner and given chase. Both British ships promptly ran aground, but thankfully got off again. Their lookouts then noticed the enemy's sloops, which they had unknowingly passed in the night; these now lay between them and Amherst's landlocked redcoats. The *Cumberland* and *Boscawen* corralled them within the confines of another west shore bay, then dropped anchor to block their escape. Next day British boats inched forward to investigate; they discovered that the French had scuttled two of their sloops and run the third aground. The crews had escaped overland. The flagship *La Vigilant* remained at large, although Loring hoped to intercept her before she could reach the refuge of Isle-aux-Noix.

Lake Champlain now unleashed its full force upon Amherst's armada. On 15 October foul weather made the lake impassable for boats. The general reported that the waves were *like the Sea in a Gale of Wind*; he could only hope that the wind would drop, as there was no time to lose. It was also growing colder; that night it froze. On 17 October the same contrary wind continued to blow; two whaleboats sent to seek Captain Loring could make no headway and were obliged to return. The following day, Amherst was finally able to move forward as far as the bay where the sloops had been netted, but this marked the limit of the army's advance. A boat now arrived from Crown Point with a letter from New York's Lieutenant Governor De Lancey. It brought the news that Amherst and his men had been awaiting for so long: a month after the event they finally learned that Québec was in British hands.

Those who had assumed that tidings of Wolfe's unexpected victory would spur the commander-in-chief to complete the conquest of Canada without delay were to be disappointed. Instead, Amherst resolved to end his offensive there and then. He explained his reasoning in his end-of-campaign despatch to Prime Minister Pitt: the wind was northerly and contrary; as winter was now setting in he determined not to lose time on the lake by attempting to reach Isle-aux-Noix, where he would arrive too late in the season to force the enemy from their *fixed Post*. He would instead return to Crown Point and strive to complete the fort before the troops dispersed to their winter quarters.

In his personal journal, Amherst admitted a more telling reason for turning back – one that reflected his pragmatic response to the news of Québec's fall. This would 'of course bring Mons de Vaudreuil & the whole Army to Montreal so that I shall decline my intended operations . . .' Amherst had no intention of pitting himself against an enemy who could be swiftly reinforced. It was the response of a cautious general, careful to keep what he already held rather than risk his field army, and all that summer's gains, on a hazardous winter campaign. Although understandable, Amherst's withdrawal ended the campaign on an inglorious note. His reaction suggests that he never intended to offer Wolfe the wholehearted support he'd been led to expect; it was fortunate for Amherst that the fiery hero of Québec did not live to demand an explanation from him.

By 21 October, Amherst and his army were back safely at Crown Point; there, as he noticed with evident satisfaction, the fortress was *going on pretty well*. At the other end of the lake, Brigadier Bourlamaque could scarcely believe that the long-feared Anglo-American offensive had come to nought. Knowing the ease with which his position could be outflanked, the brigadier was incredulous that Amherst had let him off the hook so lightly. He wrote to Lévis: 'I cannot see how he will keep his post: he is making a foolish campaign.'

Although Amherst did not know it, the approach of his ships and leading bateaux to within sight of Isle-aux-Noix had caused a serious alarm. Militiamen recently discharged from the army and returned to their farms had been recalled to meet the emergency; already exhausted by the summer's campaign, they only marched with extreme reluctance. Luckily, Amherst failed to push onwards; and it was soon apparent that he had no intention of returning that season.

Summarising the year's events in a despatch to his government, Bourlamaque conceded that New France had suffered misfortunes on her frontiers, which had contracted following the fall of Niagara and Québec. But *he* at least had the satisfaction of not sharing in those disasters and of successfully carrying out the plan of defence entrusted to him. In obedience to instructions, Carillon and St Frédéric had been abandoned, but the British had made no further headway on Lake Champlain. Thanks to unheard of labour, in which the troops had co-operated with the utmost good will, Bourlamaque had been able to 'render the post of Isle-aux-Noix sufficiently imposing to stay the progress of an army so superior and which did not want for any of the means to operate.'

Bourlamaque neglected to mention the bold enemy force that had punctured his defensive screen and marched onwards to burn St Francis; but with the threat from Amherst now receded for the winter, the brigadier's long-suffering army was well placed to settle the score with any of those raiders who might yet chance to straggle their way.

THE SAME HARSH WEATHER that had obliged Amherst's host to quit the storm-lashed surface of Lake Champlain added to the miseries of Rogers' men as they reeled across the uncharted wilderness of what is now north-eastern Vermont. Their French and Indian pursuers endured the same grim conditions. Some, like those who had bushwhacked Corporal Curtiss and his weary companions, turned back, content with their haul of scalps and captives. Others maintained the chase.

On 24 October, some three weeks after the destruction of St Francis, rumours reached Captain Méloizes at Isle-aux-Noix that the English raiders had been attacked; they'd lost fifty scalps, and the survivors remained under pursuit. This information came from the Indians, but was clarified four days later with the arrival of Captain Deganes, the Adjutant of Trois-Rivières, at the head of nineteen soldiers and thirty-three militiamen. The captain, who had apparently joined the original pursuit force cobbled together under the leadership of Dumas, provided the first reliable intelligence of the raiders to reach Bourlamaque's army. In his diary Méloizes wrote: 'He confirms the news of the chase of the English detachment that had attacked St Francis. This party divided itself into three bands in order to return later. One band of 35 was encountered and exterminated. Another band is being pursued; that group includes Rogers. As for the third group, it is not expected that one will be able to encounter them.'

Deganes' report indicated that the pursuit had been maintained with considerable determination; Abenaki oral tradition, presumably originating in the testimony of a captive, tells that this constant pressure prevented the hounded rangers from halting to hunt, and forced them to subsist on yellow lily roots. Some of the first hunters to join the chase had returned after inflicting casualties upon isolated groups of raiders; but others had continued, spurred on by the goal of catching Rogers himself. The major's name had not featured in previous French despatches: it was only after the pursuers took prisoners that they realised just *who* they were dealing with.

For all their zeal, the French and Indian bands that dogged Rogers' heels never caught up with him. Neither the major's own party or the others heading for the pre-arranged muster point on the Connecticut, succumbed to the fate of their comrades under Dunbar and Avery. Though there were no further losses to the bullets and blades of vengeful Abenakis and Frenchmen, there remained other enemies to be confronted. As Frederick Curtiss and Moses Jones had discovered, even captivity allowed some slim chance of survival; but the foes that continued to face Rogers and his men were implacable, and incapable of extending mercy towards those who sought to defy them. Arrayed in formidable alliance, the forces of nature now demanded an awful reckoning of their own.

A nightmarish ordeal ensued. Unsurprisingly, the accounts left by those who survived it are impressionistic and fragmentary. Men delirious from the effects of exposure, exhaustion and starvation were in no position to provide a meticulous daily chronicle of their experiences; and in their struggle for life, some behaved in ways that they would later try to forget. Rogers himself was close-mouthed: in his *Journals*, he characterised the trek to the Connecticut as 'many days tedious march over steep rocky mountains or thro' wet dirty swamps, with the terrible attendants of fatigue and hunger.'

Rogers had divided his party in the hope that smaller groups would stand a better chance of sustaining themselves by hunting, but as the *New-York Gazette* reported, there was little game to be had; indeed they saw scarcely any. To survive they were obliged to search for roots, bark and toadstools. Some gnawed upon old beaver skins and, in a desperate search for sustenance, even ate the flesh remaining on the scalps they had taken from the slain villagers of St Francis. In these grim circumstances, they considered themselves lucky when they could get one partridge between ten men a day.

Robert Kirkwood, who claimed to have been one of Rogers' own party, highlighted the hardships they underwent. All attempts to hunt game succeeded badly; in their weakened state they were reduced to making short marches, being much afflicted with cold and hunger. In combination, the harsh climate and punishing terrain forced a halt in the retreat: 'the deepness of the snow and the swampness of the country, made it impossible for us to stir for several days,' Kirkwood wrote. 'During this miserable period, we were obliged to scrape under the snow for acorns, and even to eat our shoes and belts, and broil our powder-horns and thought it delicious eating.'

As the major and his gaunt comrades tottered laboriously closer to the Connecticut, their minds were increasingly dominated by one thought: the supplies awaiting them at its junction with the Wells and Ammonoosuc. If all went to plan they would soon be eating their fill of civilised rations: biscuit and salt pork washed down with thick and potent New England rum. Wholesome victuals, and the fires and shelter that would surely be provided by the men sent to meet them, would warm new life into their starved, numbed and weary bodies. As men like private Andrew McNeal of the Inniskilling Regiment and ranger Andrew Wansant later stated, this was an alluring prospect that Rogers dangled before them in an effort to bolster their failing spirits. Indeed, 'Major Rogers frequently told them, upon their March, that they would meet with Provisions upon their Arrival there.'

Rogers was a leader who spared no effort to maintain the morale of his men. Neither did he shirk the physical burdens of command: he deliberately included the weakest men of the detachment within his own party, so that he could supply and support them himself. Amongst these invalids was the wounded Captain Ogden, whom the major often took on his back to carry him through rivers. Now, more than ever, the fate of Rogers' men depended upon his own courage and endurance.

MUCH INK HAS BEEN spilled in attempting to plot the paths followed by Rogers and his dispersed parties on their return from St Francis. Amidst all the speculation, Rogers' manuscript map is the sole document of value. The dotted line labelled *the Way I Came home*, shows the major's own route. He skirted the eastern shore of Lake Memphremagog, passing through what he described as *Chesnut Land*, and crossing several rivers feeding into its waters. He continued in a south-easterly direction, hugging the east side of Lake Willoughby beneath the glowering bulk of Mount Pisgah; neither of these features then bore a name, but their shape and location, as rendered on the major's map, are unmistakeable. This brought Rogers close to the west branch of the Passumpsic River; by following it, he could have reached the Passumpsic itself, and then continued to its junction with the Connecticut some ten miles above the designated rendezvous point. Tradition maintains that Rogers succumbed to the lure of that route; but his map tells a different story. It shows that he swerved in a south-westerly direction, so giving the Passumpsic a wide berth. The major's reasons for avoiding the shorter route are not hard to fathom; the obvious merits of the Passumpsic Valley – which, centuries later, formed the template for the modern US Route 5 – had long attracted Abenakis travelling southwards to farm the fertile Lower Cowass Intervales or raid the New Hampshire frontier: it was a natural conduit for war parties – and a high-risk ambush zone to be avoided at all costs.

With the Passumpsic kept at a wary ten to fifteen miles on his left, Rogers marched on until he encountered the north branch of the Wells River. He followed this to the Wells then swung south-east, proceeding along the north bank opposite Whitcher Mountain and its jostling neighbours. From there, he traced the Wells to its junction with the Ammonoosuc and the Connecticut; this, near the site of modern Woodsville, New Hampshire, was the appointed rendezvous where supplies were expected.

The major's map depicts the route taken by his own party and those stragglers who followed upon his trail. Attempts to provide detailed itineraries for other groups remain, at best, no more than educated guesswork. Yet local tradition, and the occasional tantalising scrap of anecdotal evidence, provides some clues. These suggest that the haggard bands making for the mustering point on the Connecticut fanned out from Lake Memphremagog. Splayed like the fingers of hands raised in supplication, some struck the river above the designated spot, others below.

One or more bands probably trickled down the step-like sequence of lakes and ponds leading from Memphremagog to the Nulhegan River. The Nulhegan's meeting with the Connecticut, some sixty-five miles above Rogers' specified rendezvous, lay upon the Upper Cowass Intervales. According to one early nineteenth-century account, some of the men who arrived there mistook it for the *Lower* Cowass. Benjamin Bradley, the same formidable New Hampshire ranger who had barged in upon the slumbering inhabitants of St Francis, observed that if he were in his full strength, it would take him just three days to reach his father's house. Bradley took a compass bearing; had he been where he thought he was, this would have led him to the Merrimack River, and so to home. But when taken at the *Upper* Cowass, the same bearing drew him towards the bleak wilderness of the White Mountains. Bradley left the party, accompanied by another ranger and *a Mulatto man*. Next year, the story continues, hunters found a man's bones in Jefferson, on the edge of the White Mountains. Set before the lone skeleton was a pyramid of fire-blackened sticks; scattered about were silver brooches and wampum beads. What remained of the man's hair was long, and tied with a leather ribbon such as Bradley wore. Of his two companions there was no sign.

Although Rogers himself took pains to avoid it, other members of his command no doubt wandered the tempting Passumpsic route. One of the parties, under the hard-bitten ranger Captain Joseph Wait, apparently overshot the rendezvous, striking the Connecticut some twelve miles below. Having survived the bloody Battle on Snowshoes, Wait was not the kind of man to give up easily. Tradition relates that he was fortunate enough to shoot a deer; after he and his men had satisfied their own hunger and taken some of the meat, they thoughtfully strung what remained of the carcass on trees, for the use of any others of Rogers' men who might take that route. By way of explanation, Wait carved his name on one of the trees from which the venison was suspended. This stood near a small river running into the Connecticut; the waterway is known as Wait's River to this day.

ROGERS AND HIS GROUP reached the pre-arranged rendezvous on 20 October. In their exhausted state it had taken them nine hard days to cover the one hundred miles from the point where the detachment divided.

As the long march ground inexorably onwards, it was only the prospect of food, warmth and rest that had enabled them to continue placing one foot in front of another. But when they finally reached their goal there was no one to be seen. A party had most certainly been there, and recently, for a fire was still burning; but whoever had kindled that blaze was now gone. What was far worse, they had taken their provisions with them.

Hearing guns fired at a distance down the Connecticut River, Rogers and his people responded in a desperate effort to bring them back. But the crashing reports brought no reply from the empty wilderness. It was a crushing disappointment. In his *Journals*, Rogers wrote bitterly: 'it is hardly possible to describe the grief and consternation of those of us who came to Coos Intervales . . . to find that here was no relief for us, where we had encouraged ourselves that we should find it, and have our distresses alleviated.' What made the blow all the harder to endure was the clear evidence that a party *had* been waiting for them, but hadn't stayed long enough.

By a cruel stroke of fate, as Rogers later learned to his chagrin, the relief party had left the spot just two hours before he arrived; they even heard his guns, but their commander, Lieutenant Samuel Stevens, took them for the enemy, and feared to return.

What had gone wrong? In obedience to Amherst's instructions, on 4 October Stevens had left Crown Point for Fort Number Four. There, he assembled the specified provisions and the men required to transport them to the mouth of the Ammonoosuc. Stevens later claimed that he journeyed as far as the Lower Cowass Intervales then halted at a distance of some three miles by land from the appointed spot. He judged that 'it would be as well to stop there, and not endanger the Provisions by Carrying them higher up a rapid stream.' Making camp, Stevens and his party went daily to the Wells River and fired their guns, but there was no sign of Rogers. From what Lieutenant McMullen had reported on returning from the major's party, Stevens believed that Rogers should already have reached the rendezvous, and decided against waiting any longer. By 30 October, Stevens was back at Crown Point. He told Amherst there was no probability that Rogers would ever come back that way. The general was not so sure, noting in his journal that Stevens should have waited longer.

For some of Rogers' emaciated men, the lieutenant's decision was fatal. Had Stevens delayed but a day – or even a few hours – longer, Rogers believed, he would have saved the lives of a number of men who perished in the woods.

Of all the many hardships they had endured in the six weeks since setting out from Crown Point, this last was the hardest to bear. Rogers recalled: 'Our distress upon this occasion was truly inexpressible; our spirits, greatly depressed by the hunger and fatigues we had already suffered, now almost entirely sunk within us, seeing no resource left, nor any reasonable ground to hope that we should escape a most miserable death by famine.'

Both those who had reached the deserted rendezvous, and the others who still sought a path towards it through the labyrinthine wilderness, now began to despair. The contemporary ballad of the retreat summarised their plight in stark and powerful words: 'these men did grieve and mourn and cry, wee in these howling woods must dy.'

But there was an alternative to howling and dying, and some took it. One of the bands that continued to wander aimlessly through the trackless woods was commanded by ranger Lieutenant George Campbell. At one point in their journey, Campbell recalled, he and his men spent four days without any kind of sustenance. With no idea where they were, and despairing of assistance, some now lost their senses. Others, 'who could no longer bear the keen pangs of an empty stomach, attempted to eat their own excrements.' They had already cooked and eaten their leather cartridge boxes. On 28 October, when they were more than three weeks out from St Francis, Campbell's party crossed a small river that was partially dammed by logs. Here they discovered several scalped and mangled bodies, which they assumed to be the remains of some of their comrades. This ghastly find proved their salvation. Upon them, as Campbell later told the historian Thomas Mante, 'they fell like Cannibals, and devoured part of them raw; their impatience being too great to wait the kindling of a fire to dress it by. When they had thus abated the excruciating pangs they before endured, they carefully collected the fragments, and carried them off.'

The slide into savagery was slow but inexorable. David Evans of Concord, who had been a ranger sergeant on the raid, remembered suffering every hardship men could endure. When their distresses were greatest, he said, they hardly deserved the name of human beings. Like others, Evans recollected how powder horns, bullet pouches and leather accoutrements were all successively boiled and eaten in a futile bid to combat gnawing hunger pains. One night, as the other men lay sleeping, Evans' own hunger kept him awake. Spotting a large knapsack belonging to one of his comrades, he rummaged through it in hopes of finding some last morsel. Inside were three human heads. Overcoming his revulsion, he stealthily 'cut a piece from one of them, broiled and eat it, while the men continued to sleep.' When he told his story, Evans must have been a very old man, but the decades had done nothing to diminish the guilty horror he felt upon recalling the episode; indeed, 'he would die with hunger, before he would do the like again'.

For such crazed and desperate men, it was but one step from devouring the dead to killing and consuming the living. The raiders had taken a handful of prisoners from amongst the villagers of St Francis; at least two of them – a grown woman and a young boy – were butchered for food.

In a tragic twist to the story of Chief Joseph-Louis Gill, these victims probably included both his spouse Marie-Jeanne, and his son Xavier. Judge Charles Gill, a descendant of Joseph-Louis by his second wife, related the tradition that Marie-Jeanne was murdered and eaten by her Indian captors; this may refer to the involvement of Rogers' Stockbridge

Mahicans. After cooking the mother's flesh in a pot, they forced her sons to partake of the meal. Beyond all doubt, wrote the learned judge, was the fact that neither Marie-Jeanne nor Xavier survived captivity at the hands of the men who destroyed St Francis.

The murder and cannibalism of an Indian woman also feature in the *Memoirs* of Robert Kirkwood. She had been captured on the evening following the destruction of the village, being loaded with provisions from *St Fransway*. In the coming days of strenuous marching, Kirkwood wrote, this prisoner proved of great service. Not only was she physically strong, and able to carry more than any three of Rogers' men, but she also displayed an admirable stoicism in the face of danger. Indeed, Kirkwood added, 'she bore it nobly, and was of infinite service in gathering roots and herbs, which she was better acquainted with, as she was bred among such hardships.'

Kirkwood observed that the captive was plump, having more flesh upon her than five of them. He claimed that Major Rogers several times proposed to *make away with her*, although the rest of the party would not consent. But Rogers was stronger, and in better spirits, than any of his men. When starvation reduced them to the greatest extremity, the major took matters into his own hands. Kirkwood told how Rogers 'followed the squaw who was gone out to gather roots, and there he kill'd and cut her up, and brought her to our fire, where he divided and cast lots for the shares which were distributed to each an equal part; we then broiled and eat the most of her; and received great strength thereby.'

It is easy to dismiss Kirkwood's account as a lurid figment of the author's imagination. Yet his style is simple and direct; it scarcely savours of a deliberate attempt to shock or titillate. Neither this, nor any other episode of cannibalism during the retreat from St Francis, is mentioned in the pages of Rogers' *Journals* or in newspaper accounts: the butchering and consumption of captive women and children – despite express directions that such non-combatants should be spared – was rather more than the fastidious Amherst could be expected to stomach.

Though Kirkwood's anecdote paints Rogers in a singularly ruthless light, it leaves no doubt that he alone possessed the physical strength and moral courage to keep his men alive. Of this, the major's actions were soon to provide further, unequivocal evidence.

FOR ROGERS, NO LESS THAN for his men, the crushing disappointment at the Wells River had a devastating impact; coming after so much toil, in which he had borne the added responsibility of command, it apparently resulted in temporary physical and mental collapse. Although Rogers resolved to do all he could to save what remained of his command by pressing onwards to Fort Number Four and seeking help, it was a full week before he was able to leave. Most of his men were now too feeble to go any further. He left them to grub about for 'such wretched subsistence as the barren wilderness could afford.' This consisted of 'groundnuts and lily roots, which being cleaned and boiled will serve to preserve life.' Rogers taught this crucial survival technique to Lieutenant Grant, who was left in charge of the skeletal party; he then quit his men with the promise that assistance would reach them within ten days.

Accompanied only by Captain Ogden – a tough customer who was now recovered from his wounds – an unnamed ranger, and Chief Gill's captive son Antoine, the major embarked upon a raft constructed from dry pine trees. As the Connecticut's current swirled this wretched vessel along in midstream, Rogers and his motley crew struggled to steer a course using crude paddles made from saplings or split and hewn *spires*.

On the second day of the trip they reached the White River Falls, and only narrowly escaped being swept over them along with their raft. Dragging themselves ashore, they made their way to the base of the rapids. Whilst Ogden and the ranger hunted for red squirrels, and were lucky enough to bag a partridge, Rogers laboured to build a new raft for the onward journey. Unable to fell trees with an axe, he instead brought them down by kindling fires at their bases, and thence at intervals along the trunks until he had enough logs of the correct length.

This task consumed the third day of the trip. Next day the raft was assembled, the four boarded, and were once again carried along by the

Connecticut's current. Ever mindful of the fate of their first raft, and aware that they would be unable to make a third, upon approaching the Ottaquechee Falls they cautiously made for the bank. Ogden tethered the raft using a rope made from plaited hazel bushes, then gradually lowered it down the fifty-yard falls. Rogers himself waited at the bottom, ready to swim through the icy waters to board the crude craft and paddle it ashore. The major reported the outcome in his customary terse fashion: 'I had the good fortune to succeed, and the next morning we embarked, and floated down the stream to within a small distance of No. 4 where we found some men cutting timber, who gave us the first relief, and assisted us to the fort . . .'

It was 31 October, 1759. When he arrived at Fort Number Four, so an eyewitness reported, Rogers was *scarcely able to walk after his fatigues*. Despite his exhaustion, he lost no time in despatching a canoe full of provisions to his men; the *New-Hampshire Gazette* reported that this was sent off just half an hour after his arrival. It reached the starving band four days later, 'the tenth after I left them,' as the major noted. He had honoured his pledge.

The following day, Rogers compiled his report of the raid for General Amherst; the next, 2 November, he returned up the Connecticut with more provision-laden canoes. Hiring some of the inhabitants to help him, the major hoped to meet others of his party that might be coming in that way. His efforts were rewarded. Two days later, George Campbell's band – which had spent the past week surviving on scraps of human flesh, roots and a squirrel – encountered one of the major's boats; this chance meeting saved them, and they arrived at Fort Number Four on 7 November. Rogers himself was relieved to encounter the parties led by lieutenants Abernathan Cargill, Jacob Farrington and Sergeant Evans. Stray survivors from Dunbar's ambushed band also drifted in. In an effort to help others who might have veered far eastwards across New Hampshire, the major sent couriers to Suncook and Penacook on the Merrimack River with orders that provisions be sent for their relief. Having done all that a man could do, he returned to Fort Number Four.

ROBERT ROGERS REMAINED at Fort Number Four for several days, hoping to provide assistance to any of his exhausted men who turned up. But it was not only on the Connecticut that survivors from the major's detachment were pursuing tortuous paths to safety. Far to the west, the parties ordered to make for Crown Point were not yet home and dry.

These groups experienced mixed fortunes. Remarkably, one of them came in without the loss of a man, returning by the same route that the raiders had earlier followed on their way to St Francis. According to Rogers himself, this party was guided by an Indian named Philip, later a chief of the Pequawket, or Pigwacket, tribe. His record of service in the rangers suggests that this honour was well deserved; he was reputedly the first man of Amherst's army to enter Louisbourg when that fortress was captured in 1758.

But another band that trekked westward across country from Lake Memphremagog by way of the Missisquoi River was not so lucky. Owing to the survival of several very different but complementary accounts, the fate of this party can be reconstructed with unusual confidence. The story that emerges not only highlights the appalling hardships suffered by the raiders and their captives alike, but also offers further evidence that St Francis provided a veritable nursery for renegades.

By mid-October of 1759, the French at Isle-aux-Noix were convinced that Rogers' men had given them the slip. On 2 November reports arrived that suggested otherwise. That day, as the diligent Captain Méloizes recorded, Monsieur Charles de Sabrevois of *la Marine* came in from Missisquoi Bay, where he had been hunting with the Indians. He told Brigadier Bourlamaque that women crossing the bay in bark canoes had spotted strangers stalking ducks. Another group of Indians heading overland noticed smoke rising from the abandoned Missisquoi fort. Approaching stealthily, they heard English voices and a loud noise like that made when grinding Indian corn. That same afternoon, the trusty Langis was despatched to investigate at the head of a score of Indians. Hot on his heels went Monsieur Outlas with another band of forty-five regulars and militia. This time they did not return empty-handed. Several hours later the camp was alerted by gunshots and the whoops of Indians; the detachment brought in five English prisoners. These men had come from St Francis; they had left ten others behind them, four of whom were dying of hunger and suffering.

Bourlamaque told Lévis that these prisoners were both lost and famished, having almost no food when they left St Francis. They revealed that Rogers had marched for the Connecticut River and must have reached it long since; he never had intended to return to his boats in the bay.

The starving band included Robert Lewis of Gage's Light Infantry – the same sergeant who incurred Rogers' wrath for claiming that he ordered a redistribution of rations – and Josiah Malone of the rangers. Their harrowing experiences are preserved in the evidence they gave to a court martial held upon a renegade named Jonathan Barns, alias Burns. A former soldier in the service of Massachusetts, he was 'Accused of being a Traytor to his Country, and being in Arms against it.' The nature of Barns' treason branded him an unusually heinous offender: Lewis, Malone and other survivors of the separated parties of Major Rogers' detachment all testified that he had joined their French and Indian pursuers, committing sundry cruelties upon them and their comrades.

Lewis and Malone first encountered Barns when they were being taken to Isle-aux-Noix; he was the foremost of a party of French and Indians, and armed like the rest. Lewis had already been stripped of almost everything save his leggings; Barns now demanded those too. The sergeant was in the custody of the French regulars and an officer shooed his tormentor away, but not before Barns had warned him to be ready to guide another party in search of survivors, because *his Father, the Indian Captain*, desired it.

Lewis escaped this task by feigning sickness; Malone was not so fortunate. He had divulged that another ten or eleven of Rogers' men remained in the area, and a fresh party set out to find them. It included Christopher Proudfoot, one of Rogers' Rangers who had been captured near Ticonderoga that March, and who was then living with the Missisquoi Abenakis. They discovered another group of English, sheltering in a hut and betrayed by the light of their campfire. The Indians planned to surround them and then open fire, but Malone insisted that such violence was unnecessary as their quarry were incapable of resistance. The two 'Englishmen' – the renegade Barns and the captive Proudfoot – were sent to offer them quarter. Heavily outnumbered, James Brown of Gage's regiment and his two companions surrendered; Brown remembered that they were ordered to relinquish their packs, weapons and the plunder they had got at St Francis; all were taken by canoe to the Missisquoi stockade. The next day, Proudfoot stated, they set out once more, this time to hunt a squad commanded by Sergeant Delanoe; he and two others were found by some prowling Ottawas and also brought to the fort.

Proudfoot swore to what happened next: 'an English Girl, who had been taken some time before, by the Indians, & had been Carried off from St Francis by Serjt. Delanoe's party, Informed the Indians that this Party had killed & eat a Little Boy Carried off by them from the same Place.'

Although 'rescued' by her own kind, this captive had demonstrated exactly where her loyalties now lay. According to Méloizes' journal, two of the men who had plucked her from St Francis were found to be carrying human flesh. Their throats were cut on the spot. Private Brown testified that all *three* were slain in lieu of the boy they had killed for food. Two of their scalps were brought into Isle-aux-Noix on the evening of 7 November; Barns kept the third. This dripping trophy was dashed in the face of an English prisoner named Todd. When Malone objected, Barns grabbed a hoe and struck him until the blood ran from his head. An Indian woman intervened to stop the beating and Proudfoot managed to wrestle the implement from Barns' grasp; he now flourished the fresh scalp in Malone's face, telling him 'that if it had not been for the Squaws, his Scalp might have been off too'.

Jonathan Barns was that most feared and loathed product of the colonial American frontier – the 'white Indian' who treated his countrymen worse than did the 'savages' themselves. Barns had arrived amongst the Abenakis as a prisoner-of-war, being captured on Lake George in

1756 whilst serving in Ruggles' regiment of Massachusetts provincials. On 18 September he had left Fort William Henry in a fifty-man patrol commanded by Captain Hodges; but within two days they were ambushed by French and Indians. Wounded twice, Barns was lucky to survive: the bodies of the captain and many of his men were 'found on the spot mangled in the most barbarous manner, their heads cut off and stuck upon poles.'

Despite this traumatic experience, Barns had nonetheless become thoroughly assimilated into the tribe; his own testimony suggests formal adoption. His loyalties were clear from a conversation he had at Isle-aux-Noix that October with a captured British officer, Lieutenant Hugh Meredith of Gage's Light Infantry. Barns had admitted that he was an Englishman, and that he was sorry St Francis was destroyed as its inhabitants were *always good to the English*. Meredith remembered seeing Barns amongst the Abenakis. He had no doubt where Barns' allegiance lay, having been informed that no English were allowed to stay at Isle-aux-Noix, except for those who went *with the Indians against the English*. Barns also told Josiah Malone that he had killed one of Sergeant Delanoe's party himself, saying 'the Indians would trust him now to go, where before this Action, they would not have done.' In true tribal fashion he had dressed and painted his victim's scalp, and later presented it to an elderly Indian as a gift.

All this was shocking enough, but Barns had done much worse. That same autumn of 1759, he accompanied a party of Indians who took a prisoner near Crown Point. This captive, who had been with Major Rogers at St Francis, was brought to Isle-aux-Noix. There, the Indians resolved to sacrifice him. The victim was led out a small distance from the French encampment, and then tortured in a *most barbarous Manner*. Barns had assisted in the *shocking Murder*. This display of savage cruelty had not lacked spectators; indeed, a very considerable number of the French regulars had come out to watch.

The focus of all this attention had been doubly unlucky: not only was he within an ace of salvation when his enemies caught him, but he died slowly, in the old way. His identity remains unknown. Whether ranger, redcoat or provincial, fate decreed that he above all others should atone for the sufferings of St Francis.

AMIDST SO MUCH PAIN, there remained at least some compassion. By a strange coincidence, the arrival of Robert Rogers at Fort Number Four had been witnessed by Susanna Johnson. She had only recently moved back from Massachusetts to the outpost from whence the Abenakis had dragged her five long years before. Now, Rogers and his men had destroyed the village to which she'd been taken as a frightened and bewildered captive. Before St Francis was put to the torch, one of the rangers discovered a bundle of papers that had belonged to Captain James Johnson; he presented them to the surprised and delighted Susanna. Another unexpected reminder of the past brought her even greater joy. The young captive, Antoine Gill, stopped at Susanna's house; upon seeing her he immediately cried out 'My God! My God! here is my sister!'

Susanna never forgot the emotional reunion that followed: 'It was my little brother Sabatis, who formerly used to bring the cows for me when I lived at my Indian masters,' she wrote. 'He was transported to see me, and declared that he was still my brother, and I must be his sister. Poor fellow! The fortune of war had left him without a single relation; but with his country's enemies he could find one who too sensibly felt his miseries. I felt the purest pleasure in administering to his comfort.'

CHAPTER EIGHT

Reward and Retribution

ON 2 NOVEMBER, 1759, the same day that Rogers ventured back up the Connecticut River with provisions for his starving men, Major-General Amherst finally received tidings that the major had completed the hazardous assignment with which he had been entrusted more than six weeks before.

This news issued from the mouth of the enemy, being delivered by Captain Cadillac of the *Régiment de Berri*; he approached under a flag of truce with a letter from Vaudreuil proposing an exchange of prisoners. The captain was encountered en route to Crown Point by a ranger patrol headed by Ensign Hutchins, himself only recently returned from his protracted excursion to Québec. Cadillac revealed that Rogers' detachment had burnt the settlement at St Francis and killed some Indians, women and children, although, reporting this in his journal, Amherst commented: 'I fancy he is mistaken about the women & children'.

If Cadillac was to be believed, Rogers had not had things all his own way; during his retreat, he had been harassed by Indians and Canadians who assembled and attacked him at night. Amherst's versatile aide-de-camp, James Abercrombie, was sent out to pump the Frenchman for further information. Although Cadillac took a good deal of strong beer and was in consequence quite happy to discuss such matters as the circumstances of Wolfe's death at Québec and Brigadier

Bourlamaque's hopes and fears for Isle-aux-Noix, he had nothing to add about the major's party.

No more was heard of Rogers and his men until 7 November, when Captain Ogden arrived at Crown Point bearing the major's own report from Fort Number Four. Not surprisingly, Ogden was showing signs of his recent ordeal, but although he looked very poor, the captain was nonetheless in good spirits. The weary but indomitable New Jerseyman was able to amplify Rogers' official despatch with his own personal account of events.

That afternoon an Indian from the major's detachment wandered into camp toting a scalp. To Amherst's exasperation, it was several hours before this warrior, *Indian-like*, casually remarked that he had left another sixteen of Rogers' command behind him at the mouth of the Otter River. Anxious that help should reach them as soon as possible, Amherst immediately despatched a detachment in three whaleboats, sending the taciturn Indian back to guide them down the lake. The relief party carried fifty pound of biscuit and a gallon of rum; they were to hug the lake's eastern shoreline, keeping a good lookout for others of the major's strays in need of their assistance.

The searchers returned next day with ten of those who had come from St Francis. They were a mixed bunch: four Indian and two white rangers, the freed captive woman from the German Flats, and three prisoners – two young *squaws* and an Indian boy. Unlike those making for the Connecticut River, this party had clung on to its spoils and arrived loaded with wampum and other loot; the major's Indians in particular were dressed very finely in their plundered gear. Amherst was surprised by the sheer quantity of booty harvested at what he clearly imagined to be some primitive tribal settlement. He told Governor De Lancey that some of Rogers' men had brought in more Indian riches than he thought any of their towns would have contained.

On the same day Amherst wrote to Rogers: 'Captain Ogden Delivered me Yesterday Your Letter of the 1st Instant, for which I am not only to thank You, but to assure You of the Satisfaction I had in reading it, as every step you inform me you had taken has been very well Judged and Deserves my full approbation.'

The commander-in-chief of His Britannic Majesty's forces in North America was not a man to lavish such plaudits lightly; for Major Robert Rogers, this unequivocal approval of his conduct throughout the St Francis expedition was high praise indeed.

AMHERST EXPRESSED HIS appreciation of Rogers' efforts in the measured and understated language of the English officer and gentleman. The colonial press exercised no such restraint. The men who had eradicated that *pernicious nest* at St Francis became the heroes of the hour; their leader, long since celebrated as 'the Brave Major Rogers', was now crowned with fresh laurels.

After all the rumours and misinformation that had veiled the opening phase of the operation, journalists were understandably wary about giving credence to subsequent intelligence of the major's fortunes. On 5 November, the *Boston Evening-Post* dismissed as unfounded, reports from Fort Number Four that Rogers had burned St Francis; in their next editions, on 12 November, the city's newspapers printed bulletins from Springfield, Massachusetts, stating that this was indeed fact. By 19 November, the press had its hands on hard information from the major's own mouth. With deadlines looming and pages already bulging with news from Québec and elsewhere, lack of time and space prevented publication in full, but a week later, both Boston and New York news-sheets offered full-blown coverage of the raid and its harrowing aftermath.

The report that Rogers penned to Amherst after staggering into Fort Number Four achieved wide circulation. The *New-York Mercury* carried the text of the letter on 26 November, adding a significant preface: 'The following Account of the indefatigable and brave Major ROGERS's last Scout against the St Francis Indians must be agreeable to our Readers. The Journal is authentick, wrote by himself at Number IV, November 1, 1759.' The report concluded with Rogers' name, again rendered conspicuous in capitals and bold type. That same day the *New-York Gazette* devoted two closely printed columns to a vivid letter sent from Fort Number Four on 3 November – a time when Rogers remained intent upon gathering what remained of his scattered command. It concluded: 'We all here wait impatient for the safe Arrival of all those brave Officers and Men, that have behaved so gallantly in this Affair, and in particular that indefatigable Major, and a happy Recovery of Capt. Ogden of his Wounds, such Behaviour as only Men of Constitutions like Lions could ever have went through.'

Four days later the *New-Hampshire Gazette* – a periodical that had long taken a special interest in the exploits of the colony's most famous fighting man – devoted the prime position on its front page to a lengthy account of the raid; the same report had already appeared in both the *Boston Gazette* and *Boston Evening-Post*. The prevalence of such plagiarism guaranteed that in the weeks to follow these key reports would spread far from the northern colonies whose frontiers had known the realities of the bloody war against New France, to places where the St Francis Indians were as remote as Hottentots or Tartars. By the new year they had trickled down the eastern seaboard of British North America and across the Atlantic to the mother country herself. Fresh snippets of information kept the story smouldering for months. All served to fix Robert Rogers in the spotlight of celebrity.

THE INDEFATIGABLE MAJOR initially remained oblivious to this chorus of acclaim. In the weeks following his return from St Francis he continued to fret about those of his men who were still missing, and the others who had reached the rendezvous on the Connecticut, only to die miserably of starvation when they got there. During these grim days, at the very time that the newspapers of Boston and New York were trumpeting his exploits, Rogers remained depressed and wracked with self-reproach.

The major's bleak mood was reflected in his reports to Amherst. On 21 November, Lieutenant George Campbell, the same ranger officer who had survived the wilderness by turning cannibal, arrived at Crown Point bearing a letter from Rogers at Fort Number Four: he had gathered only fifty-one men of his party in, but expected more; stragglers *did* continue to arrive – the major's subsequent claim to be reimbursed for the cost of shirts, stockings, moccasins and shoes was for fifty-nine men.

Although Rogers didn't know it, other members of his detachment who were presumed dead had come into Amherst's new fortress on 15 November, in the exchange of prisoners proposed by the affable Captain Cadillac. These lucky survivors included the men captured at Missisquoi Bay earlier that month: Sergeant Lewis and Private Brown of Gage's Light Infantry; John Crown, Jabez Burrell, John Todd, Lemuel Goddart and Daniel Rose, all of Major Rogers' Rangers; and John Jones of Fitche's provincial regiment. The same batch of prisoners included others who had played their own part in the destruction of St Francis: Captain Quinton Kennedy and Lieutenant Archibald Hamilton, whose capture by the Abenakis sparked the conflagration, and three of their men: John Humphrys of Gage's and the Stockbridge Indian rangers John Jacobs and Sergeant Abraham. Others escorted into Crown Point that day had spent far longer in enemy hands; those two veterans of the March 1758 Battle on Snowshoes, Captain Henry Pringle and Lieutenant Boyle Roche, were amongst them.

Aptly enough, the prisoners were conducted up Lake Champlain by a man they had grown to know all too well – that persistent scourge of the Anglo-Americans, Ensign Langis.

Accompanied by those of his men who had regained their strength, Rogers left Fort Number Four for Crown Point; he arrived on 1 December to find the Grand Army dispersed and Amherst already bound for New York: the increasingly mutinous provincials had been paid off and sent home and the redcoat battalions posted to their winter quarters. The Inniskilling Regiment remained in garrison. Of the six companies of rangers that had served with Amherst that summer, only two were kept up for the winter. These would remain under Rogers' command; the general was hopeful that the major would be able to recruit them with some of the good men that he had along with him.

At Crown Point, Rogers tallied up the casualties sustained since leaving the ruins of St Francis. He reckoned to have lost three officers – lieutenants Turner of the rangers, Dunbar of the regulars and Jenkins of the provincials – along with forty-six sergeants and privates. Of those men who had attacked the village on the morning of 4 October, more than a third had failed to return.

Crown Point's commandant was Rogers' old sparring partner, Colonel William Haviland of the 27th Foot. Rogers was to obey such orders as Haviland should choose to give him, although once he had rested himself thoroughly from the fatigues of his late scout, if business or inclination drew him south to Albany, he would have the colonel's leave to go there.

Rogers was glad to accept this long-awaited furlough; he clearly needed it. A French officer who encountered the major at Ticonderoga was struck by Rogers' poor condition. In his published *Memoirs*, Captain Pierre Pouchot, himself returning to Canada from New York in an exchange of prisoners, provided a vivid – if exaggerated – account of the major's casualties during the raid on St Francis. He claimed that all of the divided parties had succumbed to exposure or hunger in the forest save for that led by Rogers himself; the major and his own band only survived thanks to the services of a Mahican guide. According to Pouchot, Rogers returned with just twenty-one men, all of them haggard and emaciated.

The paltry score of hollow-cheeked scarecrows that made such an impression upon Pouchot were no doubt the regular light infantrymen that Rogers reported had come in with him; they rejoined their respective regiments as he headed south down the Hudson Valley. Rogers arrived at Albany on 11 December, and the following day penned another letter to Amherst that revealed the extent to which the gloomy aftermath of the raid continued to dampen his spirits. For all the euphoria of the newspaper coverage – of which he must by now have been aware – the major viewed his expedition in a very different light: he believed that the objective had been achieved at too high a cost, and feared that his own hard-won reputation would suffer as a result. He wrote: 'The Misfortunes attending my Retreat from Saint Francois causes me great uneasiness, the Brave men lost I most heartily lament, and fear your Excellency's Censure as the going against that place was my own proposal, and that I shall be disappointed of that Footing in the Army which I have long endeavour'd to merit.'

Rogers now volunteered his services for further arduous raids: he had procured enough skates to lead swift-moving reconnaissance patrols upon the frozen waters of Lake Champlain; and if Amherst was worried about the isolated British garrison at Québec, Rogers promised he could march a reinforcement of five hundred men there in twenty days from the mouth of the Kennebec River – provided they were fully supplied and properly equipped with snowshoes. Such eagerness to once again step into danger's way suggests that Rogers remained traumatised by the prolonged ordeal he'd so recently undergone: only by returning to the harsh wilderness and facing fresh hazards could the major blot out the horrors that still haunted him.

WHILST BRITAIN'S NORTH American colonies revelled in the fiery fate of St Francis, the beleaguered leaders of New France did their utmost to diminish the raid's significance. According to the returning British captives, the French had at first acknowledged the attack to be a *great enterprise*. However, just as the flag of truce was leaving Montréal, they changed their tune and endeavoured to downplay the raid, reporting to the prisoners that no more than forty Indians had been destroyed.

French estimates of casualties were accurate enough; despite the wishful thinking of the colonial press, the St Francis Indians had not been exterminated. Some sought sanctuary with the Mohawks at the recently established mission of St Regis, on the banks of the St Lawrence south-west of Montréal; others continued to serve with the French forces watching Québec, and many embarked upon their customary hunting trips. As for St Francis itself, although the notorious village had been plundered and torched, it would rise again from the ashes.

But the real impact of Rogers' raid was psychological, not physical: it provided a timely fillip for the Anglo-American war effort, and represented a serious loss of prestige for the Franco-Canadians. A venerable mission village in the very heart of New France had been totally destroyed; a community that had originated as a refuge from strife, and which had grown to regard itself as invulnerable during the decades in which it had disgorged warriors upon the frontiers of New England, had succumbed to a predatory raiding party. To salt the Abenakis' wounds, this grievous and humiliating blow had been landed under the very noses of their French 'father': by serving him like dutiful children, the St Francis Indians had allowed their own flesh and blood to be sacrificed.

The damaging ramifications were recognised by the embattled Governor General Vaudreuil. Reporting developments in a despatch to Versailles, he felt obliged to conclude that the affair was *very unfortunate*. Vaudreuil had strong personal reasons for such pessimism: he now faced the wrath of Indians who blamed him for their misfortunes. Two French deserters who came into the British garrison of Québec on the night of 24 November reported that the Indians were so irate at Monsieur Vaudreuil that they threatened to stone him to death because of the loss of their capital, which they blamed upon his misconduct. Such evidence of disaffection amongst Canada's hitherto loyal tribal allies was eagerly chronicled in New England newspapers; they reported that the Abenakis were well aware that Major Rogers had attacked St Francis because of their actions against Captain Kennedy: in consequence, they were now 'greatly exasperated with the French who had encouraged them thus to detain their Prisoners in View of a great Reward'.

The vengeance that fell upon St Francis delivered a clear message, not only to the Abenakis themselves, but to all the other Indian allies of New France: those stubborn and misguided tribes that persisted in their opposition to the British could expect to be chastised with equal severity; their homes would be burned and their women and children slain or carried into captivity. Robert Rogers' bold coup had demonstrated that the Anglo-Americans possessed both the resolve and the ability to seek and destroy their enemies – *wherever* they might hide. This knowledge gave teeth to the tribal diplomacy through which Sir William Johnson, Britain's superintendent of the northern Indians, now sought to seduce the Seven Nations of Canada – as the St Lawrence mission communities were known – from their traditional allegiance. As Jeffery Amherst prepared for a fresh assault upon the frontiers of New France, Johnson's offers of peace and neutrality provided an increasingly tempting alternative to an unexpected visit from the White Devil and his bloody-handed henchmen.

DURING THE CLOSING WEEKS of 1759, fallout from the St Francis expedition continued to dominate the thoughts of Major Rogers. As Lieutenant Stevens' misconduct in decamping with the provisions was the reason so many perished in the woods, Rogers had placed him under arrest. The major likewise confined Sergeant Lewis on the grounds of spreading a false report about the distribution of rations on the return from St Francis; he wanted Lewis brought before a court martial, 'that I might have Justice done me as I have nothing to depend on but my Character'.

Replying to these requests from his New York headquarters on Christmas Eve, Amherst was now aware of the true extent of the casualties suffered by the major's detachment: they would, he hoped, be a lesson to all others to secure adequate provisions 'instead of Loading themselves with Plunder, by which they must be Lost, if an Enemy pursues'. It was a pedantic admonition, but nothing more. Rogers' fears that he would be held responsible for the raiders' high death toll were unfounded. Amherst accepted that if anyone was to blame, it was Stevens; he disapproved entirely of the lieutenant's conduct in forsaking the appointed rendezvous so soon, and agreed with Rogers that he deserved to stand trial. The general had no objection to ordering a further hearing for Lewis, if that was what Rogers wanted, but as the witnesses were widely scattered, the tribunal would be unable to sit for some time. Under the circumstances, he suggested, might it not be better to let the matter drop; from what Amherst had heard of the affair, it was beyond the sergeant's power to damage Rogers' reputation.

This vote of confidence calmed the major's concerns for his character;

lucky once again, Lewis escaped prosecution. Stevens was not so fortunate. On 23 April, 1760, the lieutenant was brought before a General Court Martial at Crown Point, accused by Major Rogers of 'Neglect of Duty upon a Detachment to Wells's River in October last'. Rogers and two of his men, the redcoat Andrew McNeal and ranger Andrew Wansant, all swore that upon arrival at the appointed rendezvous on 20 October they heard gunshots at a distance down the Connecticut River; assuming these to be signals from the party entrusted with the vital provisions, they fired several times in a fruitless effort to bring them back. It was this refusal to return, Rogers asserted, that had condemned a number of his party to slow death by starvation.

For his part, Stevens maintained that he had obeyed Amherst's orders to the best of his judgement; he only quit his post when there no longer seemed to be any possibility that Rogers would march that way. The lieutenant's reason for failing to transport the provisions as far as Wells River – that the Connecticut above the Lower Cowass Intervales was dangerously rapid – and his contention that his party had travelled daily to the designated spot to fire signal guns, received support in written depositions taken from a trio of the Fort Number Four inhabitants who had accompanied him. One of them, Noah Porter, claimed that around 20 October he heard three or four shots fired from the north-east quarter; however, a bateau soon after appeared containing two hunters who said that *they* were the gunmen in question. Porter maintained that the relief party remained at the Cowass Intervales until the evening of 23 October; the other witnesses, Benjamin Sawyer and Enos Stephens, both testified that they returned two days earlier.

As these men were not available for cross-examination, there was no opportunity to reconcile their conflicting evidence. Such discrepancies may have caused the military men who composed the court to doubt this civilian testimony. In addition, Stevens' assertion that the river beyond Cowass was too hazardous to negotiate was bluntly contradicted by ranger Wansant, who was adamant that there were 'no falls in the Connecticut River above Cohass ... to prevent Canoes getting up to

Well's River, the place Major Rogers said he had appointed for the provisions to come to.'

After considering all the evidence before it, the court found Stevens guilty and decreed that he be suspended from duty during the general's pleasure. Amherst approved the verdict. In his *Journals*, Rogers noted that this finding rendered Stevens incapable of sustaining any office in His Majesty's service for the future, but given the distresses and anguish his actions had caused, he had escaped lightly enough.

Just as Rogers was adamant that wrongdoers should be punished, so he remained determined to ensure that the deserving received due recognition. From the outset he had made it clear that the men he led against St Francis were an élite band; as the *New-York Gazette* reported, the major 'never saw a better Command of Officers and Men, and thinks no Party of Men ever deserved more Encouragement for their Country['s] Service, not only for their good Courage and Behaviour, but the Fatigues and Sufferings they have undergone.'

Rogers was not slow to suggest that this encouragement would be most acceptable in the form of hard cash. On 22 March, 1760, he placed a memorial before the General Court of Massachusetts 'praying a suitable Reward may be granted by this Government to himself and his Men for their service in destroying the Indian Town of St Francois'. His petition was lodged around the same time yet another laudatory editorial was published in Boston and New York; harking back to the major's latest exploit, this had asked: 'What do we owe to such a beneficial Man; and a Man of such an enterprizing Genius?'

If this were a hint, the colony's worthy elected representatives chose to ignore it. Now that St Francis was no longer a threat to their frontiers, they decided that the major and his men deserved not a penny; instead they approved the terse minute *that this Petition be dismiss'd.*

Although denied bounties, several ranger officers were rewarded with prestigious commissions in the regulars. Unlike the ranging companies, which were wartime formations destined to be broken directly the guns fell silent, most redcoat battalions could expect to survive the end of hostilities. Even those officers who found themselves unemployed at the coming of peace would be guaranteed the coveted financial lifeline of half-pay. By the summer of 1760, George Campbell and Abernathan Cargill were both wearing the red coat of King George: Campbell now served alongside his fellow Highlanders of the Black Watch, while Cargill was commissioned ensign in another old regiment, the 17th Foot; this was a meteoric rise for a young New Englander who had begun his military career less than three years earlier as a humble private ranger under John Stark. For volunteer Hugh Wallace of the 27th Foot, a creditable role in the raid secured the officer's berth that he craved. This advancement was hard-earned: in mid-December, Colonel Haviland had begged Amherst to *remember Mr Wallace our Volunteer who is scarce recovered his long Scout.* But Wallace had not been forgotten: on 28 November, 1759, he'd already been awarded an ensigncy in the 55th Foot.

For the rank and file raiders, the material rewards were far more modest. Those who returned from St Francis without saleable plunder were obliged to remain content with the gratitude and admiration of the inhabitants in the settlements where they were billeted to recuperate. According to Robert Kirkwood, upon moving down the Connecticut from Fort Number Four, they received linen and clothes and a plentiful allowance of provisions, the better to recover from their fatigue. In an era before the institution of campaign medals for common soldiers, the hard men who had marched to *St Fransway* and back with Major Rogers received no official token of their services. But their endeavours brought other compensations: the esteem of their comrades and a fund of hair-raising anecdotes that would keep them in beer and rum for the balance of their days.

ROBERT ROGERS HAD AN especially pressing incentive to seek recompense for his services: his finances were in their customary parlous state. The new year found him mired at Albany in a morass of paperwork. Thomas Gage, a soldier with a greater flair for administration than combat, assumed a patronising stance as he contemplated the major's clumsy efforts to settle his ramshackle accounts. As Gage reported to Amherst, the major could produce receipts for the items of kit that he had provided *before* his detachment marched against St Francis, but those relating to the necessaries supplied to the men who subsequently straggled into Fort Number Four would have to be sent for. Gage tutted: 'he was told that People generally take Receipts in Payment for Goods, & it was not usual to leave them behind in strange Places.'

Unlike Gage, Rogers had always felt more at home in the field than behind a desk. Amidst all the gruelling scouts and savage skirmishes of the past five years, meticulous book-keeping had never been a priority. Under a system in which officers often borrowed cash to advance pay to their men, and then drew official warrants for reimbursement, his financial standing had frequently been precarious; it was about to become shakier still.

From Albany, Rogers had travelled downcountry to New York, where the arrival of the brave major was duly noted by an admiring press. Rogers waited upon Amherst at headquarters. He delivered a return of the detachment that had marched against St Francis, and promised to prepare a plan of his route to and from the village. According to the newspapers, Rogers also left behind a young Indian lad, one of the prisoners from St Francis; this youth, who was in all likelihood the major's rafting companion Antoine Gill, or Sabatis, was to be sent to school to learn English.

The major then headed back up the Hudson, bringing thirteen recruits for his depleted ranger force. On 12 February they accompanied a procession of fourteen provision-laden sleighs across the snow between Ticonderoga and Crown Point. Although now technically behind British lines, this remained dangerous ground; without warning, an overwhelming force of seventy Indians – or Frenchmen dressed like Indians – fell upon the vulnerable convoy. Unaccountably, the recruits had not yet been issued with muskets. Outnumbered and unarmed, they were easy prey; their attackers killed five of them and captured another four. Rogers and the survivors reached Crown Point, but Colonel Haviland refused to authorise a pursuit because the garrison was very sickly. For

Rogers this was disastrous: the enemy escaped with a rich haul of plunder that included his personal sledge; according to the major's *Journals*, this had been carrying no less than £4,761 in hard cash. Some £800 was ranger pay and later refunded; but the balance, Rogers' own money, was entirely lost. To add insult to injury, the ambush had been sprung by the major's old antagonist, Ensign Langis.

The rangers captured with Rogers' bullion included Sergeant Thomas Beverly. Several months later he escaped from Montréal, coming into Crown Point on 4 May. During his brief stay at the heart of New France the sergeant was held at the house of Governor Vaudreuil himself; he had kept his eyes and ears open and learned much. The Stockbridge Indian Captain Jacob – he who had been captured along with Quinton Kennedy – continued to languish in irons; and *Monsieur Langy*, the famous partisan, was dead. The man responsible for inflicting so much damage upon the Anglo-Americans in general, and Rogers and his rangers in particular, had drowned after falling through the ice in the St Lawrence. As the *New-Hampshire Gazette* crowed, his loss was greatly lamented by all Canada, 'as his equal is not to be found in that country'. It was a tragic end for such a redoubtable fighter. Had he known what the future held for him, Robert Rogers may have envied Langis his swift plunge into oblivion.

Sergeant Beverly reported other intelligence that exposed the dire consequences of Amherst's failure to complete the conquest of Canada in 1759. Around 10 April, he revealed, the enemy had withdrawn all of their forces from Isle-aux-Noix, except for a token garrison of three hundred men commanded by Bougainville. Every regular battalion in Canada, along with such of the militia as could be spared from their spring planting, was concentrating at Jacques Cartier under the command of the Chevalier de Lévis. His object, the sergeant warned, was nothing less than the recapture of Québec.

For New France, this last desperate roll of the dice came close to reversing the dispiriting setbacks of the previous year. Québec's governor, Brigadier-General James Murray, was keen to emulate Wolfe's recent success on the Plains of Abraham. On 28 April the glory-hungry Scot marched out with what remained of his scurvy-ridden garrison to confront Lévis on that same ground. Another desperate fight developed; but this time it was the redcoats who broke. Ably seconded by Bourlamaque and Dumas, the wily chevalier subjected the flanks of Murray's flimsy firing line to increasing pressure; after fierce fighting, both buckled. Only a garbled order prevented the Franco-Canadians from executing a pincer movement calculated to snip the British line of retreat. The Frenchmen's Indian allies played little part in the main battle: it was not their idea of war. With a mixture of admiration and disbelief they looked on as the brave but foolhardy white men traded volleys and blows and churned the snow beneath their feet into crimson slush.

It was a gallant effort, but courage and determination alone were not enough to save New France. A reprieve for the colony depended upon prompt and significant aid from the old country; what arrived was too little and too late. When the first ship to drop anchor in the thawed St Lawrence flaunted British colours, Lévis had no option but to abandon his trenches and raise the siege.

Unaware of Murray's deliverance, Amherst once again looked to Rogers to stage a diversionary strike capable of causing mayhem within Canada. On 25 May, the major was ordered to take three hundred men – twenty-five light infantry, the rest rangers – on a fresh mission down Lake Champlain; they were directed to land on the west shore, bypass Isle-aux-Noix, and then fall upon the forts and supply depots above at St Jean and Chambly. One officer and fifty of the men were to branch off eastwards to seek and destroy the elusive community of Wigwam Martinique.

Amherst added specific instructions that harked back to the harsh lessons of the St Francis raid. Provided the command stuck together, he cautioned, nothing could hurt them; the major's Indians were to be restrained from killing women or children; and all should refrain from burdening themselves with plunder: upon their return they would be rewarded as they deserved.

Rogers left Crown Point on 1 June. As the Stockbridge Indians were still marching up from Albany, his command numbered two hundred and fifty men. Personnel, provisions and whaleboats were all loaded aboard three sloops and a brig. On 4 June, this task force halted some twelve miles south of Isle-aux-Noix; a brace of sloops probed forward to distract the enemy until Rogers could get into their country. A day later the detachment lay stalled by heavy rain; on 6 June French gunboats edged as near as they dared to the British sloops. Having discovered the major's landing place, the enemy now sent a detachment to cut him off. Rogers' scouts tallied the opposition as they crossed over from the fortified island to the west shore; they numbered about three hundred, chiefly Indians. Warned of the impending attack, Rogers disposed his men with their right flank anchored upon the lake and screened by a bog. The enemy shunned the marsh but assaulted the left flank briskly; Rogers promptly riposted by sending seventy men, under the St Francis raider Lieutenant Jacob Farrington, along the lakeside to take them in the rear. When Farrington's strike hit home the major pushed onward; caught between two fires the French and Indians broke and ran. The pursuit was maintained for a mile before the enemy scattered within the shelter of a thick cedar swamp.

In pouring rain Rogers gathered his men and totalled casualties: he had suffered seventeen dead and eleven wounded; the enemy conceded thirty-two killed outright and another nineteen disabled. The high proportion of slain to injured indicated a close-range fire-fight. One ranger officer reported that the opposing forces drew so near to each other that they swapped shots across the hulls of the major's beached boats. With the benefit of quick-loading cartridges Rogers' men laid down a blistering fusillade. Unable to match this rate of fire the Indians threw rocks, 'on which our men haloo'd to them that they would likewise fight with stones and give them an equal chance.' The opposition were routed just the same.

After burying his dead and sending back one of the sloops with the wounded and a plea for fresh provisions, the major set off again, determined to follow his orders *at all adventures*.

Now reinforced by the tardy Stockbridge company, Rogers led two hundred and twenty officers and men on this second *excursion*. At midnight on 9 June the detachment landed on the lake's west shore, opposite Isle la Motte. They marched hard, and by the evening of 15 June were within two miles of their target, St Jean. Careful reconnaissance revealed that the sentries were too numerous and alert to be rushed. At 2.00 a.m. on the 16th the command instead pushed downriver to St Thérèse, where daybreak revealed a settlement containing two large storehouses surrounded by a stockade. The enemy were busy carting hay into the fort. Employing a timeless ruse, Rogers waited until the haywain was blocking the gateway, then darted within before the passage could be cleared. At that same moment, scattered parties fell upon the settlement's houses, securing them all without firing a shot. Several young men scampered off to raise the alarm, but two dozen soldiers and another seventy-eight civilians were captured. Prisoner interrogation revealed that it was impracticable to proceed north to Chambly, so Rogers torched St Thérèse and the stores stockpiled within it; horses and livestock were slaughtered and anything else of possible value to the enemy was destroyed, except for eight bateaux which Rogers used to ferry the command over the Richelieu River. Soon after they had crossed, six hundred French and Indians drew up on the opposite bank; with no means of following, the enemy could only watch in mortification as Rogers' men staved in the boats.

Sending the captured old folk, women and children off to Montréal, Rogers now marched along the east side of Lake Champlain. Near Missisquoi Bay his scouts clashed with the advance guard of a pursuit force from Isle-aux-Noix; luckily, the main body recoiled. That same day, 20 June, 1760, the major's party arrived at the rendezvous arranged with the British vessels; no sooner had they embarked than the frustrated French once again lined the shore.

Ordering back the prisoners and fifty of his men to Crown Point in one of the vessels, Rogers and the rest waited to cover the retreat of the party that had been despatched to eradicate Wigwam Martinique. That settlement continued to lead a charmed life: the rangers sent against it missed their way, but all returned safely to the muster point. Having gathered in every last member of his command, Rogers returned up the lake to arrive at Crown Point on 23 June.

Haviland reported the agreeable news of Rogers' arrival without the loss of a single man. Amherst was fulsome in his praise. This ungrudging applause from critical professional soldiers was well merited: the expedition had been a spectacular success. In the three-week period behind enemy lines the major's command had inflicted maximum disruption at minimum cost. There had been hard fighting, in which Rogers' tactical acumen was matched by the motivation and proficiency of his men; the forced marches, stealthy surprise attacks and cool evasion of pursuit all followed principles delineated in the major's own Rules for Ranging; and in a fashion remarkable for that age – or any other – the entire mission was characterised by flawless co-operation between land and naval forces. It was a classic combined operation that showed both Rogers and his men at the peak of their form. Here was proof positive that the major had conquered the demons that had dogged him since his return from St Francis.

On 11 June, Jeffery Amherst received tidings that the Union flag continued to fly over Québec. Mightily relieved, he finalised plans for a fresh assault upon the limbless trunk of Canada. This time there could be no margin for error. Three armies would converge upon Montréal from the south, east and west. Murray's regulars were to be ferried up the St Lawrence from Québec; Haviland, with promotion to brigadier-general, would move via Lake Champlain, whilst Amherst himself advanced from Oswego, taking the path that Gage had refused to follow. Historians have likened this three-pronged strike to an overwhelming juggernaut – a monstrous sledgehammer wielded to smash a puny nut – but the logistical problems were not to be underrated. Once again Amherst faced the headaches of mustering his war-weary provincial troops on schedule, and accumulating the transport and supplies required to keep his forces in the field for long enough to breach the battered defences of New France.

And for all the odds ranged against them, honour demanded

that Canada's defenders could not submit without a fight; in the coming months, Robert Rogers and his rangers would find further scope for their skills.

AS THE ANGLO-AMERICAN war machine moved in for the kill, New France's Indian allies began to melt away. The signs had been evident at Québec before the end of May, when Governor Murray reported how, in the wake of Lévis' decision to abandon his siege of the city, an unspecified nation of Indians had surrendered and entered into an alliance with the British. To the west, as summer approached, it was much the same story: according to intelligence from Montréal, the Indians in general had grown very insulting to the French. The Iroquois of Caughnawaga, hitherto amongst the staunchest of New France's allies, were succumbing to Johnson's entreaties; they were now divided amongst themselves – half poised to join the British, the remainder resolved to take to the woods and adopt a neutral stance. And in July, ten French Indians from Oswegatchie came into Amherst's camp at Oswego to seek peace on behalf of their nation; as it was clear that the English would take their country anyway, they even promised sixty warriors to guide him along the St Lawrence.

During August, when the three British armies finally moved forward, the desertions began in earnest. Amherst's own force now fielded an intimidating host of seven hundred warriors drawn from the Iroquois League and other nations. The army advanced from Oswego until it came up against the newly constructed Fort Lévis, on Isle Royale near Oswegatchie, which was only subdued after an intensive bombardment. Whilst the siege was underway, representatives of the Seven Nations of Canada came into camp to confer with Johnson; they agreed to remain neutral on condition that they were treated as friends in the future.

On 29 August, as he took stock of the battered island fortress, Amherst received a further deputation. 'At night Capt Jacobs who was taken with Capt Kennedy came to me,' the general reported. He arrived 'with Indians from the French & brought me a letter from a Priest to offer Peace on the Indian side.' The author of the letter was none other than the missionary of St Francis, Pierre Roubaud. Since the destruction of his church and the dispersal of his flock, Roubaud had followed a controversial and convoluted path. On 23 May, whilst at Montréal, he delivered an inflammatory sermon that castigated the French regulars for their low morals and blamed them for the failure to recapture Québec. Officers amongst the congregation were outraged at this unwarranted verbal flaying, particularly as it came from a priest who was reputed to take a more than spiritual interest in his female parishioners; to save his skin the outspoken cleric was obliged to flee, first to the Jesuits' residence in Montréal and then to Caughnawaga.

By the time he composed his peace proposal, Roubaud was apparently at St Regis, the Iroquois mission community where members of his homeless flock had sought safety following Rogers' raid. As the British and their fearsome tribal allies approached, most of the village's inhabitants and guests had understandably decamped; but the priest was very happy to stay there, in peace with those Indians that remained, and to vouch for their good behaviour. Roubaud's overtures marked the beginning of his attempts to ingratiate himself with the victorious British. He initially offered his services as an authority on Canadian Indian affairs; in due course his defection became far more profound as he renounced his catholicism and embarked upon a truly bizarre career in which acting, forgery and espionage all played a part.

Once Amherst had taken Fort Lévis, only the notorious Cedar Rapids lay between him and the prize of Montréal; these natural defences were daunting enough in their own right; if the French took up position on either bank and raked the river with gunfire, his army would stand no chance. Far from opposing the descent, Indians who had recently fought alongside the French now helped to pilot the British bateaux down the river. Despite their expertise, the descent was so hazardous that the experience left a deep impression upon those who survived it. Lieutenant John Grant of the Black Watch recalled how his own boat was caught by the suction and whirled about; he and his men only escaped a watery grave by frantically bailing out their craft with camp kettles; the blue bonnets of Highlanders who were not so lucky joined the provision casks that swirled and bobbed amongst the eddies. Eighty-four men drowned in running the wild waters. Amherst himself admitted that the rapids cost them dear. But things could have been much worse: Bourlamaque subsequently observed that only the defection of the Indians and militia assigned to defend the rapids saved Amherst's army from utter annihilation.

On the Lake Champlain front, Haviland's army at last laid siege to Isle-aux-Noix; the famous Nut Island finally cracked under an intensive bombardment coupled with a ranger sweep that hunted the remnants of the evasive French fleet and eventually ran them aground. Before the fortress fell, some five hundred mission Indians had gathered at St Jean to consider proposals to march to Bougainville's aid; but these warriors refused to budge without independent verification of the enemy's strength. When news arrived that their brethren facing Amherst had opted for neutrality, they too withdrew their services. By early September, Lévis and his regulars were left to fight on alone.

As the trio of British armies converged upon Montréal, the last act in the drama unfolded. Faced by such overwhelming force, the embattled colony had no option but to capitulate. All that remained was to settle the surrender terms. Vaudreuil sought to safeguard the inhabitants' property, religion and legal rights, and to obtain passage back to France for the remaining troops, with full honours of war so they could march off with muskets shouldered and standards flying.

Colonel Bougainville presented the French proposals to General Amherst. Although ready to accept most of Vaudreuil's conditions, the British commander was adamant that the French regulars must not only surrender themselves as prisoners, but also forgo the expected marks of honour: he refused to concede this point because of 'the infamous part the troops of France had acted in exciting the savages to perpetrate the most horrid and unheard of barbarities in the whole progress of the war'.

Lévis, who had risked his own life to save British prisoners from Indian vengeance at Fort William Henry, was outraged. He demanded that Vaudreuil at least allow him and his men to stage a last stand of their own to uphold the reputation of the King's arms, but the governor general refused to sanction the sacrifice of further lives. The articles of surrender were signed on 8 September, 1760. The chevalier snapped his sword rather than relinquish it to the unbending Amherst; to the same end, his veterans made a bonfire of the silk regimental colours that had billowed above them during four long years of victory and defeat.

It was not only Lévis and his regulars who sought to salvage some martial pride from the wreckage of New France. Like others of Canada's erstwhile Indian allies, the Abenakis had withdrawn from the conflict in a pragmatic bid to secure their own future under the new régime: in return for forsaking the French and allowing the British to descend the St Lawrence River without interruption, the tribe had received solemn assurances that it should be numbered amongst King George's friends and allowed to 'enjoy our right and possessions and the free exercise of our Religion forever'; these privileges were promised under the Articles of Capitulation.

But *realpolitik* was one thing, the dictates of tribal honour quite another. Even as their familiar world collapsed around them, the St Francis Indians could not allow the recent sack of their village to go unanswered. That same summer, a last war party of the *St Francois Tribe* followed the familiar trail to the New Hampshire frontier, bent upon a retaliatory raid.

On 7 June these warriors fell upon an unsuspecting Fort Number Four. Joseph Willard, his wife Huldah – Susanna Johnson's sister – and their five children were all seized and bustled off like so many others before them. They were the very last New Englanders taken captive to Canada during the long saga of the French and Indian wars – a distinction that the Willards would have happily forgone. After two weeks they arrived at Montréal; within months, New France had surrendered and the family was freed.

When the Willards returned to their home at the edge of the Great Meadow, they brought back their niece, Susanna Johnson's namesake daughter, who had been captured with her in 1754; after five years' absence, she spoke only French and no longer recognised her own mother. Susanna was already inured to such quirks of frontier life; by the time her son Sylvanus finally returned from his sojourn with the Abenakis in the autumn of 1758, he had entirely forgotten the English language, though he was fluent in Indian and well able to brandish a tomahawk or bend the bow. As the stoical Susanna observed, these habits wore off by degrees. She now remained content that her changeling daughter was likewise safe and well. The Willards must have envied her. For them, the last symbolic act of vengeance by the St Francis Abenakis had taken its toll: on the northbound trek through the wilderness their six-week-old baby Samuel perished in a manner known only to the Indians; his brother James, aged two, survived the hard journey to Canada, only to die at Crown Point on his return. These pathetic little victims were the last casualties of the St Francis raid.

THAT SUMMER, MORE OF the men captured during that celebrated expedition were released. They returned to the astonishment and delight of friends and relations who had long since thought them dead.

Those resurrected in this startling fashion included Frederick Curtiss, the Connecticut corporal who had come so close to losing his life at the hands of the vengeful villagers of St Francis. After escaping their clutches he had remained at Trois-Rivières until December 1759, when he was transferred to Montréal. In mid-June he journeyed back to Crown Point amongst a batch of one hundred and twenty-eight prisoners. He finally arrived home to Canterbury in early July. On 4 October, 1760 – a year to the day after he had helped to burn St Francis – Curtiss swore to the truth of a declaration made before Justice of the Peace Stephen Fuller, which was duly considered by the Connecticut General Assembly at New Haven: he now sought compensation for his suffering and losses while detained in captivity. Not only had the Indians taken away his gun, which he had provided himself, but also a blanket, two shirts and a good jacket. Curtiss had left most of his clothes behind at Crown Point when he went out on the scout. After he failed to return these were purloined: a good-as-new blanket and three pairs of good stockings had vanished; what few items remained were ruined, having been *Worn by ye Soldiers thro the woods & no due care taken of them*. After deliberating upon his doleful memorial, the Assembly's Lower House resolved to grant Curtiss the princely sum of fifteen pounds and ten shillings out of the public treasury.

Another St Francis raider freed that same June was the ranger Josiah Malone. Shortly before his exchange, whilst housed in the hospital at Montréal, Malone once again met the renegade Jonathan Barns. A contrite Barns now asked Malone's pardon for his callous treatment of him; he in his turn endeavoured to persuade Barns to return home to his friends, in company with the released prisoners. Barns answered darkly that he could not, having *done such things that he durst not go home*.

Just what Barns *had* done only became apparent in March of 1761, after he came into Oswegatchie as interpreter for a party of Abenakis. Lieutenant Meredith of Gage's Light Infantry, who had last seen Barns at Isle-aux-Noix back in October 1759, urged him to leave the Indians and seek his livelihood at Montréal. Such attention made Barns nervous; he sought to hide himself amongst the Indians, seemingly frightened. Of course, Barns had good cause to be jittery. Men of Gage's regiment on detachment at Oswegatchie soon assured the lieutenant that 'the Prisoner had been Guilty of Several Crueltys against some of Major Rogers's Party on their Return from St Francis'. This information, allied with his own suspicions, persuaded Meredith to order Barns' detention.

Taken to Montréal, Barns was brought before a General Court Martial. Over three days in April a damning body of evidence accumulated against him. Barns made a desperate plea to justify his actions:

> that whatever can be Laid to his Charge, was the effects of Compulsion,
> by the Indians, whom he durst not disobey, as his Life then was at
> their mercy, and that he was very young when he was taken, and
> Living so long among them, had entirely Subjected him to them.
> That when he was ordered by them to do any Act of Cruelty it was
> very much against his Inclination, & thro fear of them, and a desire

to gain more of their Affections; and was in hope by that means to find an opportunity to escape from them; And humbly submits himself to the Mercy of the Court.

That clemency was not forthcoming. Having pondered the gruesome testimony before them, the court members had no hesitation in finding Barns guilty of the crimes laid to his charge and sentencing him to death. Two days later, on 6 April, 1761, Major-General Gage approved of the verdict and ordered that Jonathan Barns, alias Burns, be hanged by the neck until dead.

With the gallows rearing above him, Barns decided to unload his sins upon the clergyman appointed to ease his path to eternity. As minister to two challenging martial congregations – the Mohawk Indians and the redcoats of the Royal American Regiment – the Reverend John Ogilvie was not easily shocked; but the words that tumbled from the mouth of the condemned man left a lasting impression upon him: Barns now confessed his participation in the murder of the unknown St Francis raider who had been tortured to death at Isle-aux-Noix in the fall of 1759. Determined to meet his Maker with the slate wiped clean, the wretched Barns assured Ogilvie, *as a dying Man*, that the grim story was all true; when he subsequently arrived at Montréal, he had received clothes and other goods as a reward for his services.

Jeffery Amherst was horrified to learn the details of the case; he could scarcely credit the commission of such *Cruelties and Barbarities*. But as Amherst himself was to discover, the American frontier could find and untether the savage that lay within even the most civilised of men.

CHAPTER NINE

Endings

OF ALL THE MANY THOUSANDS of men who had fought to subdue New France, few served harder, longer or more effectively than Robert Rogers. But Canada's conquest brought no end to the major's labours; his peculiar talents denied him any such respite. It remained for the British to impose the surrender terms upon the former French possessions in the far west, and on 13 September, 1760 – exactly a year after Rogers set out to destroy St Francis – Jeffery Amherst sent him from Montréal to do just that. With two hundred rangers at his back, he carried orders to relieve the far-flung garrisons at Detroit, Michilimackinac and other still more distant posts, and to secure oaths of loyalty from King George's sullen new subjects.

Proceeding via the Great Lakes Ontario and Erie, and collecting a company of Royal Americans en route, Rogers' command rowed their whaleboats deep within territory dominated by tribes that had always been inveterate foes of the British. As Rogers neared Detroit, Ottawas reported that the post's defiant commander, Captain François-Marie Picoté de Belestre, had erected a flagstaff: this supported a wooden effigy of a man's head with a crow sitting on top. The sinister bird represented Belestre; the head designated Rogers: the meaning of the whole, as the major wryly commented in his *Journals*, was that 'he would scratch out my brains'. The Indians interpreted the grisly ensemble differently; they maintained that the reverse would be true. And so it proved. Luckily for Belestre, when he relinquished his command to Rogers on 29 November, the symbolism remained no more than that.

Although ice prevented Rogers from pushing on to Michilimackinac, the perilous mission added another feather to the major's cap: it had required all of his hardihood, resolution and nerve; a bold front and firm grasp of tribal diplomacy underpinned its spectacular success. His biographer summed up the magnitude of the achievement: 'With the skill of a natural woodsman he had taken an expedition in open boats over eight hundred miles into a region totally unknown to him, in a perilous season of the year and with only one casualty. It was done so simply that only the disasters of other expeditions make it seem other than a pleasant Sunday afternoon row.'

Having performed his duty with vigour and despatch, Rogers returned via the Ohio to a hero's welcome. At Philadelphia, the arrival of the brave Major Rogers after his long and fatiguing march prompted the local populace to *testify their Sense of his distinguished Merit*: they ordered the church bells to peal out in welcome. Coming so soon after the St Francis raid, the western expedition boosted Rogers to the very pinnacle of his fame. For a man who had yet to enter his thirties, these were heady days indeed.

By Valentine's Day, 1761, Rogers was back in New York. There, he finally received the *Footing in the Army* that he had sought for so long; Amherst rewarded him with a regular captain's commission in one of the independent companies based in South Carolina. During the previous two years, that colony had become embroiled in hostilities as exasperated Cherokees retaliated against encroachments upon their lands. By the time Rogers joined his new unit in August 1761, the Cherokee War was already over, but several of his old comrades had played conspicuous parts in the conflict. When fighting escalated in early 1760, Amherst had responded by despatching piecemeal reinforcements from his veteran regular battalions; they included the light infantry company of the Royals, commanded by Captain Manley Williams. Having survived the gunshot wound sustained on the journey to St Francis, Williams was less fortunate when he encountered the Cherokees on 27 June, 1760; skirmishing through thick brushwood hard by the banks of an ugly muddy river, he fell, riddled with bullets. As Williams lay dying he encouraged his men, crying: 'Advance, my brave boys, never mind me'. The gallant captain was lamented – as the newspapers pointed out – by all who knew him.

Ensconced amidst daunting mountainous terrain and armed with rifles that outranged the British smoothbores, the stubborn Cherokees were not easily chastised. In 1761 Amherst was obliged to send a second, more formidable, expedition against them. The new force included Captain Quinton Kennedy, who headed a corps of Indians; this unique formation embraced not only Stockbridges and Mohawks, but also southern Indians, redcoat volunteers and a handful of Rogers' Rangers. According to his commanding officer, Colonel James Grant, Kennedy's specialists worked wonders in screening the expedition from ambush whilst it brought fire and sword to the Cherokee homelands.

No sooner were the Cherokees obliged to sue for peace than a fresh zone of conflict opened in the Caribbean; troops from South Carolina, including Kennedy and his multiracial band of frontier-fighters, were now sent against the French sugar-island of Martinique. There, the zealous Kennedy commanded the ranging companies that spearheaded the amphibious landing on 16 January, 1762; these units were captained by Amos Ogden and Joseph Wait, both hardened veterans of the St Francis raid.

In the brisk campaign that followed, the light infantry, grenadiers and rangers bore the brunt of the fighting in Martinique's ravines and cane fields. Seasoned and aggressive, they made short work of their intimidated opponents. Kennedy himself was wounded when these élite units stormed strong enemy positions on 24 January; his services once more secured him a mention in despatches.

With the island safely gathered within Britain's bulging imperial net, Kennedy paused to ponder his future. Before sailing for the West Indies he had sought Lord Loudoun's backing for his appointment as Britain's superintendent to the southern tribes; he believed that his intimate and varied knowledge of Indians and their ways would make him *very Easy* in such a post. But what Quinton Kennedy craved more than anything was the company of his old friends back in Ayrshire; after seven long years of campaigning in America he did not lack tales with which to regale them over a fireside dram or two. But both ambitions lay beyond his reach: like many other veterans of the army that had subdued Canada, Kennedy left his bones in the fever-ridden Caribbean, being quite worn out by his exertions.

Robert Rogers had also hoped to secure the potentially lucrative superintendency of the southern Indians. Disappointed when that plum post went elsewhere, and out of sorts with the sultry Carolinian climate, Rogers badgered Amherst for a transfer. He was pining, not only for lungfuls of crisp northern air, but also for Elizabeth Browne, the fetching daughter of a New Hampshire clergyman; Rogers had briskly courted and wed her before heading south. It was the following spring before he could sell his existing captaincy and buy another in one of the New York independent companies, but when news arrived of the official end of the war with France, in February 1763, all the independents were axed. Now surplus to requirements, Rogers had at least secured the benefit of half-pay; as his debts mounted, this slender allowance provided an increasingly threadbare safety net.

PEACE IN EUROPE DID NOT end strife in America. Early that summer, a fresh Indian war engulfed the west; unlike the unilateral Cherokee struggle of resistance, this conflict aligned diverse tribes possessing common grievances. Following the elimination of French power on the continent, many Indians had resented the increasingly high-handed stance of the victors. Obliged to retrench in the wake of the ruinously expensive conquest of Canada, Jeffery Amherst sought economies by pruning the hefty costs incurred in making the customary gifts to Indians. Although understandable from the perspective of a hard-pressed imperial administrator, this response revealed a woeful ignorance of Indian value-systems; interpreted as gross disrespect, it led all too swiftly to disaster. All along the western frontier, tribes vented their spleen by slaying settlers, slaughtering isolated garrisons and blockading key forts. With his veteran army winnowed by tropical disease and peacetime demobilisations, Amherst struggled to douse the conflagration.

Scratch forces were despatched to relieve the beleaguered forts Pitt and Detroit. Armed with his recent knowledge of the west, Rogers joined the Detroit column headed by Amherst's current aide-de-camp, Captain James Dalyell. An experienced and forceful soldier, Dalyell had fought under Rogers' command five years earlier, but now *he* would be giving the orders. His force reached Detroit on 29 July. Confident that he could rout the besiegers with one bold strike, Dalyell lost no time in orchestrating a sortie. A picked command sallied forth on the night of 31 July, only to encounter determined opposition from warriors under the direction of the charismatic Ottawa war chief Pontiac. Brave but bewildered, Dalyell rapidly lost control of the situation. With casualties mounting as bullets and arrows scythed into the column from out of the darkness, retreat became inevitable.

Rogers, however, was in his element. Barricading a house with bales of beaver-skins, he helped to mount a rearguard action that covered the withdrawal of the survivors. The feisty Dalyell was not amongst them: he was killed whilst leading a counter-attack. Impressed by the captain's courage, if not his tactics, Pontiac's exultant warriors roasted and ate his heart.

Throughout that summer of 1763, Amherst's New York headquarters were bombarded with reports confirming the massacre of trusted officers. Many of these men were not merely subordinates, but also close companions. For Amherst, the Indian war soon became a personal vendetta. Writing to the commander of Detroit, he would hear of no 'Accommodations with the savages ... until they have felt our Just Revenge'. Amherst himself placed a reward of one hundred pounds New York currency on Pontiac's head, with a like bounty for whoever slew the Indian murderer of Captain Donald Campbell.

There was no longer any talk of tempering retribution against the guilty with mercy towards the innocent – in stark contrast to the orders Amherst had issued when he sent Rogers against St Francis. In the eyes of his peers, Amherst was technically justified in adopting a stern stance: as both 'rebels' *and* 'heathen savages', the Indians fell outside the parameters of protection offered by the Laws of War. But the measures he took were harsh indeed: that July he gave orders for *all* hostile Indians to be slain – as 'no punishment we can Inflict is Adequate to the Crimes of those Inhumane Villains'. Always uneasy amongst Indians, the general now gave free rein to his latent prejudices: he wished 'there was not an Indian settlement within a Thousand miles of our Country, for they are only fit to live with the Inhabitants of the Woods, being more nearly allied to the Brute than the Human Creation.'

As the crisis worsened, Amherst was willing to consider any method that would *extirpate this execrable race*; proposals included a scheme to infect the tribes with smallpox. Such indiscriminate solutions brooked no distinction between warriors and their families. In his rage, grief and unvarnished thirst for vengeance, Jeffery Amherst displayed the savagery that he had so often deplored in others.

Pontiac's War sullied the clean sheet that Amherst had maintained for so long. He returned to England that November leaving an ugly conflict festering in his wake. Writing from London in the new year, Sir William Johnson's agent, the semi-literate George Croghan, reported that the general's reputation was in tatters: indeed, his conduct was condemned by everybody, 'and has been pelted away in ye. papers . . . in Short he is No body heer Nor has he been askt aqustion with Respect to ye. affairs of amerrica Sence he Came over which a gentleman might nott ask his footman'.

WHILST FALLING SHORT OF A true pan-Indian struggle for independence, the war associated with Pontiac's name was nevertheless remarkable because it overcame linguistic and cultural barriers to embrace disgruntled tribes from the Great Lakes to northern New York. But for all their long-standing hatreds, the St Francis Abenakis, those sworn enemies of the English, were not amongst the rebels. Inside what was now the most heavily garrisoned sector of British America, they had little alternative to inaction: ever since the fall of New France, they had been carefully watched. Amherst harboured no illusions about their true feelings: provided they remained quiet, they would be left in peace; if they strayed, he would know how to punish them. Coming from the man who had unleashed Rogers upon St Francis, Amherst's blunt warning was loaded with menace.

Like the other Indian nations of Canada, the chastened Abenakis now fell within the bailiwick of Sir William Johnson, Britain's superintendent of the northern tribes. Aided by his enthusiastic informant Father Roubaud, Johnson kept them under close observation. As an extra precaution, a company of hard-bitten redcoats was billeted upon the village and the Indians had no choice but to endure their drunkenness and debauchery.

The humiliating position that the St Francis Abenakis were obliged to occupy in the post-war world was all too soon demonstrated by an episode of wrangling with the Stockbridge Mahicans, or River Indians. This centred upon retribution for Peter, the warrior who had been captured with Quinton Kennedy in August 1759 and slain when he refused to return to his people. Captain Jacob Cheeksaunkun, the Stockbridge leader, had festered in irons for the best part of a year because of the St Francis Indians, and he was determined to exact his pound of flesh from them. For all their former notoriety, they were no longer in any position to ignore the demands of a tribe that had backed the victorious British and now enjoyed the advocacy of the omnipotent Johnson.

Negotiations dragged on until March 1762, before the Stockbridges were at last placated. In place of the murdered man, the St Francis Abenakis produced a young *Panis* – an Indian slave from a far-flung western nation who had been bought for that very purpose. The final deal was brokered by Johnson and the ever-ready Roubaud, and sealed with the customary offerings of wampum. The weighty belts and strings of drilled and polished shells signified a desire to remove the axe that had been buried, metaphorically, in the heads of the River Indians as a people, but all too literally in the skull of the obstinate Peter himself; henceforth the offending hatchet would be sunk in a rapid stream and swept down to the 'bottomless sea, that it can never again be found'. With that, all the past might be forever forgotten.

In his efforts to bolster his standing with the British, the renegade Roubaud had no qualms about informing against his flock. Writing from St Francis in October 1761, he warned Johnson that the *Abinaquis* had hardly shown themselves in the village during the summer. Instead, they had been conspicuous at Caughnawaga, holding frequent talks with the Iroquois there. These councils had discussed speeches brought to them from the Ohio by some Ottawas, and even by the Cherokees from Carolina. The messages sought to unite all the Indians . . .

Despite these ominous signs of a looming Indian confederacy, when Pontiac's War ignited, the St Francis Abenakis took pains to affirm their loyalty to the British. Those seeking to steer the battered tribe through these difficult times included Chief Gill. With his own family ravaged by Rogers' raid, Joseph-Louis might have been forgiven for nurturing dreams of vengeance against the British; but if he held such personal cravings, they were subsumed by concern for the greater good of his people. Gill assured the governor of Trois-Rivières, Brigadier-General Frederick Haldimand, that his tribe had nothing but peaceful intentions towards the British. They joined the other Indian Nations of Canada in sending a wampum belt to the western tribes, castigating them for having foolishly and rashly taken up the hatchet against the English.

Collaboration with the old enemy was unavoidable, but galling all the same: in truth, the Abenakis shared common cause with the tribes fighting to eject the land-hungry whites from their territories. Following the conquest of New France, migrant settlers had swarmed up the Connecticut Valley in an 'unprecedented invasion of western Abenaki lands'.* The St Francis expedition had done much to stimulate this onslaught;

* The verdict of Professor Colin G. Calloway.

not only did the major's bloody strike warn Indians of the consequences of future defiance, but his celebrated exploit focused attention upon the region's natural riches. Rogers' own manuscript map of his march depicted these in an alluring light: whilst 'the land of the Upper Cohorse [Cowass]' was undoubtedly 'Very good, and [was] made a Rich Soil, by the Wash of the High Mountains all Round it', the Lower Cowass was more attractive still: 'the greatest Part of it is Clear from Trees,' Rogers noted, 'and in my Opinion the best Lands that ever I have Travell'd Over.'

By blazing a trail for future settlement, Rogers delivered a far more grievous wound against the St Francis Indians than any he inflicted during those frenzied early hours of 4 October, 1759. It was a gutting blow that laid bare the very vitals of their heartlands, and in doing so, it sounded the death-knell for a traditional way of life. Within a few short years, white families were flocking to farm soil long sacred to the Abenakis, and now freshly fertilised by the blood and bones of the major's *chosen men.*

IN SHUNNING CONFRONTATION with redcoats and settlers alike, Abenaki leaders sought to evolve a strategy for meeting the challenges posed by rapidly changing times. Amidst such shifting sands, the firm path forwards could prove difficult to identify; those who struggled to find it included Robert Rogers, who now experienced problems in adjusting to the twin concepts of peace and civilisation.[*]

Above all, Rogers' future was dominated by a battle against a foe as implacable as any he ever encountered on the frontier: debt. Indeed, 1764 had scarcely begun before his creditors were closing in for the kill. Within weeks he was inside a New York prison, though the major's incarceration was brief. Sympathetic soldiers of the Royal Americans and Black Watch soon battered their way into the New Gaol and freed him. The *New-York Gazette*, which heartily disapproved of the *atrocious affair*, remained unconvinced by claims that Rogers was merely the hapless victim of his own popularity. During the riot, reported the paper, he was

[*] As Stanley Pargellis put it in his pungent sketch for the *Dictionary of American Biography.*

heard to give a signal of one, two, or three Indian yells to his accomplices; amidst the ensuing pandemonium he jumped upon a waiting horse and, *Indian-like, went the Lord knows where.* Irate New Yorkers offered a substantial reward of two hundred pounds for his apprehension, but Rogers was soon beyond their reach in neighbouring Connecticut.

The rank and file redcoats who engineered the jailbreak respected Rogers for his sterling qualities as a fighting man, but the men responsible for winning the war were not those who would administer the peace. Amherst's successor as commander-in-chief was none other than Thomas Gage, that same officer who had failed so dismally during the campaign of 1759. The paper-shuffling Gage had never seen eye to eye with the unruly Rogers; an outspoken critic of the rangers, the general possibly resented the fact that his own regiment of light infantry had never replaced them. His continuing coolness was soon apparent. When Rogers sought the captain's pay due for his services at Detroit in 1763, Gage initially refused to approve the claim; as Rogers was technically a volunteer, he would receive nothing. After further lobbying, the payment was eventually authorised, but the episode provided an ominous warning of attitudes at headquarters. Rogers would have to look elsewhere for patronage.

Stymied at home, in 1765 Rogers resolved to capitalise upon his wartime celebrity by seeking his fortune in London, at the very hub of the British Empire. He hoped to secure a position and financial backing for an ambitious expedition to locate the Northwest Passage – the fabled route between the Atlantic and Pacific that would provide a lucrative short cut to the riches of the Orient. In several respects this transatlantic foray was a stunning success. Rogers was a picturesque figure whose backwoods ruggedness was highlighted by the sartorial excesses of the fops then strutting the capital's streets. He quickly won the friendship of many influential men, including the Paymaster-General Charles Townshend, the hard-drinking and effervescent 'Champagne Charlie' whose own brother had been killed serving alongside Rogers at Ticonderoga in 1759. Once again, Major Rogers was lionised by society, and in a crowning mark of official favour, he was summoned to kiss the hand of King George III himself.

All this was progress enough, but Rogers' months in the metropolis were marked by other achievements that testified to his remarkable character. At his own expense he published two books. Both *The Journals of Major Robert Rogers* and another, more expansive, work entitled *A Concise Account of North America* left little doubt of Rogers' qualifications to undertake fresh employment on the wilder bounds of Britain's expanding domains.

In a time and place where literary critics derived a more than usual satisfaction from butchering the efforts of deluded tyros, Rogers' volumes acquitted themselves well. The *Monthly Review* believed the *Journals* to be 'as authentic as they are important and necessary'. In addition, its critic considered that Rogers wrote like an honest, a sensible, and a modest man. Of the same book the *Critical Review* remarked that the fatigues Rogers claimed to have undergone 'would be incredible, were they not confirmed by the unquestionable relations of persons in the like circumstances'. These impartial verdicts provide interesting counterpoints to those who, both in his lifetime and since, branded him a liar and a braggart. That Rogers had scored a direct hit upon one of his primary targets was clear from the reviewer's concluding comment: 'If the author has obtained a government in the country he was so instrumental in reducing, we very heartily wish him joy.'

But it was *A Concise Account* that attracted the lion's share of interest. According to the *Monthly Review*, the book provided a timely reminder of the possibilities offered by the interior parts of that immense continent which victory had so lately added to the British Empire. In introducing its thirteen-page selection of extracts, the same journal provided striking proof of Rogers' enduring fame throughout the English-speaking world: 'Few of our Readers, we apprehend, are unacquainted with the name, or ignorant of the exploits, of Major Rogers; who, with so much reputation, headed the provincial troops called *Rangers*, during the whole course of our late successful wars in America.'

Reviewers were particularly struck by a passage describing Pontiac, whom Rogers claimed to have encountered during his western expedition of 1760. As one of them noted, his picture of the *emperor Ponteack* was new and curious; the Ottawa sachem would appear to vast advantage in the hands of a great dramatic genius.

This suggestion may explain the swift emergence of a third publication associated with Rogers' sojourn in London: a blank verse drama entitled *Ponteach; or, The Savages of America. A Tragedy*. No author was named on the title page, but commentators attributed it to Major Rogers; given its gritty subject matter, he had at least some hand in the production; a greater share may have stemmed from the imagination of his secretary, the Princeton graduate Nathaniel Potter. The first native-authored play to feature an American setting, *Ponteach* represented a literary milestone. Sadly, its artistic quality fell short of the subject's potential, and this time the critics were merciless. The *Gentleman's Magazine* deplored the crude language – 'such *damning* and *sinking*, and calling *bitch*' was not to be endured in any production, least of all a tragedy – while the *Critical Review* slammed the piece as the most insipid and flat drama it had ever perused. But the *coup de grâce* was administered by the *Monthly Review*, which thought it 'a great pity that so brave and judicious an officer should thus run the hazard of exposing himself to ridicule, by an unsuccessful attempt to entwine the poet's bays with the soldier's laurel. His journal, and account of our western acquisitions, were not foreign to his profession and opportunities; but in turning bard, and writing a tragedy, he makes just as good a figure as would a Grubstreet rhymester at the head of our Author's corps of North-American Rangers.'

It's unlikely that these excoriating verdicts preyed overly upon Rogers' mind; by the time they surfaced, he was already back in North America, in possession of what he had travelled so far to find: an appointment as commandant of Michilimackinac, a frontier post from where he could pursue his dreams of finding the Northwest Passage.

This longed-for theatre of opportunity was the backdrop for the opening scene of Rogers' own personal tragedy. By gaining command of

Michilimackinac, Rogers alienated two of the most powerful men in America. Gage resented the fact that Rogers had secured the posting without his prior knowledge; as the appointment also conveyed a loose superintendency over neighbouring Indians, it also raised the hackles of Sir William Johnson. Back in 1755, Rogers' daring scouts had helped to salvage Johnson's crumbling reputation as his army languished at the Lake George camp, but now Sir William chose to forget such former services. Above all, he would tolerate no encroachment upon an Indian department that he regarded as his own personal fiefdom.

Gage and Johnson shared prejudices that left them all too willing to credit correspondence that implicated Rogers in a far-fetched plot to foment Indian rebellion and betray his post to the French. The allegations originated in a letter that bore all the hallmarks of a clumsy attempt to smear his name, but when Rogers' estranged former secretary Nathaniel Potter swore to his evil intentions, Gage had no hesitation in arresting him on a charge of high treason. On 6 December, 1767, Rogers was clapped in irons within his own guardhouse, where he suffered severely throughout the harsh winter. When the lakes thawed in the spring, Rogers was taken east for trial. During the ten-day voyage by sloop to Detroit he lay in chains upon the rough ballast in the hold. The court martial finally opened at Montréal on 20 October, 1768. After a lengthy hearing, during which Rogers spoke fluently against the *Infamous Accusation* that had blasted his reputation, the court acquitted him on all counts.

This finding failed to clear Rogers' name. Although the king approved the verdict, his official response included the damning observation that there had nevertheless been good grounds for suspecting 'an improper and dangerous Correspondence'.

IF GOSSIP IS TO BE BELIEVED, Rogers was himself a gambler; yet there was something remorseless about the hard cards that fate now dealt him. Tainted by the stigma of treason, Rogers regained neither his command nor his character. From that point forwards, his fortunes went into a tailspin decline.

Frustrated and embittered, Rogers returned to London in the summer of 1769; he sought pay that he maintained was owing to him, and redress for the wrongs he had endured. But there would be no repeat of his triumphs of 1765. To be sure, there were flashes of the old Rogers, and he had a way with malefactors that endeared him to Georgian London's crime-lashed inhabitants: in October, 1771, whilst travelling by post-chaise through Kent, Rogers' nervous coachman warned him that a high-wayman was lurking. When this unsuspecting Gentleman of the Road demanded his due, the major grabbed his hand, hauled him into the coach and delivered him to the authorities at Gravesend.

But this time such dashing interludes were rare; more typical were lengthy and demoralising stints in debtors' prison. The poignancy of Rogers' continuing fall from grace did not fail to move those who remembered the indomitable major of earlier days. When he published his own *Memoirs* in 1775, the Scottish soldier Robert Kirkwood remarked, 'Whatever may have influenced his actions since, [he] was when I knew him an enterprizing, hardy soldier, and really deserved better usage from the English.'

Increasingly desperate, in 1774 Rogers sued Thomas Gage for false imprisonment; the suit was later withdrawn when Rogers eventually secured a major's half-pay. Gage, who spent the winter of 1773–4 on leave in England, had more on his mind than Rogers' writs; he was concerned with nothing less than the fate of British North America. Ever since the triumphant close of the Seven Years' War in 1763, the colonists had raised increasingly vociferous objections to imperial taxation; a decade later, it was apparent that a crisis was fast approaching. As commander-in-chief of Britain's forces across the Atlantic, Gage's views carried considerable influence in London. On 4 February, 1774, during an audience with King George III, he argued that a firm hand would overawe the obstreperous inhabitants of Massachusetts, who were viewed as the chief troublemakers. Gage told the king that the New Englanders would be *lyons, whilst we are lambs*; but if the government was resolute, they would become *very meek*. This was a fatal misreading of the colonists' temper.

IN AUGUST, 1775, AT THE END of five dispiriting years, Rogers returned to America. Much had changed since his last Atlantic crossing: taking a leaf from Pontiac's book, and contrary to Gage's predictions, Britain's North American colonies had risen up in defence of their liberties.

Jeffery Amherst's conquest of Canada had marked a crucial milestone on the road to revolution: the elimination of French power on the continent not only freed the colonists from the menace of a traditional enemy, but likewise severed their umbilical reliance upon the military might of the mother country. Such an outcome had long been predicted, not least by that astute outsider Peter Kalm. In 1749, Englishmen born on both sides of the Atlantic had assured him that within thirty or fifty years the American colonies 'would be able to form a state by themselves, entirely independent of Olde England'. The Swede was convinced that only the presence of their dangerous neighbours, the French, prevented the connection between the colonies and their mother country from being quite broken off. Kalm died in 1779, just four years before a humbled Great Britain was obliged to recognise an independent republic in the stead of its former colonies.

For many of those who had fought through the Seven Years' War, the revolution that it begat meant nothing less than a world turned upside down: in an era of changing loyalties, old friends became enemies, old enemies friends. The first set-piece encounter of the conflict, the battle of Bunker Hill in June 1775, established a pattern destined to be repeated in years to come. The British grenadiers sent to storm the Yankee breastwork were commanded by James Abercrombie; the men facing them looked to their orders from other veterans of the French and Indian War: these included the redoubtable John Stark. In their youth, Abercrombie and Stark had shared the hardships of ranger patrols in the hazardous no-man's-land around lakes George and Champlain. Now they were foes.

Never short on courage, Abercrombie led on his bold grenadiers in person; like many others, he died of wounds received on that bloody day. But John Stark, who had steadied his men with the eminently practical advice to aim for the redcoats' waist-belts, survived to fight again. Two years later, his destruction of a British foraging expedition at Bennington, Vermont, presaged the subsequent elimination of General John Burgoyne's army at Saratoga. This, the turning point of the war, ensured that Stark's old enemies the French joined the fray, thereby escalating colonial rebellion into a world war that Britain could scarcely expect to win.

Men who had once defended Canada now returned to help determine the future of Britain's prized American domains. They included Louis-Antoine de Bougainville. Following the fall of New France, Montcalm's aide-de-camp had followed a glittering career that satisfied all of his scientific ambitions. He transferred to the navy and, between 1766 and 1769, circumnavigated the globe, returning with tales of an idyllic South Pacific and bearing a lush bloom that was named bougainvillea in his honour.

A decade later, after France threw her resources behind the American rebels, Bougainville took part in the botched assault on Savannah. Promoted to rear admiral in September 1781, he played a distinguished role in the battle of Chesapeake Bay. The Royal Navy's failure to seize control of that waterway doomed the British army trapped within Yorktown; the garrison's surrender broke Britain's resolve to prosecute an unpopular war. France now savoured some belated measure of vengeance for her own humiliation in 1760.

Those obliged to weather this bewildering era of fluctuating alliances included the Abenakis of St Francis. Traditional enemies of *all* the English, they were naturally viewed with suspicion by rebels and royalists alike. But the tribe's base in a strategically important region betwixt British Canada and rebel New England, combined with their formidable warrior past, also guaranteed that both camps would court them as allies or at least seek to secure their neutrality. Conscious that wholehearted allegiance to just one side in this English civil war could lead to disaster, the Abenakis of St Francis exploited their flexible tribal structure of rambling bands to flirt with both.

Whilst carefully avoiding situations that would bring them into direct conflict with each other, the tribe's warriors simultaneously provided scouts for the British and information for the rebels. Some families accepted an invitation from the Americans to settle at Haverhill, on the Lower Cowass Intervales. Within twenty years of Rogers' raid, they were patrolling the upper Connecticut Valley alongside just such New Hampshire rangers as had torched their village.

Abenaki ambivalence was epitomised by the vacillating role of Joseph-Louis Gill. The White Chief emerged as the leader of a pro-rebel faction, and George Washington himself backed a recommendation that he should receive a captain's commission in the Continental Army. But Britain's Indian Department maintained a strong presence in St Francis and obliged Gill to demonstrate his loyalty to King George. He did this by leading a band of warriors on a covert operation that captured the rebel Major Benjamin Whitcomb. Snared on the Connecticut, Whitcomb was allowed to escape whilst being taken back to St Francis; the price of liberty was an assurance that if his countrymen invaded Canada, Gill's village would be spared.

Like the wily Joseph-Louis himself, the St Francis Abenakis survived the maelstrom of the Revolutionary war by placing a tentative foot in either camp. But not every tribe, community or individual embroiled in the conflict was able to adopt such a stance. From celebrated fighting men like Robert Rogers, unequivocal choices were required. If, like John Stark, Rogers had wholeheartedly embraced the patriot cause, it is likely that he too would have remained a hero to his countrymen, revered in his mellow twilight years and ultimately elevated to membership of the select fraternity of Revolutionary stalwarts. Instead, he followed a very different path.

WHEN HE RETURNED TO America, Rogers initially wandered Pennsylvania and New England as if oblivious to the conflagration igniting all around him. When he called upon Eleazer Wheelock, the President of New Hampshire's Dartmouth College, in November, 1775, he appeared chiefly interested in encouraging that establishment to invest in a land grant. As Wheelock reported to Washington, the famous Major Rogers claimed that he had been urged to accept an officer's commission in favour of the colonies, but as he remained on British half-pay, had thought best to decline. There were signs of Rogers' continuing money problems: the major tarried all night at a neighbouring tavern and by the next morning was unable to settle his score; he promised to pay the landlord on his return.

Rogers never came back, but some weeks later, Wheelock received startling news that his visitor was actually right-hand man to Britain's commander in Canada, Brigadier-General Guy Carleton; not only that, but in a ruse reminiscent of earlier days, Rogers had donned Indian habit and infiltrated the patriots' encampment at St Jean.

Washington ordered an investigation into this sensational claim. Although he was inclined to believe it false, he continued to be chary of a man 'much suspected of unfriendly views to this Country'; he directed that Rogers' 'Conduct should be attended to with some Degree of Vigilance & Circumspection'.

As an officer upon British half-pay, Rogers did invite scrutiny. Yet several other men who had previously served King George gained commissions from Congress. The outright rejection of this fading hero apparently stemmed from a deeper distrust, rooted in his failure to reveal any obvious enthusiasm for the patriot cause. So sceptical did Washington remain that, in June 1776, he ordered Rogers' arrest in Philadelphia as a suspected enemy agent. This was the turning point: when Rogers escaped soon after, he sought employment with the Royal army at New York. His old comrade John Stark, who did not doubt Rogers' courage, maintained that he would have proved a true man to his native country had he not been denounced before he could avow his principles.

Major Rogers was now commissioned lieutenant-colonel in command of a loyalist battalion named the Queen's American Rangers. In such scant fighting as it saw, the unit's performance was undistinguished: these were not the men who had fought the Battle on Snowshoes or marched to St Francis and back; neither was Rogers his old forceful self.

Long years of grinding frustration and bitter disappointment had bequeathed him a legacy of drunkenness. Swiftly adjudged unfit to command, he was once again retired on half-pay.

Rogers' personal life was equally dismal. Betsy had not seen her roving husband for years; at their last meeting he was in such a state that she was obliged to *shun & fly from him* for her own safety. She divorced him in 1778, retaining custody of their young son Arthur.

Two years later, on passage from Nova Scotia to New York, Rogers was captured by a rebel privateer; another miserable spell in prison followed. At the war's end in 1783 he returned to England, probably evacuated with the last diehard British garrison of New York.

Rogers ended his days a lonely exile, seeking blessed oblivion in the bottle. He died in Southwark, London, on 18 May, 1795. There, even in the midst of a conflict with Revolutionary France, his passing did not go completely unnoticed. *The Oracle and Public Advertiser* reported that Lieutenant-Colonel Rogers 'served in America during the late war, where he had the command of a body of Rangers, with which he performed prodigious feats of valour. He was a man of uncommon strength, but adversity, and a long confinement in the Rules of the King's Bench, had reduced him to the most miserable state of wretchedness.'

Perhaps, when the broken old ranger lifted the numbing glass, he had recaptured some distant recollection of the time when he was brave Major Rogers, the toast of His Britannic Majesty's North American Colonies. It can only be hoped that this was so.

JOSEPH-LOUIS GILL, the White Chief of the Abenakis, died at his beloved St Francis in 1798. That same year, his adopted daughter, Susanna Johnson, reflected upon her own dramatic past. Now a great-grand-mother, she had recently published an account of her captivity at the hands of the St Francis Indians; she was encouraged to do so by the numerous progeny who pestered her for exciting tales of bygone days. The stories that Susanna dictated were vivid, believable and unbiased, making her book amongst the most valuable of all such captivity narratives. She told of her terror at being plucked from her home at Fort Number Four; the unexpected kindnesses she had encountered amongst her enemies; and of witnessing Robert Rogers returning from his most famous exploit, the destruction of St Francis in 1759.

Half a lifetime later, when Susanna Johnson's recollections appeared in print, much had changed in the Connecticut Valley. Fort Number Four was now a peaceful settlement, long since known by the less belligerent name of Charlestown; the 'savages' had been driven off, and the young republic of the United States of America faced no enemies. Susanna wrote of how the passing decades had wrought a dramatic transformation: 'The gloomy wilderness, that forty years ago secreted the Indian and the beast of prey, has vanished away, and the thrifty farm smiles in its stead; the Sundays, that were then employed in guarding a fort, are now quietly devoted to worship; the tomahawk and scalping knife have given way to the sickle and ploughshare; and prosperous husbandry now thrives where the terrors of death once chilled us with fear.'

Susanna Johnson had survived all the perils of war to witness a bright new era of peace. But the harsh environment that provided her formative experiences, and which fashioned the likes of Joseph-Louis Gill, John Stark and Robert Rogers, had itself succumbed to the remorseless advance of civilisation. For whites and Indians alike, the violent but liberating world of New England's northern frontier would soon exist in nothing more than memories of hardship, courage and loss.

Notes

Abbreviations used in Notes

AB Abercromby Papers, Huntington Library, San Marino, California

BFTM *Bulletin of the Fort Ticonderoga Museum*

BEP *Boston Evening-Post*

BG *Boston Gazette and Country Journal*

BNL *Boston [Weekly] News-Letter*

CO Colonial Office Papers, Public Record Office (National Archives), Kew

DCB *Dictionary of Canadian Biography*

DHNY *Documentary History of the State of New-York*

GD Gifts and Deposits, National Archives of Scotland, Edinburgh

GM *Gentleman's Magazine and Historical Chronicle*

JP *Papers of Sir William Johnson*

JR *The Jesuit Relations and Allied Documents*

LO Loudoun Papers, Huntington Library, San Marino, California

NAC National Archives of Canada, Ottawa

NHG *New-Hampshire Gazette*

NYCD *Documents Relative to the Colonial History of the State of New York*

NYG *New-York Gazette*

NYM *New-York Mercury*

RH Register House (Microfilms), National Archives of Scotland, Edinburgh

VH *Vermont History*

WMQ *William and Mary Quarterly* (Third Series)

WO War Office Papers, Public Record Office (National Archives), Kew

Note: Where manuscript material must now be consulted on microfilm, the reel reference is given in preference to the original archival citations.

Preface

– *Robert Rogers*. See Stanley Pargellis, 'Rogers, Robert', in *Dictionary of American Biography*, ed. Allen Johnson and Dumas Malone (20 vols, New York, 1928–36), XVI, (1935), 108–9. The standard biography remains John R. Cuneo, *Robert Rogers of the Rangers* (New York, 1959; reprinted, Ticonderoga, New York, 1988). An excellent short sketch is C.P. Stacey, 'Rogers, Robert', in *Dictionary of Canadian Biography*, ed. F.G. Halpenny (13 vols, Toronto, 1966–94), IV, 679–83.

– *Rogers' Journals*. The full title is *The Journals of Major Robert Rogers, containing an account of the several excursions he made under the Generals who commanded upon the continent of North America during the late war* (London, 1765). There have been several reprints, including that introduced by Howard H. Peckham (New York, 1961). The Dublin edition of 1769 forms the basis for a valuable and handsome work, *The Annotated and Illustrated Journals of Major Robert Rogers*, eds. Timothy J. Todish and Gary S. Zaboly (Fleischmanns, New York, 2002).

– *Thomas Mante*'s book provides the most detailed and thoughtful contemporary account of the American campaigns of the Seven Years' War. See *The History of the Late War in North America and the Islands of the West Indies* . . . (London, 1772), pp. 221–4.

– *Ranger recollections*. See *Reminiscences of the French War with Robert Rogers'*

Journal and a Memoir of General Stark, ed. Luther Roby (Concord, New Hampshire, 1831; republished Freedom, New Hampshire, 1988).

– *Parkman's interest in Rogers*. See *The Journals of Francis Parkman*, ed. Mason Wade (2 vols, New York, 1947), I, 55; 60; 271; and Wade's biography, *Francis Parkman: Heroic Historian* (New York, 1942), pp. 60; 191. Also *Montcalm and Wolfe* (2 vols, Boston, 1884), I, 447; II, 261–9.

– *Northwest Passage* was first published in 1936. The two-volume limited edition (New York, 1937) includes detailed appendices of the sources that Kenneth Roberts used in researching his novel. For the film see R. Durgnot and S. Simmon, *King Vidor, American* (Berkeley, California, 1988).

– *'military legend and popular fascination'*. See Fred Anderson, *Crucible of War: The Seven Years' War and the Fate of Empire in British North America, 1754–1766* (New York, 2000), p. 769. On prototypes for the modern Rangers, see Burt Garfield Loescher, *Genesis: Rogers Rangers – The First Green Berets* (San Mateo, California, 1969; repr. Bowie, Maryland, 2000), ix. For an example of television coverage, see 'Ray Mears' Extreme Survival: Rogers's Rangers'. First screened by the BBC in March 2002, this programme focused upon the St Francis raid. For information on the extent of ranger re-enacting I remain indebted to Tim Todish.

– *Reassessments of the rangers*. Stacey's verdict is contained within his essay, 'The British Forces in North America during the Seven Years War', in *DCB*, III, xxix. For Eccles' comments see his review of Douglas Edward Leach, *Arms for Empire: A Military History of the British Colonies in North America, 1607–1763* (New York, 1973) in *William and Mary Quarterly* (3rd Series), XXXVI (1974), 502.

– *Francis Jennings' views.* See his *Empire of Fortune: Crowns, Colonies, and Tribes in the Seven Years War in America* (New York, 1988), p. 200; also 'Francis Parkman: A Brahmin Among Untouchables', in *WMQ*, XLII (1985), 305–28.

– *My Lai.* For the events at My Lai as part of a long 'tradition of atrocity' in North American military history, see Kendrick Oliver, 'Atrocity, Authenticity and American Exceptionalism: (Ir)rationalising the Massacre at My Lai', in *Journal of American Studies*, XXXVI, 2 (2003), 247–68; especially p. 257.

– *Textbook verdict.* See Richard Middleton, *Colonial America. A History, 1585–1776* (2nd edition, Oxford, 1996), pp. 432–3.

– *Difficulty of representing Indian perspective.* See Richard White, 'On the Beaches', a review of Daniel Richter's *Facing East from Indian Country: A Native History of Early America* (Cambridge, Massachusetts, 2001), in *London Review of Books*, XXIV, 6 (21 March, 2002), 25–6.

– *Indian Oral History.* Gordon Day was himself quick to emphasise that such oral evidence falls into various categories of trustworthiness, and that it is important to differentiate between them. Statements from 'literate informants', which may themselves have originated in published works, must be eliminated at the outset. More useful

are 'statements of unknown origin which appear to be common property'; such stories were known to almost everyone from the mouths of the 'older people'. However, the most valuable category of all comprises 'detailed narratives obtained from conservative, tradition-conscious Indians who in turn had obtained them from known and named sources.' It is fortunate that significant oral evidence relating to the St Francis raid falls within this most credible classification. See Day's important article, 'Rogers' Raid in Indian Tradition', in *Historical New Hampshire*, XVII (June, 1962), 3–17; especially 8–9.

– *'spurious evidence'.* An example includes the 'diary' attributed to a known participant in the raid, ranger Lieutenant George Campbell. Both the language used and information recorded in published extracts have long raised doubts about the authenticity of this account. Verifiable documents from the period support the contention that it is a carefully crafted fake. It should not be confused with the genuine account that Campbell gave to Thomas Mante, and which is used here.

Chapter One: *Conflict and Coexistence*

– *Susanna Johnson.* See 'A Narrative of the Captivity of Mrs Johnson, 1754, with the deposition of James Johnson, 1757', in *North Country Captives: Selected Narratives of Indian Captivity from Vermont and New Hampshire*, ed. Colin G. Calloway (Hanover, New Hampshire, 1992), pp. 45–87.

– *Flip.* This was a favourite tipple throughout Britain's North American colonies. It could be 'sweetened with sugar, molasses or dried pumpkin, according to individual taste or capabilities'. Eggs and cream might also be added to thicken the brew. See Alice Morse Earle, *Stage-Coach & Tavern Days* (New York, 1900; repr. 1969), pp. 108–9.

– *Fort St Frédéric.* See Timothy Titus, *An Illustrated History of Crown Point State Historic Site* (New York, 1994); *The America of 1750: Peter Kalm's Travels in North America, The English Version of 1770*, ed. Adolph B. Benson (2 vols, New York, 1966), I, 392; 'Narrative of James Johnson', in *North Country Captives*, pp. 85–7; 86. For the fort and its civilian settlement, see 'Sparta on the Lake: The Success of the St. Frederic Community', Chapter 7 of Theodore G. Corbett's *A Clash of Cultures on the Warpath of Nations: The Colonial Wars in the Hudson-Champlain Valley* (Fleischmanns, New York, 2002), pp. 165–93.

– *Lusignan.* See J.R. Turnbull, 'Dazemard De Lusignan, Paul-Louis', in *DCB*, III, 168–9.

– *Lake Champlain.* See *Kalm's Travels*, I, 393–6. See also the explanatory notes included on 'A Survey of Lake Champlain . . . By William Brassier [Brasier], Draughtsman 1762' (published August 1776) reproduced in *Atlas of the American Revolution*, eds. Kenneth Nebenzahl and Don Higginbotham (Chicago, 1974), pp. 62–3. This map provides the best contemporary depiction of both Lake George and Lake Champlain.

– *'pernicious nest'.* See Lt Gov James De Lancey of New York to Maj-Gen Jeffery Amherst, New York, 8

November, 1759 (WO/34/29, fol. 124).

– *'widowed land'.* See Francis Jennings, *The Invasion of America: Indians, Colonialism, and the Cant of Conquest* (New York, 1976), p. 30.

– *Escalation of tribal warfare.* See Daniel K. Richter, 'War and Culture: The Iroquois Experience', *WMQ*, XL (1983), 528–59.

– *King Philip's War.* For a brief discussion see Ian K. Steele, *Warpaths: Invasions of North America* (New York, 1994), pp. 96–109.

– *Evolution of St Francis.* This section, and much that follows, is indebted to two key works: Gordon M. Day, *The Identity of the Saint Francis Indians* (Hull, Québec, 1981); and Colin G. Calloway, *The Western Abenakis of Vermont, 1600–1800: War, Migration, and the Survival of an Indian People* (Norman, Oklahoma, 1990).

– *Jesuits.* See Alan Taylor, *American Colonies: The Settlement of North America to 1800* (London, 2001), pp. 107–11. Professor Taylor's book provides an excellent overview of both New France and the British colonies.

– *Deerfield raid.* For an atmospheric account of the raid and its ramifications see John Demos, *The Unredeemed Captive: A Family Story From Early America* (New York, 1994).

– *Sébastien Rasles.* See Rasles to his brother, 'Narantsouak' [Norridgewock], 12 October, 1723, in *The Jesuit Relations and Allied Documents*, ed. Reuben Gold Thwaites (73 vols, Cleveland, 1896–1901), LXVII, 203–5; Rasles to his nephew, Narantsouak, 15 October, 1722 (Ibid, 105).

– *Scalping and scalp bounties.* Descriptions by the first Europeans to visit North America, and scarified skulls excavated from prehistoric sites along the Mississippi and Missouri, leave no doubt that scalping was a pre-Columbian Indian practice. Like the Celts of Iron Age Europe, Indians gathered the heads of vanquished enemies; for Indians on long-distance raids, scalps were convenient substitutes for such spiritually significant trophies. The colonists' practice of offering bounties for scalps undoubtedly led to the spread and intensification of the custom amongst Indians and whites alike. For a balanced discussion of this emotive topic, see J. Axtell and W. C. Sturtevant, 'The unkindest cut, or who invented scalping?' *WMQ*, XXXVII, 3 (July, 1980), 451–72.

– *Killing of Rasles.* See 'Letter from Father de la Chasse, Superior-General of the Missions in New France', Québec, 29 October, 1724 (*JR*, LXVII, 233–5).

– *Grey Lock.* See Gordon M. Day in *DCB*, II, 265–6.

– *'Onontio'*. The relationship between 'Onontio' and those of his 'children' who adjoined New France's western outposts is examined in Richard White's *The Middle Ground: Indians, Empires, and Republics in the Great Lakes Region, 1650–1815* (Cambridge, 1991). Rasles' comment is contained in his letter to his nephew of 15 October, 1722 (*Jesuit Relations*, LXVII, 101).

– *Martial ethos of Canadian society.* See 'The Social, Economic, and Political Significance of the Military Establishment in New France', in W.J. Eccles,

Essays on New France (Toronto, 1987), pp. 110–23.

– *Events at 'No 4' in 1746–7.* See 'Narrative of Mrs Johnson', p. 50; also Calloway, *Western Abenakis of Vermont*, pp. 154–5.

– *Vengeance and independence.* See *French and Indian Cruelty; Exemplified in the Life and Various Vicissitudes of Fortune, of Peter Williamson, A Disbanded Soldier* ... (4th ed, London, 1759), p. 26.

– *Ateawanto's warning.* See 'Conference of Captain Phineas Stevens with the St. Francis Indians', in *Documents Relative to the Colonial History of the State of New York*, ed. E.B. O'Callaghan and B. Fernow (15 vols, Albany, 1853–87), X, 252–4; see also Thomas M. Charland, 'Atecouando (Jerome)', in *DCB*, III, 20–1.

– *'Fort Wentworth'*. The most telling evidence against the construction of 'Fort Wentworth' at Cowass in 1754 is the fact that as late as the autumn of 1759 Wentworth was still urging the establishment of a post there. See Wentworth to Amherst, Portsmouth, 8 September, 1759 (CO/5/56, fol. 281).

– *Running the gauntlet.* See Henry Grace, *The History of the Life and Sufferings of Henry Grace* ... (2nd ed, Reading, 1765), pp. 13; 30; 41–2. Describing the customs of the Iroquois in the early 1720s, the Jesuit priest Pierre de Charlevoix maintained that the gauntlet was *never* intended to prove mortal. See *Journal of a Voyage to North America ... by Pierre Francois Xavier de Charlevoix* (2 vols, London, 1761) I, 369–70. However, as Grace's narrative makes clear, the treatment of those obliged to 'run' could vary dramatically.

At the hands of excited warriors, adult male war captives might fare very badly indeed; fatalities were not unknown.

– *The market for captives*. See Ian K. Steele, 'Surrendering Rites: Prisoners on Colonial North American Frontiers', in *Hanoverian Britain and Empire: Essays in Memory of Philip Lawson*, eds. S. Taylor, R. Connors and C. Jones (Woodbridge, Suffolk, 1998), pp. 137–57; 141–2.

– *Fate of captives*. This hinged upon a wide variety of factors, but for a good general discussion see June Namias, *White Captives: Gender and Ethnicity on the American Frontier* (Chapel Hill, North Carolina, 1993), especially pp. 1–5; also very useful is Wilcomb E. Washburn's 'Introduction' to *Narratives of North American Indian Captivity: A Selective Bibliography*, ed. Alden T. Vaughan (New York, 1983). A valuable overview of conditions on the northern frontiers of New England is provided by Colin G. Calloway's article 'An Uncertain Destiny: Indian Captivities on the Upper Connecticut River', *Journal of American Studies*, XVII, 2 (1983), 189–210. For captivity amongst the North American Indians as part of a wider phenomenon of British contact with non-Europeans, see Linda Colley, *Captives: Britain, Empire and the World, 1600–1850* (London, 2002).

– *Adoption of whites by Indians*. See *Kalm's Travels*, II, 456–7. In an influential article, James Axtell estimated that about fifteen per cent of captives were totally assimilated into tribal society. See 'The White Indians of Colonial America', *WMQ*, XXXII (1975), 55–88. Atxell's findings have been questioned

by Alden T. Vaughan and Daniel Richter in 'Crossing the Cultural Divide: Indians and New Englanders, 1605–1763', *American Antiquarian Society Proceedings*, XC (1980), 23–99. This reckons the rate of complete cultural transition far lower, at just 3.2 per cent. See also J. Norman Heard, *White Into Red: A Study of the Assimilation of White Persons Captured by Indians* (Metuchen, New Jersey, 1973).

– *Coleman on St Francis captives*. See Emma Lewis Coleman, *New England Captives Carried to Canada Between 1677 and 1760 During the French and Indian Wars* (2 vols, Portland, Maine, 1925), I, 28–9.

– *Wampum*. See Elisabeth Tooker, 'The League of the Iroquois: Its History, Politics and Ritual', in *Handbook of the North American Indians: Volume 15, The North East*, ed. B.G. Trigger (Washington, 1978–9), 418–41; 422–4.

– *Joseph-Louis Gill*. See John C. Huden, 'The White Chief of the St. Francis Abnakis – Some Aspects of Border Warfare: 1690–1790', in *Vermont History*, XXIV (1956), 199–210; 337–55; Thomas M. Charland, 'Gill, Joseph-Louis', in *DCB*, IV, 293–4. The maiden name of Gill's mother Rosalie, given here as 'James', remains the subject of debate amongst genealogists.

– *St Francis and Chartres*. See Thomas M. Charland, *Histoire des Abénakis d'Odanak, 1675–1937* (Montréal, 1964), p. 87.

– *The village, or 'town', of St Francis*. See Day, 'Rogers' Raid in Indian Tradition', *Historical New Hampshire*, (June 1962), 15; 'Narrative of James Johnson', p. 86; Day, *Identity of the St Francis Indians*,

p. 42. The 1704 plan of the original stockaded village is reproduced in Charland, *Abénakis d'Odanak*, facing p. 64. The community to which the Johnsons were brought fifty years later was located some two and a half miles closer to the mouth of the St Francis River.

– *Frontier-Tidewater divide.* See *Kalm's Travels*, I, 119. Study of North America's colonial frontier, or 'back-country', has become something of an academic growth industry in recent decades. The outpouring of scholarly articles and monographs shows no sign of slackening. For a useful grounding in some of the key issues see Gregory H. Nobles, 'Breaking into the Backcountry: New Approaches to the Early American Frontier, 1750–1800', *WMQ*, XLVI (1989), 641–70, while recent research is synthesised in Eric Hinderaker and Peter C. Mancall, *At the Edge of Empire: The Backcountry in British North America* (Baltimore, 2003).

– *Frontier coexistence.* See Calloway, *Western Abenakis of Vermont*, pp. 24–7.

– *Expansion of New Hampshire.* See Jere R. Daniell, *Colonial New Hampshire: A History* (New York, 1981), pp. 140–2.

– *'Scotch-Irish'.* A recent survey of this movement, albeit concentrating upon Pennsylvania, is Patrick Griffin, *The People With No Name: Ireland's Ulster Scots, America's Scots Irish, and the Creation of a British Atlantic World, 1689–1764* (Princeton, 2001), pp. 1–2; 71.

– *Anglo-Scots borderers.* See David Hackett Fischer, *Albion's Seed. Four British Folkways in America* (New York, 1989). Professor Fischer's controversial but stimulating book treats the Scotch-

Irish as part of a broader movement from a region deemed to include the northern counties of England, Northern Ireland and most of Scotland. See 'Borderlands to the Backcountry: The Flight from North Britain, 1717–1775' (Ibid, pp. 605–782; 630).

– *'Memoir' of Stark.* This was included in Roby's *Reminiscences of the French War*, pp. 194–7; see also Coleman, *New England Captives*, II, 292–4.

– *Rogers on cross-cultural interaction.* See *Rogers' Journals*, vi.

– *Rogers' activities in 1754.* See Cuneo, *Robert Rogers*, p. 4. *Rogers' Journals*, vi–vii, describe his early ramblings. Parkman also recorded the tradition that 'Rogers himself was a hunter and wanderer from his youth up' (*Journals of Francis Parkman*, I, 270).

Chapter Two: *Making Reputations*

– *Ambush of Jumonville.* This interpretation follows the reconstruction in Anderson, *Crucible of War*, pp. 5–7; 53–9.

– *Fort Necessity.* See Lawrence Henry Gipson, *The British Empire Before the American Revolution* (15 vols, New York, 1936–70), *VI, The Great War for the Empire: The Years of Defeat, 1754–1757*, pp. 41–2. The Indian perspective is explored in D. Peter MacLeod, *The Canadian Iroquois and the Seven Years' War* (Toronto, 1996), pp. 43–9.

– *Thomas Gage.* His culpability for Braddock's defeat has prompted much debate. Whilst agreeing that the 'hill' was crucial, Gage's sympathetic biographer absolves him of any negligence on the grounds that he had received no orders to seize it. See John Richard Alden, *General Gage in America: Being Principally a History of his Role in the American Revolution* (Baton Rouge, 1947), p. 27. For harsher judgements see Robert L. Yaple, 'Braddock's Defeat: The Theories and a Reconsideration', *Journal of the Society for Army Historical Research*, XLVI (1968), 194–201; also Paul Kopperman, *Braddock at the Monongahela* (Pittsburgh), pp. 114–5.

– *Dumas*. See Étienne Taillemite's entry in *DCB*, IV, 242–3. Dumas' account is given in Kopperman, *Braddock at the Monongahela*, pp. 251–2.

– *Account of the anonymous British soldier*. This has been published as 'The Journal of Captain Robert Cholmley's Batman', in *Braddock's Defeat*, ed. Charles Hamilton (Norman, Oklahoma, 1959), p. 28.

– *Indian tactics*. See Robert Rogers, *A Concise Account of North America* (London, 1765), p. 229. Also Leroy V. Eid, '"A Kind of Running Fight": Indian Battlefield Tactics in the Late Eighteenth Century', *Western Pennsylvania Historical Magazine*, LXXI (1988), 147–71. A convincing thesis for the effectiveness of such 'skulking methods' throughout the colonial era and beyond is presented by Armstrong Starkey, *European and Native American Warfare 1675–1815* (London, 1998).

– *Cameron's verdict*. See *The Life, Adventures, And Surprizing Deliverances of Duncan Cameron, Private Soldier in the Regiment of Foot, late Sir Peter Halket's* (3rd ed, Philadelphia, 1756), pp. 11–13.

– *Official report*. See the 'Inquiry into

the Behaviour of the Troops at the Monongahela', Albany, 21 November 1755 (WO/34/73, fols. 45–6); for Shirley's comments to Fox see fols. 38–40. This was prepared in conjunction with another officer, Lt-Col Thomas Dunbar of the 48th Foot. As Dunbar wasn't even present at the battle, the views reflected must be attributed primarily to Thomas Gage.

– *Treatment of Monongahela captives*. See *An Account of the Remarkable Occurrences In the Life and Travels of Col. James Smith . . .* (Lexington, Kentucky, 1799), p. 9.

– *Torture*. A perceptive analysis of the functions of torture amongst the Indians of the north-east is provided in Gregory Evans Dowd, *A Spirited Resistance: The North American Indian Struggle for Unity, 1745–1815* (Baltimore, 1992), pp. 13–16. For a detailed account of these rituals as practised by the Iroquois in the early 1720s, see Charlevoix's *Journal of a Voyage to North America*, I, 368–77. On Indian stoicism see Rogers, *Concise Account*, pp. 212–13.

– *Eyre's views*. See his letter to Robert Napier, Camp near Albany, 27 July, 1755, in *Military Affairs in North America*, ed. S. Pargellis (New Haven, 1933), pp. 128–9.

– *'Braddock's Instructions'*. See *The History of an Expedition Against Fort Duquesne in 1755 . . .* ed. W. Sargent (Philadelphia, 1855), p. 396; for Johnson's commission, see *The Papers of Sir William Johnson*, eds. J. Sullivan and A.C. Flick (14 vols, Albany, 1921–65), I, 496. The original 'Five Nations' of the Iroquois Confederacy – the Mohawks, Onondagas, Oneidas, Senecas and

Cayugas – increased to six following the admission of the Tuscaroras during the 1720s.

– *William Johnson.* For a balanced assessment of this controversial figure, see Julian Gwyn, 'Johnson, Sir William', in *DCB*, IV, 394–8.

– *Naming Lake George.* See Johnson to the Lords of Trade, Lake George, 3 September, 1755 (*NYCD*, VI, 997).

– *Vaudreuil* has received a mixed press at the hands of historians. For a sympathetic treatment see the lengthy article by W.J. Eccles in *DCB*, IV, 662–74.

– *Dieskau.* The baron's thirst for action is clear from his letter to Commissary Doreil, Montréal, 16 August, 1755 (*NYCD*, X, 311–12).

– *Battle of Lake George.* Dieskau's experience of this encounter and its. aftermath is best conveyed in an imagined 'Dialogue' in the 'Elysian Fields' between the baron and his old commander, Marshall Saxe (Ibid, 340–45). See also 'Letter from a Gunner to his Cousin', Lake George, 10 September, 1755 (*NYCD*, VI, 1005).

– *Mourning at St Francis.* King's account is cited in MacLeod, *Canadian Iroquois*, p. 7.

– *Vaudreuil's response to Dieskau's defeat.* See his letter to de Machault, Montréal, 25 September, 1755 (*NYCD*, X, 318–27).

– *Wraxall's pessimistic assessment.* See his letter to Henry Fox, Camp at Lake George, 27 September, 1755, in *Military Affairs*, pp. 137–45.

– *Rogers' and Sullivan.* See Cuneo, *Robert Rogers*, pp. 12–15.

– *Rogers' appearance and demeanour*, as recorded in Stark family tradition, is cited by Cuneo (Ibid, pp. 17–18).

– *Patrol of 14 September, 1755.* See 'A Journal of the New Hampshire Scout . . .', in *A Documentary History of the State of New-York*, ed. E.B. O'Callaghan (4 vols, Albany, 1849–51), IV, 259–60. This is the report compiled by Rogers immediately upon his return. His published *Journals* (pp. 1–3) include other details and state that the scout departed on 24 September. There are several discrepancies between the dates of these early intelligence reports and those in the published *Journals*. These anomalies have never been satisfactorily explained. There is no obvious motive for distorting the record; they may result from editorial errors.

– *Scout to Ticonderoga.* See *Rogers' Journals*, pp. 3–5, and *DHNY*, IV, 260–61.

– *Symes' report.* From the Lake George camp, dated 22 October, 1755, Ibid, 268–9.

– *Conflicting reports of Ticonderoga.* See: 'Examination of a French Deserter', Camp at Lake George, 16 October, 1755 (*Johnson Papers*, II, 200–202); 'Report of Capt Rodgers' and Co's Scout' (*DHNY*, IV, 269–70); Goldsbrow Banyar to Johnson, Albany, 18 and 27 October, 1755 (*JP*, II, 203; 244); Cuneo, *Robert Rogers*, pp. 26–7. *Rogers' Journals*, p. 8. Whether or not Rogers actually saw the future Fort Carillon during his scout in late September, or instead spied an entrenchment constructed at the foot of the portage, remains a moot point.

– *Newspaper coverage of Rogers' scouts.*

See *Boston Gazette*, 13 October (Supplement) and 3 November, 1755; letters from Albany dated 22 and 23 January, in *Boston Weekly News-Letter*, 12 February, 1756.

– *Growing recognition of Rogers.* See *BNL*, 26 February and 11 March, 1756.

– *Shirley's orders.* See *Rogers' Journals*, pp. 14–15.

– *Whaleboat portage mission.* See news from 'Albany, August 12', in *BNL*, 2 September, 1756; *Rogers' Journals*, pp. 20–22. For Rogers' original report see 'Journal of a Scout' in *DHNY*, IV, 285–7. This once again differs from the *Journals* regarding dates and details.

– *Montcalm and his staff* all receive coverage in the *DCB*: on Montcalm and Lévis see W.J. Eccles (III, 458–69: IV, 477–82); for Bourlamaque see C.P. Stacey (III, 84–87); and on Bougainville, Étienne Taillemite in V, 102–6. Bougainville's invaluable journal has been published as *Adventure in the Wilderness: The American Journals of Louis Antoine De Bougainville, 1756–60*, ed. E.P. Hamilton (Norman, Oklahoma, 1964).

– *Killings at Oswego.* See *The Military History of Great Britain, for 1756, 1757. Containing A Letter From An English Officer at Canada, Taken Prisoner at Oswego . . . Also, A Journal of the Siege of Oswego* (London, 1757), pp. 41–2. Also 'Letter from an Officer, Camp at Chouaguen [Oswego]', 22 August, 1756 (*NYCD*, X, 456).

– *Newspapers.* See Middleton, *Colonial America*, pp. 299–300; Carl Bridenbaugh, *Cities in Revolt: Urban Life in America, 1743–1776* (New York, 1955), pp. 185–8. For the distribution of newspapers in 1760, see *Atlas of Early American History: The Revolutionary Era, 1760–1790*, ed. Lester J. Cappon (Princeton, 1976), p. 34. Despite its title, the *Boston Evening-Post* was a weekly publication. Strictly speaking, the *first* American newspaper was *Publick Occurences Both Forreign and Domestick*, published in Boston in 1690; however, only one issue, that of 25 September, was printed before the authorities ordered its suppression.

– *Lord Loudoun.* See S. Pargellis, *Lord Loudoun in North America* (New Haven, 1933). For Loudoun's views on the rangers cited here see his letter to Henry Fox, begun Albany, 22 November, finished New York, 26 December, 1756 (CO/5/48, fols 1; 4–5).

– *Capture of the sentry.* See *Rogers' Journals*, pp. 34–5; *New-Hampshire Gazette*, 26 November, 1756.

– *Importance of prisoners.* See Loudoun to Maj-Gen Phineas Lyman, Albany, 13 September, 1756 (LO 1798). The testimony of 'Laverdure', dated Fort Edward, 31 October, 1756 is in CO/5/48, fols. 29–31.

– *Rogers' vision of the rangers' role* is presented in his proposal to Loudoun, Fort Edward, 19 October, 1756 (LO 2043). In advocating a strike against St Francis, it is possible that Rogers was spurred on by hopes of emulating a recent raid, boldly executed by Pennsylvanian provincial troops, against the Delaware settlement of Upper Kittanning, on the Allegheny River beyond Fort Duquesne. During early September 1756, after a week-long approach march through difficult terrain, Colonel John Armstrong and three hundred men surprised the town in a dawn attack. The raiders burned Kittanning, killed many Indians – including the war leader Captain Jacobs – and freed a handful of captives. But it was a costly mission: the attackers suffered some thirty slain and wounded, with another nineteen captured. Fred Anderson emphasises that whilst Armstrong's daring raid was 'the only successful Anglo-American offensive' of 1756, it was a Pyrrhic victory that merely intensified assaults by vengeful Ohio Indians (*Crucible of War*, pp. 163–4). The expedition nonetheless gave a badly needed boost to the colonists' spirits, and was reported as a major victory (Matthew C. Ward, *Breaking the Backcountry: The Seven Years' War in Virginia and Pennsylvania, 1754–1765* (Pittsburgh, 2003), pp. 106–7). Above all, Armstrong's raid underlined the daunting hazards involved in mounting long-range strikes against Indians on their own ground.

– *Combat of 21 January, 1757.* This reconstruction draws upon the following sources: Rogers' original report, written at the 'Island near Fort Edward' on 25 January, 1757, in CO/5/48, fols. 108–9; a slightly edited version, omitting all reference to the killing of prisoners, was sent from Albany to Boston and published by newspapers (see for example, *NHG*, 11 February, 1757); in a more heavily amended form, it provided the basis for the account in *Rogers' Journals* (pp. 38–45). For the French perspective, see, for example, 'Relation de l'action . . . Le 21 Janvier 1757', in 'The Bourlamaque

Collection', V, 309–11 (NAC, Microfilm C - 363); also 'Account of two Expeditions in Canada, in the course of the winter of 1757' (*NYCD*, X, 569–70). Although not a participant, Bougainville recorded eyewitness details in his journal under the date of 1 February (*Adventure in Wilderness*, pp. 80–82). The recollections of Shute and Eastman are in *Reminiscences of French War*, pp. 135; 231. For Stark's role see Ibid, pp. 199–200. Shute and Eastman were both residents of Concord, New Hampshire. Luther Roby apparently interviewed them, and other former rangers, in old age. Testimonies made many years after the event in question must of course be treated with great caution, and they are used so here. However, those collected by Roby include vivid details that carry the ring of truth. In addition, it's sometimes possible to corroborate such anecdotes from contemporary sources. For example, the casualty list included with Rogers' report of 25 January gives *J[oh]n Shoot* as wounded *in the Head* – just as he claimed many years later.

– *French casualties.* It was subsequently reported, on the testimony of French prisoners, that Rogers killed '28 of the Enemy on the Spot, of which 15 were Indians, and 28 more died afterwards of their Wounds' (*NHG*, 29 April, 1757, under heading 'New-York', April 18).

– *Thomas Brown.* His story is told in *A Plain Narrative of the Uncommon Sufferings, and Remarkable Deliverance of Thomas Brown* . . . (Boston, 1760). Brown's book was clearly popular: a second edition surfaced before the year was out.

– *Tattooing*. Whilst Brown's tattooing was apparently enforced, other white men on the colonial American frontier adopted this bodily decoration with enthusiasm. Peter Kalm noted that Canadians, especially those involved in the fur trade, followed the Indian example by tattooing their torsos and limbs, although they jibbed at the native custom of facial tattooing. Indian 'masters of the art' adorned the Frenchmen, who favoured designs composed of stripes, suns, crucifixes or 'something else which their fancy may dictate'. Black dye, made from the charcoal of alder, was the most popular colour employed (*Kalm's Travels*, II, 577–8). A decade later, Bougainville reported that the tough *voyageurs* were universally tattooed 'with figures of plants or animals'. Such designs were imprinted by burning powder in holes pricked by needles. It was a painful rite of passage: 'One would not pass for a man among the Indians of the Far West if he had not had himself tattooed,' Bougainville observed. See *Adventure in Wilderness* (p. 288).

– *Burning of prisoners no longer the fashion*. Montcalm expressed this opinion to his mother, Le Marquise de St Véran, on 16 June, 1756, shortly after arriving in New France. He added, with grim humour, that the Indians had burned one prisoner near the Ohio River, 'so as not to lose the habit'. See 'Montcalm's Correspondence', in *Report on the Public Archives [of Canada] for 1929* (Ottawa, 1930), pp. 31–108; 44–5. A year later, Bougainville maintained that whilst Canada's mission Indians had been 'softened by the glimmerings of Christianity', such *cruelties* remained 'frequent enough' amongst the Shawnees and Delawares of the Ohio (*Adventure in Wilderness*, p. 114).

– *Loudoun's strategy*. See Guy Frégault, *Canada: the war of the conquest*, trans. Margaret M. Cameron (Toronto, 1969), pp. 146–9. Although Loudoun was ultimately given discretion to attack either Louisbourg *or* Québec, Pitt's interference in his original plan undoubtedly complicated an already difficult situation.

– *Montcalm's 1757 campaign*. For a detailed and thoughtful account see Ian K. Steele, *Betrayals: Fort William Henry and the 'Massacre'* (New York, 1990).

– *Bougainville on 'western' Indians and Abenakis*. See *Adventure in Wilderness*, p. 45 (entry for 3 October, 1756); p. 118 (20–25 June, 1757).

– *Composition of Montcalm's Indian contingent*. See Ibid pp. 150–51 (28 July, 1757).

– *Roubaud*. The remarkable Roubaud included a lengthy retrospective account of his eventful career at St Francis within a memoir to France's Minister for Foreign Affairs, the Comte de Vergennes, in March 1776. See 'Histoire de Pierre Roubaud, ci-devant, de la societe de jesus' (NAC Microfilm C - 12551, under MG 5/A1, Vol. 515, pp. 21–38). See also Auguste Vachon, 'Roubaud, Pierre-Joseph-Antoine', in *DCB*, IV, 685–7; Jane M. Lape, 'Pere Roubaud, Missionary Extraordinary', *Bulletin of the Fort Ticonderoga Museum*, XII, 1 (March, 1966), 63–71.

– *'Cannibal feast' at Ticonderoga*. See 'Letter from Father * * * [Roubaud], Missionary to the Abnakis, Saint

François, October 21, 1757', in *JR*, LXX, 91–203; 125–9. For Bougainville's observations see *Adventure in Wilderness*, pp. 142–3. See also Pierre Pouchot, *Memoirs on the Late War in North America Between France and England*, trans. M. Cardy, ed. B.L. Dunnigan (Youngstown, New York, 1994), p. 480. For cannibalism as a means of assuming an enemy's strength see G.M. Sayre, *Les Sauvages Americains: Representations of Native Americans in French and English Colonial Literature* (Chapel Hill, 1997), p. 298; also Starkey, *European and Native American Warfare*, p. 30.

– *Shouted Abenaki warning.* See *Adventure in Wilderness*, pp. 159–60.

– *Roubaud's account of Fort William Henry 'massacre'.* See *JR*, LXX, 175–91. Professor Steele calculates that a minimum of sixty-nine soldiers and civilians were killed, with a maximum of one hundred and eighty-four (*Betrayals*, p. 144).

– *Montcalm's letter to Loudoun.* Written from the 'Camp before Fort George [Fort William Henry]' on 14 August, 1757 (LO 4182).

– *Phips' proclamation against the Penobscots.* In *BG*, 10 November, 1755.

– *Laws of War.* This was the term used for the various conventions – intended to introduce some restraint into warfare – which slowly gained recognition in Europe during the century and a half before 1700. They theoretically extended protection to civilians, and sought to guarantee the humane treatment of prisoners and the wounded. Issues embraced under their aegis included the specified 'honours of war'

that were prized so highly by European soldiers – and which meant so little to Indian warriors. See *The Laws of War: Constraints on Warfare in the Western World*, eds. M. Howard, G.J. Andreopoulos and M.R. Shulman (New Haven, 1994), especially Chapter 5, 'Colonial America', by Harold E. Selesky (pp. 59–85).

– *Press coverage of the 'massacre'.* See, for example, 'Extract of a Letter from Albany, dated August 15' and the ensuing editorial, in *New-York Mercury*, 22 August, 1757.

– *Richard Rogers' fate.* See *Rogers' Journals*, pp. 55–6 (note).

– *Biological legacy of Fort William Henry.* See D. Peter MacLeod, 'Microbes and Muskets: Smallpox and the Participation of the Amerindian Allies of New France in the Seven Years' War', in *Ethnohistory*, XXXIX (winter, 1992), 42–64; 49. In the following year, prisoners who escaped from Canada reported that the French didn't expect many of the *distant Indians.* Indeed, 'the Small Pox that they got . . . at Fort William Henry . . . made such Havock among them, that out of 1500 that were there, it was believed 1200 died.' See Dr Richard Huck to Brig-Gen John Forbes, Albany, 28 June, 1758 (GD 45/2/23/5).

Chapter Three: *The Ranging Way of War*

– *Criticism of British.* See 'Letter from a Correspondent at New York', 26 August, 1757, in *Gentleman's Magazine*, 1757 (October), 442–3.

– *Proposed war-winning strategies.* See Pownall to Robert Napier, Boston,

4 September, 1757 (LO 4400); Loudoun to Cumberland, New York, 17 October, 1757, in *Military Affairs*, p. 404; Loudoun to Lord Colville, New York, 8 February, 1758 (LO 5554).

– *Forbes' bush-fighting suggestions* are contained within an undated memorandum from the early summer of 1757. See RH 4/86/2.

– *Lord Howe and the rangers.* See *Rogers' Journals*, p. 56.

– *Rogers' 'Rules for Ranging'.* Cuneo's verdict is in *Robert Rogers*, p. 55. The Rules were eventually published in *Rogers' Journals*, pp. 60–70 (see Appendix 1 here). Benjamin Church's Indian-fighting techniques are outlined in his *Diary of King Philip's War 1675–76*, with an introduction by Alan and Mary Simpson (Chester, Connecticut, 1975), p. 140. I remain very grateful to Gerald Orvis for discussing the issuing of Rogers' Rules for Ranging during the Vietnam War.

– *Original manuscript version of the ranging rules.* See Robert Rogers, 'Methods used in disciplining the Rangers … with their manner and practices in Scouting and Fighting in the Woods', Fort Edward, 25 October, 1757 (LO 4701).

– *Pringle on Rogers and his men.* See 'Henry Pringle Letterbook, 1747–1782' (NAC Microfilm H - 1954), pp. 64–5.

– *Black rangers.* See Scott A. Padeni, 'Forgotten Soldiers: The Role of Blacks in New York's Northern Campaigns of the Seven Years' War', *BFTM*, XVI, 2 (1999), 152–69; 165. Boston 'Burns' appears in the muster roll of Captain Charles Bulkley's Company of Rangers

[pre March 1758] in *BFTM*, VI, 1 (1941), 17. For 'Jacob' see *NYM*, 30 July, 1759.

– *Eyewitness descriptions of rangers.* See *An Historical Journal of the Campaigns in North America for the Years 1757, 1758, 1759, and 1760, by Captain John Knox*, ed. A.G. Doughty (3 vols, Toronto, 1914), I, 34; also 'An authentick Account of the Reduction of Louisbourgh', in *London Magazine*, 1758 (December), 615. A well-documented discussion of the evidence is provided by Gary Zaboly in 'Rogers' Rangers and Their Uniforms: Fact to Legend, Legend to Misconceptions', in *Annotated Journals of Rogers*, pp. 292–322; see also the treatment of ranger clothing in Gerry Embleton and Philip Haythornthwaite, 'The British Infantry of the Seven Years' War (3)', in *Military History Illustrated*, XXXIX (August, 1991), 39–46.

– *Capabilities of smoothbore weapons.* One authority on flintlock weapons states that both the 'Brown Bess' and its French equivalent, the 'Charleville' musket, were 'capable of hitting a target the size of a man quite consistently at 50 or even 60 yards'. See E.P. Hamilton, *The French Army in America* (Ottawa, 1967), p. 7.

– *British muskets and carbines.* See Anthony D. Darling, *Red Coat and Brown Bess* (Bloomfield, Ontario, 1971); Harold L. Peterson, *Arms and Armor in Colonial America, 1526–1783* (New York, 1956), pp. 159–70.

– *Rifles.* The use of rifles by volunteers with Rogers is documented in orders given at Fort Edward, 9 November, 1757, in 'Loudoun's Order Books'

(RH4/86/1); on metal-detector finds see Bob Bearor, *French and Indian War Battlesites: A Controversy* (Bowie, Maryland, 2000), pp. 81–4.

– *Status of rangers in British Army.* The first ranger unit to be officially recognised was the 'Corps of Rangers in North America', formed in September 1761 under Major-Commandant Joseph Gorham. See *Army List*, 1762.

– *Fallout from Stark's patrol.* See Capt. Abercrombie to Loudoun, Albany, 29 November, 1757 (LO 4915); Abercrombie to Colonel Forbes, undated (c. November, 1757), and Maj-Gen Abercromby to Forbes, Albany, 29 November and 14 December, 1757 (RH4/86/1). Although Captain Abercrombie was the nephew of General Abercromby, they spelled their surnames differently.

– *Whipping post mutiny.* See 'Court of Inquiry', Island near Fort Edward, 8–11 December, 1757, signed R. Rogers (LO 4969); Haviland to Abercromby, Fort Edward, 16 December, 1757 (LO 6859). The island in question was soon named Rogers' Island. The notorious severity of British Army discipline earned the redcoats their nickname of 'bloody backs'. See Stephen Brumwell, *Redcoats: The British Soldier and War in the Americas, 1755–1763* (Cambridge, 2002), pp. 100–12.

– *Abercromby's praise of Rogers.* See his letter to Loudoun, Albany, 2 January, 1758 (LO 5316).

– *Rogers' cattle killing foray.* See Doreil to Marshal de Belle Isle, in *NYCD*, X, 703; 'Journal of Occurrences in the Garrisons or Camps occupied by the

Regiment of Béarn, from the 20th October, 1757, to the 20th of October, 1758 [by Captain and Adjutant Anne-Joseph-Hippolyte de Maurès de Malartic]', in Ibid, 837.

– *Expansion of the rangers.* See Loudoun to Rogers, New York, 11 January, 1758, in *Rogers' Journals*, pp. 75–7; Loudoun to Pitt, New York, 14 February, 1758. See *The Correspondence of William Pitt, when Secretary of State, with Colonial Governors and Military and Naval Commissioners in America*, ed. G.S. Kimball (2 vols, London, 1906), I, 190–91; see also 'Engagement of the Stockbridge Indians' [February] 1758 (LO: 5799). The Mohegans and Mahicans represent two distinct tribes of the Algonquian language group. Both are sometimes referred to as 'Mohicans', a term that gained currency after 1826 with the publication of James Fenimore Cooper's popular novel. See T.J. Brasser, 'Mahican', in *Handbook of North American Indians: North East*, pp. 198–212. By the early summer of 1758, Jacob Cheeksaunkun and Jacob Naunauphtaunk each held the rank of captain (Patrick Frazier, *The Mohicans of Stockbridge* (Lincoln, Nebraska, 1992), pp. 124–5). British commentators called both men 'Captain Jacobs'.

– *Drafted veterans of the 27th Foot* expressed their gripes in a petition to Loudoun on 14 November, 1757 (LO 4833).

– *Langis' ambush outside Fort Edward.* See Massy to Forbes, Albany, 14 February, 1758 (LO 5596); *Pouchot's Memoirs*, p. 129; 'Extract of a Letter from Albany dated 14 February, 1758', in *NHG*, 10 March, 1758.

– *Chelsea pensioner Hugh Smith*. For his appearance on the Royal Hospital's admission rolls, see WO/116/5, fol. 30. Smith wasn't the only redcoat to survive the loss of his 'night cap' in America; for example, Lawrence Ranton and Sergeant William Wattson of the 45th Foot, who were examined at Chelsea on 21 January, 1757, were both wounded and 'Scalp'd by the Indians'. Ranton, thirty-six, was a shoemaker from Fifeshire; Wattson, thirty-four, a labourer from Spalding in Lincolnshire (WO/120/4, pp. 540–41). For a contemporary description of Chelsea Hospital see *The Diary of a Journey to England in the Years 1761–1762, By Count Frederick Kielmansegge*, trans. Countess Kielmansegge (London, 1902), pp. 275–6. The treatment of army veterans in Britain during the second half of the eighteenth century is addressed in Stephen Brumwell, 'Home from the Wars', *History Today*, LII, 3 (March, 2002), 41–7.

– *'The Battle on Snowshoes'*. This account draws upon the following contemporary sources: 'Journal of a Scout of Capt. Robert Rogers … Island near Fort Edward, 17 March, 1758', in *NHG*, 7 April, 1758; *Rogers' Journals*, pp. 79–90; *Adventure in Wilderness*, pp. 198–9; *Pouchot's Memoirs*, pp. 130–31; Extract of a letter from d'Hébécourt, 18 March, 1758, enclosed in de Massiac to Bourlamaque, Montréal, 19 March, 1758, in 'Bourlamaque Collection', I, 233–6 (NAC microfilm C - 362); Montcalm to M. de Paulmy, Montréal, 10 April 1758, in *NYCD*, X, 693; 'Journal of Occurrences in Canada, 1757–58', in Ibid, 837–8. For an imaginative reconstruction, incorporating

personal experience of the terrain and climate, see Bob Bearor, *The Battle on Snowshoes* (Bowie, Maryland, 1997).

– *Pringle's experiences*. See his letter to Haviland, Carillon, 28 March, 1758, in 'Pringle Letter Book', pp. 68–80. On the fate of the volunteers of the 27th Foot see Burt Garfield Loescher, *The History of Rogers' Rangers, Volume III: Officers and Non-Commissioned Officers* (1957; repr. Bowie, Maryland, 2001), 39; also undated memorial (c. 1762–3) of Major John Wrightson to Governor William Rufane at Martinique (WO/1/19, fol. 224).

– *Rogers' escape*. For a detailed discussion see Gary Zaboly's essay, 'The Legend of Rogers' Slide', in *Annotated Journals of Rogers*, pp. 97–103; also *Journals of Parkman*, I, 55.

– *Newspaper praise for Rogers*. See *The American Magazine and Monthly Chronicle for the British Colonies*, 1758 (March), 299–300.

– *French casualties*. See Montcalm to de Paulmy, Montréal, 10 April, 1758, in *NYCD*, X, 693; *Adventure in Wilderness*, pp. 199–200.

– *Doubts over Rogers' combat report and his subsequent vindication*. See Huck to Loudoun, 29 May, 1758 (LO 5837), and 'Pringle Letter Book', p. 68.

– *Rogers' promotion*. See *Rogers' Journals*, p. 104.

– *Gage's Light Infantry*. See Cuneo, *Robert Rogers*, pp. 60–61; Alden, *General Gage*, pp. 41–3. Gage's men were clearly a tough and motley crew. Whilst the regular regiments in North America theoretically shunned Indians,

Gage's recruiting criteria were apparently more flexible. A list of eleven deserters from the regiment during early 1762 included four Indians. Of the remainder, two were English, two Irish and three colonial Americans – one each from New England, Maryland and Pennsylvania. See list of deserters 'from His Majesty's 80th or Regiment of Light arm'd Foot', enclosed in Maj-Gen Amherst to Lieutenant Newland of the 80th Foot, New York, 22 March, 1762 (WO/34/92, fol. 65).

– *Transformation of Abercromby's army.* See *Scots Magazine*, 1758 (August), 442; 'Extract of a Letter from Flat Bush', 12 June, in *NHG*, 7 July 1758; Huck to Loudoun, Albany, 29 May, 1758 (LO 5837); Gates to Colonel Henry Bouquet, 8 September, 1759, cited in Sir John Fortescue, *A History of the British Army, Volume II* (London, 1910), 330 (note); orders, Albany, 8 and 11 May, 1758, in 'The Monypenny Orderly Book', *BFTM*, XII, 5 (December, 1969), 328–357; 335–7.

– *Reluctance of regular officers to undertake scouts.* See Huck to Loudoun, Albany, 29 June, 1758 (LO 5866).

– *Howe's death* is recounted in Captain Alexander Monypenny's letter to Mr Calcraft, Camp at Lake George, 1758, in Stephen H.P. Pell, 'Lord Howe', *BFTM*, II, 2 (July, 1930), 44–54.

– *Panic of 6 July.* See Major William Eyre, 44th Foot to Robert Napier, Lake George, 10 July, 1758, in *Military Affairs*, pp. 418–19.

– *Assault on the French lines.* See *Adventure in Wilderness*, p. 229–34; 'Copy of a letter from North America', in *Scots*

Magazine, 1758 (Appendix), 698–9, given in '"Like roaring lions breaking from their chains." The Highland Regiment at Ticonderoga', (documents compiled and edited by Nicholas Westbrook), *BFTM*, XVI, 1, (1998), 16–91; 54–8.

– *Major Eyre's gloomy letter to Napier.* See *Military Affairs*, pp. 421–2.

– *Trials of Susanna Johnson.* See 'Narrative of Mrs Johnson', pp. 69–79; *NHG*, 3 February, 1758 (under heading 'New-Haven, January 7'); Coleman, *New England Captives*, II, 306–9. 'Capt. Johnson' is listed as killed in the official casualty return for the action 'near Tienderoga, July 8th 1758' (WO/1/1, fol. 203).

– *Unruly Abenakis and Halfway Brook raid.* See *Adventure in Wilderness*, pp. 242–3.

– *Abenaki-Iroquois lacrosse match.* See Ibid, p. 249. For a plan of the Lake of the Two Mountains mission see B.G. Trigger, 'Native Settlement, 1635–1800', Plate 47 in *Historical Atlas of Canada 1: From the Beginning to 1800*, ed. R. Cole Harris (Toronto, 1987). The origins of lacrosse and its rise in Canada, are discussed in Dane Lanken, 'Lacrosse: "Little brother of war," the Indians called it', in *Canadian Geographic*, CIV, 5 (October–November, 1984), 36–43.

– *Skirmish near Old Fort Anne.* See *Rogers' Journals*, pp. 117–19; Lieutenant Thomas Barnsley of the 1/60th Foot to Colonel Bouquet, Albany, 7 September, 1758 in *The Papers of Henry Bouquet*, eds. S.K. Stevens et al (6 vols, Harrisburg, 1951–94), II, 480–81; 'Diary of

Abel Spicer' in *Chronicles of Lake George: Journeys in War and Peace*, ed. Russell P. Bellico (Fleischmanns, New York, 1995), pp. 91–119; 109; letter from Philadelphia, 24 August, in *Gentleman's Magazine*, 1758 (October), 498–9; Abercromby to Pitt, Camp at Lake George, 19 August, 1758, *Correspondence of Pitt*, I, 319–22; Abercromby to Governor De Lancey of New York, 10 August, 1758 (AB 522).

– *Abercromby's thanks.* See 'Monypenny Orderly Book', Lake George Camp, 12 August, 1758, in *BFTM*, XIII, 1 (December 1970), 89–116; 91.

– *Rogers' treat* to his men is recorded in the Orderly Book of Sergeant-Major Edmund Munroe of the rangers, entry for 28 August, 1758, at camp near Lake George, cited in *Annotated Journals of Rogers*, p. 147.

– *The onset of Amherst.* See *The Journal of Jeffery Amherst: Recording the Military Career of General Amherst in America from 1758 to 1763*, ed. J. Clarence Webster (Toronto, 1931), pp. 85–98; Abercrombie to Loudoun, New York, 17 December, 1758 (LO: 5977).

Chapter Four: *Amherst and Wolfe*

– *Character of Amherst.* See *Rogers' Journals*, pp. 88–90; LO 6043: Huck to Loudoun, Philadelphia, 20 February, 1759; LO 6041: Abercrombie to Loudoun, New York, 4 February, 1759. See also C.P. Stacey, 'Amherst, Jeffery, 1st Baron Amherst', in *DCB*, III, 20–26.

– *British strategy for 1759.* See Pitt to Amherst, 29 December, 1758, in *Correspondence of Pitt*, I, 432–42.

– *Wolfe's views on coming campaign.* See Wolfe to Amherst, Bath, 29 December, 1758 and *Neptune* at sea, 6 March, 1759 in WO/34/46B, fols. 287; 293; and to Major Walter Wolfe, Louisbourg, 19 May, 1759, in Beckles Willson, *The Life and Letters of James Wolfe* (London, 1909), p. 427.

– *British criticism of the rangers.* See Wolfe to Major Wolfe (Ibid, 427); Huck to Loudoun, 19 June, 1759 (LO 6113); Abercrombie to Loudoun, Fort Edward, 20 June, 1759 (LO 6115).

– *Ticonderoga enchanted.* See *Journal of William Amherst in America, 1758–1760*, ed. John Clarence Webster (Shediac, New Brunswick, 1927), p. 47; 'Robert Webster's Journal, April 5 to November 23, 1759', in *BFTM*, II, 4 (July, 1931), 120–53; 132. Alongside 'bogus' or 'cali-bogus', another favoured beverage was a blend of rum and molasses known as 'black-strap' (Earle, *Stage-Coach and Tavern Days*, p. 104–5).

– *Naval aspects of Amherst's campaign.* See Russell P. Bellico, *Sails and Steam in the Mountains: A Maritime and Military History of Lake George and Lake Champlain* (Fleischmanns, New York, 1992; revised ed. 2001), pp. 85–111.

– *Bourlamaque's position.* See G.F.G. Stanley, *New France: The Last Phase 1744–1760* (Toronto, 1959), p. 235; Thomas M. Charland, 'The Lake Champlain Army and the Fall of Montreal', *Vermont History*, XXVIII, 1 (January, 1960), 293–301; 294–5.

– *Highlanders' praise of Amherst.* See GD/87/1/87 and GD/170/1067/2.

– *Abercrombie's gripe.* See letter of 27 July, 1759 (LO 6128).

– *Conquest of Crown Point.* See Amherst to Pitt, 5 August, 1759, in *Knox's Journal*, III, 47–8; Campbell's letter from Camp at Crown Point, 6 August, 1759 (GD/87/1/88); *Amherst's Journal*, p. 151.

– *Press euphoria at Amherst's gains.* See *New-York Gazette*, 24 September and 3 December, 1759.

– *British dissatisfaction with progress of campaign.* For Huck see LO 6134; also Abercrombie to Loudoun, Crown Point, 13 August, 1759 (LO 6137).

– *Mounting criticism of Amherst.* See for example, *NHG*, 21 September, 1759; *NYG*, 24 September, 1759 (both under heading Boston, 17 September, 1759).

– *Impact of Niagara's conquest.* See C.P. Stacey, *Quebec, 1759: The Siege and the Battle* (Toronto, 1959), pp. 86–7.

– *Gage's orders to attack La Galette.* See Alden, *General Gage*, p. 49.

– *Amherst's caution.* See John Shy, *Toward Lexington: The Role of the British Army in the Coming of the American Revolution* (Princeton, 1965), p. 94–5.

– *Wolfe's efforts to aid Amherst.* See Wolfe to Pitt, HQ of Montmorencie in the River St Lawrence, 2 September, 1759, in *Correspondence of Pitt*, II, 156.

– *Rumours from Québec.* See *Diaries of Lemuel Wood, of Boxford*, ed. Sidney Perley (Salem, 1882), pp. 26–7; 36; 40.

– *Ensign Hutchins' mission to Québec.* See *Amherst's Journal*, pp. 152; 178; Amherst to Pitt, Crown Point, 22 October, 1759, in *Knox's Journal*, III, 50; Amherst to Wolfe, Camp of Crown Point, 7 August, 1759, in CO/5/56, fols. 201–202; letter from Point Lévis (Québec), 4 September,

1759, in *NHG*, 12 October, 1759; *BG*, 8 October, 1759.

– *Kennedy/Hamilton mission to Wolfe.* See Amherst to Pitt, *Knox's Journals*, III, 50. Amherst reported that the British officers would leave in company with four Indians; in fact their escort numbered seven. Besides 'Captain Jacobs' himself there were Sergeant Abraham Wnaumpos and privates John Maunaummaug, Jacob Miscouhukk and Jeremiah Maunhgaumpoo. See 'Accot. Of Pay due to Captain Jacob Cheek-saunkun, and those, of his Company of Stockbridge Indians, who were taken Prisoners by the Enemy Indians …' (WO/34/198, fol. 309). The party was completed by another Indian, possibly named Peter, and private John Humphrys of Gage's Light Infantry. See 'List of People Returned from being Prisoners in Canada 15th November 1759' (CO/5/57, fol. 118); also Frazier, *Mohicans of Stockbridge*, p. 143.

– *Kennedy's career.* See *London Gazette*, no 9505, 23–26 August, 1755; letter from 'Camp at Lake George, Sept. 20, 1756', in *BNL*, 7 October, 1756; *Military Affairs*, p. 242; *Scots Magazine*, 1756 (November), 559; *Army List*, 1758, p. 134 and 1762, p. 70.

– *Kennedy's 'Instructions'.* See 'Instructions for Captain Quinton Kennedy', Camp at Crown Point, 8 August, 1759, CO/5/56, fol. 177; Amherst to Gage, Crown Point, 14 August, 1759, in Ibid, fol. 213; Amherst to Pitt, *Knox's Journal*, III, 50. For the wampum belt see WO/34/198, fol. 309. The genesis of Kennedy's 'Instructions' is uncertain. Amherst was not noted for his interest in Indians and their affairs, so it is highly unlikely that they originated with him. Ensign Hutchins carried no such document; it is probable that Kennedy himself suggested the ploy when he volunteered his services.

– *Departure of Kennedy mission.* See *Diaries of Lemuel Wood*, pp. 27–8; 'Journal Militaire tenu par Nicolas Renaud D'Avène Des Méloizes', in *Rapport De L'Archiviste de la Province de Québec Pour 1928–1929* (1929), p. 64.

- *Kennedy's progress.* See Amherst to Pitt, Crown Point, 22 October, 1759, in *Knox's Journal*, III, 50–51; *Amherst's Journal*, pp. 154; 159.

– *Hopkins' fishing ruse.* Letter from Albany, dated 30 September, in *NYG*, 8 October, 1759; *Amherst's Journal*, p. 163.

– *Naval arms race.* See Ibid, pp. 163–4; 'Extract of a Letter from the Camp at Crown-Point', 7 September, 1759, in *NYG*, 24 September, 1759.

– *Hopkins' attempted sloop sabotage.* See WO/34/81, fol. 2: 'Orders for Sergeant Hopkins of the Rangers', Crown Point, 4 September, 1759; 'Méloizes' Journal', p. 73; *Amherst's Journal*, p. 168; Amherst to Pitt, in *Knox's Journal*, III, 58–9. Sergeant-Major Munson's exploits are recounted in 'Extracts of Letters, not of a very late Date, from the Westward', in *BNL*, 26 October, 1759.

– *Reactions to Kennedy's capture.* See *Amherst's Journal*, p. 167; Amherst to Pitt (*Knox's Journal*, III, 58–9); Montcalm to Amherst, August (undated), 1759, in *Collection Des Manuscripts du Maréchal de Lévis*, ed. H.R. Casgrain (10 vols, Montréal, 1889–95), IV, 255–6; Amherst to Montcalm, Crown Point, 10 September, 1759, in

Ibid, 258. That same autumn of 1759, a British Army lieutenant from Guadeloupe who was sent in disguise to report on the French defences of Martinique received short thrift upon detection, suffering 'the Common fate of Spies and Traitors'. See General Byam Crump to Pitt, Guadeloupe, 26 December, 1759, in *Correspondence of Pitt*, II, 227–8.

– *Discovery of Kennedy's party.* This reconstruction of events draws upon the following French sources: Rigaud to Bourlamaque, Montréal, 23 August, 1759, in 'Bourlamaque Collection', IV (NAC, Microfilm C - 362), 105; Vaudreuil to Bourlamaque, 'au Quartier General', 25 August (Ibid, II, 369). Also three letters sent to Lévis and contained in the *Lévis MSS*: from Vaudreuil, 'Au Quartier General', 26 August (VIII, 89–91); from Bigot, 26 August (IX, 49–50); and from Rigaud, Montréal, 31 August (X, 46). For French translations of letters taken with Kennedy see 'Meloizes' Journal', pp. 67–70.

– *Treatment of Kennedy's party.* See Montcalm's journal entries for 25–6 August in *Lévis MSS*, VII, 596–7; Vaudreuil to Brig-Gen Robert Monckton, Montréal, 13 October, 1759 (Ibid, IV, 266–7); Charland, 'Lake Champlain Army', *VH* (1960), 297; Frazier, *Mohicans of Stockbridge*, p. 143. A hint of Peter's grim fate is suggested by rumours that circulated within Wolfe's army. According to Lieutenant John Knox of the 43rd Foot, a French deserter who arrived on 31 August reported the capture of 'two Officers and four Mohawk Indians, who were coming express from General Amherst to this army'. In a note, Knox added the grisly detail that: 'Two of these Mohawks were roasted to death by the French at Trois Rivieres, in the presence of the other two, who were scalped alive, carried to Montreal, and hanged in chains; the Officers, I have been informed, were put in irons, and otherwise very rigorously treated' (*Knox's Journals*, II, 55).

– *Vaudreuil triumphant*. See Vaudreuil to Lévis, 26 August, 1759 (*Lévis MSS*, VIII, 89–91).

Chapter Five: *Chosen Men*

– *Amherst's disclaimer*. See for example, *NHG*, 1 February, 1760 (reporting intelligence from New York, dated 14 January).

– *Rogers' scheme for attacking St Francis*. See Rogers to Amherst, Albany, 12 December, 1759 (WO/34/78, fol. 182).

– *Targets of the raid*. See *Amherst's Journal*, p. 168.

– *Importance of La Galette*. See Amherst to De Lancey, Camp of Crown Point, 25 September, 1759 (WO/34/30, fol. 82).

– *Composition and size of the force*. For 250 men 'from the whole Army' see *NHG*, 1 February, 1760. The *BNL* (27 September, 1759) also gives 250, whilst the *BEP* (8 October, 1759) quotes a very precise 207. Amherst's '220 chosen men' (*Amherst's Journals*, p. 168) may reflect the total of privates, NCOs and volunteers. The addition of officers would raise this to around 230 of all ranks; this is the figure given in the most detailed newspaper account of the force's composition, in the *NYG* of 26

November, 1759 (see Appendix 2 here). Although the evidence is conflicting, it's clear that Rogers' command was *at least* 200-strong.

– *Manpower problems of Rogers' Rangers in the summer of 1759*. A 'List of People Returned from being Prisoners in Canada' on 15 November, 1759, names no less than thirty-eight of Rogers' Rangers who had been captured prior to the St Francis expedition (CO/5/57, fols. 118–19); also 'List of Deserters ... belonging to Major Rogers's Rangers', *BNL*, 20 September, 1759. Orders issued at Lake George on 16 July, 1759, required the provincial regiments to contribute a total of one hundred and thirty-two men for the rangers. Rogers chose the designated number from all who volunteered. See 'Monypenny Order Book', *BFTM*, II, 6 (July, 1932), 219–52; 222–3. Writing to Rogers from Crown Point on 24 November, 1759, Amherst characterised the majority of rangers who now demanded their discharges as 'the Worst Trash that I believe was ever Collected in any Corps' (WO/34/81, fol. 185).

– *Veteran ranger officers*. See Loescher, *History of Rogers' Rangers*, III, 23–4; 44–5.

– *Provincials*. 'Extract of a Letter from Crown Point, dated Sept. 28', in *NYG*, 8 October, 1759; 'Extract of a Letter from Number 4, to a Gentleman at Crown-Point, dated November 5, 1759', in *NYG*, 26 November, 1759; 'Memorial of Frederick Curtiss', Windham, 4 October, 1760, Connecticut State Archives: Colonial War Records, Vol. VIII, pp. 314–16. I am indebted to Robert J. Andrews for generously providing me with a transcript of Curtiss' invaluable manuscript.

– *British regulars.* For 'Draughts from the Regulars' joining the St Francis raiders see *NYG*, 24 September, 1759 ('Extract of a Letter from Albany, dated Sept. 20, 1759'). The British Army's gradual adaptation to American conditions is explored in Brumwell, *Redcoats*, especially pp. 191–263.

– *Inniskilling Regiment.* The first surviving muster rolls of the 27th Foot, dated at Crown Point , 28 May, 1760, and covering the period from 25 October, 1759 to 24 April, 1760, record that private 'Andrew McNale' was 'On Command'. The same comment, denoting detached service, was given alongside the names of no less than thirty-three other officers, NCOs and men from McNeal's company commanded by Captain James Holmes junior. The regiment's remaining companies included a further nine men 'On Command'. Given McNeal's known participation in the St Francis operation, it's likely that others of his comrades joined him. See muster rolls of the 27th Foot (1759–77), in WO/12/4328, fols. 1–10 (McNeal at fol. 10).

– *Robert Kirkwood.* See *The Memoirs and Adventures of Robert Kirk, Late of the Royal Highland Regiment, Written by Himself* ... (Limerick, 1775), pp. 5–41. The author of this intriguing but little-known book remains a mysterious figure. By his own account 'Robert Kirk' was drafted from Montgomery's Highlanders to the 42nd, or Royal Highland Regiment, in the winter of 1763–4 (Ibid, p. 80). As the surviving

muster rolls of the Black Watch record that a 'Robt Kirkwood' was enlisted from Montgomery's on 25 October 1763, it seems extremely likely that Kirkwood and Kirk are the same man (see WO/12/5478/part 1, fol. 96). This conclusion is bolstered by the fact that Kirkwood's subsequent duties and whereabouts, as recorded on the muster roll, match those recorded in *Kirk's Memoirs*. Although the exact date of composition cannot be established, Kirkwood clearly wrote his account of the *St Fransway* expedition some years after the event. Imprecise in terms of geography, dates, numbers and the spelling of proper names, but vivid when recounting specific events, it displays all the characteristics of a work composed from memory alone. In the fashion of his age, Kirkwood padded his text with swathes of material plagiarised from earlier travel writers. However, his book contains lengthy passages that are unique, and obviously based upon personal experience. In his preface, Kirkwood sought to assure his readers that he'd 'not inserted any lying or fabulous story in his *Memoirs*'. Coming from authors seeking to make a living, such statements must be taken with a healthy pinch of salt. Yet Kirkwood's account of his months amongst the Shawnees is one of the most credible of all captivity narratives. Other sections of his memoirs are equally fresh and convincing, and can be corroborated from independent contemporary sources. Although detailed and coherent, Kirkwood's treatment of the St Francis raid remains difficult to square with Rogers' own *Journals*; however, the fact that it was obviously written without access to them, or any other published account, is a strong argument in their favour. Until a muster roll of Rogers' command is unearthed, it remains impossible to say whether or not Kirkwood actually witnessed the events he describes, or merely reported the recollections of others. The fact that Kirkwood served in both the 77th and 42nd suggests that even if *he* didn't participate in the raid, he knew men who *were* with Rogers at St Francis. He would therefore have been aware of anecdotes that circulated within the army in the wake of the raid, and may have drawn upon them to spice his narrative. Whilst undoubtedly a problematic source, for all its flaws Kirkwood's extraordinary little book provides a voice for a private soldier who campaigned in the Americas during the 1750s and 60s. Such a rare survival deserves careful consideration here.

– *Kirkwood's account of events at Fort Duquesne* is confirmed by that of another soldier captured that same night, Ensign Thomas Gist of the Virginia Regiment. Gist saw several prisoners forced to undergo an extreme form of the 'gauntlet'. These men were 'beat and drove' until they 'could not stand; then they were tomohawked, scelped and in short was massacred in the most barbarous manner that can be immajined'. See 'Thomas Gist's Indian Captivity 1758–1759', ed. Howard H. Peckham, in *The Pennsylvania Magazine of History and Biography*, LXXX (1956), 285–311; 294.

– *Equipping the raiders*. Rogers was subsequently reimbursed 'for the Equipment of the Detachment, that went with him against St François …'

(WO/34/197/part 2, fol. 464).

– *Amherst's instructions*. See *Rogers' Journals*, pp. 144–5. Although Amherst couched his call for vengeance in broad terms, the 'barbarities' that he urged Rogers to remember undoubtedly included the most notorious of them all – the 'massacre' at Fort William Henry: the most detailed analysis of that episode and its legacies observes that Amherst's instructions 'recalled' the infamous events of 1757 (Steele, *Betrayals*, p. 147).

– *Previous orders to spare women and children*. See orders, Fort Edward, 12 June, and Camp at the Island of Orleans, 5 July, 1759 in *Knox's Journals*, I, 468; 400.

– *Whaleboats*. In 1759 Amherst himself described whaleboats as '28 feet in the Keel, 5 feet 2 inches broad, 25 Inches Deep, 34 feet from stem to Stern … with Seven Oars besides the Ste[e]ring Oar.' See Bellico, *Sails and Steam*, p. 90 (note).

– *Departure from Crown Point*. I remain extremely grateful to Tom Nesbitt, Ranger at Crown Point State Park, for his opinion on this point. The bay concerned was a favoured harbour throughout the French régime. Many wrought-iron mooring pins, showing heavy wear from lines, have been found there. The remains of two such pins came to light when I visited the site in May 2002.

– *Bogus Orders*. In fact, surviving records of the official orders issued within Amherst's army at Crown Point make no mention of any such ploys. See for example, *Commissary Wilson's Orderly Book: Expedition of the British and Provincial Army … Against Ticon-deroga and Crown Point, 1759* (Albany, 1857), entries for 12–13 September, pp. 155–6; manuscript order book kept by a regular officer [Major Alexander Monypenny of the 55th Foot] Crown Point, 4 August, 1759 to 'Legonier Bay', 17 October, 1759, in a private North American collection. I am very grateful to the owner of this document for allowing me to inspect it. Despite the lack of deliberate misinformation in official orders, Amherst was clearly close-mouthed about the operation. A letter written by an officer at Crown Point on 14 September observed that 'the General keeps every Thing very secret' (*BNL*, 27 September, 1759).

– *Camp rumours.* See 'Robert Webster's Journal', in *BFTM*, II, 4 (July, 1931), 120–53; 141; *Diaries of Lemuel Wood*, p. 37.

– *'Suagothel' and Oswegatchie.* See Gary Zaboly's discussion of the evidence in *Annotated Journals of Rogers*, pp. 183–4.

– *The St Francis raid.* The entire operation is covered in *Rogers' Journals* (pp. 150–58). The two most valuable and extensive newspaper reports appeared on 26 November, 1759, in the *New-York Gazette* ('Particulars of Major Rogers's last Scout, sent us from Numb. 4' (given as Appendix 2 here); and in both the *Boston Gazette* and *Boston Evening-Post* ('Number IV, November 1, 1759'). These sources underpin my narrative of the raid.

– *The French flotilla.* See Dennis M. Lewis, 'The Naval Campaign of 1759 on Lake Champlain', in *BFTM*, XIV (fall, 1983), 203–16; 206–8; Bellico, *Sails and Steam*, p. 93.

– *Wounding of Williams.* See *BEP*, 1 October, 1759; *BG*, 1 and 8 October, 1759. For the injured Highlanders, see *Amherst's Journal*, p. 170. Although contemporary newspapers reported that Williams was injured in a firearms accident, other theories have since been put forward. Perhaps the unlucky captain fell foul of some fiendish French booby-trap out on the lake? Or were he and others scorched by the accidental detonation of a powder keg? It's also been suggested that Williams and Rogers had clashed in the past, and remained at loggerheads; Rogers therefore welcomed an opportunity to send the captain back to Crown Point. This theory is expounded by Burt Garfield Loescher, *History of Rogers' Rangers, Volume 4, The St Francis Raid* (Bowie, Maryland, 2002), 14–15; 126. Rogers *had* been involved in wrangling with a regular captain over a question of precedence whilst out on a scout to Ticonderoga earlier that year (see Cuneo, *Robert Rogers*, pp. 92–3). But the officer concerned was Samuel Williamos of the 4th Battalion Royal *American* Regiment, *not* Manley Williams of the Royals. In September 1759, the 4/60th was at Oswego, and Williamos was with it; he'd left Niagara for that post on 22 August. See 'Private Diary Kept by Sir William Johnson at Niagara and Oswego, 1759', in *Knox's Journals*, III, 193. In his coverage of the raid, John Cuneo also confused Williams with Williamos (*Robert Rogers*, p. 103); in *Northwest Passage*, novelist Kenneth Roberts identified Williams correctly.

– *Firearms accidents.* See orders, Lake George Camp, 14 August, 1758, in

'Monypenny Orderly Book', *BFTM*, XIII, 1 (December, 1970), 89–116; 92; General Court Martial, Louisbourg, 24 August, 1758 (WO/71/66, pp. 420–22). For the shooting of Sergeant Kerr, see *BNL*, 6 and 13 July, 1758. Humph, of the Royal Americans, was acquitted of the killing. See General Court Martial, Fort Edward, 22 June, 1758 (WO/71/66).

– *Illness*. See 'Robert Webster's Journal', p. 139. For sickness amongst the Jersey Blues, see 'Extract of a Letter from Crown-Point, dated Sept. 28', in *NYG*, 8 October, 1759.

– *False reports*. See 'Extract of a Letter from Crown-Point, dated September 18, 1759' and 'Extract of a Letter from Albany, dated Sept. 20, 1759', in *NYG*, 24 September, 1759; and for the rebuttal, 'Extract of a Letter from Albany, dated Sep. 26', in *BG*, 8 October, 1759; also *Diaries of Lemuel Wood*, pp. 38–9.

– *Gage's failed mission to La Galette/Oswegatchie*. See Amherst to Gage, Camp at Crown Point, 21 September, 1759 (CO/5/56, fol. 223); *Amherst's Journal*, pp. 170–71; Amherst to Pitt, Crown Point, 22 October, 1759, in *Knox's Journal*, III, 60–61; Pitt to Amherst, Whitehall, 11 December, 1759, in *Correspondence of Pitt*, II, 216–17; Alden, *General Gage*, pp. 50–52; Shy, *Toward Lexington*, pp. 131–2.

– *Weather conditions*. See *Diaries of Lemuel Wood*, p. 38; 'Robert Webster's Journal', p. 142; *Amherst's Journal*, p. 171 (entries for 19–22 September, 1759). In the course of researching *Northwest Passage*, Kenneth Roberts presented data culled from Webster's diary and

Amherst's journal to W.R. Gregg, Chief of the United States Weather Bureau in Washington. Gregg concluded that the severe weather noted by both was caused 'by a series of storms advancing up the Atlantic Coast'. The resulting 'general gales and widespread precipitation' would have prevailed not only on Lake Champlain, but also throughout the region encompassed within the St Francis expedition. See Roberts, *Northwest Passage*, II, 25–6 (note).

– *Bears*. See *NYG*, 3 September, 1759, under heading 'Boston, August 27'; 24 September ('Boston, September 17'); and 8 October.

– *Rain at Missisquoi Bay*. At nearby Isle-aux-Noix it had rained all night. See 'Méloizes' Journal', p. 75.

– *Rogers' landing place* was near modern-day Phillipsburg, Canada. The exact location was later identified by British engineers who surveyed the area in 1762 and found the remnants of some of Rogers' whaleboats. This spot was marked on the manuscript version of William Brassier's map of Lake Champlain. A copy of the original (in the William L. Clements Library, Ann Arbor, Michigan) is held in the Thompson-Pell Research Centre, Fort Ticonderoga.

– *French patrols at Missisquoi Bay*. See 'Méloizes' Journal', pp. 73–5; Charland, 'Lake Champlain Army', *VH* (1960), 295.

– *Labelling of boats*. On 17 July, 1759, at Lake George Camp, orders had been issued for 'Whale Boats to be mark'd by the Corps they are given to, in the same manner as the Batteaus.' See 'Monypenny Orderly Book', in *BFTM*,

(1932), 223.

– *French reaction to discovery of boats.* See 'Méloizes' Journal', pp. 75–6; Bourlamaque to Lévis, Isle-aux-Noix, 27 and 29 September, 1759 (*Lévis MSS*, V, 47–50).

Chapter Six: *Search and Destroy*

– *Rogers' map of the St Francis raid.* This remarkable document has been described as 'a landmark in the early mapping of New England'. See David Bosse, 'The Maps of Robert Rogers and Jonathan Carver', in *The American Magazine and Historical Chronicle*, II, 1 (Spring/Summer, 1986), 45–61; 46–7. Although signed by Rogers, annotations are not in his hand. The map is either a copy of the original, or was drawn up under Rogers' supervision. I remain greatly indebted to the present owner of the map for generously providing me with a facsimile for my own researches.

– *McMullen's arrival at Crown Point.* See *Amherst's Journal*, p. 175.

– *Amherst's orders for Rogers' reception.* See his letters from Crown Point to Lieutenant Stevens and Major Bellows, 4 October, 1759 (WO/34/81, fols. 52–3).

– *Rogers' recommendation of Stevens.* See his letter to Colonel Roger Townshend, Albany, 28 January, 1759. The lieutenant's surname is sometimes spelled 'Stephens' or 'Stephans', but he signed himself as given in the text.

– *Crossing the swamps.* See *NHG*, 1 February, 1760, under 'New York, 14 January'.

– *Langis' fruitless pursuit.* See 'Méloizes' Journal', p. 79. It is baffling that Rogers' Indian scouts can have reported that two hundred of the enemy were on his trail just two days after he set out from Missisquoi Bay, when French sources indicate that the pursuit force only *left* the Bay three days later, on 26 September. Of course it's possible that the major's Indians witnessed Langis' discovery of the whaleboats on the 24th, then left *immediately* under the assumption that the French would do likewise.

– *Abenaki recollections.* See Gordon M. Day, 'Rogers' Raid', in *Historical New Hampshire* (June, 1962), 8.

– *Abandoned rafting plan.* This is the conclusion of Burt Garfield Loescher in *History of Rogers' Rangers*, IV, 30. Another prominent historian of the rangers, Tim Todish, considers it highly unlikely that Rogers' numerous party would have had the equipment – or time – to even consider such an undertaking (*Annotated Journals of Rogers*, p. 174). However, in an age when swimming remained an unusual accomplishment, rafting was a common method of crossing unfordable rivers. Rogers himself recommended this technique to a party of rangers who were sent to Québec in June 1760, and expected to encounter the St Francis River en route. But as he explained, at the (unspecified) point where these men would strike the river it was 'very still water' and therefore 'easily rafted'. Lower down, the St Francis River was 'so swift and rapid' that they shouldn't attempt to cross it ('Instructions for Sergeant Beverly of his Majesty's Rangers', in *Rogers' Journals*, p. 176–8). This sage advice went unheeded: 'in crossing the River St Francis, on a Raft', the 'Express of Rangers' were 'carried down the Falls', losing their crucial despatches in the process. See *NYM*, 18 August, 1760, under heading 'Philadelphia, August 14'.

– *Crossing the St Francis.* Local tradition places Rogers' crossing point at the cascades some twelve miles upstream from St Francis, roughly midway between the modern communities of Pierreville and Drummondville, and not far from the village of St Joachim de-Courval (Roberts, *Northwest Passage*, II, 17). Tantalising support for this location was provided in the late nine-teenth century when a local farmer unearthed two rusted muskets whilst digging a ditch (Charland, *Abénakis d'Odanak*, p. 112, note 11).

– *Rigaud's precautions and Vaudreuil's anxiety.* See Rigaud to Bourlamaque, Montréal, 27 September, 1759 ('Bourla-maque Collection', IV, 145–6); Vau-dreuil to Bourlamaque and Lévis, Montréal, 3 October, 1759 (Ibid, II, 395–6; *Lévis MSS*, VIII, 112).

– *French moves to protect St Francis.* See Charland, *Abénakis d'Odanak*, p. 111.

– *Hunger of raiders.* See 'Memorial of Frederick Curtiss'. Corroboration for Curtiss comes from the most detailed and convincing newspaper report of the raid; this stated that the raiders 'expended' their rations 'three Days before they arrived at the Town' (*NYG*, 26 November, 1759).

– *Rogers' reconnaissance.* See 'Extract of a Letter from New York, dated Nov 22, giving an authentic Account of Major Rogers's Expedition against the Indians', in *Derby Mercury*, 1–8

February, 1760; *BG*, 26 November; *NYG*, 26 November, 1759. The *New-York Gazette*'s report claimed that Rogers entered St Francis at midnight. Events from this point onwards are covered in Rogers' letter to Amherst upon 'his return from St Francis', given in his *Journals* (pp. 146–150) under the date of 5 November, 1759, but actually dated 1 November. This report was published in the *New-York Mercury* of 26 November, 1759. Strangely enough, the original letter is missing from the very comprehensive Amherst Papers (WO/34) in the Public Record Office, Kew. Also important are the comments of Ogden, as reported to Lt Gov De Lancey of New York by Amherst from Crown Point on 13 November, (WO/34/30, fol. 93), and included within Amherst's despatch to Pitt of 16 December, 1759 (*Knox's Journal*, III, 71–2).

– *Abenaki accounts of a warning.* See Day, 'Rogers' Raid', *Historical New Hamp-shire* (June, 1962), 9–14. Both of these narratives satisfy Day's criteria for the most valuable category of oral testi-mony – that told by 'tradition-conscious' individuals and derived from 'known and named sources'. Day suggests that the 'little woods' men-tioned in the narrative of Elvine Royce, where Rogers' men allegedly hid, were 'probably the 50 year-old second growth' that had sprouted on the site of the original Abenaki village depicted in the 1704 plan; this was some two and a half miles upstream from the St Francis of 1759. Himself a forester, Day was surely correct here; the location cer-tainly squares with the contemporary newspaper report that Rogers halted his men 'within 2 or 3 Miles' of the village (*NYG*, 26 November, 1759). Day also suggested that the mysterious *Mahigan* who gave the warning hailed from Schaghticoke; although originally a Mahican village, it had subsequently attracted inhabitants from many other tribes including the Sokoki Abenakis. On the close links between Abenakis and Mahicans during Queen Anne's War, see Calloway, *Western Abenakis of Vermont*, p. 106.

– *Absence of St Francis' warriors.* Writing to William Pitt on 8 October, 1759, the British commander at Québec, Brig-Gen Monckton reported that although St Francis had been destroyed, 'as some of the Indians were not returned home from the French Army, they escaped' (*Correspondence of Pitt*, II, 178).

– *The attack on St Francis.* This reconstruction of the assault employs the key sources already cited. Particularly important is the letter from New York, dated 22 November, 1759, in the *Derby Mercury* of 1–8 February, 1760. In addition, *Kirk's Memoirs* (pp. 44–5) contribute several vivid and convincing details: they're used here on the basis that whilst they *may* not reflect the author's personal experience, they *probably* preserve information current within Amherst's army following the raid. Other anecdotes are taken from *Reminiscences of French War*, pp. 179–80.

– *Date of the attack.* Although reliable contemporary sources make it clear that the attack was launched before dawn on 4 October, many secondary works state that it occurred two days later. These follow Rogers' statement in

his *Journals* that he arrived within sight of St Francis on the evening of the twenty-second day after leaving Crown Point; this would place the attack itself on 6 October. For a very thorough discussion of the dating evidence see Thomas M. Charland, 'C'est Arrivé Le 4 Octobre 1759', in *Revue d'Histoire de l'Amérique Française*, XIII, 3 (December, 1959), 328–34. A commemorative plaque for the victims of the raid at the modern village of Odanak gives the correct date.

– *Fate of the 'priest'.* See *The London Chronicle or Universal Evening Post*, 12–15 January, 1760, (under 'Philadelphia, Nov 22'); Amherst to Pitt, New York, 16 December, 1759, in *Knox's Journal*, III, 71–72; 'Histoire de Roubaud', pp. 32–3. For Rogers' recollection see 'Gentleman from London', under dateline 'Williamsburg, Sept. 8', in *NHG*, 10 October, 1775, cited in John Cuneo's manuscript notes for *Robert Rogers* (Thompson-Pell Research Centre, Fort Ticonderoga), Chapter 9, note 26. On La Brosse's whereabouts see Loescher, *History of Rogers' Rangers*, IV, 241 (note 93).

– *Destruction of mission church.* See 'An Imperfect Description of the Misery of Canada. By Bishop de Pontbriand', Montréal, 5 November, 1759, in *NYCD*, X, 1057–9; 1058; Charland, *Abénakis d'Odanak*, p. 113. From the historian's perspective, not least of the losses was the incineration of the mission's manuscript records.

– *Plunder.* See Rogers to Amherst, Albany, 1 January, 1760 (WO/34/82, fol. 2).

– *Rogers' casualties.* Abenaki oral

tradition suggests that the major's sole fatality, the Stockbridge Indian, was not yet dead when the raiders quit the village. According to the story related by Theophile Panadis, Abenakis who returned to St Francis in the wake of the attack found an injured Indian 'stranger'. They were about to finish him off with a hatchet when he asked them to pause, as he wished to be baptised. He identified himself as a *Mahigan* named Samadagwis. As he'd no Christian name, the Abenakis invited him to select one. He chose Sabadis. These formalities over, the Abenakis promptly killed him. Gordon Day speculates that this wounded raider was a Schaghticoke – and none other than the Indian ranger who'd recently delivered the mysterious warning to the villagers. See 'Oral Tradition as Complement', in *In Search of New England's Native Past: Selected Essays by Gordon M. Day*, eds. Michael K. Foster and William Cowan (Amherst, Massachusetts, 1998), pp. 127–35; 133–4.

– *'English' scalps at St Francis.* See 'Extract of a Letter from Crown-Point, dated Nov. 16, 1759', in *NYG*, 26 November, 1759.

– *Ballad evidence.* See 'A Ballad of Rogers' Retreat, 1759', ed. T.D. Seymour Bassett, in *VH*, XLVI, 1 (winter, 1978), 21–3. The opening line 'The thirteenth of Septembr last …' indicates that this fascinating literary relic was composed within the year. Besides Rogers himself, it names two individuals – Nathan Brigham and 'Eben Wheler' (Ebenezer Wheeler). Of these two, only Brigham survived; even if he was not the ballad's author, he

probably provided the grim testimony upon which it draws. Whoever wrote it, the ballad conveys a strong eyewitness flavour. Amongst much other information it fixes the timing of Rogers' assault upon St Francis at about 5.00 a.m. ('He was but just two Hours space / in takeing of this fatal place'). As noted, Rogers himself reported that the *affair* was over by 7.00 a.m. The ballad also provides striking contemporary evidence of the degree to which the recent killings at Fort William Henry were not only seared upon the psyche of survivors, but also deemed to justify the heaviest retribution against those held responsible.

– *French reports of casualties.* See for example, Lt-Col Nicolas Sarrebource de Pontleroy to Bourlamaque, Trois-Rivières, 6 October, 1759 ('Bourlamaque Collection', III, 159); Bishop de Pontbriand's letter of 5 November, 1759 (*NYCD*, X, 1058). Roubaud was precise: ten men and twenty-two women and children were killed ('Histoire de Roubaud', p. 33).

– *Discrepancies over death toll.* Gordon Day observes that the oral tradition 'that the Indians were warned, that some hid, and some, disbelieving, did not' also offers the best explanation for Rogers' belief that he'd taken the village by surprise: those who stayed behind *were* surprised (*In Search of New England's Native Past*, p. 132).

– *Gill family captives.* See Huden, 'White Chief', *VH* (1956), 202; Charland, *Abénakis d'Odanak*, p. 117. A brief note of the raid penned by one of the Connecticut provincials states that Rogers took 6 *Prisners* at *Sant fransways*. See

'Diary of Ebenezer Dibble', ed. Rev. E.C. Starr, *Proceedings of the Society of Colonial Wars for the State of Connecticut*, I (1903), 313–29; 322.

– *George Barnes*. See Coleman, *New England Captives*, II, 362. Coleman erred in suggesting that the liberated prisoners included Quinton Kennedy (Ibid, I, 29). As has been seen, after capture he was taken to Trois-Rivières.

– *Information from 'German woman'*. See *London Chronicle*, 12–15 January, 1760. It's interesting to note that the original letter to Amherst of 1 November, 1759 quoted here, and contemporary newspaper reports, suggest that it was only at this point, *after* Rogers sacked St Francis, that he learned that the whaleboats left hidden at Missisquoi Bay had been discovered by the French. Elsewhere in his *Journals*, Rogers maintained that he received this news two days after heading inland from Lake Champlain; and in an explanatory footnote appended to the report of 1 November in his *Journals*, he stated that an officer was sent back to Crown Point on the basis of 'some intelligence that I had when going out'; this gave 'reason to believe we should be deprived of our boats'. Rogers certainly despatched Lieutenant McMullen to request that supplies be sent to Wells River, and Amherst responded accordingly. Yet there's nothing in the general's personal journal or official correspondence to indicate that Rogers lodged his request on the basis that his boats and supplies had been *captured*. Indeed, Amherst sent an officer and one hundred men to Missisquoi Bay to secure the boats (*Amherst's Journal*, p. 184; *Knox's Journal*, III, 69); this

would be a futile exercise if he *already* knew that the French had found them. Having gauged the intensity of enemy patrolling around Missisquoi Bay, Rogers possibly feared that the discovery of his boats was inevitable and therefore requested supplies as a contingency plan. If so, Rogers deserves credit for his foresight, if not his veracity. As with other aspects of the story for which his own *Journals* remain the sole source, there is little option but to take the major at his word.

Chapter Seven: *Retreat and Pursuit*

– *French responses to the destruction of St Francis*. In the wake of the raid, a copious correspondence crackled between the men responsible for Canada's defence. This analysis draws upon the following letters and journals: Vaudreuil to Lévis, Montréal, 5 and 7 October, 1759 (*Lévis MSS*, VIII, 116; 119–20); Bourlamaque to Lévis, Isle-aux-Noix, 7 October (Ibid, V, 55); 'Journal Des Campagnes Du Chevalier De Lévis' (Ibid, I, 223–4); 'Méloizes' Journal' (6 October), p. 79; Vaudreuil to Bourlamaque, Montréal, 5 (two letters), 6 and 7 October ('Bourlamaque Collection', II, 401; 405–7; 411; 413–14); Pontleroy to Bourlamaque, Trois-Rivières, 6 October (Ibid, III, 159–60); Lévis to Bourlamaque, 6 October (Ibid, 156–7); 'Histoire de Roubaud', p. 33. See also, 'Extract of a journal kept at the army commanded by the late Lieutenant-General de Montcalm', in *NYCD*, X, 1042; and Charland, *Abénakis d'Odanak*, p. 115.

– *Timing of Rogers' departure from*

village. See *NYG*, 26 November, 1759.

– *Rogers' complaint against Sergeant Lewis.* See Rogers to Amherst, Albany, 12 December, 1759 (WO/34/78, fol. 182).

– *Treasure trail.* See Leonard A. Auger, 'St Francis Through 200 Years', in *VH*, XXVII (1959), 287–304; 290; Cuneo, *Robert Rogers*, p. 115.

– *Splitting the detachment.* Although Rogers stated that his detachment marched together for eight days before splitting into foraging parties, Frederick Curtiss recalled a very different scenario. He testified that Rogers ordered the division *immediately* after St Francis was reduced to ashes: the raiders were then told 'to make off to Disperse into small Partys about Eight in each … & to get Back thro' ye Woods as we could'. When Curtiss delivered his sworn statement, exactly a year had passed. In that short span it's unlikely that his memory would have clouded on such a basic point. The memoirs of Robert Kirkwood offer partial corroboration for Curtiss; they maintain that the decision was made by a council-of-war directly the command regrouped after burning the village: it was then 'agreed for our mutual safety, to divide into three parties, and so make the best of our way to the english settlements' (*Kirk's Memoirs*, p. 45). As already conjectured, Kirkwood's narrative of the St Francis expedition may reflect no more than a colourful melange of camp gossip. However, it receives some support from an unexpected source: intelligence received at Isle-aux-Noix at the end of October stated that the raiders had divided into three bands for their return, although it does not specify at which point this split occurred ('Méloizes' Journal', 28 October, 1759, pp. 83–4). As members of the rank and file, neither Curtiss nor Kirkwood had any obvious motive for distorting the record. Rogers, by contrast, was commander of a force that suffered casualties in consequence of his decision to divide it. He may have considered it important for his professional reputation to establish that this course was necessitated by the shortage of rations, and not made at the outset. Although Rogers' *Journals* are once again difficult to reconcile with other sources, his version of events is accepted here.

– *Compasses.* See *Knox's Journal*, I, 34.

– *Fate of Dunbar's party.* Authentic details are limited to a footnote in Rogers' own *Journals* (p. 158) and a brief comment by Amherst to Pitt in his lengthy despatch from New York of 16 December, 1759 (in *Knox's Journals*, III, 74–5); this is apparently based upon information in a letter from Rogers, delivered to Amherst by Lieutenant George Campbell on 21 November (*Amherst's Journal*, p. 193); the original despatch, like Rogers' letter of 1 November, doesn't survive amongst the general's papers in the Public Record Office. The contemporary ballad of the raid provides close corroboration for the dating of the attacks: '… & when ten days were spent in vain/ the indians ovre took them again/ Near thirty men as som do cry/ Now by the indians their did dy.' See 'Ballad of Rogers' Retreat', *VH* (1978), 22.

– *The ordeal of Frederick Curtiss* is

described in his 'Memorial'.

– *Anonymous French journal.* See *NYCD*, X, 1042. The journalist's claim exaggerates the casualties inflicted.

– *Langis' unsuccessful scout.* See 'Méloizes' Journal', pp. 79–80 (entries for 10/14 October).

– *British patrols to Isle-aux-Noix.* See *Amherst's Journal*, p. 177. Both of these parties returned on 23 October, having failed to reach their destinations.

– *Amherst's Lake Champlain thrust.* See Amherst to Ligonier, Camp of Crown Point, 22 October, 1759 (Amherst Family Papers, Centre for Kentish Studies, Maidstone, item U1350/035/13). Also Amherst's despatch to Pitt from Crown Point, 22 October, 1759 (*Knox's Journal*, III, 64–7); *Amherst's Journal*, pp. 178–183; Bellico, *Sails and Steam*, pp. 98–101; Bourlamaque to Marshal de Belle Isle, Isle-aux-Noix, 1 November, 1759 (*NYCD*, X, 1056); Dennis Lewis, 'The Naval Campaign of 1759 on Lake Champlain', *BFTM*, XIV, 4 (fall, 1983), 203–16; 210–13; Charland, 'Lake Champlain Army', *VH* (1960), 295; 'Extract of a Journal …' (*NYCD*, X, 1042–3).

– *Deganes' report.* See 'Méloizes' Journal' (24/28 October, 1759), pp. 83–4.

– *Yellow lily roots.* See Day, 'Rogers' Raid', *Historical New Hampshire* (June, 1962), 8. Day speculates that this information originated with the captive Antoine Gill.

– *'deepness of the snow'.* As Kirkwood alone mentions heavy snow, it's tempting to discount this detail as a hyperbolic flourish. However, as has been emphasised, the autumn of 1759 was exceptionally cold. Crown Point soon experienced 'Very cold weather & frost' (30 October); 'very hard' frost (31 October – 1 November); and 'Frost & Snow' (7 November). On 8 November snow was 'visible on all the mountains round'. See *Amherst's Journal*, pp. 185–9. One hundred miles or more to the north, in the rugged regions traversed by Rogers' men, such conditions would have registered sooner.

– *Testimony of McNeal and Wansant.* See Roberts, *Northwest Passage*, II, 36–7.

– *Traditional support for the Passumpsic route.* See *Vermont: A Guide to the Green Mountain State* (Federal Writers' Project, Boston, 1937), p. 159: 'Where now the sleek, powerful automobiles of a great nation race smoothly along winding ribbons of cement [US 5], less than two centuries ago a band of fighting woodsmen, facing death from wounds, starvation, and exposure, struggled through a dense wilderness.'

– *Wells-Ammonoosuc rendezvous.* In 1968 an Historic Marker was placed two miles south of Woodsville Village, on the west side of Route 10. It reads in part: 'ROGERS RANGERS. This river's junction two miles north was the rendezvous for Rogers Rangers after their destruction of St Francis, Que, on October 4, 1759 …' Rogers' chosen rendezvous lay at the head of that conspicuous stretch of meadows, the Lower Cowass Intervales. Indeed, a map of the Connecticut River region, given as an inset in a larger chart published in 1754, mentions just two place names on that river – 'No 4' and 'Cowass'. It also names the St Francis River and indicates Lake Memphremagog and the waterways running between it and the Connecticut. The map concerned was dedicated to William Shirley; it's highly likely that Rogers knew of it. See 'Plan of the Kennebeck & Sagadahook Rivers, & Country adjacent', engraved by Thomas Johnston (Boston, November 20, 1754).

– *The Nulhegan route and the fate of Sergeant Bradley*. See *Reminiscences of French War*, p. 180. A monument at Groteton, New Hampshire, which lies between Jefferson and North Stratford (where the Nulhegan enters the Connecticut), claims the Connecticut's junction with the *Upper* Ammonoosuc as the rendezvous of the rangers returning from St Francis.

– *Joseph Wait's party*. See Silas McKeen, *A History of Bradford, Vermont* (Montpelier, Vermont, 1875), p. 39, cited in *Annotated Journals of Rogers*, p. 187. Also *Vermont: A Guide to the Green Mountain State*, pp. 173–4.

– *Lt Stevens' premature return*. See *Amherst's Journal*, p. 185. Stevens' subsequently sought to explain his conduct when he was charged with neglect of duty. The court-martial proceedings are given in Roberts, *Northwest Passage*, II, 35–9. An 'Extract of a Letter from Crown-Point, Oct 16', published in the *BEP* of 29 October, 1759 noted that Rogers was 'not expected sooner than the 24th of this Month'; a party with provisions had gone to meet him 'at the Head of Connecticut River, where he is expected to be at a certain Day.' It's unclear from the context whether the date specified refers to his arrival at the

rendezvous, or at Crown Point; the latter is probably intended.

– *Campbell's cannibals*. See Mante, *History of the Late War*, pp. 223–4.

– *Account of David Evans*. See *Reminiscences of French War*, pp. 180–81.

– *Fate of Marie-Jeanne and Xavier Gill*. See Huden, 'White Chief', *VH* (1956), 203; and Charland, *Abenakis d'Odanak*, p. 117. Judge Gill published his *Notes historiques sur l'origine de la famille Gill et histoire de ma propre famille* in 1887.

– *Kirkwood's account of cannibalism*. See *Kirk's Memoirs*, pp. 45–7. As already noted, whilst Rogers maintained that he took five prisoners at St Francis, the actual total was six. Kirkwood's grisly anecdote *may* explain the fate of this sixth captive; it also provides a possible explanation for the death of Marie-Jeanne Gill.

– *Rogers' arrival at 'No 4'*. See *NYG*, 26 November, 1759; *NHG*, 30 November (under heading 'Boston, November 26').

– *Campbell's salvation*. See Mante, *History of the Late War*, p. 224.

– *Philip's party*. Rogers' comment is included as a note to Roby's version of the major's *Journals* but doesn't appear in the 1765 or 1769 editions. Roby himself reported Philip's role at Louisbourg, adding that his *squaw*, Mary Missle, was still remembered by old folk in northern New Hampshire as 'an excellent moccasin maker' (*Reminiscences of French War*, pp. 143; 179).

– *Fate of the Missisquoi captives*. This reconstruction draws upon the General Court Martial of Jonathan Barns, Montréal, 1–4 April, 1761

(WO/71/68). See also 'Méloizes'
Journal', pp. 84–5 (entries for 2/7
November, 1759); Bourlamaque to
Lévis, Isle-aux-Noix, 2 and 3
November, 1759 (*Lévis MSS*, V, 76–8);
Vaudreuil to Lévis, 6 November, 1759
(Ibid, VIII, 154).

– '*Killed & eat a Little Boy*'. It is likely
that this lad was Chief Gill's son
Xavier.

– *Hodges' doomed patrol*. See *NHG*,
7 October, 1756 (from 'Camp at Lake
George, Sept 20. 1756'); also 'Proceed-
ings of the Campaign in North
America, 1756', in *Journals of the Hon.
William Hervey, in North America and
Europe, from 1755 to 1814; with Order
Books at Montreal, 1760–1763* (Bury St
Edmunds, Suffolk, 1906), p. 40.

– *Torture at Isle-aux-Noix*. See 'The
Substance of Jonathan Burns's Confession, a few Minutes before his Execu-
tion on the 7th of April last …'; and
Gage to Amherst, Montréal, 23 August,
1762 (WO/34/5, fols. 194; 196).

– *Susanna Johnson's reunion with Antoine
Gill*. See 'Narrative of Mrs Johnson',
p. 80.

Chapter Eight: *Reward and Ret-
ribution*

– *Cadillac's information*. See *Amherst's
Journal*, pp. 186–7; also Amherst to De
Lancey, Crown Point, 2 November,
1759 (WO/34/30, fol. 91).

– *Ogden's arrival*. See 'Extract of a
Letter from Crown-Point, dated Nov.
16, 1759', in *NYG*, 26 November, 1759.

– *Otter Creek relief party*. See *Amherst's
Journal*, pp. 188–9; also Amherst to the

'Officer Commanding a Party of
Rangers to go to the Otter River …',
Camp of Crown Point, 7 November,
1759 (WO/34/81, fol. 134). According
to a letter from Crown Point dated 12
November, another three of Rogers'
party came in that evening, leaving 'two
others about 5 miles off' (*NHG*, 30
November, 1759).

– *Amherst's praise of Rogers*. See letter
from Camp of Crown Point, 8
November, 1759 (WO/34/81, fol. 140).
This glowing tribute was published in
Rogers' *Journals* (pp. 158–9).

– *Press reports*. See *BEP*, 5, 12 and 19
November, 1759; *BG*, 19 November,
1759. At Crown Point on 7 November,
an officer of Ruggles' provincials
reported 'that Majr. Rogers is Come
into No 4. with his party, Lost but 1
Man'. See 'The Orderly Book of Lieut
William Henshaw', in *Transactions and
Collections of the American Antiquarian
Society*, XI (1909), pp. 180–254; 251.

– *Rogers' post-raid mood*. In the 'Introduction' to his *Journals*, (p. vi), Rogers
had written with feeling of 'that depres-
sion of spirits which is the natural consequence of exhausting fatigue'. After
all the horrors and privations of the St
Francis expedition, it would be surprising if what is now diagnosed as post-
traumatic stress disorder did not play
some part in his reaction to its aftermath.

– *Rogers' stragglers*. See *Amherst's
Journal*, p. 193; Amherst to Pitt, 16
December, 1759, in *Knox's Journal*, III,
74–5; 'Account of Expenses by Major
Robert Rogers for the Relief of the
Detachment on their return from St
Francis …' (WO/34/197, part 2,

fol. 466). On 30 November the *NHG* reported that sixty-three of the major's men had come safe into 'No. 4', 'and the Remainder were soon expected'.

– *Returning prisoners.* See 'List of Officers …' and 'List of People Returned from being Prisoners in Canada 15th November 1759' (CO/5/57, fols. 118–19). Crown, Burrell, Todd, Goddart and Rose were all listed as captured 'near Nutt Island [Isle-aux-Noix]' on 4 November. John Jones was described as 'of Rogers's party, 4th Novr, 1759'; despite the date, it seems probable that this was actually *Moses* Jones. Three of these men – Lewis, Brown and Todd – subsequently testified against the renegade Jonathan Barns.

– *Rogers' casualties.* See *Rogers' Journals*, p. 159. Although the circumstances remain obscure, Lieutenant George Turner in fact survived, and was later commissioned into one of the South Carolina independent companies of regulars. See Amherst to Lt-Col Grant of the 40th Regiment, New York, 30 April, 1762 (WO/34/92, fol. 106).

– *Permission for leave.* See Amherst to Rogers, Crown Point, 24 November, 1759 (WO/34/81, fol. 185). The general left for Ticonderoga on the 25th (*Amherst's Journal*, pp. 193–4).

– *Pouchot's account.* See *Pouchot's Memoirs*, p. 249.

- *Rogers' continuing despondency.* See Rogers to Amherst, Albany, 12 and 17 December, 1759 (WO/34/78, fols. 182; 188).

– *French downplay raid.* See *BG*, 17 December, 1759.

– *Survival of St Francis Abenakis.* See Charland, *Abénakis d'Odanak*, p.119. Henry Hamilton of the 48th Foot, charged with deserting from Wolfe's army at Québec, claimed to be a captive who was subsequently taken out hunting by the St Francis Indians. See General Court Martial, Crown Point, 24 July, 1761 (WO/71/68).

– *Vaudreuil and Indian anger.* See Parkman, *Montcalm and Wolfe*, II, 269; *Knox's Journal*, II, 286–7; *BNL* ('Extraordinary'), 7 February, 1760.

– *St Francis a warning to other Indians.* See MacLeod, *Canadian Iroquois*, pp. 17–18.

– *Arrest of Stevens and Lewis.* See Rogers to Amherst, Albany, 12 December, 1759 (WO/34/78, fol. 182).

– *Amherst's letters of 24 December, 1759.* See WO/34/81, fols. 201–2. The decision to drop the case against Lewis was a happy outcome for the sergeant, less so for the historian: had he stood trial, the resulting testimonies would undoubtedly have thrown much new light upon the St Francis raid. Members of the detachment whom Rogers intended to call as witnesses included lieutenants Campbell, Farrington and Cargill of the rangers; Captain Ogden and Lieutenant Brigham of the provincials; and of the regulars, Lieutenant Grant and Volunteer 'Mr Grant' of Montgomery's Highlanders, and Volunteer Hugh Wallace of the 27th Foot (Rogers to Amherst, Albany, 17 December, 1759, in WO/34/78, fol. 188).

– *Stevens' court martial.* See the proceedings published in Roberts, *Northwest*

Passage, II, 35–9.

– *Fate of Stevens*. See *Rogers' Journals*, p. 155 (note). According to a subsequent petition to Amherst, Stevens had received no pay from 25 November, 1759 to 24 May, 1760, when he was 'dismissed the service' at Crown Point. See 'The Memorial of Samuel Stevens formerly Lieutenant in the late Captain Burbanks Independent Company of Rangers' (undated, in WO/34/100, fol. 18).

– *Rejection of Rogers' petition*. See *Journals of the House of Representatives of Massachusetts* (55 vols, Boston, 1919–90), XXXVI (1759–60), 274. For newspaper praise of Rogers see *NHG*, 1 February, 1760 (under heading 'New York, January 14').

– *Promotions of St Francis raiders*. See Loescher, *History of Rogers Rangers*, III, 39; Haviland to Amherst, Crown Point, 14 December, 1759 (WO/34/51, fol. 2). I am very grateful to Dr John Houlding and Robert J. Andrews for confirming details of these officers' service records.

– *Reception of returning raiders*. See *Kirk's Memoirs*, pp. 49–50.

– *Rogers' finances*. See Gage to Amherst, Albany, 30 December, 1759 (WO/34/46A, fol. 69).

– *Captured Indian boy sent to school*. See *BNL* ('*Extraordinary*'), 7 February, 1760. For others of the major's captives, contact with civilisation proved more fleeting. The same report noted that the two Indian girls brought back from St Francis 'died lately with the small-pox at Albany'.

– *Langis' ambush*. See *Rogers' Journals*, p. 161 (which give the date of 13 February, 1760); Amherst to Pitt, New York, 8 March, 1760, in *Correspondence of Pitt*, II, 263–4.

– *Sergeant Beverly's report*. See *Rogers' Journals*, pp. 168–71. See also 'Intelligence supplied by an officer taken prisoner at Quebec on 28 April' in *NHG*, 11 July, 1760 (under 'Boston, July 7').

– *Second battle of Québec*. This was dubbed the battle of St Foye to distinguish it from the previous action. For a detailed account see Brumwell, *Redcoats*, pp. 255–61.

– *The Richelieu raid*. See *Rogers' Journals* pp. 173–6; 178–87. See also letter from 'Point Rogers, June 26, 1760', in *NHG*, 12 September, 1760. Brassier's 1762 map of Lake Champlain locates Rogers' brisk fight of 6 June at Point au Fer.

– *Praise of Rogers*. See Amherst to Rogers, 'Canajoharie', 26 June, 1760, in *Rogers' Journals*, pp. 187–8; Haviland to Amherst, Crown Point, 29 June, 1760 (WO/34/51, fol. 52).

– *Disaffection of 'French Indians'*. See Murray to Pitt, Québec, 25 May, 1760 (*Correspondence of Pitt*, II, 297); 'Extract of a Letter from Oswego, dated July 16, 1760', in *NYM*, 11 August, 1760. News of developments at Caughnawaga reached Crown Point by two escaped prisoners on 19 June. One of them was Christopher Proudfoot, the same ranger captive of the Abenakis who'd been obliged to help hunt the famished St Francis raiders discovered at Missisquoi Bay. See 'Intelligence Enclosed in Some of Colonel Haviland's Letters of June 1760' (WO/34/51, fol. 47).

– *Conferences with Johnson.* See Johnson to Pitt, 24 October, 1760, in *JP*, III, 273; also the anonymous journal given in *Knox's Journal*, II, 553.

– *Roubaud's overtures.* See *Amherst's Journal*, pp. 241–3; Frazier, *Mohicans of Stockbridge*, p. 143. There's no full-length biography of Roubaud, although his adventures certainly deserve one. For brief sketches of his convoluted career see Vachon, 'Roubaud', in *DCB*, IV, 685, and Lape, 'Pere Roubaud, Missionary Extraordinary', in *BFTM* (1966), 63–71. See also 'Mr Roubaud's Deplorable Case', introduced by J.G. Shea, *Historical Magazine* (second series), VIII, 5 (November, 1870), 282–91.

– *Running the Cedar Rapids.* See 'Journal of Lieutenant John Grant, 2nd Battalion, 42nd Regiment' (RH4/77), pp. 60–61; *Amherst's Journal*, p. 244 (4 September, 1760); 'Memoir on Canada by M. de Bourlamaque [1762]', in *NYCD*, X, 1142.

– *Vacillation of mission Indians.* See MacLeod, *Canadian Iroquois*, pp. 171–2.

– *Surrender at Montréal.* See *Knox's Journal*, II, 561; 'Protest of the Chevalier de Levis …', in *NYCD*, X, 1106.

– *Abenaki pragmatism.* See Calloway, *Abenakis of Western Vermont*, pp. 192–3; 'Articles of Capitulation for the Surrender of Canada' (Article 40), in *NYCD*, X, 1117.

– *Charlestown raid.* See 'Extract of a Letter from Charlestown, or No. Four, in this Province, dated the 17th Instant', in *NHG*, 27 June, 1760; Coleman, *New England Captives*, II, 329; 'Narrative of Mrs Johnson', pp. 79–81.

– *Return of Curtiss.* See his 'Memorial' of 4 October, 1760. 'A List of the English Prisoners, June 14th, 1760' (WO/1/5, fols. 116–17) mistakenly describes 'Frederick Courtis' as 'Of the Rangers', and lists ranger 'Joshiah Malone' amongst the provincials.

– *Fate of Barns.* See the court-martial proceedings in WO/71/68, and Ogilvie's recollection of his final confession (WO/34/5, fol. 194); also, Daniel Claus to William Johnson, Montréal, 9 April, 1761 (*JP*, III, 377).

– *Amherst aghast.* See his letter to Pitt, New York, 4 May, 1761, in *Correspondence of Pitt*, II, 426.

Chapter Nine: *Endings*

– *Rogers' Detroit expedition.* See Cuneo, *Robert Rogers*, pp. 129–41 (quotation on p. 141).

– *Reception of Rogers.* See *NYM*, 16 February, 1761 (under 'Philadelphia, February 12'). An instance of the awe inspired by the mere invocation of the major's name at this time is provided by the case of a former ranger who was court-martialled at Montréal on 19 February, 1762, on a charge of extorting money and goods from local *habitants*. James Hamilton bolstered his racket by claiming that *he* was Robert Rogers. Hamilton, who'd served in the major's own company, denied the scam, but was found guilty and sentenced to one thousand lashes (WO/71/70).

– *Death of Williams.* See David H. Corkran, *The Cherokee Frontier: Conflict and Survival, 1740–62* (Norman, Oklahoma, 1962), p. 212.

– *Kennedy's Indian corps.* See Extract of a letter from Lt-Col Grant to Amherst, Camp near Fort Prince George, 10 July, 1761 (CO/5/61, fol. 377). Grant was the same officer who had been defeated and captured outside Fort Duquesne in September 1758.

– *Fate of Kennedy.* See Ensign John Carden, 17th Foot, to Sir William Johnson, Martinique, 8 February, 1762 (*JP*, III, 625); Maj-Gen Robert Monckton to the Earl of Egremont, Fort Royal, Martinique, 9 February, 1762, in *GM*, 1762 (March), p. 126; Kennedy to Loudoun, from Beaver Dams, 23 October and Charlestown, South Carolina, 14 November, 1761 (LO 6318 and 6328); and Brig-Gen Haviland to Amherst, Fort Royal, Martinique, 20 March, 1762 (WO/34/55, fol. 127).

– *British officers and the genesis of 'Pontiac's War'.* See Gregory Evans Dowd, *War Under Heaven: Pontiac, the Indian Nations & The British Empire* (Baltimore, 2002), pp. 63–75.

– *Action outside Detroit.* For Rogers' own report of this fight, dubbed the battle of 'Bloody Run', see 'A Letter from Detroit, August 8, 1763', in *The Pennsylvania Gazette*, 8 September, 1763. His key role is emphasised in a 'Journal of the Siege of Detroit, By Lieutenant James MacDonald of the 60th Regt' (WO/34/49, fols. 7–9). British captives witnessed the consumption of Dalyell's heart. See *The Siege of Detroit in 1763, comprising the Journal of Pontiac's Conspiracy and John Rutherfurd's Narrative of a Captivity,* ed. M. Quaiffe (Chicago, 1958), p. 264.

– *Amherst's bounties.* See Amherst to

Major Henry Gladwin, New York, 10 August, 1763 (WO/34/49, fols. 332–3). For the other comments cited here, see Amherst to Colonel Bouquet, from New York, 16 July and 7 August, 1763 (WO/34/41, fols. 113; 117). Even within mainland Britain itself, the treatment meted out to rebels by victorious royal forces could be very harsh. The last set-piece battles fought on English and British soil – respectively Sedgemoor in 1685, and Culloden in 1746 – both witnessed summary executions of wounded rebels. See Peter Earle, *Monmouth's Rebels: The Road to Sedgemoor 1685* (London, 1977), pp. 133–7; John Prebble, *Culloden* (London, 1961), pp. 114–30.

– *Smallpox.* For a thorough discussion of the notorious 'smallpox episode' see Elizabeth A. Fenn, 'Biological Warfare in Eighteenth-Century North America: Beyond Jeffery Amherst', in *Journal of American History*, LXXXVI, 4 (March, 2000), 1552–80.

– *Fall of Amherst.* See Croghan to Johnson, London, 24 February, 1764 (*JP*, IV, 341).

– *Amherst's warning to Abenakis.* See Amherst to Roubaud, Camp at Montréal, 16 September, 1760 (Ibid, X, 187).

– *Stockbridge retribution for 'Peter'.* See Roubaud to Johnson, St Francis, 13 November, 1760 (Ibid, III, 281); Daniel Claus to Johnson, Montréal, 10 June, 1761 (Ibid, 402–3); Johnson to Amherst, Fort Johnson, 6 February, 1762 (Ibid, 623); 'Journal of Indian Affairs', 24–30 March, 1762 (Ibid, X, 409–13).

– *Roubaud turns informer.* See Roubaud

to Johnson, St Francis, 30 October, 1761 (Ibid, III, 555). Roubaud's mention of an approach from the Cherokees is intriguing in view of information relayed by the captive 'German girl' who was freed during Rogers' raid. She claimed that the St Francis Indians 'had resolved on the first fall of snow, to go to the back parts of Carolina, on an invitation from the Cherokees' (*London Chronicle*, 12–15 January, 1760).

– *Abenaki response to 'Pontiac's War'*. See Charland, *Abénakis d'Odanak*, p. 134; 'Message of the Canada to the Western Indians', in *NYCD*, VII, 544.

– *Inrush of settlement*. See Calloway, *Western Abenakis of Vermont*, pp. 183–8 (quote at page 185). As early as 1764, some eighteen white families were already settled at Newbury, on the Lower Cowass Intervales (Ibid, p. 188). The natural bounties of the Connecticut River Valley were extolled in 'An Accurate Map of His Majesty's Province of New Hampshire', drawn by Joseph Blanchard and Samuel Langdon, and engraved by Thomas Jefferys (London, c. 1761). The notation 'Choice White Pines and Good Lands' occurs twice.

– *Rogers' jailbreak*. See *NYG*, 16 January and 23 January, 1764.

– *Gage's hostility*. John Cuneo argued that Gage's antipathy rested upon professional jealousy of Rogers and his rangers; when Rogers earned promotion to major he 'gained a powerful enemy for life'. Whilst this probably exaggerates affairs, there was clearly no love lost between these two very different soldiers. See *Robert Rogers*, pp. 91–7.

– *Rogers in London*. It is quite plausible

– though impossible to prove – that whilst in London, Rogers also posed for the artist Benjamin West, modelling one of the figures that would subsequently feature in the Pennsylvanian prodigy's epoch-making painting, *The Death of Wolfe*. Although West's finished oil painting was not exhibited until 1771, a preliminary ink and watercolour sketch is dated 1765 – the very year Rogers descended upon London society. There are significant differences between the two versions, but the left-hand figure clad in the green ranger-style uniform is conspicuous in both. Certain characters in the composition are known to represent men who were actually present with Wolfe at Québec, others were elsewhere at the time, or remain unidentified. The identity of the 'ranger' has never been established. The painting has generated a considerable literature. For a useful overview, which reproduces both the 1765 and 1771 versions, see Ann U. Abrams, *The Valiant Hero: Benjamin West and Grand-Style History Painting* (Washington, 1985), especially pp. 161–84.

– *Rogers' books*. On the *Journals* and *Concise Account* see *Critical Review, or Annals of Literature*, 1765 (November), 387–8; *Monthly Review*, 1766 (January), 9–22; 79–80; also *GM*, 1765 (October), 584–5.

– *Ponteach*. A new edition of *Ponteach*, with an introduction and biographical sketch of Rogers, was produced by Allan Nevins (Chicago, 1914). For the comments cited here see: *Critical Review*, 1766 (February), 150; *GM*, 1766, 90; *Monthly Review*, 1766 (March), 242.

– *Treason trial.* John Cuneo, who was himself a lawyer, provides extensive and thoughtful coverage of this episode (*Robert Rogers*, pp. 215–46). See also *Treason? At Michilimackinac: The Proceedings of a General Court Martial held at Montreal in October 1768 for the Trial of Major Robert Rogers*, ed. David A. Armour (Mackinac Island, Michigan, 1967), with quotes at p. 59. Gage's biographer believed he was justified in taking such drastic action. See Alden, *General Gage*, p. 77. John Shy observes: 'Whether Rogers was guilty or innocent, the whole affair was a travesty of justice' (*Toward Lexington*, p. 228).

– *Rogers and the highwayman.* See *The General Evening Post* [London], 10–12 October, 1771.

– *Kirkwood's high opinion of Rogers.* See *Kirk's Memoirs*, p. 50.

– *Gage's advice to George III.* See Alden, *General Gage*, p. 200; also Shy, *Toward Lexington*, p. 407.

– *Predicted rift between Crown and colonies.* See *Kalm's Travels*, I, 139–40.

– *Abercrombie and Stark at Bunker Hill.* As he lay dying of his wounds, Abercrombie conceded that 'the Rebells Behaved most Gallantly'. See his letter to Amherst of 20 June, 1775 (Amherst Family Papers, U1350/080/3). On Stark see Philip H. Viles Jr, 'Stark, John', in *American National Biography*, eds. John A. Garratye and Mark C. Carnes (24 vols, New York, 1999), XX, 573–4.

– *Bougainville* lived to enjoy a venerated old age under the Napoleonic régime. His funeral in 1811 merited full military honours. See Étienne

Taillemite's article in *DCB*, V, 102–5.

– *St Francis and the Revolutionary war.* See 'Odanak: Abenaki ambiguity in the North', Chapter 2 of Colin G. Calloway's *The American Revolution in Indian Country: Crisis and Diversity in Native American Communities* (Cambridge, 1995), pp. 65–84; also Huden, 'White Chief', *VH* (1956), 206–8; 337–47.

– *'Patriot' suspicions of Rogers.* See Wheelock to Washington, Dartmouth College, 2 December, 1775, in *The Papers of George Washington: Revolutionary War Series*, ed. W.W. Abbot (Charlottesville, Virginia, 1987), II, 473–4; Washington to Maj-Gen Philip Schuyler, Cambridge, Massachusetts, 16 January, 1776, in Ibid, III (1988), 112.

– *Stark's verdict.* See 'Notice of Major Rogers', in *Reminiscences of French War*, p. 161.

– *Rogers' marital problems.* See Cuneo, *Robert Rogers*, pp. 275–6.

– *Rogers' obituary.* See *The Oracle and Public Advertiser*, 26 May, 1795.

– *Susanna Johnson remembers.* See 'Narrative of Mrs Johnson', p. 84. Susanna died in 1810, aged 80.

Appendices

(1) Rogers' 'rules to be observed in the Ranging service'

From the *Journals of Major Robert Rogers* (1765), pp. 60–70.

I All Rangers are to be subject to the rules and articles of war; to appear at roll-call every evening on their own parade, equipped, each with a fire-lock, sixty rounds of powder and ball, and a hatchet, at which time an officer from each company is to inspect the same, to see they are in order, so as to be ready on any emergency to march at a minute's warning; and before they are dismissed the necessary guards are to be drafted, and scouts for the next day appointed.

II Whenever you are ordered out to the enemy's forts or frontiers for discoveries, if your number be small, march in a single file, keeping at such a distance from each other as to prevent one shot from killing two men, sending one man, or more, forward, and the like on each side, at the distance of twenty yards from the main body, if the ground you march over will admit of it, to give the signal to the officer of the approach of an enemy, and of their number, &c.

III If you march over marshes or soft ground, change your position, and march abreast of each other, to prevent the enemy from tracking you (as they would do if you marched in a single file) till you get over such ground, and then resume your former order, and march till it is quite dark before you encamp, which do, if possible, on a piece of ground that may afford your sentries the advantage of seeing or hearing the enemy at some considerable distance, keeping one half of your whole party awake alternately through the night.

IV Some time before you come to the place you would reconnoitre, make a stand, and send one or two men in whom you can confide, to look out the best ground for making your observations.

V If you have the good fortune to take any prisoners, keep them separate, till they are examined, and in your return take a different route from that in which you went out, that you may the better discover any party in your rear, and have an opportunity, if their strength be superior to yours, to alter your course, or disperse, as circumstances may require.

VI If you march in a large body of three or four hundred, with a design to attack the enemy, divide your party into three columns, each headed by a proper officer, and let these columns march in single files, the columns to the right and left keeping at twenty yards distance or more from that of the centre, if the ground will admit, and let proper guards be kept in the front and rear, and suitable flanking parties at a due distance as before directed, with orders to halt on all eminences, to take a view of the surrounding ground, to prevent your being ambushed, and to notify the approach or retreat of the enemy, that proper dispositions may be made for attacking, defending, &c. And if the enemy approach in your front on level ground, form a front of your three columns or main body with the advanced guard, keeping out your flanking parties, as if you were marching under the command of trusty officers, to prevent the enemy from pressing hard on either of your wings, or surrounding you, which is the usual method of the savages, if their number will admit of it, and be careful likewise to support and strengthen your rear-guard.

VII If you are obliged to receive the enemy's fire, fall, or squat down, till it is over, then rise and discharge at them. If their main body is equal to yours, extend yourselves occasionally; but if superior, be careful to support and strengthen your flanking parties, to make them equal to theirs, that if possible you may repulse them to their main body, in which case push upon them with the greatest resolution, with equal force in each flank and in the centre, observing to keep at a due distance from each other, and advance from tree to tree, with one half of the party before the other ten or twelve yards. If the enemy push upon you, let your front fire and fall down, and then let your rear advance thro' them and do the like, by which time those who before were in front will be ready to discharge again, and repeat the same alternately, as occasion shall require; by this means you will keep up such a constant fire, that the enemy will not be able easily to break your order, or gain your ground.

VIII If you oblige the enemy to retreat, be careful, in your pursuit of them, to keep out your flanking parties, and prevent them from gaining eminences or rising grounds, in which case they would perhaps be able to rally and repulse in their turn.

IX If you are obliged to retreat, let the front of your whole party fire and fall back, till the rear has done the same, making for the best ground you can; by this means you will oblige the enemy to pursue you, if they do it at all, in the face of a constant fire.

X If the enemy is so superior that you are in danger of being surrounded by them, let the whole body disperse, and every one take a different road to the place of rendezvous appointed for that evening, which must every morning be altered and fixed for the evening ensuing, in order to bring the whole party, or as many of them as possible, together, after any separation that may happen in the day; but if you should happen to be actually surrounded, form yourselves into a square, or if in the woods, a circle is best, and, if possible, make a stand till the darkness of the night favours your escape.

XI If your rear is attacked, the main body and flankers must face about to the right or left, as occasion shall require, and form themselves to oppose the enemy, as before directed; and the same method must be observed, if attacked in either of your flanks, by which means you will always make a rear of one of your flank-guards.

XII If you determine to rally after a retreat, in order to make a fresh stand against the enemy, by all means endeavour to do it on the most rising ground you can come at, which will give you greatly the advantage in point of situation, and enable you to repulse superior numbers.

XIII In general, when pushed upon by the enemy, reserve your fire till they approach very near, which will then put them into the greater surprise and consternation, and give you an opportunity of rushing upon them with your hatchets and cutlasses to the better advantage.

XIV When you encamp at night, fix your sentries in such a manner as not to be relieved from the main body till morning, profound secrecy and silence being often of the last importance in these cases. Each sentry, therefore, should consist of six men, two of whom must be constantly alert, and when relieved by their fellows, it should be done without noise; and in case those on duty see or hear any thing, which alarms them, they are not to speak, but one of them is silently to retreat, and acquaint the commanding officer thereof, that proper dispositions may be made; and all occasional sentries should be fixed in like manner.

XV At the first dawn of day, awake your whole detachment; that being the time when the savages choose to fall upon their enemies, you should by all means be in readiness to receive them.

XVI If the enemy should be discovered by your detachments in the morning, and their numbers are superior to yours, and a victory doubtful, you should not attack them till the evening, as then they will not know your numbers, and if you are repulsed, your retreat will be favoured by the darkness of the night.

XVII Before you leave your encampment, send out small parties to scout round it, to see if there be any appearance or track of an enemy that might have been near you during the night.

XVIII When you stop for refreshment, chuse some spring or rivulet if you can, and dispose your party so as not to be surprised, posting proper guards and sentries at a due distance, and let a small party waylay the path you came in, lest the enemy should be pursuing.

XIX If, in your return, you have to cross rivers, avoid the usual fords as much as possible, lest the enemy should have discovered, and be there expecting you.

XX If you have to pass by lakes, keep at some distance from the edge of the water, lest, in case of an ambuscade, or an attack from the enemy, when in that situation, your retreat should be cut off.

XXI If the enemy pursue your rear, take a circle till you come to your own tracks, and there form an ambush to receive them, and give them the first fire.

XXII When you return from a scout, and come near our forts, avoid the usual roads, and avenues thereto, lest the enemy should have headed you, and lay in ambush to receive you, when almost exhausted with fatigues.

XXIII When you pursue any party that has been near our forts or encampments, follow not directly in their tracks, lest you should be discovered by their rear-guards, who, at such a time, would be most alert; but endeavour, by a different route, to head and meet them in some narrow pass, or lay in ambush to receive them when and where they least expect it.

XXIV If you are to embark in canoes, bateaux, or otherwise, by water, chuse the evening for the time of your embarkation, as you will then have the whole night before you, to pass undiscovered by any parties of the enemy, on hills, or other places, which command a prospect of the lake or river you are upon.

XXV In paddling or rowing, give orders that the boat or canoe next the sternmost, wait for her, and the third for the second, and the fourth for the third, and so on, to prevent separation, and that you may be ready to assist each other on any emergency.

XXVI Appoint one man in each boat to look out for fires, on the adjacent shores, from the numbers and size of which you may form some judgment of the number that kindled them, and whether you are able to attack them or not.

XXVII If you find the enemy encamped near the banks of a river, or lake, which you imagine they will attempt to cross for their security upon being attacked, leave a detachment of your party on the opposite shore to receive them, while, with the remainder, you surprize them, having them between you and the lake or river.

XXVIII If you cannot satisfy yourself as to the enemy's number and strength, from their fire, &c. conceal your boats at some distance, and ascertain their number by a reconnoitring party, when they embark, or march, in the morning, marking the course they steer, &c. when you may pursue, ambush, and attack them, or let them pass, as prudence shall direct you. In general, however, that you may not be discovered by the enemy on the lakes and rivers at a great distance, it is safest to lay by, with your boats and party concealed all day, without noise or show, and to pursue your intended route by night; and whether you go by land or water, give out parole and countersigns, in order to know one another in the dark, and likewise appoint a station for every man to repair to, in case of any accident that may separate you.

(2) *New-York Gazette*, **Monday 26 November, 1759**

'Particulars of Major Rogers's last Scout, sent us from Numb. 4, (via Crown-Point).'

'Extract of a Letter from Number 4, to a Gentleman at Crown-Point, dated November 3, 1759.

SIR,

I HAVE the Pleasure to send you the Particulars of the late Scout under the Command of Major Rogers, with a Party of Rangers, and Capt. Ogden, of the New-Jersey Regiment, with a Detachment from 5 Provincial Regiments, viz. Col. Schuyler's, Col. Fitch's, Col. Whiting's, Col. Babcock's, and Col. Ruglass's, and Lieut. Dunbar, with a Party of Light Infantry, the whole consisting of 230 Men, when they departed from Crown-Point. On the 13th of September, with 30 Days Provisions, they embarked in Whale-boats, and proceeded down Lake-Champlain 10 Days, only rowing in the Night, for Fear of the Enemy's Vessels on the Lake: They then landed, and hawled their Boats out of the Lake, and set out on their March for St. Francois, an Indian Town, so called, on the River St. Francois. They marched 12 Days; when, just before Night, Major Rogers climb'd up a Tree, and saw the Smoak about 5 or 6 Miles distant. He then halted his Party until the Dusk of the Evening, and then march'd on again, until he came within 2 or 3 Miles, when he halted his Party a second Time, and took two Men with him, leaving the Command with Capt. Ogden, and went to Reconnoiter the Town, where he arrived about 12 o'Clock, finding the Indians in a great Frolick, singing and having the War Dance, as the whole Town intended to come up the River on a Scout the next Day: The Major stayed until about Two in the Morning, and then returned to his Party, leaving them in the Dance; then march'd on with his Party within 300 Yards of the Town, when he and all his Men threw off their Packs, and prepared themselves for the Attack, dividing themselves in three Divisions, himself on the Right, Capt. Ogden on the Left, and

Lieut. Dunbar in the Center; the Number then reduced to only 142, Officers included.

'At Half between Day-break and Sun-rise, they march'd up to the Town, where finding the Indians all asleep, never stood to ask Entrance, but burst open their Doors, and saluted them with Tomahawks and Bayonets, so that in the Space of 2 Hours, we had cleared the whole Town of them, some of which attempted to run off, were shot down immediately, others trying to cross the River in Canoes were killed, and their Boats sunk; so that out of between Two and Three Hundred People, old and young, not above Six made their Escape, besides about TWENTY taken Prisoners: The Loss on our Side was one Indian killed and six men slightly wounded; besides Capt. Ogden who was wounded in the Head, and a Ball went through his Body, and his Powder-horn shot from his Side in the Beginning of the Engagement; but it did not hinder him from doing his Duty, he took his Handkerchief and bound it round the Wound in his Body; two or three Men being near him, asked him if he was wounded, he answered only scratched, and encouraged them on. The Major who was never known to be idle in such an Affair, was in every Part in the Engagement encouraging his Men and giving Directions, and who says he never saw a better Command of Officers and Men, and thinks no Party of Men ever deserved more Encouragement for their Country Service, not only for their good Courage and Behaviour, but the Fatigues and Sufferings they have undergone. After the Action was over, they supplied themselves with Corn, as there was no other Provisions to be found, their own being expended three Days before they arrived at the Town; they set the Town all in Flames, thinking there was none left alive; afterwards we heard dreadful Cries and Screeches, as though there were Numbers of them in the Flames, who had concealed themselves in their upper Rooms and By-places, thinking to Escape. After seeing the Town in ashes, about 11 o'Clock, they set out on their Return back, but finding by the Prisoners that their Boats on the Lake were Way-laid by a large Number of French and Indians, which we had Reason to believe was true, by their giving us an exact Number of Boats and other Remarks, and 215 Indians had been out three Days after us up Wigwamortineack, a River 10 miles on this side St. Francois; so that our People was obliged to return by Way of Number Four and in Connecticut. They marched eight Days, and then parted themselves into small Parties, as their Corn was almost expended, and every Party took his Way; the Rest of their Corn was soon gone, and they were obliged to live on Roots and Barks, Toad-stools, some old Beaver skins, and Scalps, as there was but little Game to be had, it was seldom they saw any: They thought themselves well supplied, when they could get one Partridge between 10 Men a Day. In this Manner they lived until they arrived at Connecticut River, where Major Rogers left all his Party, except Capt. Ogden and one man, (this was about 80 Miles above Number Four). They then made a Raft with some Pieces of Wood and floated down on them, until they came to Number Four, to which Place they arrived in 29 Days from St. Francois, it being between 3 and 400 Miles; through excessive bad travelling. They were 20 Days in a continued Swamp, with their feet in the Mud and water, and could scarcely get a dry Place to sleep on. When the Major arrived at this Place, he was scarcely able to walk after his fatigues, as he took with him the Poorest of the Men, to supply and support them himself, and having Capt. Ogden with him, who was wounded, and whom he used often to take on his Back and carry him through Rivers. Immediately after the Majors arrival here, he provided Canoes with Provision, and sent them up the River to the Relief of the Party he had left, and within two days set out himself up the River to recollect his wearied Men; the same Day Capt. Ogden set out for Crown-Point. This Town had a beautiful Situation, on a fine River, about half a Mile wide; it was regular built with Timber and Boards, in two Rows, with a fine large Church, at the Head of the Town: It was vastly rich, which our poor People's Scalps had pur-chased for them.

'This Nation of Indians have always been at War with us, and have committed more cruel Barbarities on our poor People, than all the Rest of the Indian Nations in America; and it is the most happy Thing for them, as could have been done, as they cannot commit any more Cruelties.

'We all here wait impatient for the safe Arrival of all those brave Officers and Men, that have behaved so gallantly in this Affair, and in particular that indefatigable Major, and a happy Recovery of Capt. Ogden of his Wounds, such Behaviour as only Men of Constitutions like Lions could ever have went through.'

Dramatis Personae

Abercrombie, James (1732–75).
Aggressive captain in the Black Watch. He was aide-de-camp to Loudoun, Abercromby and Amherst successively, and the author of lively and candid letters.

Abercromby, James (1706–81).
Plodding Scottish soldier. Commander-in-chief of British forces in North America during most of 1758, he was recalled following his disastrous defeat at Ticonderoga.

Amherst, Jeffery (1717–97).
Cautious British general. After conquering Louisbourg (1758), Amherst was appointed to the chief command in North America. He orchestrated the methodical conquest of Canada, 1759–60.

Ateawanto (or 'Jerome Atecuando') (flourished 1749–57).
Renowned chief and orator of the St Francis Abenakis. In 1752 at Montréal, he famously warned the English to desist from encroachments upon Abenaki lands.

Aubery, Joseph (1673–1756).
Long-serving Jesuit missionary at St Francis. He was instrumental in maintaining an alliance between the Abenakis and the French government.

Barns (Burns), Jonathan (d. 1761).
Boston-born provincial soldier, captive and ultimately renegade amongst Abenakis. He helped to hunt the St Francis raiders.

Bougainville, Louis-Antoine de (1729–1811).
Well-born French army officer, gifted scientist and future explorer. He was Montcalm's devoted aide-de-camp, and the author of a lively journal.

Bourlamaque, François-Charles de (1716–64).
Professional soldier and tenacious defender of New France's Lake Champlain frontier in 1759. He was Lévis' right-hand man in 1760.

Braddock, Edward (1695–1755).
Brave but stubborn British major-general. Braddock died of wounds received on the Monongahela River whilst leading the first Anglo-American expedition against Fort Duquesne.

La Brosse, Jean-Baptiste de (1724–82).
Scholarly and revered Jesuit missionary. The assistant to Roubaud at St Francis, 1758–9, and parish priest at Yamaska (Wigwam Martinique), he also prepared an important dictionary of Abenaki language.

Brown, Thomas (b. 1740).
Boston-born private in Rogers' Rangers. He wrote a vivid narrative of his active service and subsequent captivity.

Cheeksaunkun, Jacob (Captain Jacobs) (flourished 1759).
Trusted officer of the Stockbridge Mahicans operating alongside the rangers. He accompanied Kennedy's 1759 mission to Wolfe, and was captured with him.

Dieskau, Jean-Armand, Baron de (1701–67).
Bold Saxon veteran in service of France. A major-general and field commander of Canada's forces in 1755, he was defeated and captured at the Battle of Lake George.

Dumas, Jean-Daniel (1721–94).

Tough French-born captain of Canadian regular troops. He played a key role in the defeat of Braddock, fought at Québec, and led the pursuit of the St Francis raiders.

Forbes, John (1707–59).

Determined Scottish soldier. A valued adjutant general to Loudoun, he battled chronic illness to capture Fort Duquesne in 1758.

Gage, Thomas (c. 1720–87).

Indecisive British officer. He survived Braddock's defeat to form Gage's Light Infantry. In 1759, as brigadier-general, Gage incurred Amherst's wrath for failing to take La Galette.

Gill, Joseph-Louis (1719–98).

Celebrated White Chief of the St Francis Abenakis. The son of New England captives, he became a successful warrior and trader. He was the husband of Marie-Jeanne Nanamaghemet and father of Xavier and Antoine (Sabatis).

Grey Lock (flourished 1675–1740).

Wily and determined chief, originally from an Indian tribe in Massachusetts. During the 1720s he led raids from Missisquoi that stemmed the inroads of English settlers.

Haviland, William (1718–84).

Irish professional soldier. As lieutenant-colonel of the 27th Foot, he clashed with Rogers at Fort Edward in 1757. Promoted brigadier-general, Haviland commanded the British advance against Isle-aux-Noix in 1760.

Howe, George Augustus, Viscount (c. 1724–58).

Aristocratic and popular British officer. A dynamic brigadier under the sluggish Abercromby, he was killed in action near Ticonderoga.

Johnson, Susanna (1730–1810).

Resilient trader's wife on New Hampshire frontier. Captured, with her husband and children, by St Francis Abenakis in 1754, she later wrote a remarkable narrative of her experiences.

Johnson, William (c. 1715–74).
Irish trader and landowner on New York's frontier. Influential amongst the Mohawks, he led provincial forces to victory at the Battle of Lake George (1755). From 1756 Johnson was Britain's superintendent to the northern Indian tribes.

Kalm, Peter (Pehr or Petter) (1716–79).
Distinguished and observant natural historian, born in Sweden of Finnish-Scots stock. Kalm's journals of his travels in North America between 1748 and 1751 offer valuable glimpses of Canada and the British colonies.

Kennedy, Quinton (d. 1762).
Versatile Scottish officer. A veteran of Braddock's defeat, he became a daring leader of scouts. In 1759, Kennedy volunteered to carry despatches from Amherst to Wolfe. His capture by the Abenakis triggered the St Francis raid.

Kirkwood (Kirk), Robert (flourished 1757–67).
Private soldier in Montgomery's Highlanders, 1757–63. Captured by the Shawnees at Fort Duquesne (1758). His published *Memoirs* preserve unique and vivid details of the St Francis raid.

Langis (Langy), Jean-Baptiste Levrault de Langis Montegron (1723–60).
Fearless Canadian officer of colonial regulars. Langis never rose beyond the rank of ensign, but was widely acknowledged as a master of guerrilla warfare.

Lévis, François-Gaston, Duc de (1719–87).
Capable French officer of poor but noble birth. The Chevalier de Lévis served as Montcalm's second-in-command. After the marquis' death, he led Canada's forces to victory outside Québec in April 1760.

Loudoun, John Campbell, Earl of (1705–82).
Conscientious but curmudgeonly Scottish soldier. As Britain's commander-in-chief in North America from mid-1756 to early 1758, he
presided over an era of defeat. Loudoun nonetheless laid the logistical
and strategic foundations for future victory.

Lusignan, Paul-Louis Dazemard de (1691–1764).
Competent and refined Canadian-born officer of colonial regulars. He
was commandant at Fort St Frédéric, and later Ticonderoga.

Montcalm, Louis-Joseph, Marquis de (1712–59).
Experienced French soldier of noble family. He led Canada's forces to
victories at Oswego (1756), Fort William Henry (1757) and Ticonderoga (1758). Defeated by Wolfe at Québec (1759), he died of his
wounds.

Pontiac (c. 1720–69).
Ottawa war chief. He was an important figure in the western Indian
uprising (Pontiac's War) against the Anglo-Americans in 1763–4.

Rasles (Rale), Sébastien (1658–1724).
Dedicated and influential Jesuit missionary to the eastern Abenakis.
Rasles was hated by New Englanders for allegedly inciting his congregation against them. He was killed during a surprise attack on his Norridgewock mission.

Rigaud de Vaudreuil, François Pierre de (1703–79).
Son of one governor general of New France, and brother of another.
An experienced officer in the colonial regulars, he participated in the
campaign against Oswego (1756) and led an abortive raid on Fort
William Henry in early 1757. From 1758–9, Rigaud was governor of
Montréal.

Rogers, Robert (1731–95).
Native of Massachusetts, but long linked with New Hampshire. Rogers
emerged as the paramount leader of rangers during the campaigns

against New France. Indomitable and ruthless, his exploits brought him fame on both sides of the Atlantic.

Roubaud, Pierre-Joseph-Antoine (1724–c. 1789).
Controversial Jesuit priest. He served as missionary to the St Francis Abenakis, 1756–60, often joining them on the warpath.

Stark, John (1728–1822).
Hardy New Hampshire frontiersman. Stark was an experienced ranger officer and a trusted henchman of Rogers.

Vaudreuil, Pierre de Rigaud de Vaudreuil de Cavagnial, Marquis de (1698–1778).
Resourceful last governor general of New France. Born in Canada, Vaudreuil served in the colony regulars before becoming governor of Louisiana, and from 1756, governor general of the whole colony.

Wolfe, James (1727–59).
Fiery and ambitious British Army officer. After serving as a brigadier-general at Louisbourg (1758), Wolfe was promoted major-general to command the troops in the crucial 1759 Québec expedition. He was killed winning the battle on the Plains of Abraham.

Acknowledgements

This book results from the sudden rekindling of an old interest. In the autumn of 2001, shortly after moving from England to the Netherlands, I was surprised and delighted to find a copy of the 1961 reprint edition of Robert Rogers' *Journals* in the library of the University of Amsterdam. In those then unfamiliar surroundings, this was like unexpectedly bumping into a long lost friend. Decamping to a nearby bar, I settled down with my beer and began to re-read Rogers' vivid accounts of waging the French and Indian War. Over the next few hours, the idea for this book was roughed out.

Like many of his contemporaries, I was struck by Rogers' account of the St Francis raid – not only for the understated power of the narrative itself, but for the many questions that it left unanswered. I became increasingly interested in attempting to fill those gaps, and particularly to reflect the perspective of Rogers' Indian and French foes.

My first findings were presented as a research paper – 'The bloodiest scene in all America: Reassessing the St Francis Raid of 1759' – given to the Annual Conference of the British Association for American Studies, held at St Anne's College, Oxford, in April 2002. Questions and suggestions from the conference delegates were valuable in helping me to refine my ideas.

In the following month, the project received a decisive boost when I attended the Annual College of the Seven Years' War, held at Fort Ticonderoga, New York. I remain extremely grateful to the fort's Director, Nicholas Westbrook, for inviting me to speak. That trip enabled me to visit places featured in these pages, and meet many enthusiasts who could not have been more generous with their time, knowledge and friendship. I owe a particular debt to Christopher D. Fox, Curator of Fort Ticonderoga's Thompson-Pell Research Centre; his courtesy and expertise maximised the time I spent perusing that outstanding resource for the military history of colonial America. Wes Red Hawk Dikeman offered valuable insights into Abenaki views on Rogers and his raid; in doing so, he also gave me the title for my book.

At Crown Point State Historic Site – surely one of the most atmospheric ruins in North America – Parks and Recreation Supervisor Thomas L. Nesbitt volunteered his services as an entertaining and informative guide. Tim J. Todish, a leading authority on Rogers' Rangers, kindly allowed me to pick his brains. Robert J. Andrews and Dr John Houlding both shared their immense knowledge of the British Army's officer corps.

J. Robert Maguire, of Shoreham, Vermont, and Lt-Col Ian McCulloch of the Canadian Defence Headquarters, not only helped to locate vital evidence, but also provided a detailed critique of my original manuscript. I am likewise extremely grateful to Professor Colin G. Calloway of Dartmouth College, Hanover, New Hampshire, for casting an expert eye over my efforts. I couldn't have asked for a finer trio of readers. Their interest has improved the book immensely; the responsibility for what lies within it of course remains my own.

The staffs of the research institutions mentioned in the notes were uniformly helpful. Although an ever-increasing proportion of primary source material has now understandably been microfilmed, it's still possible to walk into an archive and inspect unique original documents: the opportunity to read an intelligence report penned by Rogers just hours after returning from a scout is not to be underestimated.

In Amsterdam I benefited from the extensive American history library holdings of the city's university, and the assistance of that institution's inter-library loan department. The library of the Rijksmuseum voor Volkenkunde (National Museum of Ethnology) at Leiden was another veritable treasure trove of rare books and journals.

For precise translations of key French documents I owe an immense debt to Marijke van der Meer. Her enthusiastic assistance was crucial to the completion of the book. I'm also very grateful to my brother-in-law, Philip Durnford, who provided timely and invaluable computing help. In addition, I've much appreciated the patient encouragement of my commissioning editor, Ian Drury, and remain very grateful for the efforts of his colleagues at Weidenfeld & Nicolson who also worked on the project.

The final stages of writing *White Devil* coincided with the arrival of my daughter Milly. During the busy days before that event, my wife Laura cheerfully read through each chapter as it churned out of the printer, checking style and content with an eagle eye. Like Laura, little Milly has proved herself to be a real gem. Together, they offered the unconditional affection and support I needed to finish the job. This book is dedicated to them both with all my love.

Index